TH CRICKE WHO'S 1991

compiled and edited by
IAIN SPROAT

Introduction by the
Rt Hon John Major, MP

CollinsWillow
An Imprint of HarperCollins*Publishers*

ACKNOWLEDGEMENTS

The Editor is indebted to Mr Richard Lockwood, Editor of the TCCB/Bull Computer official cricket statistics service, for providing the statistics and for his help in the production of the book; and to Mr Bill Smith, FRPS, who personally took most of the photographs. Above all the Editor is grateful to the cricketers themselves without whose support this book could not have been compiled.

First published in Great Britain in 1991 by
Collins Willow
an imprint of HarperCollins Publishers
London
© Iain Sproat 1991

A CIP catalogue record for this book is available from the British Library.
ISBN 0 00 218396 X

Cover photographs of
Devon Malcolm and Michael Atherton
by Graham Morris
Portraits by Bill Smith
Statistics: TCCB / Bull Computer Statistics Service
Pre-print production by Richard Lockwood

Typesetting by Michael Mepham, Frome, Somerset
Printed and bound in Great Britain by
Butler and Tanner Ltd,
Frome, Somerset

PREFACE

The cricketers listed in this volume include those who played for their county at least once last season in the County Championship. Those who played only in one-day games are not included. All statistics are complete to the end of the last English season. Figures about 1000 runs and 50 wickets in a season refer to matches in England only. First-class figures do not include figures for Test matches which are listed separately. One-day 100s and 50s are for the English domestic competitions and all One-Day Internationals, home and abroad. The RAL figures include both League and Cup matches.

The following abbreviations apply: * means not out; 1ST first-class; INT One-Day Internationals; RAL Refuge Assurance League/Cup; N.W. NatWest Trophy; B&H Benson & Hedges Cup. The figures for batting and bowling averages refer to the full first-class English list for 1990, followed in brackets by the 1989 figures. Inclusion in the batting averages depends on a minimum of six completed innings, and an average of at least 10 runs; a bowler has to have taken at least 10 wickets. The same qualification has been used for compiling the bowlers' strike rate.

Readers will notice certain occasional differences in the way the same kind of information is presented. This is because I have usually tried to follow the way in which the cricketers themselves have provided the relevant information.

Each year in *The Cricketers' Who's Who*, in addition to those cricketers who are playing during the current season, I also include the biographical and career details of those who played in the previous season but retired at the end of it. The purpose of this is to have, on the record, the full and final cricketing achievements of every player when his career has ended. Full batting statistics are provided for every player and bowling statistics for all those who have taken at least five first-class wickets.

A book of this complexity and detail has to be prepared several months in advance of the cricket season, and occasionally there are recent changes in a player's circumstances which cannot be included in time. Many examples of facts and statistics which can quickly become outdated in the period between the actual compilation of the book and its publication, months later, will spring to the reader's mind, and I ask him or her to make the necessary commonsense allowance and adjustments.

Iain Sproat
January 1991

FOREWORD

MIKE SMITH
Director and General Manager, Refuge Assurance p.l.c.

The Cricketers' Who's Who is a great read for two main reasons – the facts and the figures.

The facts speak for themselves. Cricket, more than any other sport, attracts people who are interested in statistics. If you want to find out what Surrey did against Sussex at The Oval on 11 August, 1888* it's all documented somewhere.

This book has got fascinating facts galore ... but to me it's the 'figures' that bring it to life, the people who play in our national game. Here you can find the batsman who was a Birmingham copper, the bowler who 'always salutes magpies', and the wicket-keeper who swallowed Graham Cowdrey's contact lens!

The Refuge Assurance League and Cup gave us some thrilling facts in 1990 – with Derbyshire winning the League in the last match of the season with three balls to spare ... then losing to Middlesex in the Cup with only two balls to spare.

Now we can look forward to 1991, with *The Cricketers' Who's Who* to turn the facts and figures into people.

* They beat them by an innings and 485 runs.

INTRODUCTION

I AM DELIGHTED to be asked to write the introduction to Iain Sproat's 1991 volume. Its arrival is an annual delight and its well thumbed pages are a tribute to the increasing charm of the most elegant game in the world. I write this foreword against the background of some very disappointing news from Australia. England have just lost the second test at Melbourne, and go two down with three to play. As the newspapers keep reminding us, no English side has yet won the Ashes from that position.

Whatever happens in Australia, however, all English cricket-lovers can take consolation: a few more months will bring the start of another season here. This will see some new features: Tuesday and Friday starts to county games, a contest between the county champions and the winners of the Sheffield Shield, and a restriction of overseas players to one per county. In other respects, 1991 will be similar to previous years: a mixture of three- and four-day county championship matches, the usual array of one-day competitions, and – more controversially – covered wickets.

Once more the main tourists are the West Indies. In the late summer there is a brief visit from the Sri Lankans, who are to play a Test at Lord's.

I make no predictions about the new season, because cricket is always capable of producing the unexpected. But one thing is certain: in the coming months there will be no shortage of words written and spoken about England's Test teams. Should we rely on the Ashes veterans? Do some of the England A team merit promotion? Should the selectors look further afield – such as to Worcester where there is a batsman called Hick?

Like every follower of the game, I have my own views. But I do not intend to offer selectoral advice here. Indeed, my present concern – like that of this publication – is with the English county game rather than the international arena.

We need surely to keep international cricket and cricketers in proper perspective. There will be six Test matches this summer. Probably fewer than twenty players will represent England, unless, delightful thought, a host of young talent forces its way into the teams. In contrast, there will be well over 200 first-class county matches; and over 300 players will take part in them. Although I enjoy Test matches as much as anybody, it is self-evident that the overwhelming majority of first-class and one-day matches in England continue to be county cricket. And some 90 per cent of those taking part will be county rather than current Test cricketers.

I do not see this as a drawback. On the contrary, herein lies the richness and charm of the English game. Of course we are drawn by the best that

England has to offer – the batting of Graham Gooch, or the bowling of Angus Fraser. But the attraction of county cricket goes far wider and deeper than the (relatively few) players who for much of the summer will be away representing their country. The same is true of grounds. Old Trafford, Headingley and Trent Bridge will always have their place; but so too will Taunton, Swansea, Bournemouth, Chesterfield, Wellingborough....

In my view, the skill and variety of the individuals to be seen in the county game are unrivalled anywhere in the world.

There are a number of cricket followers who maintain that cricket is not what it was and that players are not what they were. I do not subscribe to this view, even though I was lucky enough to grow up watching Surrey in the 1950s – surely one of the best county sides of all time. In those days, too, there were critics who alleged that standards had fallen. If all such nostalgia were accepted at face value, it would be difficult to avoid the conclusion that cricket had been in continuous decline since the middle of the last century.

In 1991 county cricket offers as exciting a prospect as it has ever done. Consider, for example, what is on show even when the England team are absent. There are the talented overseas players who enrich our game – Jimmy Cook, Wasim Akram, Tom Moody, Mohammed Azharuddin. There is an up and coming generation of English players – John Stephenson, Nasser Hussain, Mark Ramprakash, Warren Hegg, Mark Alleyne, Richard Blakey, Richard Illingworth.... At the other end of the age spectrum are the senior statesmen who have been part of the county scene for so many years. If pride of place here goes to David Hughes (who alas will retire at the end of 1991), others quickly come to mind – Phil Carrick, Derek Randall, Peter Willey, Alan Butcher. And then there are the stalwarts – the players who always have and always will make up the backbone of county cricket. Is the championship conceivable without the day-in day-out virtues of players like Richard Williams, Geoff Holmes, Dermot Reeve, Phil Neale, Paul Parker, Nigel Briers, Paul Johnson, Mark Benson, Simon Hughes...?

I could mention many more players in each category. I have omitted, for example, some of the particular successes of last year – Neil Fairbrother, Tim Munton, Hugh Morris, Richard Davis. Nor do I have space to talk of the delightful eccentricities of the county game – the only arena that offers in the same team batting of the quality of both Allan Lamb and Mark Robinson.

In a sense, any omissions only underline the point I am trying to make. The distinctive quality of the English county game is the unique variety and diversity of its players. Whatever legislators and administrators do, it is on the county professionals that we rely for our entertainment.

This publication is, in essence, the book of those players. It is an honour to introduce them. I wish them and their supporters well in the summer of 1991.

If my editor's objectivity allows, perhaps I might also be permitted to express one hope. I have studiously refrained from mentioning above any Surrey players, in order to avoid accusations of bias. But I cannot, in concluding, resist the temptation to point out that under those famous gasometers can be seen all the ingredients of county cricket. We have an outstanding overseas international, England Test players, a number of very promising youngsters, and some dependable county stalwarts. The blend is there. I trust I may end with the hope that, with a little good fortune, Surrey will number among the successful counties this year.

John Major

January 1991

Name: Christopher John Adams
Role: Right-hand bat, off-break bowler
Born: 6 May 1970, Whitwell, Derbyshire
Height: 6ft **Weight:** 13st 7lbs
Nickname: Grizzly, Ninja Turtle – 'don't ask why!'
County debut: 1988
1st-Class 50s scored: 6
1st-Class 100s scored: 2
One-Day 50s: 1
Place in batting averages: 157th av. 31.06 (1989 131st av. 26.10)
1st-Class catches: 25 (career 36)
Parents: John and Lynn
Marital status: Single
Family links with cricket: Brother David played 2nd XI cricket for Derbyshire, Somerset and Gloucestershire. Father played Yorkshire Schools cricket
Education: Chesterfield School and Repton College
Qualifications: 6 O-levels
Off-season: 'Abroad in New Zealand or some other exotic country.'
Cricketers particularly admired: Allan Lamb, Viv Richards, Ian Botham and Gary Sobers. 'Allan Hill was very inspirational as far as preparation and attitude towards the game were concerned.'
Other sports followed: Soccer (Southend FC), golf and every other sport
Relaxations: Cinema, reading and crosswords
Extras: 'Hold record for runs scored in a season at Repton, beating Richard Hutton's 25-year-old record.' ESCA and MCC Schools
Opinions on cricket: 'We have not found the right balance between bat and ball. We should have wickets that benefit both batsmen and bowlers. Four-day cricket is much better for the game, allowing teams to realise their full potential.'

LAST SEASON: BATTING

	I.	N.O.	R.	H. S.	AV.
TEST					
1ST	34	4	932	111*	31.06
INT					
RAL	16	6	243	58*	24.30
N.W.	1	0	0	0	0.00
B&H	4	1	80	44	26.66

CAREER: BATTING

	I.	N.O.	R.	H.S.	AV.
TEST					
1ST	46	5	1214	111*	34.50
INT					
RAL	19	7	290	58*	24.16
N.W.	1	0	0	0	0.00
B&H	4	1	80	44	26.66

Best batting: 111* Derbyshire v Cambridge University, Fenner's 1990
Best bowling: 1–5 Derbyshire v Glamorgan, Cardiff 1990

AFFORD, J. A.   Nottinghamshire

Name: John Andrew Afford
Role: Slow left-arm bowler;
'don't bat or field'
Born: 12 May 1964, Crowland,
nr Peterborough
Height: 6ft 2 1/2in **Weight:** 13st
Nickname: Aff
County debut: 1984
50 wickets in a season: 1
1st-Class 5 w. in innings: 7
1st-Class 10 w. in match: 1
Place in bowling averages: 114th av.
46.28 (1989 71st av. 30.54)
Strike rate: 93.28 (career 72.70)
1st-Class catches: 7 (career 22)
Parents: Jill
Wife and date of marriage: Lynn,
1 October 1988
Education: Spalding Grammar School;
Stamford College for Further Education
Qualifications: 5 O-levels, NCA coaching certificate
Off-season: Playing and coaching in New Zealand
Overseas tours: England A to Zimbabwe 1989–90
Cricketers particularly admired: Richard Hadlee, Bishen Bedi, Derek Underwood

LAST SEASON: BATTING

	I.	N. O.	R.	H. S.	AV.
TEST					
1ST	22	7	16	5	1.06
INT					
RAL	1	1	0	0*	-
N.W.	1	1	2	2*	-
B&H	-	-	-	-	-

LAST SEASON: BOWLING

	O.	M.	R.	W.	AV.
TEST					
1ST	688	209	1944	42	46.28
INT					
RAL	55	2	305	7	43.57
N.W.	11	6	26	0	-
B&H	66	9	240	5	48.00

CAREER: BATTING

	I.	N. O.	R.	H. S.	AV.
TEST					
1ST	70	31	124	22*	3.17
INT					
RAL	3	2	0	0*	0.00
N.W.	2	2	2	2*	-
B&H	1	1	1	1*	-

CAREER: BOWLING

	O.	M.	R.	W.	AV.
TEST					
1ST	2278.2	655	6484	188	34.48
INT					
RAL	92	6	474	10	47.40
N.W.	35	11	86	4	21.50
B&H	107	12	415	11	37.72

Other sports followed: 'Will give anything a whirl, but nothing too serious. Able to watch most things. Follow Peterborough United FC and the Seattle Seahawks.'
Injuries: 'Broken toe kicking cricket case at Derby.'
Relaxations: 'Determined to go fishing more regularly.'
Opinions on cricket: 'When a batting side continues after the 100-over mark bowling points should continue.'
Best batting: 22* Nottinghamshire v Leicestershire, Trent Bridge 1989
Best bowling: 6–81 Nottinghamshire v Kent, Trent Bridge 1986

AGNEW, J. P. Leicestershire

Name: Jonathan Philip Agnew
Role: Right-hand bat, right-arm medium-fast bowler
Born: 4 April 1960, Macclesfield, Cheshire
Height: 6ft 4in **Weight:** 12st 6lbs
Nickname: Spiro, Aggers, Aggy
County debut: 1978
County cap: 1984
Test debut: 1984
Tests: 3
One-Day Internationals: 3
50 wickets in a season: 7
1st-Class 50s scored: 2
1st-Class 5 w. in innings: 37
1st-Class 10 w. in match: 6
Place in batting averages: 264th av. 12.23 (1989 245th av. 12.13)
Place in bowling averages: 73rd av. 37.22 (1989 85th av. 33.17)
Strike rate: 62.23 (career 53.16)
1st-Class catches: 5 (career 39)
Parents: Philip and Margaret
Wife and date of marriage: Beverley, 8 October 1983
Children: Jennifer, 31 October 1985; Rebecca, 18 September 1988
Family links with cricket: First cousin, Mary Duggan, captain of England's Women's XI in 1960s. Father very keen cricketer
Education: Taverham Hall Prep School; Uppingham School
Qualifications: 9 O-levels, 2 A-levels in German and English
Career outside cricket: Retired at the end of 1990 to become Cricket Correspondent for *Today* newspaper
Overseas tours: Young England to Australia 1978–79; England to India and Australia 1984–85; England B to Sri Lanka 1986

Cricketers particularly admired: Imran Khan, Wayne Larkins
Other sports followed: Hockey, golf
Relaxations: 'I became very interested in game viewing in Zimbabwe. I spent days driving around to study and photograph – particularly elephants.'
Extras: One of *Wisden's* Five Cricketers of the Year, 1987. Wrote *Eight Days a Week*, published in 1988. Wrote a weekly column for *Today* while still playing and previously spent winters working for Radio Leicester
Opinions on cricket: 'Just a thank you to everyone who helped to make my thirteen years in the game so much fun.'
Best batting: 90 Leicestershire v Yorkshire, Scarborough 1987
Best bowling: 9–70 Leicestershire v Kent, Leicester 1985

LAST SEASON: BATTING

	I.	N. O.	R.	H. S.	AV.
TEST					
1ST	26	5	257	46*	12.23
INT					
RAL	5	0	8	5	1.60
N.W.	-	-	-	-	-
B&H	1	1	1	1*	-

LAST SEASON: BOWLING

	O.	M.	R.	W.	AV.
TEST					
1ST	612	108	2196	59	37.22
INT					
RAL	88.1	10	370	11	33.63
N.W.	12	1	44	2	22.00
B&H	28	4	103	4	25.75

CAREER: BATTING

	I.	N. O.	R.	H. S.	AV.
TEST	4	3	10	5	10.00
1ST	228	46	2108	90	11.57
INT	1	1	2	2*	-
RAL	38	15	206	23*	8.95
N.W.	7	4	34	8*	11.33
B&H	13	4	65	23*	7.22

CAREER: BOWLING

	O.	M.	R.	W.	AV.
TEST	92	22	373	4	93.25
1ST	5809.2	1108	19112	662	28.87
INT	21	0	120	3	40.00
RAL	566.5	43	2485	84	29.58
N.W.	168	26	604	19	31.78
B&H	303.2	46	1099	42	26.16

ALIKHAN, R. I. Surrey

Name: Rehan Iqbal Alikhan
Role: Right-hand bat, off-break bowler
Born: 28 December 1962, London
Height: 6ft 2in **Weight:** 'Varies between 13st and 14st.'
Nickname: Prince, Old Boy, Munch
County debut: 1986 (Sussex), 1989 (Surrey)
1st-Class 50s scored: 22
1st-class 100s scored: 2
One-Day 50s: 2
Place in batting averages: 44th av. 51.85 (1989 150th av. 23.40)
1st-Class catches: 3 (career 44)
Parents: Akbar and Farida
Marital status: Single

Family links with cricket: Father played at university and at club level
Education: King's College School, Wimbledon
Qualifications: 8 O-levels, 2 A-levels
Off-season: Playing cricket in Perth, Western Australia
Overseas teams played for: Pakistan International Airlines 1986–87
Cricketers particularly admired: Zaheer Abbas, Imran Khan, Sunil Gavaskar
Other sports followed: Rugby, soccer
Relaxations: Playing squash, tennis or golf
Extras: Released by Sussex at end of 1988 season. Surrey 2nd XI Player of the Year

LAST SEASON: BATTING

	I.	N. O.	R.	H. S.	AV.
TEST					
1ST	16	2	726	138	51.85
INT					
RAL					
N.W.					
B&H					

LAST SEASON: BOWLING

	O.	M.	R.	W.	AV.
TEST					
1ST	20	1	83	1	83.00
INT					
RAL					
N.W.					
B&H					

CAREER: BATTING

	I.	N. O.	R.	H. S.	AV.
TEST					
1ST	136	12	3427	138	27.63
INT					
RAL	8	2	72	23	12.00
N.W.	8	1	125	41	17.85
B&H	3	0	137	71	45.66

CAREER: BOWLING

	O.	M.	R.	W.	AV.
TEST					
1ST	52.5	2	231	5	46.20
INT					
RAL	9	0	47	0	-
N.W.					
B&H					

1989. Scored first first-class 100 in 1990
Opinions on cricket: 'Four-day cricket and truer wickets are a much better preparation for Test cricket.'
Best batting: 138 Surrey v Essex, The Oval 1990
Best bowling: 2–19 Sussex v West Indians, Hove 1988

ALLEYNE, M. W. Gloucestershire

Name: Mark Wayne Alleyne
Role: Right-hand bat, medium pace bowler, cover fielder, occasional wicket-keeper
Born: 23 May 1968, Tottenham
Height: 5ft 10 1/2in **Weight:** 12st 10lbs
Nickname: Boo-Boo
County debut: 1986
1st-Class 50s scored: 15
1st-Class 100s scored: 4
1st-Class 200s scored: 1
Place in batting averages: 105th av. 40.66 (1989 99th av. 30.04)
Place in bowling averages: 9th av. 24.43
Strike rate: 42.00 (career 65.10)
1st-Class catches: 11 (career 68 & 1 stumping)
Parents: Euclid Clevis and Hyacinth Cordeilla
Marital status: Single
Family links with cricket: Brother played for Gloucestershire 2nd XI and

LAST SEASON: BATTING

	I.	N. O.	R.	H. S.	AV.
TEST					
1ST	21	0	854	256	40.66
INT					
RAL	13	5	203	39*	25.37
N.W.	1	1	9	9*	-
B&H	3	1	64	30	32.00

CAREER: BATTING

	I.	N. O.	R.	H. S.	AV.
TEST					
1ST	118	17	2896	256	28.67
INT					
RAL	54	20	822	49*	24.17
N.W.	8	4	20	9*	5.00
B&H	12	3	175	36	19.44

LAST SEASON: BOWLING

	O.	M.	R.	W.	AV.
TEST					
1ST	112	29	391	16	24.43
INT					
RAL	107.5	2	589	20	29.45
N.W.	29	4	114	6	19.00
B&H	24.5	1	151	4	37.75

CAREER: BOWLING

	O.	M.	R.	W.	AV.
TEST					
1ST	401.5	84	1529	37	41.32
INT					
RAL	313.5	9	1594	57	27.96
N.W.	66	8	258	8	32.25
B&H	92	5	423	20	21.15

Middlesex YCs. Father played club cricket in Barbados and England
Education: Harrison College, Barbados and Cardinal Pole School, E. London
Qualifications: 6 O-levels, NCA senior coaching award, and volleyball coaching certificate
Overseas tours: England YC to Sri Lanka 1987 and Australia 1988
Cricketers particularly admired: Gordon Greenidge, Viv Richards
Other sports followed: Football, volleyball, athletics
Relaxations: Watching films and sport; listening to music
Extras: Youngest player to score a century for Gloucestershire. In 1990 also became the youngest to score a double hundred for the county. Graduate of Haringey Cricket College
Best batting: 256 Gloucestershire v Northamptonshire, Northampton 1990
Best bowling: 4–48 Gloucestershire v Glamorgan, Bristol 1988

ALLOTT, P. J. W. Lancashire

Name: Paul John Walter Allott
Role: Right-hand bat, right-arm fast-medium bowler
Born: 14 September 1956, Altrincham, Cheshire
Height: 6ft 4in **Weight:** 15st
Nickname: Walt
County debut: 1978
County cap: 1981
Benefit: 1990
Test debut: 1981
Tests: 13
One-Day Internationals: 13
50 wickets in a season: 5
1st-Class 50s scored: 10
1st-Class 5 w. in innings: 30
Place in bowling averages: 102nd av. 40.55 (1989 36th av. 25.65)
Strike rate: 88.66 (career 59.20)
1st-Class catches: 9 (career 129)
Parents: John Norman and Lillian Patricia
Wife and date of marriage: Helen, 27 October 1979
Children: Ben and Susie
Family links with cricket: Father was dedicated club cricketer for twenty years with Ashley CC and is now active with Bowdon CC as a selector, administrator and junior organiser
Education: Altrincham Grammar School; Bede College, Durham

Qualifications: Qualified teacher and cricket coach
Off-season: Winding up benefit year
Overseas tours: With England to India 1981–82; India and Australia 1984–85
Cricketers particularly admired: Dennis Lillee
Injuries: Groin and back strains
Relaxations: Playing golf, watching all sports, listening to music, eating out, photography
Extras: Played football as goalkeeper for Cheshire schoolboys
Opinions on cricket: 'Too varied to be contained in one paragraph!'
Best batting: 88 Lancashire v Hampshire, Southampton 1987
Best bowling: 8–48 Lancashire v Northamptonshire, Northampton 1981

LAST SEASON: BATTING

	I.	N. O.	R.	H. S.	AV.
TEST					
1ST	6	2	114	55*	28.50
INT					
RAL	1	0	12	12	12.00
N.W.	-	-	-	-	-
B&H	-	-	-	-	-

CAREER: BATTING

	I.	N. O.	R.	H. S.	AV.
TEST	18	3	213	52*	14.20
1ST	236	59	3084	88	17.16
INT	6	1	15	8	3.00
RAL	60	28	536	43	16.75
N.W.	12	5	65	19*	9.28
B&H	22	7	153	23*	10.20

LAST SEASON: BOWLING

	O.	M.	R.	W.	AV.
TEST					
1ST	266	77	730	18	40.55
INT					
RAL	105	5	466	11	42.36
N.W.	34	10	93	4	23.25
B&H	67	12	190	6	31.66

CAREER: BOWLING

	O.	M.	R.	W.	AV.
TEST	370.5	75	1084	26	41.69
1ST	5924.5	1642	15065	612	24.61
INT	136.3	19	552	15	36.80
RAL	981	85	3833	142	26.99
N.W.	266	61	763	47	16.23
B&H	466.5	82	1450	60	24.16

AMBROSE, C. E. L. Northamptonshire

Name: Curtly Elconn Lynwall Ambrose
Role: Left-hand bat, right-arm
fast bowler; 'like the gully area'
Born: 21 September 1963, Antigua
Height: 6ft 7in **Weight:** 14st 4lbs
Nickname: Ambie
County debut: 1989
Test debut: 1987–88
Tests: 19
One-Day Internationals: 37
1st-Class 50s scored: 2
1st-Class 5 w. in innings: 13
1st-Class 10 w. in match: 3
Place in batting averages: 248th av.
15.61 (1989 228th av. 14.11)
Place in bowling averages: 6th av.
23.16 (1989 59th av. 28.39)
Strike rate: 49.54 (career 51.24)
1st-Class catches: 1 (career 13)
Parents: Jasper (deceased) and Hillie
Marital status: Single

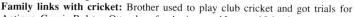

Family links with cricket: Brother used to play club cricket and got trials for
Antigua. Cousin Rolston Otto plays for Antigua and Leeward Islands
Education: Swetes Primary School; All Saints Secondary School
Qualifications: 3 O-levels, 3 A-levels, qualified carpenter
Off-season: Touring Pakistan with West Indies, then playing cricket in the
Caribbean
Overseas tours: West Indies to England 1988; Australia 1988–89; India for Nehru

LAST SEASON: BATTING

	I.	N. O.	R.	H. S.	AV.
TEST					
1ST	18	5	203	55*	15.61
INT					
RAL	-	-	-	-	-
N.W.	3	0	70	48	23.33
B&H	3	2	34	12	34.00

LAST SEASON: BOWLING

	O.	M.	R.	W.	AV.
TEST					
1ST	503.4	127	1413	61	23.16
INT					
RAL	7	1	31	0	-
N.W.	54.1	11	136	4	34.00
B&H	44	9	100	9	11.11

CAREER: BATTING

	I.	N. O.	R.	H. S.	AV.
TEST	30	7	333	44	14.47
1ST	59	14	783	59	17.40
INT	18	10	124	26*	15.50
RAL	6	1	23	13*	4.60
N.W.	3	0	70	48	23.33
B&H	4	3	51	17*	51.00

CAREER: BOWLING

	O.	M.	R.	W.	AV.
TEST	749	164	1948	80	24.35
1ST	1394.5	378	3768	171	22.03
INT	336.5	39	1220	63	19.36
RAL	84.5	13	285	10	28.50
N.W.	88	16	227	10	22.70
B&H	55	9	166	10	16.60

Cup 1989–90; Pakistan 1990–91
Overseas teams played for: Leeward Islands
Cricketers particularly admired: 'David Gower, Richard Hadlee, and of course my West Indian colleagues.'
Other sports followed: Basketball and tennis – 'Boris Becker is my favourite player.'
Relaxations: Listening to music, relaxing on the beach, going to the cinema
Extras: A basketball player who only began playing cricket seriously at age 17. Took a wicket with his first ball on Championship debut for Northamptonshire against Glamorgan in 1989. Figures of 8 for 45 are the best in Tests for West Indies v England
Opinions on cricket: 'Too many games played in county cricket. The wickets are too slow so do not encourage the bowlers a lot. It should be an even contest.'
Best batting: 59 West Indians v Sussex, Hove 1988
Best bowling: 8–45 West Indies v England, Bridgetown 1989–90

ANDREW, S. J. W. Essex

Name: Stephen Jon Walter Andrew
Role: Right-hand bat, right-arm medium bowler
Born: 27 January 1966, London
Height: 6ft 3in **Weight:** 13st
Nickname: Rip
County debut: 1984 (Hampshire), 1990 (Essex)
1st-Class 5 w. in innings: 5
Place in batting averages: 258th av. 13.22
Place in bowling averages: 105th av. 41.23 (1989 101st av. 40.23)
Strike rate: 65.60 (career 57.40)
1st-Class catches: 1 (career 16)
Parents: Jon and Victoria
Marital status: Single
Education: Hordle House Prep. School; Milton Abbey Public School
Qualifications: 3 O-levels
Off-season: 'Abroad in Australia.'

Overseas tours: Young England to West Indies 1985
Cricketers particularly admired: Dennis Lillee, Malcolm Marshall
Other sports followed: Interested in most sports
Relaxations: Music, video and TV, reading Wilbur Smith and Viz
Opinions on cricket: 'I think the balance between bat and ball has swayed too much to the batsman's favour. Keep wickets white but bring back the '89 ball to give the

bowler a chance at least to swing it.'
Best batting: 35 Essex v Northamptonshire, Chelmsford 1990
Best bowling: 7–92 Hampshire v Gloucestershire, Southampton 1987

LAST SEASON: BATTING

	I.	N. O.	R.	H. S.	AV.
TEST					
1ST	16	7	119	35	13.22
INT					
RAL	1	0	5	5	5.00
N.W.	-	-	-	-	-
B&H					

LAST SEASON: BOWLING

	O.	M.	R.	W.	AV.
TEST					
1ST	503	75	1897	46	41.23
INT					
RAL	19	2	121	2	60.50
N.W.	12	2	34	2	17.00
B&H					

CAREER: BATTING

	I.	N. O.	R.	H. S.	AV.
TEST					
1ST	48	25	224	35	9.73
INT					
RAL	2	1	6	5	6.00
N.W.	1	1	0	0*	-
B&H	3	3	5	4*	-

CAREER: BOWLING

	O.	M.	R.	W.	AV.
TEST					
1ST	1846.3	361	6148	193	31.85
INT					
RAL	146.3	3	756	14	54.00
N.W.	62	7	219	7	31.28
B&H	109	11	363	20	18.15

ANTHONY, H. A. G.   Glamorgan

Name: Hamesh Aubrey Gervase Anthony
Role: Right-hand bat, right-arm fast-medium bowler
Born: 16 January 1971, Walings Village, Antigua
Height: 6ft 1in **Weight:** 12st 7lbs
Nickname: Hot-shot, Hamo
County debut: 1990
Place in batting averages: 247th av. 15.87
Place in bowling averages: 84th av. 38.83
Strike rate: 66.33 (career 56.41)
1st-Class catches: 0 (career 4)
Parents: Emelda Williams and Alfred Anthony
Marital status: Single
Family links with cricket: Brothers Junie and Joshua play; George Ferris is cousin
Education: Urlings Primary School, Jennings Primary School, Antigua
Qualifications: Carpentry certificate
Off-season: Playing cricket with Leeward Islands

19

Overseas tours: West Indies Youth to Canada 1989
Overseas teams played for: Leeward Islands (debut 1990)
Cricketers particularly admired: Viv Richards, Andy Roberts, Eldine Baptiste, David Gower
Other sports followed: Football, basketball, tennis
Injuries: Strained side – out for two weeks
Relaxations: Listening to music, TV, films
Opinions on cricket: 'Too much cricket is crammed into an English season.'
Best batting: 39 Glamorgan v Lancashire, Colwyn Bay 1990
Best bowling: 5–40 Leeward Islands v Jamaica, Kingston 1989–90

LAST SEASON: BATTING

	I.	N. O.	R.	H. S.	AV.
TEST					
1ST	8	0	127	39	15.87
INT					
RAL					
N.W.					
B&H					

LAST SEASON: BOWLING

	O.	M.	R.	W.	AV.
TEST					
1ST	142.4	32	466	12	38.83
INT					
RAL					
N.W.					
B&H					

CAREER: BATTING

	I.	N. O.	R.	H. S.	AV.
TEST					
1ST	15	0	174	39	11.60
INT					
RAL					
N.W.					
B&H					

CAREER: BOWLING

	O.	M.	R.	W.	AV.
TEST					
1ST	301.3	64	894	31	28.83
INT					
RAL					
N.W.					
B&H					

1. Who won the County Championship in 1990?

2. Who won the Refuge Assurance League in 1990?

3. Who came last in the County Championship in 1990?

ASIF DIN, M.   Warwickshire

Name: Mohamed Asif Din
Role: Right-hand bat, leg-break bowler
Born: 21 September 1960, Kampala, Uganda
Height: 5ft 9in **Weight:** 10st 7lbs
Nickname: Gunga 'and many others'
County debut: 1981
County cap: 1987
1000 runs in a season: 2
1st-Class 50s scored: 37
1st-Class 100s scored: 6
1st-Class 5 w. in innings: 1
One-Day 50s: 16
One-Day 100s: 3
Place in batting averages: 180th av. 27.82 (1989 101st av. 29.92)
Place in bowling averages: 145th av. 63.50
Strike rate: 95.49 (career 85.80)
1st-Class catches: 10 (career 98)
Parents: Jamiz and Mumtaz
Wife and date of marriage: Ahmevin, 27 September 1987
Family links with cricket: Brothers Khalid and Abid play in local leagues
Education: Ladywood Comprehensive School, Birmingham
Qualifications: CSEs and O-levels
Cricketers particularly admired: Zaheer Abbas, Majid Khan
Other sports followed: American football, basketball

LAST SEASON: BATTING

	I.	N. O.	R.	H. S.	AV.
TEST					
1ST	39	4	974	100*	27.82
INT					
RAL	14	3	545	113	49.54
N.W.	2	0	124	66	62.00
B&H	4	0	123	50	30.75

LAST SEASON: BOWLING

	O.	M.	R.	W.	AV.
TEST					
1ST	159.1	30	635	10	63.50
INT					
RAL	2	0	17	0	-
N.W.	11	2	54	5	10.80
B&H					

CAREER: BATTING

	I.	N. O.	R.	H. S.	AV.
TEST					
1ST	294	42	7559	158*	29.99
INT					
RAL	114	20	2683	113	28.54
N.W.	21	7	584	94*	41.71
B&H	30	4	758	107	29.15

CAREER: BOWLING

	O.	M.	R.	W.	AV.
TEST					
1ST	972.3	159	3956	68	58.17
INT					
RAL	28.3	1	182	4	45.50
N.W.	20.1	3	78	7	11.14
B&H	11	0	62	1	62.00

Opinions on cricket: 'Too much cricket. Would like to see 16 four-day matches.'
Best batting: 158* Warwickshire v Cambridge University, Fenner's 1988
Best bowling: 5–100 Warwickshire v Glamorgan, Edgbaston 1982

ATHERTON, M. A.   Lancashire

Name: Michael Andrew Atherton
Role: Right-hand bat, leg-spin (!) bowler, slip fielder
Born: 23 March 1968, Manchester
Height: 6ft **Weight:** 12st 5lbs
Nickname: Athers
County debut: 1987
Test debut: 1989
Tests: 8
One-Day Internationals: 2
1000 runs in a season: 4
1st-Class 50s scored: 23
1st-Class 100s scored: 16
1st-class 5w. in innings: 3
One-Day 50s: 11
One-Day 100s: 1
Place in batting averages: 9th av. 71.25 (1989 92nd av. 31.36)
Place in bowling averages: 34th av. 31.06 (1989 103rd av. 40.60)
Strike rate: 57.80 (career 82.21)
1st-Class catches: 24 (career 65)
Parents: Alan and Wendy
Marital status: Single
Family links with cricket: 'Dad plays cricket at local club Woodhouses.'
Education: The Manchester Grammar School; Downing College, Cambridge
Qualifications: 10 O-levels, 3 A-levels; BA Cantab.
Off-season: Touring Australia with England
Overseas tours: Young England to Sri Lanka 1987 and Australia 1988; England A to Zimbabwe 1989–90; England to Australia 1990–91
Cricketers particularly admired: 'Many, especially in the Lancashire dressing room – Gehan Mendis, Neil Fairbrother and Wasim Akram who are all exciting and often brilliant cricketers.'
Other sports followed: Golf, squash, football, rugby
Relaxations: Golf, squash, reading
Extras: In 1987 was first player to score 1000 runs in his debut season since Paul Parker in 1976. Youngest Lancastrian to score a Test century (151 v NZ at Trent Bridge in 1990); second Lancastrian to score a Test century at Old Trafford (138 v

India in 1990). First captained England U–19s aged 16

Opinions on cricket: 'Over-rate fines should be abolished. Four-day cricket is extremely boring. County cricket too often takes the brunt for failures in Test cricket.'

Best batting: 191 Lancashire v Surrey, The Oval 1990

Best bowling: 6–78 Lancashire v Nottinghamshire, Trent Bridge 1990

LAST SEASON: BATTING

	I.	N. O.	R.	H. S.	AV.
TEST	11	0	735	151	66.81
1ST	20	4	1189	191	74.31
INT	2	0	66	59	33.00
RAL	10	1	462	111	51.33
N.W.	5	1	156	55	39.00
B&H	7	2	288	74	57.60

LAST SEASON: BOWLING

	O.	M.	R.	W.	AV.
TEST	38	9	178	1	178.00
1ST	395.3	94	1220	44	27.72
INT					
RAL	29	0	190	5	38.00
N.W.	18	1	59	4	14.75
B&H	14	1	52	3	17.33

CAREER: BATTING

	I.	N. O.	R.	H. S.	AV.
TEST	15	0	808	151	53.86
1ST	114	15	4621	191	46.67
INT	2	0	66	59	33.00
RAL	13	1	487	111	40.58
N.W.	6	1	191	55	38.20
B&H	19	2	619	74	36.41

CAREER: BOWLING

	O.	M.	R.	W.	AV.
TEST	46	9	212	1	212.00
1ST	1269.3	266	3781	95	39.80
INT					
RAL	29	0	190	5	38.00
N.W.	20	1	71	4	17.75
B&H	33	1	168	7	24.00

ATHEY, C. W. J. Gloucestershire

Name: Charles William Jeffrey Athey

Role: Right-hand bat, right-arm medium bowler

Born: 27 September 1957, Middlesbrough

Height: 5ft 10in **Weight:** 12st 3lbs

Nickname: Bumper, Wingnut, Ath

County debut: 1976 (Yorks), 1984 (Gloucs)

County cap: 1980 (Yorks), 1985 (Gloucs)

Benefit: 1990

Test debut: 1980

Tests: 23

One-Day Internationals: 31

1000 runs in a season: 8

1st-Class 50s scored: 86

1st-Class 100s scored: 35

One-Day 50s: 63

One-Day 100s: 8

Place in batting averages: 43rd av. 52.64 (1989 118th av. 27.88)
1st-Class catches: 18 (career 332 & 2 stumpings)
Parents: Peter and Maree
Wife and date of marriage: Janet Linda, 9 October 1982
Family links with cricket: 'Father played league cricket in North Yorkshire and South Durham League for twenty-nine years, twenty-five of them with Middlesbrough. President of Middlesbrough CC since 1975. Brother-in-law Colin Cook played for Middlesex, other brother-in-law (Martin) plays in Thames Valley League. Father-in-law deeply involved in Middlesex Youth cricket.'
Education: Linthorpe Junior School; Stainsby Secondary School; Acklam Hall High School
Qualifications: 4 O-levels, some CSEs, NCA coaching certificate
Off-season: Completing benefit year; watching England in Australia
Overseas tours: England U–19 to West Indies 1976; England to West Indies 1980–81; Australia 1986–87; Pakistan, Australia and New Zealand 1987–88; England B to Sri Lanka 1985–86; unofficial English XI to South Africa 1989–90
Cricketers particularly admired: Gordon Greenidge, Malcolm Marshall, Chris Smith
Other sports followed: Most sports
Relaxations: Music, good films, good food
Extras: Played for Teesside County Schools U–16s at age 12. Played for Yorkshire Colts 1974. Played football for Middlesbrough Schools U–16 and Junior XIs. Offered but declined apprenticeship terms with Middlesbrough FC. Captain of Gloucestershire in 1989
Opinions on cricket: 'Should play four-day cricket, playing each county once. Over-rate fines are not realistic.'
Best batting: 184 England B v Sri Lanka XI, Galle 1985–86
Best bowling: 3–3 Gloucestershire v Hampshire, Bristol 1985

LAST SEASON: BATTING

	I.	N. O.	R.	H. S.	AV.
TEST					
1ST	35	7	1474	131	52.64
INT					
RAL	15	2	546	113	42.00
N.W.	3	1	111	81*	55.50
B&H	3	1	152	83*	76.00

LAST SEASON: BOWLING

	O.	M.	R.	W.	AV.
TEST					
1ST	50.5	10	145	2	72.50
INT					
RAL					
N.W.	3	0	14	0	-
B&H					

CAREER: BATTING

	I.	N. O.	R.	H. S.	AV.
TEST	41	1	919	123	22.97
1ST	599	62	18969	184	35.32
INT	30	3	848	142*	31.40
RAL	179	15	5601	121*	34.15
N.W.	33	6	1091	115	40.40
B&H	55	8	1691	95	35.97

CAREER: BOWLING

	O.	M.	R.	W.	AV.
TEST					
1ST	745.4	112	1966	41	47.95
INT	1	0	10	0	-
RAL	103.4	1	581	22	26.40
N.W.	22.1	1	120	1	120.00
B&H	56.4	4	242	12	20.16

ATKINS, P. D.   Surrey

Name: Paul David Atkins
Role: Right-hand bat, right-arm bowler
Born: 11 June 1966, Aylesbury
Height: 6ft 1in **Weight:** 13st 11lbs
Nickname: Ripper
County debut: 1988
1st-Class 50s scored: 1
1st-Class 100s scored: 1
One-Day 50s: 1
1st-Class catches: 0 (career 3)
Parents: Brian Alan Arthur and Thelma
Marital status: Single
Family links with cricket: Father plays club cricket for Dinton CC
Education: Aylesbury Grammar School
Qualifications: 7 O-levels, 3 A-levels
Off-season: 'Relaxing, coaching cricket and working on my game.'
Cricketers particularly admired: Gordon Greenidge
Other sports followed: Golf and football. Supports Portsmouth FC
Relaxations: Listening to music, and 'socialising with Jonathan Robinson and Neil Kendrick.'
Extras: Played for Buckinghamshire CCC 1985–90, scoring 97* in Holt Cup final win in 1990. Seventh Surrey player to score hundred on debut. Also scored 99 on County Championship debut
Opinions on cricket: 'Avoid politics and play cricket with all races and anywhere in the world. 2nd XI wickets must improve.'
Best batting: 114* Surrey v Cambridge University, Fenner's 1988

LAST SEASON: BATTING

	I.	N. O.	R.	H. S.	AV.
TEST					
1ST	2	1	23	23	23.00
INT					
RAL					
N.W.					
B&H					

CAREER: BATTING

	I.	N. O.	R.	H. S.	AV.
TEST					
1ST	18	3	471	114*	31.40
INT					
RAL	1	0	2	2	2.00
N.W.	2	0	82	82	41.00
B&H	3	1	15	9	7.50

AUSTIN, I. D. Lancashire

Name: Ian David Austin
Role: Left-hand bat, right-arm medium bowler
Born: 30 May 1966, Haslingden, Lancs
Height: 5ft 10in **Weight:** 14st 7lbs
Nickname: Oscar, Bully
County debut: 1986
1st-Class 50s scored: 3
1st-Class 5 w. in innings: 1
One-Day 50s: 2
Place in batting averages: 161st av. 30.66 (1989 210th av. 17.10)
Place in bowling averages: 135th av. 55.16 (1989 28th av. 22.52)
Strike rate: 122.50 (career 69.09)
1st-Class catches: 0 (career 3)
Parents: Jack and Ursula
Family links with cricket: Father opened batting for Haslingden CC
Education: Haslingden High School
Qualifications: 3 O-levels; NCA coaching certificate
Off-season: Playing in Sydney with Renwick CC
Cricketers particularly admired: Ian Botham, Clive Lloyd
Other sports followed: Football, golf
Injuries: Thigh and groin strains
Relaxations: Listening to music, playing golf, reading
Extras: Holds amateur Lancashire League record for highest individual score
Opinions on cricket: 'Should abolish over-rate fines. Lengthen tea-time.'

LAST SEASON: BATTING

	I.	N.O.	R.	H.S.	AV.
TEST					
1ST	15	6	276	58	30.66
INT					
RAL	8	5	36	10*	12.00
N.W.	1	1	13	13*	-
B&H	5	4	88	61*	88.00

LAST SEASON: BOWLING

	O.	M.	R.	W.	AV.
TEST					
1ST	245	76	662	12	55.16
INT					
RAL	108.1	2	622	16	38.87
N.W.	53	5	205	7	29.28
B&H	65	11	244	11	22.18

CAREER: BATTING

	I.	N.O.	R.	H.S.	AV.
TEST					
1ST	40	11	704	64	24.27
INT					
RAL	31	14	239	41	14.05
N.W.	2	1	23	13*	23.00
B&H	9	4	199	80	39.80

CAREER: BOWLING

	O.	M.	R.	W.	AV.
TEST					
1ST	621.5	180	1610	54	29.81
INT					
RAL	333.5	8	1624	51	31.84
N.W.	65	1	255	7	36.42
B&H	115	11	441	14	31.50

Best batting: 64 Lancashire v Derbyshire, Old Trafford 1988
Best bowling: 5–79 Lancashire v Surrey, The Oval 1988

AYLING, J. R. Hampshire

Name: Jonathan Richard Ayling
Role: Right-hand bat, right-arm medium bowler
Born: 13 June 1967, Portsmouth
Height: 6ft 4in **Weight:** 14st
Nickname: Victor
County debut: 1988
1st-Class 50s scored: 7
Place in batting averages: 69th av. 46.00
Place in bowling averages: 133rd av. 52.00
Strike rate: 93.45 (career 62.43)
1st-Class catches: 2 (career 7)
Parents: Christopher and Mary
Marital status: Single
Education: Portsmouth Grammar School
Qualifications: 8 O-levels, 1 A-level
Off-season: 'Coaching, training and moving house.'

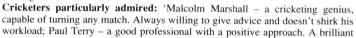

Cricketers particularly admired: 'Malcolm Marshall – a cricketing genius, capable of turning any match. Always willing to give advice and doesn't shirk his workload; Paul Terry – a good professional with a positive approach. A brilliant

LAST SEASON: BATTING

	I.	N. O.	R.	H. S.	AV.
TEST					
1ST	11	3	368	62*	46.00
INT					
RAL	10	6	144	47*	36.00
N.W.	4	1	54	29	18.00
B&H	1	0	14	14	14.00

LAST SEASON: BOWLING

	O.	M.	R.	W.	AV.
TEST					
1ST	181.2	46	572	11	52.00
INT					
RAL	91	3	450	15	30.00
N.W.	45	5	197	7	28.14
B&H	10	0	63	3	21.00

CAREER: BATTING

	I.	N. O.	R.	H. S.	AV.
TEST					
1ST	44	7	1079	88*	29.16
INT					
RAL	20	7	312	47*	24.00
N.W.	7	3	87	29	21.75
B&H	2	0	15	14	7.50

CAREER: BOWLING

	O.	M.	R.	W.	AV.
TEST					
1ST	603.3	143	1670	58	28.79
INT					
RAL	188	5	879	30	29.30
N.W.	92	14	351	12	29.25
B&H	61	7	162	6	27.00

all-round fielder and a genuinely nice guy.'
Other sports followed: Athletics, soccer, snooker
Injuries: 'Still recovering from knee reconstruction operation in 1989.'
Relaxations: 'Many types of music; good food; evenings out with friends.'
Extras: Wicket with first ball in first-class cricket; missed all of 1989 season with a serious knee injury
Opinions on cricket: 'The 1990 season's pitches favoured batsmen too much; either the balls or pitches should return to previous types to redress the balance. An alternative to the present benefit system should exist: regardless of whether he has had ten years' capped service a player should be rewarded financially at the end of his first-team career. This would prevent capped players 'hanging on' simply to gain a benefit and would promote younger and more ambitious players.'
Best batting: 88* Hampshire v Lancashire, Liverpool 1988
Best bowling: 4–57 Hampshire v Gloucestershire, Cheltenham 1988

AYMES, A. N. Hampshire

Name: Adrian Nigel Aymes
Role: Right-hand bat, wicket-keeper
Born: 4 June 1964, Southampton
Height: 6ft **Weight:** 13st 3lbs
Nickname: Adi
County debut: 1987
1st-Class 50s scored: 4
Parents: Michael and Barbara
Marital status: Engaged to Marie
Education: Shirley Middle; Bellemoor Secondary; Hill College
Qualifications: 4 O-levels, 1 A-level
Off-season: 'Building Robin Smith's house.'
Cricketers particularly admired: Bob Taylor, Malcolm Marshall, Gordon Greenidge, David Turner 'for playing for thirty-four years'
Other sports followed: Football, American and Australian Rules football, martial arts
Injuries: Dislocated finger
Relaxations: 'Watching films; swimming, keeping as fit as possible.'
Extras: Half century on debut v Surrey; equalled club record of 6 catches in an innings and 10 in a match
Opinions on cricket: '12-strand ball with good wickets might help level out the game. I would also be in favour of one hour for lunch and half an hour for tea. Second

XI sides are far too scared to lose and feel a draw is a success.'
Best batting: 75* Hampshire v Glamorgan, Pontypridd 1990

LAST SEASON: BATTING

	I.	N. O.	R.	H. S.	AV.
TEST					
1ST	8	4	317	75*	79.25
INT					
RAL	1	1	15	15*	-
N.W.					
B&H					

LAST SEASON: WICKET-KEEPING

	CT	ST	
TEST			
1ST	9	3	
INT			
RAL	-	-	
N.W.			
B&H			

CAREER: BATTING

	I.	N. O.	R.	H. S.	AV.
TEST					
1ST	10	5	399	75*	79.80
INT					
RAL	1	1	15	15*	-
N.W.					
B&H					

CAREER: WICKET-KEEPING

	CT	ST	
TEST			
1ST	23	3	
INT			
RAL	2	1	
N.W.			
B&H			

BABINGTON, A. M.   Gloucestershire

Name: Andrew Mark Babington
Role: Left-hand bat, right-arm
fast-medium bowler
Born: 22 July 1963, London
Height: 6ft 2in **Weight:** 13st 3lbs
Nickname: Hagar, Vinny, Turbo
County debut: 1986 (Sussex)
1st-Class 5 w. in innings: 2
1st-Class catches: 2 (career 21)
Parents: Roy and Maureen
Wife and date of marriage: Lisa,
30 September 1989
Family links with cricket: Father
played club cricket. Brother also plays
Education: Reigate Grammar School;
Borough Road PE College
Qualifications: 5 O-levels, 2 A-levels;
NCA coaching certificate; Member of
Institute of Legal Executives; holds con-
sumer credit licence and is licensed to
work for insurance company
Off-season: Working for Homeowners Advisory Bureau
Cricketers particularly admired: Dennis Lillee, John Snow, Richard Hadlee

Other sports followed: Motor racing, boxing, football, golf

Injuries: Missed six weeks with torn intercostal and stomach muscles

Relaxations: 'Spending time at home with my wife and friends. Playing golf and driving.'

Extras: Took hat-trick v Gloucestershire in 1986, with second, third and fourth balls in Championship cricket. Released by Sussex at end of 1990 season – joined Gloucestershire

Opinions on cricket: 'The authorities should now decide whether they wish to continue with contrived cricket due to the seamless balls, to uncover pitches and run-ups or to keep pitches as they are and bring back the old ball. We should play 16 four-day games.'

Best batting: 20 Sussex v Glamorgan, Hove 1990

Best bowling: 5–37 Sussex v Lancashire, Liverpool 1989

LAST SEASON: BATTING

	I.	N. O.	R.	H. S.	AV.
TEST					
1ST	2	0	28	20	14.00
INT					
RAL	-	-	-	-	-
N.W.					
B&H					

LAST SEASON: BOWLING

	O.	M.	R.	W.	AV.
TEST					
1ST	63	7	256	3	85.33
INT					
RAL	4	0	21	0	-
N.W.					
B&H					

CAREER: BATTING

	I.	N. O.	R.	H. S.	AV.
TEST					
1ST	61	26	224	20	6.40
INT					
RAL	8	3	2	1*	0.40
N.W.	2	2	4	4*	-
B&H	4	2	15	9	7.50

CAREER: BOWLING

	O.	M.	R.	W.	AV.
TEST					
1ST	1495.3	275	4671	135	34.60
INT					
RAL	272	10	1275	34	37.50
N.W.	64	1	280	11	25.45
B&H	105.2	13	423	19	22.26

BAILEY, R. J.   Northamptonshire

Name: Robert John Bailey
Role: Right-hand bat, off-break
bowler, county vice-captain
Born: 28 October 1963, Biddulph,
Stoke-on-Trent
Height: 6ft 3in **Weight:** 14st
Nickname: Bailers, Nose Bag ('I eat
a lot!')
County debut: 1982
County cap: 1985
Test debut: 1988
Tests: 4
One-Day Internationals: 4
1000 runs in a season: 7
1st-Class 50s scored: 53
1st-Class 100s scored: 26
1st-Class 200s scored: 3
One-Day 50s: 30
One-Day 100s: 5
Place in batting averages: 17th av.

64.09 (1989 76th av. 33.42)
Place in bowling averages: 134th av. 54.90 (1989 121st av. 55.20)
Strike rate: 91.81 (career 78.25)
1st-Class catches: 16 (career 134)
Parents: Marie, father deceased
Wife and date of marriage: Rachel, 11 April 1987
Family links with cricket: Father played in North Staffordshire League for thirty
years for Knypersley and Minor Counties cricket for Staffordshire as wicket-keeper

LAST SEASON: BATTING

	I.	N. O.	R.	H. S.	AV.
TEST					
1ST	39	8	1987	204*	64.09
INT					
RAL	16	1	477	71	31.80
N.W.	5	1	123	72*	30.75
B&H	4	1	140	92*	46.66

LAST SEASON: BOWLING

	O.	M.	R.	W.	AV.
TEST					
1ST	168.2	29	604	11	54.90
INT					
RAL	8	0	51	1	51.00
N.W.	12	2	49	4	12.25
B&H					

CAREER: BATTING

	I.	N. O.	R.	H. S.	AV.
TEST	8	0	119	43	14.87
1ST	305	48	10728	224*	41.74
INT	4	2	137	43*	68.50
RAL	101	13	3142	125*	35.70
N.W.	22	6	553	86*	34.56
B&H	31	3	1224	134	43.71

CAREER: BOWLING

	O.	M.	R.	W.	AV.
TEST	456.3	83	1618	35	46.22
1ST					
INT	6	0	25	0	-
RAL	21.1	0	159	4	39.75
N.W.	16	2	71	5	14.20
B&H	10	3	29	1	29.00

Education: Biddulph High School
Qualifications: 6 CSEs, 1 O-level, NCA senior coach
Off-season: 'Finding a job!'
Overseas tours: England to Sharjah 1985 and 1987; West Indies 1989–90
Other sports followed: Stoke City and Coventry City FCs
Relaxations: Listening to music
Extras: Played for Young England v Young Australia 1983. Selected for cancelled tour of India 1988–89. Youngest Northamptonshire player to score 10,000 runs
Opinions on cricket: 'NatWest finals are becoming a farce with early starts in September. Sixty overs is far too long – why are we the only country in the world to play so many overs?'
Best batting: 224* Northamptonshire v Glamorgan, Swansea 1986
Best bowling: 3–27 Northamptonshire v Glamorgan, Wellingborough 1988

BAINBRIDGE, P.   Gloucestershire

Name: Philip Bainbridge
Role: Right-hand bat, right-arm medium bowler
Born: 16 April 1958, Stoke-on-Trent
Height: 5ft 9 1/2in **Weight:** 12st 7lbs
Nickname: Bains, Robbo
County debut: 1977
County cap: 1981
Benefit: 1989
1000 runs in a season: 8
1st-Class 50s scored: 69
1st-Class 100s scored: 22
1st-Class 5 w. in innings: 7
One-Day 50s: 21
One-Day 100s: 1
Place in batting averages: 83rd av. 44.28 (1989 89th av. 31.83)
Place in bowling averages: 116th av. 46.81 (1989 70th av. 30.48)
Strike rate: 88.72 (career 72.86)
1st-Class catches: 4 (career 110)
Parents: Leonard George and Lilian Rose
Wife and date of marriage: Barbara, 22 September 1979
Children: Neil, 11 January 1984; Laura, 15 January 1985
Family links with cricket: Cousin, Stephen Wilkinson, played for Somerset
Education: Hanley High School; Stoke-on-Trent Sixth Form College; Borough Road College of Education

Qualifications: 9 O-levels, 2 A-levels, BEd
Career outside cricket: Partner in a corporate hospitality and travel company
Off-season: 'Building up business.'
Overseas tours: English Counties XI to Zimbabwe 1985
Cricketers particularly admired: Mike Procter, Brian Brain, Zaheer Abbas
Other sports followed: All sports, particularly soccer and rugby
Injuries: Back injury early season, hand injury in August
Relaxations: 'Music, drinking and eating, my children.'
Extras: Played for four 2nd XIs in 1976 – Gloucestershire, Derbyshire, Northamptonshire and Warwickshire. Played for Young England v Australia 1977. Scored first century for Stoke-on-Trent aged 14. One of *Wisden's* Five Cricketers of the Year, 1985
Opinions on cricket: 'Too much cricket is being played. There should be a 16 four-day match Championship. Durham should be made first-class.'
Best batting: 169 Gloucestershire v Yorkshire, Cheltenham 1988
Best bowling: 8–53 Gloucestershire v Somerset, Bristol 1986

LAST SEASON: BATTING

	I.	N. O.	R.	H. S.	AV.
TEST					
1ST	28	3	1107	152	44.28
INT					
RAL	11	2	228	59*	25.33
N.W.	2	1	69	56*	69.00
B&H	3	1	65	55	32.50

LAST SEASON: BOWLING

	O.	M.	R.	W.	AV.
TEST					
1ST	162.4	30	515	11	46.51
INT					
RAL	74.1	0	410	11	37.27
N.W.	17.1	1	53	0	-
B&H	24	3	108	2	54.00

CAREER: BATTING

	I.	N. O.	R.	H. S.	AV.
TEST					
1ST	424	60	12353	169	33.93
INT					
RAL	144	25	2531	106*	21.26
N.W.	21	3	610	89	33.88
B&H	42	9	967	96	29.30

CAREER: BOWLING

	O.	M.	R.	W.	AV.
TEST					
1ST	3315.3	40	1265	38	33.28
INT					
RAL	932.4	31	4754	159	29.89
N.W.	238.1	27	807	27	29.88
B&H	355.3	40	1265	38	33.28

BAIRSTOW, D. L.   Yorkshire

Name: David Leslie Bairstow
Role: Right-hand bat, wicket-keeper, occasional medium pacer
Born: 1 September 1951, Bradford
Height: 5ft 10in **Weight:** 14st 7lbs
Nickname: Bluey
County debut: 1970
County cap: 1973
Benefit: 1982 (56,913)
Testimonial: 1990
Test debut: 1979
Tests: 4
One-Day Internationals: 21
1000 runs in a season: 3
1st-Class 50s scored: 73
1st-Class 100s scored: 10
One-Day 50s: 19
One-Day 100s: 1
Wife and date of marriage: Janet, 14 October 1988
Children: Andrew David, September 1989
Family links with cricket: Father, Leslie, played cricket for Laisterdyke
Education: Hanson Grammar School, Bradford
Qualifications: O and A-levels
Career outside cricket: Runs his own office automation company
Overseas tours: England to Australia 1978–79 and 1979–80; West Indies 1981
Overseas teams played for: Griqualand West 1976–77 and 1977–78

LAST SEASON: BATTING

	I.	N.O.	R.	H.S.	AV.
TEST					
1ST	6	0	179	61	29.83
INT					
RAL	6	3	72	21*	24.00
N.W.					
B&H	2	1	10	9	10.00

LAST SEASON: WICKET-KEEPING

	CT	ST			
TEST					
1ST	13	0			
INT					
RAL	2	1			
N.W.					
B&H	1	0			

CAREER: BATTING

	I.	N.O.	R.	H.S.	AV.
TEST	7	1	125	59	20.83
1ST	640	118	13836	145	26.50
INT	20	6	206	23*	14.71
RAL	227	51	3677	83*	20.89
N.W.	27	5	492	92	22.36
B&H	59	14	945	103*	21.00

CAREER: WICKET-KEEPING

	CT	ST			
TEST	12	1			
1ST	949	137			
INT	17	4			
RAL	231	24			
N.W.	38	3			
B&H	117	5			

Relaxations: Gardening, playing golf
Extras: Turned down an offer to play for Bradford City FC. Played for MCC Schools at Lord's in 1970. First Yorkshire wicket-keeper to get 1000 runs in a season (1982) since Arthur Wood in 1935. Set Yorkshire record of seven catches v Derbyshire at Scarborough, 1982. His 145 for Yorkshire v Middlesex is the highest score by a Yorkshire wicket-keeper. Allowed to take an A-level at 6am in order to make Yorkshire debut. Published *A Yorkshire Diary – A Year of Crisis* 1984. Yorkshire captain 1984–1986. Completed 1000 dismissals for Yorkshire in 1988. Released at end of 1990 season
Best batting: 145 Yorkshire v Middlesex, Scarborough 1980
Best bowling: 3–25 Yorkshire v MCC, Scarborough 1987

BAKKER, P-. J. Hampshire

Name: Paul-Jan Bakker
Role: Right-hand bat, right-arm medium pace bowler
Born: 19 August 1957, Vlaardingen, Holland
Height: 6ft 1in **Weight:** 14st
Nickname: Nip, Barry, Dutchie
County debut: 1986
50 wickets in a season: 1
1st-Class 5 w. in innings: 7
Place in bowling averages: 87th av. 38.89 (1989 27th av. 22.49)
Strike rate: 70.75 (career 56.27)
1st-Class catches: 3 (career 7)
Parents: Hubertus Antonius Bakker and Wilhelmina Hendrika Bakker-Goos
Marital status: Single
Family links with cricket: 'Father is scorer for my club in the Hague – Quick CC.'

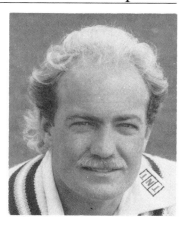

Education: Ie VCL and Hugo de Groot College, The Hague, Holland
Qualifications: 'We have a different school system but finished my HAVO schooling.' Ski-instructor
Career outside cricket: Tour-guiding in the Swiss Alps
Off-season: MCC tour to USA, golf in Zimbabwe, four months in Switzerland
Overseas tours: Several tours to England with Dutch clubs and with Holland national side
Cricketers particularly admired: Malcolm Marshall ('he has the ball on a string'), Michael Holding ('he has the most beautiful run up ever'), Graham Gooch

Other sports followed: Formula One motor racing, Dutch football, golf and most other sports

Injuries: Torn calf muscle during pre-season training in Barbados

Relaxations: Bars and restaurants, newspapers, golf 'if I'm playing well', skiing

Extras: First ever Dutch player to play professional cricket. Played for Holland in 1986 and 1990 ICC Trophy competitions

Opinions on cricket: 'As a bowler who tries to hit the seam, I found it an almost impossible task to get any movement out of the ball in 1990. I realise it doesn't have to seam all over the place but a little bit is not too much to ask. The wickets were dry and flat so I could count the studs on the batsman's front foot after every delivery. No, it wasn't much fun. Keep the same wickets but bring back the old ball.'

Best batting: 22 Hampshire v Yorkshire, Southampton 1989

Best bowling: 7–31 Hampshire v Kent, Bournemouth 1987

LAST SEASON: BATTING

	I.	N. O.	R.	H. S.	AV.
TEST					
1ST	9	4	95	20	19.00
INT					
RAL	3	2	11	9	11.00
N.W.	2	1	5	3*	5.00
B&H	-	-	-	-	-

CAREER: BATTING

	I.	N. O.	R.	H. S.	AV.
TEST					
1ST	41	16	247	22	9.88
INT					
RAL	9	8	22	9	22.00
N.W.	3	1	7	3*	3.50
B&H	-	-	-	-	-

LAST SEASON: BOWLING

	O.	M.	R.	W.	AV.
TEST					
1ST	436.2	90	1439	37	38.89
INT					
RAL	65	6	363	13	27.92
N.W.	43	6	164	3	54.66
B&H	10	3	21	1	21.00

CAREER: BOWLING

	O.	M.	R.	W.	AV.
TEST					
1ST	1519.2	376	4310	162	26.60
INT					
RAL	222.1	16	973	50	19.46
N.W.	110.4	19	363	11	33.00
B&H	115	16	186	6	31.00

BALL, M. C. J. Gloucestershire

Name: Martyn Charles John Ball
Role: Right-hand bat, off-break bowler
Born: 26 April 1970, Bristol
Height: 5ft 9in **Weight:** 11st 4lbs
Nickname: Benny, Scarrot
County debut: 1988
1st-Class catches 1989: 4 (career 9)
Parents: Kenneth Charles and Pamela
Wendy
Marital status: Single
Education: King Edmund Secondary
School, Yate; Bath College of Further
Education
Qualifications: 6 O-levels, 3 AO-levels
Off-season: Playing and coaching in
Zimbabwe
Cricketers most admired: Ian
Botham, John Emburey, Vic Marks,
David Graveney, Jack Russell
Other sports followed: All sports
except synchronised swimming and show jumping
Relaxations: Following Manchester City FC and listening to music
Extras: Played for Young England against New Zealand in 1989
Opinions on cricket: 'The 1990 season was too much in the batsmen's favour – we
should keep hard, brown and flat wickets, but use a better ball.'
Best batting: 17* Gloucestershire v Hampshire, Portsmouth 1989
Best bowling: 4–53 Gloucestershire v Kent, Maidstone 1989

LAST SEASON: BATTING

	I.	N. O.	R.	H. S.	AV.
TEST					
1ST	5	0	39	15	7.80
INT					
RAL	1	0	1	1	1.00
N.W.					
B&H	-	-	-	-	-

LAST SEASON: BOWLING

	O.	M.	R.	W.	AV.
TEST					
1ST	62	15	201	3	67.00
INT					
RAL	16	0	86	1	86.00
N.W.					
B&H	10	0	68	0	-

CAREER: BATTING

	I.	N. O.	R.	H. S.	AV.
TEST					
1ST	14	3	72	17*	6.54
INT					
RAL	2	0	5	4	2.50
N.W.	-	-	-	-	-
B&H	-	-	-	-	-

CAREER: BOWLING

	O.	M.	R.	W.	AV.
TEST					
1ST	251	49	795	23	34.56
INT					
RAL	24	0	135	1	135.00
N.W.	12	1	42	3	14.00
B&H	10	0	68	0	

37

BARNES, S. N. Gloucestershire

Name: Stuart Neil Barnes
Role: Right-hand bat, right-arm
medium-fast bowler
Born: 27 June 1970, Bath
Height: 6ft 1in **Weight:** 12st 7lbs
Nickname: Digger, Digs
County debut: 1989 (RAL), 1990
(1st-class)
Place in bowling averages: 77th av.
37.62
Strike rate: 77.62 (career 77.62)
1st-Class catches: 3 (career 3)
Parents: Hedley George and Georgina
Marital status: Single
Family links with cricket: 'Father
plays village cricket for Dunkerton CC.
Brother Darren represents the county.'
Education: Fosse Way Junior and
Beechen Cliff School, Bath

Qualifications: CSEs
Career outside cricket: 'Worked in Barclays Bank, Bath, for three years before
having a six-week trial in 1989.'
Off-season: 'Working in Bath as a sales rep.'
Cricketers particularly admired: Ian Botham, Richard Hadlee
Other sports followed: Football, rugby
Relaxations: Watching sport on TV, listening to music
Best batting: 12* Gloucestershire v Indians, Bristol 1990
Best bowling: 4–51 Gloucestershire v Cambridge University, Fenner's 1990

LAST SEASON: BATTING

	I.	N. O.	R.	H. S.	AV.
TEST					
1ST	9	2	23	12*	3.28
INT					
RAL	1	1	0	0*	-
N.W.	1	0	0	0	0.00
B&H					

LAST SEASON: BOWLING

	O.	M.	R.	W.	AV.
TEST					
1ST	207	45	602	16	37.62
INT					
RAL	41	1	211	7	30.14
N.W.	18	1	93	1	93.00
B&H					

CAREER: BATTING

	I.	N. O.	R.	H. S.	AV.
TEST					
1ST	9	2	23	12*	3.28
INT					
RAL	2	2	11	11*	-
N.W.	1	0	0	0	0.00
B&H					

CAREER: BOWLING

	O.	M.	R.	W.	AV.
TEST					
1ST	207	45	602	16	37.62
INT					
RAL	49	1	265	7	37.85
N.W.	18	1	93	1	93.00
B&H					

BARNETT, K. J. — Derbyshire

Name: Kim John Barnett
Role: Right-hand bat, leg-break bowler, county captain
Born: 17 July 1960, Stoke-on-Trent
Height: 6ft 1in **Weight:** 13st 7lbs
County debut: 1979
County cap: 1982
Test debut: 1988
Tests: 4
One-Day Internationals: 1
1000 runs in a season: 8
1st-Class 50s scored: 85
1st-Class 100s scored: 32
1st-Class 200s scored: 1
1st-Class 5 w. in innings: 1
One-Day 50s: 42
One-Day 100s: 8
Place in batting averages: 49th av. 49.93 (1989 65th av. 35.54)
Place in bowling averages: 26th av. 29.11 (1989 79th av. 31.30)
Strike rate: 67.73 (career 79.81)
1st-Class catches: 14 (career 186)

Parents: Derek and Doreen
Marital status: Single
Children: Michael Nicholas, 24 April 1990
Education: Leek High School, Staffs
Qualifications: 7 O-levels
Off-season: 'Resting'
Overseas tours: With England Schools to India 1977; Young England to Australia 1978–79; England B to Sri Lanka 1986 (vice-captain); unofficial English XI to South Africa 1989–90
Overseas teams played for: Boland 1982–83, 1984–85, 1987–88
Cricketers particularly admired: Gordon Greenidge, Richard Hadlee
Other sports followed: Horse racing
Relaxations: Watching racing on TV, eating and sleeping
Extras: Played for Northamptonshire 2nd XI when aged 15, Staffordshire and Warwickshire 2nd XI. Became youngest captain of a first-class county when appointed in 1983. Banned from Test cricket after joining tour to South Africa
Opinions on cricket: 'It's time pitches were created to provide a decent balance between bat and ball instead of flat, slow, nothing wickets which only produce boredom for everyone concerned. County cricket should be left to run itself with variation in pitches around the country. County cricket should not be blamed for

failure at Test level. Maybe Test pitches should be more like county pitches and not too much in favour of the bat.'

Best batting: 239* Derbyshire v Leicestershire, Leicester 1988
Best bowling: 6–115 Derbyshire v Yorkshire, Bradford 1985

LAST SEASON: BATTING

	I.	N.O.	R.	H.S.	AV.
TEST					
1ST	39	6	1648	141	49.93
INT					
RAL	18	0	824	127	45.77
N.W.	2	0	60	59	30.00
B&H	4	0	124	94	31.00

CAREER: BATTING

	I.	N.O.	R.	H.S.	AV.
TEST	7	0	207	80	29.57
1ST	458	40	15619	239*	37.36
INT	1	0	84	84	84.00
RAL	164	23	4928	131*	34.95
N.W.	25	2	798	88	34.69
B&H	46	2	1418	115	32.22

LAST SEASON: BOWLING

	O.	M.	R.	W.	AV.
TEST					
1ST	293.3	54	757	26	29.11
INT					
RAL	25	0	132	3	44.00
N.W.					
B&H	1	0	9	0	-

CAREER: BOWLING

	O.	M.	R.	W.	AV.
TEST	6	0	32	0	-
1ST	1497.1	299	4546	113	40.23
INT					
RAL	85.5	3	480	12	40.00
N.W.	29.4	5	107	11	9.72
B&H	10	2	42	2	21.00

BARTLETT, R. J. Somerset

Name: Richard James Bartlett
Role: Right-hand bat, off-spin bowler
Born: 8 October 1966, Ash Priors, Somerset
Height: 5ft 9in **Weight:** 12st 7 lbs
Nickname: Pumpy
County debut: 1986
1st-Class 50s scored: 5
1st-Class 100s scored: 2
One-Day 50s: 8
1st-Class catches: 0 (career 27)
Parents: Richard and Barbara
Family links with cricket: 'Dad used to play club cricket but now umpires in the Somerset League.'
Education: Taunton School
Qualifications: 8 O-levels, 3 A-levels
Off-season: Playing and coaching in Horowhenua, New Zealand
Cricketers particularly admired: Jimmy Cook, Steve Waugh, Adrian Jones, Trevor Gard, Viv Richards

Other sports followed: Golf, hockey (county U–21 player) and most others
Injuries: Groin and hamstring strains, and 'a closed right eye from a vicious bouncer from Jonathan North.'
Relaxations: Music, socialising, playing golf
Extras: First Somerset player to score a century on first-class debut since Harold Gimblett. Represented England Schools and England Young Cricketers. Rapid Cricketline 2nd XI Player of the Season 1990
Opinions on cricket: 'Last season was loaded in the favour of batsmen due to the changes to the pitches and ball. To even this out we should revert to the old ball and keep the wickets as they were in 1990.... but it's a great game when you're doing well!'
Best batting: 117* Somerset v Oxford University, The Parks 1986
Best bowling: 1–9 Somerset v Glamorgan, Taunton 1988

LAST SEASON: BATTING

	I.	N. O.	R.	H. S.	AV.
TEST					
1ST	2	0	85	73	42.50
INT					
RAL	8	0	211	55	26.37
N.W.					
B&H					

CAREER: BATTING

	I.	N. O.	R.	H. S.	AV.
TEST					
1ST	62	5	1327	117*	23.28
INT					
RAL	31	1	787	55	26.23
N.W.	3	1	147	85	73.50
B&H	7	1	80	36	13.33

4. Who came last in the Refuge Assurance League in 1990?

5. Who won the Benson & Hedges Cup in 1990?

6. Who won the NatWest Trophy in 1990?

BARWICK, S. R.   Glamorgan

Name: Stephen Royston Barwick
Role: Right-hand bat, right-arm
medium bowler
Born: 6 September 1960, Neath
Height: 6ft 2in **Weight:** 13st 2lbs
Nickname: Baz
County debut: 1981
County cap: 1987
50 wickets in a season: 2
1st-Class 5 w. in innings: 9
1st-Class 10 w. in match: 1
1st-Class catches: 0 (career 30)
Parents: Margaret and Roy
Wife and date of marriage: Margaret,
12 December 1987
Family links with cricket: 'My Uncle
David played for Glamorgan 2nd XI.'
Education: Cwrt Sart Comprehensive,
Dwr-y-Felin Comprehensive
Qualifications: 'Commerce, human
biology, mathematics, English.'
Career outside cricket: Ex-steel worker
Other sports followed: Watches Swansea City FC. Plays football, badminton,
squash and table tennis
Injuries: Surgery on knee meant that he missed most of the 1990 season
Opinions on cricket: 'I think there should be more four-day cricket played.'
Best batting: 30 Glamorgan v Hampshire, Bournemouth 1988
Best bowling: 8–42 Glamorgan v Worcestershire, Worcester 1983

LAST SEASON: BATTING

	I.	N. O.	R.	H. S.	AV.
TEST					
1ST	2	2	2	2*	-
INT					
RAL	1	1	0	0*	-
N.W.					
B&H	2	1	14	13*	14.00

LAST SEASON: BOWLING

	O.	M.	R.	W.	AV.
TEST					
1ST	158.4	43	441	9	49.00
INT					
RAL	32.1	3	182	5	36.40
N.W.					
B&H	41	3	193	8	24.12

CAREER: BATTING

	I.	N. O.	R.	H. S.	AV.
TEST					
1ST	137	57	629	30	7.86
INT					
RAL	29	19	156	48*	15.60
N.W.	6	3	18	6	6.00
B&H	19	10	70	18	7.77

CAREER: BOWLING

	O.	M.	R.	W.	AV.
TEST					
1ST	3718.5	924	10537	314	33.55
INT					
RAL	578.1	38	2623	87	30.14
N.W.	104.4	26	279	18	15.50
B&H	283.3	41	1067	40	26.67

BASE, S. J.   Derbyshire

Name: Simon John Base
Role: Right-hand bat, right-arm medium bowler
Born: 2 January 1960, Maidstone
Height: 6ft 3in **Weight:** 14st
Nickname: Basey, Bok
County debut: 1986 (Glamorgan), 1988 (Derbys)
50 wickets in a season: 1
1st-Class 50s: 2
1st-Class 5 w. in innings: 10
1st-Class 10 w. in match: 1
Place in batting averages: 225th av. 19.54
Place in bowling averages: 97th av. 50.05 (1989 34th av. 24.18)
Strike rate: 91.05 (career 49.14)
1st-Class catches: 4 (career 25)
Parents: Christine and Peter
Wife and date of marriage: Louise Ann, 23 September 1989
Family links with cricket: Grandfather played
Education: Fish Hoek Primary School, Fish Hoek High School, Cape Town, South Africa
Qualifications: High School, School Certificate Matriculation. Refrigeration and air conditioning technician
Career outside cricket: Hall-Thermotank in South Africa as a technician and S. A. Sea Products, G. S. P. K. Electronics in North Yorkshire, England

LAST SEASON: BATTING

	I.	N. O.	R.	H. S.	AV.
TEST					
1ST	13	2	215	58	19.54
INT					
RAL	4	2	3	2	1.50
N.W.					
B&H	2	1	15	15*	15.00

LAST SEASON: BOWLING

	O.	M.	R.	W.	AV.
TEST					
1ST	414.3	68	1402	35	40.05
INT					
RAL	104	3	549	20	27.45
N.W.					
B&H	40	4	176	7	25.14

CAREER: BATTING

	I.	N. O.	R.	H. S.	AV.
TEST					
1ST	96	26	834	58	11.91
INT					
RAL	17	4	54	19	4.15
N.W.	2	0	6	4	3.00
B&H	7	3	45	15*	11.25

CAREER: BOWLING

	O.	M.	R.	W.	AV.
TEST					
1ST	2023.1	324	6593	250	26.37
INT					
RAL	304.4	8	1395	56	24.91
N.W.	15	0	61	2	30.50
B&H	109	9	495	12	41.25

Off-season: Playing for Border in South Africa
Overseas teams played for: Western Province B 1982–83; Boland 1986–89; Border 1989–91
Cricketers particularly admired: Eddie Barlow, Graham Gooch, Graeme Pollock
Other sports followed: Golf, tennis, snooker, all sports
Relaxations: Windsurfing, golf, reading science fiction, watching films, music
Extras: Suspended from first-class cricket for ten weeks during 1988 season for a supposed breach of contract, joining Derbyshire when he was still said to be contracted to Glamorgan. The TCCB fined Derbyshire 2000. Banned from playing Test cricket for continuing to play in South Africa
Opinions on cricket: 'I feel that politics should not interfere with international sport at any level.'
Best batting: 58 Derbyshire v Yorkshire, Chesterfield 1990
Best bowling: 7–60 Derbyshire v Yorkshire, Chesterfield 1989

BASTIEN, S.   Glamorgan

Name: Steven Bastien
Role: Right-hand bat, right-arm fast-medium bowler, outfielder
Born: 13 March 1963, Stepney
Height: 6ft 1in **Weight:** 12st 7lbs
Nickname: Bassie
County debut: 1988
1st-Class 5 w. in innings: 3
Place in bowling averages: 31st av. 30.43
Strike rate: 48.79 (career 58.27)
1st-Class catches: 0 (career 1)
Parents: Francisca and Anthony
Marital status: Single
Family links with cricket: Brother Roger plays in the Essex League
Education: St Mary's Academy School, Dominica; St Bonaventure School, London
Qualifications: 3 CSEs; NCA coaching certificate; carpentry and CCPR course

Cricketers particularly admired: Viv Richards, David Gower, Robin Smith, Michael Holding, Malcolm Marshall
Other sports followed: Football, boxing, athletics
Injuries: Side strain in June – out for two weeks
Relaxations: Watching movies, listening to reggae, soul and calypso music

Extras: Took five wickets on first-class debut in 1988. Member of Haringey Cricket College

Opinions on cricket: 'There is still too much three-day cricket. I think we should have more four-day games instead, because there is a better chance of getting a result.'

Best batting: 36* Glamorgan v Warwickshire, Edgbaston 1988

Best bowling: 6–75 Glamorgan v Worcestershire, Worcester 1990

LAST SEASON: BATTING

	I.	N. O.	R.	H. S.	AV.
TEST					
1ST	9	3	47	12	7.83
INT					
RAL	-	-	-	-	-
N.W.					
B&H					

LAST SEASON: BOWLING

	O.	M.	R.	W.	AV.
TEST					
1ST	317.1	57	1187	39	30.43
INT					
RAL	4	0	21	1	21.00
N.W.					
B&H					

CAREER: BATTING

	I.	N. O.	R.	H. S.	AV.
TEST					
1ST	8	4	58	36*	14.50
INT					
RAL	1	0	1	1	1.00
N.W.					
B&H	1	0	7	7	7.00

CAREER: BOWLING

	O.	M.	R.	W.	AV.
TEST					
1ST	495.2	104	1678	51	32.90
INT					
RAL	19	0	86	1	86.00
N.W.					
B&H	11	1	64	0	

7. Who won the Refuge Assurance Cup in 1990?

8. Which English county did Tom Moody play for last season?

9. Who has been an England selector for the most Test series, and how many?

BATTY, J. D. Yorkshire

Name: Jeremy David Batty
Role: Right-hand bat, off-spin bowler, outfielder
Born: 15 May 1971, Bradford
Height: 6ft 1in **Weight:** 12st 2lbs
Nickname: Bullfrog, Chip
County debut: 1989
1st-Class 5 w. in innings: 1
Place in bowling averages: 141st av. 60.16
Strike rate: 97.50 (career 77.75)
Parents: David and Rosemary
Marital status: Single
Family links with cricket: 'Father is a good league cricketer.'
Education: Parkside Middle School; Bingley Grammar School
Qualifications: 5 O-levels; BTec Leisure Studies; coaching certificate
Off-season: Playing club cricket and coaching in Zimbabwe
Overseas tours: England Young Cricketers to Australia 1989–90
Cricketers particularly admired: Allan Lamb, John Emburey
Other sports followed: Rugby League
Relaxations: Watching Leeds RFC and playing golf
Extras: Took five wickets on first-class debut v Lancashire in 1989
Opinions on cricket: 'I think efforts should be made to make cricket more exciting to watch for younger players – playing in coloured clothing on Sundays with name and number on back.'

LAST SEASON: BATTING

	I.	N. O.	R.	H. S.	AV.
TEST					
1ST	5	2	30	21	10.00
INT					
RAL					
N.W.					
B&H					

LAST SEASON: BOWLING

	O.	M.	R.	W.	AV.
TEST					
1ST	195	29	722	12	60.16
INT					
RAL					
N.W.					
B&H					

CAREER: BATTING

	I.	N. O.	R.	H. S.	AV.
TEST					
1ST	7	3	34	21	8.50
INT					
RAL					
N.W.					
B&H					

CAREER: BOWLING

	O.	M.	R.	W.	AV.
TEST					
1ST	259.1	46	915	20	45.75
INT					
RAL					
N.W.					
B&H					

Best batting: 21 Yorkshire v Middlesex, Headingley 1990
Best bowling: 5–118 Yorkshire v Lancashire, Scarborough 1989

BELL, R. M.   Gloucestershire

Name: Robert Malcolm Bell
Role: Right-hand bat, right-arm medium
bowler
Born: 26 February 1969, St Mary's,
Isles of Scilly
Height: 6ft 1in
County debut: 1990
1st-class catches: 0 (career 0)
Marital status: Single
Education: Truro School
Extras: Played for Kent 2nd XI in 1989
and for Cornwall in the Minor Counties
Championship in 1990
Best batting: 0* Gloucestershire v
Worcestershire, Worcester 1990
Best bowling: 2–38 Gloucestershire v
Worcestershire, Worcester 1990

LAST SEASON / CAREER: BATTING

	I.	N. O.	R.	H. S.	AV.
TEST					
1ST	2	1	0	0*	-
INT					
RAL	-	-	-	-	-
N.W.					
B&H					

LAST SEASON / CAREER: BOWLING

	O.	M.	R.	W.	AV.
TEST					
1ST	44	7	114	3	38.00
INT					
RAL	4	0	38	0	-
N					
B&H.W					

BENJAMIN, J. E.   Warwickshire

Name: Joseph Emmanuel Benjamin
Role: Right-hand bat, right-arm
fast-medium bowler
Born: 2 February 1961, St Kitts,
West Indies
Height: 6ft 1in **Weight:** 12st
Nickname: Boggy
County debut: 1988
1st-Class 5 w. in innings: 4
Place in batting averages: 187th av.
26.85 (1989 93rd av. 36.07)
Place in bowling averages: 18th av.
28.02
Strike rate: 54.20 (career 61.31)
1st-Class catches: 4 (career 6)
Parents: Henry and Judith
Marital status: Single
Education: Cayon High School, St Kitts;
Mount Pleasant, Highgate, Birmingham
Qualifications: 4 O-levels
Off-season: Working in advertising

Opinions on cricket: 'With the seam on balls having been lowered and wickets very flat, average batsmen have been getting double centuries when they struggled before.'
Best batting: 41 Warwickshire v Surrey, The Oval 1990
Best bowling: 5–29 Warwickshire v Cambridge University, Fenner's 1990

LAST SEASON: BATTING

	I.	N. O.	R.	H. S.	AV.
TEST					
1ST	14	7	188	41	26.85
INT					
RAL	7	4	65	24	21.66
N.W.	2	2	3	2*	-
B&H	1	0	20	20	20.00

LAST SEASON: BOWLING

	O.	M.	R.	W.	AV.
TEST					
1ST	388.3	68	1205	43	28.02
INT					
RAL	79	4	334	11	30.36
N.W.	14	2	49	0	-
B&H	22	6	72	3	24.00

CAREER: BATTING

	I.	N. O.	R.	H. S.	AV.
TEST					
1ST	18	8	213	41	21.30
INT					
RAL	8	5	74	24	24.66
N.W.	4	2	27	19	13.50
B&H	1	0	20	20	20.00

CAREER: BOWLING

	O.	M.	R.	W.	AV.
TEST					
1ST	582.3	118	1763	57	30.93
INT					
RAL	95	4	391	11	35.54
N.W.	37	6	151	3	50.33
B&H	22	6	72	3	24.00

BENJAMIN, W. K. M.   Leicestershire

Name: Winston Keithroy Matthew Benjamin
Role: Right-hand bat, right-arm fast bowler
Born: 31 December 1964, All Saints, Antigua
County debut: 1986
Test debut: 1987–88
Tests: 8
One-Day Internationals: 47
50 wickets in a season: 1
1st-class 100s scored: 1
1st-Class 50s scored: 10
1st-Class 5 w. in innings: 17
1st-Class 10 w. in match: 2
Place in batting averages: 142nd av. 33.61 (1989 214th av. 16.05)
Place in bowling averages: 33rd av. 30.64 (1989 6th av. 17.94)
Strike rate: 60.96 (career 52.81)
1st-Class catches: 3 (career 43)
Education: All Saints School, Antigua
Off-season: Playing cricket in West Indies
Overseas teams played for: Leeward Islands since 1985
Injuries: Tendonitis in his knee on and off for two years made him decide to quit county cricket at the end of the 1990 season
Extras: Played Minor Counties cricket for Cheshire
Best batting: 101* Leicestershire v Derbyshire, Leicester 1990

LAST SEASON: BATTING

	I.	N. O.	R.	H. S.	AV.
TEST					
1ST	15	2	437	101*	33.61
INT					
RAL	4	1	21	11*	7.00
N.W.	1	0	7	7	7.00
B&H	1	0	2	2	2.00

CAREER: BATTING

	I.	N. O.	R.	H. S.	AV.
TEST	10	1	125	41*	13.88
1ST	108	28	1969	101*	24.61
INT	22	3	92	31	4.84
RAL	26	7	232	41*	12.21
N.W.	4	1	31	17	10.33
B&H	7	2	62	21	12.40

LAST SEASON: BOWLING

	O.	M.	R.	W.	AV.
TEST					
1ST	284.3	63	858	28	30.64
INT					
RAL	57	5	264	8	33.00
N.W.	12	4	34	1	34.00
B&H	9	3	29	2	14.50

CAREER: BOWLING

	O.	M.	R.	W.	AV.
TEST	208	38	564	26	21.69
1ST	2300.3	514	6538	259	25.24
INT	331.1	32	1382	37	37.35
RAL	253.2	18	1066	36	29.61
N.W.	81	17	243	10	24.30
B&H	107.4	19	357	24	14.87

Best bowling: 7–54 Leicestershire v Australians, Leicester 1989

BENSON, J. D. R. Leicestershire

Name: Justin David Ramsay Benson
Role: Right-hand bat, right-arm medium bowler
Born: 1 March 1967, Dublin
Height: 6ft 3in **Weight:** 15st
Nickname: Rambo, Archie
County debut: 1988
1st-Class 50s scored: 3
1st-Class 100s scored: 1
One-Day 50s: 2
Place in batting averages: 133rd av. 34.52
1st-Class catches: 12 (career 13)
Parents: Malcolm and Liz
Marital status: Single
Family links with cricket: Father is a qualified first-class umpire
Education: The Leys, Cambridge; Cambridge College of Further Education

Qualifications: 10 O-levels
Off-season: 'Resting'
Cricketers particularly admired: Chris Hawkes, Mark Gilliver and Jimmy Cook
Other sports followed: All sport on TV – except racing
Injuries: Hamstring strain – out for two weeks
Relaxations: 'Drinking games and sleeping'
Extras: Scored 85 and won the Man of the Match Award for Cambridgeshire in his first NatWest Trophy match in 1986
Opinions on cricket: 'A professional cricketer should be able to play anywhere in the world if he so chooses – without being banned!'
Best batting: 106 Leicestershire v Indians, Leicester 1990
Best bowling: 1–44 Leicestershire v Hampshire, Bournemouth 1989

LAST SEASON: BATTING

	I.	N. O.	R.	H. S.	AV.
TEST					
1ST	27	6	725	106	34.52
INT					
RAL	15	5	230	67	23.00
N.W.	1	0	11	11	11.00
B&H	2	0	44	43	22.00

CAREER: BATTING

	I.	N. O.	R.	H. S.	AV.
TEST					
1ST	36	6	838	106	27.93
INT					
RAL	25	7	439	67	24.38
N.W.	2	0	96	85	48.00
B&H	3	1	81	43	40.50

BENSON, M. R.   Kent

Name: Mark Richard Benson
Role: Left-hand bat, off-break
bowler, county captain
Born: 6 July 1958, Shoreham, Sussex
Height: 5ft 9 1/2in **Weight:** 12st 7lbs
Nickname: Benny
County debut: 1980
County cap: 1981
Benefit: 1991
Test debut: 1986
Tests: 1
One-Day Internationals: 1
1000 runs in a season: 9
1st-Class 50s scored: 76
1st-Class 100s scored: 34
One-Day 50s: 32
One-Day 100s: 4
Place in batting averages: 55th av.
48.79 (1989 12th av. 54.12)
1st-Class catches: 5 (career 96)
Parents: Frank and Judy
Wife and date of marriage: Sarah, 20 September 1986
Children: Laurence Mark Edward, 16 October 1987
Family links with cricket: Father played for Ghana
Education: Sutton Valence School
Qualifications: O and A-levels and 1 S-level. Qualified tennis coach
Career outside cricket: Marketing assistant with Shell UK Oil; financial adviser
Cricketers particularly admired: Malcolm Marshall, Jimmy Cook, Chris Tavare
Other sports followed: Football, horse racing
Relaxations: Windsurfing, tennis, golf and bowls
Extras: Scored 1000 runs in first full season. Record for most runs in career and
season at Sutton Valence School. Appointed Kent captain at end of 1990 season
Opinions on cricket: 'Four-day cricket, with each county playing each other once.'
Best batting: 162 Kent v Hampshire, Southampton 1985
Best bowling: 2–55 Kent v Surrey, Dartford 1986

LAST SEASON: BATTING

	I.	N. O.	R.	H. S.	AV.
TEST					
1ST	25	1	1171	159	48.79
INT					
RAL	3	0	83	55	27.66
N.W.	1	0	7	7	7.00
B&H	2	0	203	118	101.50

CAREER: BATTING

	I.	N. O.	R.	H. S.	AV.
TEST	2	0	51	30	25.50
1ST	352	27	13173	162	40.53
INT	1	0	24	24	24.00
RAL	99	1	2723	97	27.78
N.W.	24	1	839	113*	36.47
B&H	44	6	1507	118	39.65

BENT, P. Worcestershire

Name: Paul Bent
Role: Right-hand bat, off-break
bowler
Born: 1 May 1965, Worcester
Height: 6ft **Weight:** 13st
Nickname: Benty, Bodell
County debut: 1985
1st-Class 50s scored: 5
1st-Class 100s scored: 1
Place in batting averages: 173rd av.
28.83 (1989 144th av. 24.09)
1st-Class catches: 0 (career 1)
Parents: Emily and Roy
Wife and date of marriage:
Lynne, 29 September 1990
Family links with cricket: Brother plays
local club cricket, as did father-in-law
Education: Worcester Royal Grammar
School

Qualifications: 7 O-levels, 2 A-levels;
senior award coach
Off-season: 'Trying to find employment. Also helping in the production of Mr R.
D. Stemp's first novel, *The Art of Excuses.*'
Cricketers particularly admired: Graeme Hick, Ian Botham, John Bracewell, Tim
Curtis, Richard Stemp
Other sports followed: Supports West Bromwich Albion
Relaxations: Sleeping in, listening to music, gardening
Extras: Hat-trick v Leicestershire 2nd XI, 1988. Fielded as 12th man for England v
India in 1986 while on Lord's ground staff
Opinions on cricket: 'I would like to see a minimum wage level from day one of a
contract, not after two years. I would also like to see the TCCB listen more to players'
views before implementing new rules.'
Best batting: 144 Worcestershire v Kent, Worcester 1989

LAST SEASON: BATTING

	I.	N.O.	R.	H.S.	AV.
TEST					
1ST	12	0	346	79	28.83
INT					
RAL					
N.W.					
B&H					

CAREER: BATTING

	I.	N.O.	R.	H.S.	AV.
TEST					
1ST	31	1	686	144	22.86
INT					
RAL	3	0	51	36	17.00
N.W.					
B&H					

BERRY, P. J. Yorkshire

Name: Philip John Berry
Role: Right-hand bat, off-break
bowler
Born: 28 December 1966, Saltburn
Height: 6ft **Weight:** 11st 10lbs
Nickname: Chuck, Goose, Charlie
County debut: 1986
1st-Class catches: 1 (career 6)
Parents: John and Beryl
Marital status: Single
Family links with cricket: Brother
used to play league cricket for Saltburn
Education: Saltscar Comprehensive
School; Longlands College of FE
Qualifications: 1 O-level, City &
Guilds passes in Recreational
Management
Career outside cricket: 'Worked with
my father on Redcar racecourse.'
Off-season: 'Staying fit, improving my
house, watching Middlesbrough FC,
winning money on the horses.'

Cricketers particularly admired: Brian Bainbridge, John Emburey
Other sports followed: Rugby Union, football, snooker, horse racing
Injuries: Torn stomach muscles
Relaxations: 'Reading autobiographies or Dick Francis racing stories; my favourite
book is John Francome's *Born Lucky.*'
Opinions on cricket: 'At last we are down to one overseas player per side; would

LAST SEASON: BATTING

	I.	N. O.	R.	H. S.	AV.
TEST					
1ST	4	4	45	31*	-
INT					
RAL					
N.W.					
B&H	-	-	-	-	-

LAST SEASON: BOWLING

	O.	M.	R.	W.	AV.
TEST					
1ST	44.3	4	172	2	86.00
INT					
RAL					
N.W.					
B&H	5	0	28	0	-

CAREER: BATTING

	I.	N. O.	R.	H. S.	AV.
TEST					
1ST	7	6	76	31*	76.00
INT					
RAL					
N.W.					
B&H	-	-	-	-	-

CAREER: BOWLING

	O.	M.	R.	W.	AV.
TEST					
1ST	135.5	33	401	7	57.28
INT					
RAL					
N.W.					
B&H	5	0	28	0	-

also like to see return of old ball with bigger seam.'
Best batting: 31* Yorkshire v Northamptonshire, Headingley 1990
Best bowling: 2–35 Yorkshire v Cambridge University, Fenner's 1988

BEVINS, S. R. Worcestershire

Name: Stuart Roy Bevins
Role: Right-hand bat, wicket-keeper
Born: 8 March 1967, Solihull
Height: 5ft 6 1/2in **Weight:** 10st 5lbs
Nickname: Tot
County debut: 1989
Parents: Roy and Gwen
Marital status: Single
Family links with cricket: 'Grandad and father played club cricket. Brother Martyn has played for Warwickshire U19s, English Schools and Worcestershire 2nd XI.'
Education: Solihull School; Solihull College of Technology
Qualifications: 5 O-levels; Diploma in Business Studies
Off-season: Playing and coaching in South Africa
Cricketers particularly admired: Alan Knott, Rodney Marsh, Richard Hadlee, Ian Botham
Other sports followed: Hockey, football, golf. Warwickshire U–21 hockey player

LAST SEASON: BATTING

	I.	N. O.	R.	H. S.	AV.
TEST					
1ST	3	1	17	10	8.50
INT					
RAL	-	-	-	-	-
N.W.					
B&H	1	1	0	0*	-

CAREER: BATTING

	I.	N. O.	R.	H. S.	AV.
TEST					
1ST	5	2	28	10	9.33
INT					
RAL	-	-	-	-	-
N.W.					
B&H	1	1	0	0*	-

LAST SEASON: WICKET-KEEPING

	CT	ST
TEST		
1ST	6	0
INT		
RAL	3	1
N.W.		
B&H	2	1

CAREER: WICKET-KEEPING

	CT	ST
TEST		
1ST	13	0
INT		
RAL	4	1
N.W.		
B&H	2	1

Injuries: Broken finger – out for three weeks
Relaxations: Eating out and playing golf
Opinions on cricket: 'I think the cricketing public are far too eager to criticise county players when they are struggling for form. With so much cricket being crammed into a season, plus all the travelling, it is inevitable that players will become weary occasionally.'
Best batting: 10 Worcestershire v New Zealand, Worcester 1990

BICKNELL, D. J. Surrey

Name: Darren John Bicknell
Role: Left-hand opening bat, left-arm bowler, close fielder
Born: 24 June 1967, Guildford
Height: 6ft 5in **Weight:** 13st
Nickname: Denzil
County debut: 1987
County cap: 1990
1000 runs in a season: 2
1st-Class 50s scored: 18
1st-Class 100s scored: 10
One-Day 50s: 3
One-Day 100s: 2
Place in batting averages: 12th av. 69.31 (1989 61st av. 35.69)
1st-Class catches: 2 (career 25)
Parents: Vic and Valerie
Marital status: Engaged to Rebecca
Family links with cricket: Brother Martin 'is fairly well known'; Stuart plays for Normandy CC; father is a qualified umpire
Education: Robert Haining County Secondary; Guildford County College of Technology
Qualifications: 2 O-levels, 5 CSEs, City and Guilds qualification in Recreation and Administration
Off-season: Touring Pakistan with England A; 'moving into my new flat.'
Overseas tours: England A to Zimbabwe and Kenya 1989–90; Pakistan 1990–91
Cricketers particularly admired: 'Too many to mention.'
Other sports followed: 'I watch Aldershot FC and also follow the fortunes of West Ham.'
Injuries: Out for six weeks with broken right hand and injured same hand again while batting
Relaxations: 'Eating out, and quiet evenings in, with my fiancee.'

Extras: 'I was capped during Sunday match against Warwickshire along with David Ward and Chris Bullen and all three made duck.' Shared county record third wicket stand of 413 with David Ward v Kent at Canterbury in 1990 as both made career bests

Opinions on cricket: 'Four-day cricket on good pitches will undoubtedly prove which are the best sides; it will allow batsmen to build large innings and prevent average bowlers picking up cheap wickets in run chases. All second team games should be played on county grounds to provide young players with the best possible facilities.'

Best batting: 186 Surrey v Kent, Canterbury 1990
Best bowling: 1–73 Surrey v Kent, Canterbury 1989

LAST SEASON: BATTING

	I.	N. O.	R.	H. S.	AV.
TEST					
1ST	23	4	1317	186	69.31
INT					
RAL	5	0	128	75	25.60
N.W.	1	0	12	12	12.00
B&H	4	0	215	119	53.75

CAREER: BATTING

	I.	N. O.	R.	H. S.	AV.
TEST					
1ST	112	15	3703	186	38.17
INT					
RAL	13	1	310	75	25.83
N.W.	4	1	195	135*	65.00
B&H	8	0	264	119	33.00

BICKNELL, M. P. Surrey

Name: Martin Paul Bicknell
Role: Right-hand bat, right-arm fast-medium bowler
Born: 14 January 1969, Guildford
Height: 6ft 4in **Weight:** 14st
Nickname: Bickers, Spandau
County debut: 1986
50 wickets in a season: 3
1st-Class 50s scored: 1
1st-Class 5 w. in innings: 8
Place in batting averages: 113th av. 38.75 (1989 241st av. 13.00)
Place in bowling averages: 14th av. 27.26 (1989 41st av. 26.41)
Strike rate: 60.10 (career 56.98)
1st-Class catches: 8 (career 26)
Parents: Vic and Valerie
Marital status: Single
Family links with cricket: Brother

Darren 'occasional cricketer'; father is qualified umpire and younger brother Stuart also plays

56

Education: Robert Haining County Secondary

Qualifications: 2 O-levels, 5 CSEs

Off-season: Touring Australia with England

Overseas tours: England YC to Sri Lanka 1986–87 and Australia 1987–88; England A to Zimbabwe and Kenya 1989–90; England to Australia 1990–91

Cricketers particularly admired: Richard Hadlee, Dennis Lillee, Ian Botham

Other sports followed: 'Leeds United, and generally most sports.'

Injuries: Recurring hamstring problem, neck spasm

Relaxations: Golf, snooker, watching videos. 'Listening to Tony Murphy's theories on cricket.'

Extras: Youngest player to play for Surrey since David Smith. His figures of 9 for 45 were the best for the county for thirty years

Opinions on cricket: 'Four-day cricket is wanted by all players and makes for better cricket. Hopefully then we will need fewer declarations and the better team will generally win. At the moment we often get to the last day and it becomes a one-day game to get a result.'

Best batting: 50* Surrey v Sussex, Hove 1990

Best bowling: 9–45 Surrey v Cambridge University, Fenner's 1988

LAST SEASON: BATTING

	I.	N. O.	R.	H. S.	AV.
TEST					
1ST	16	8	310	50*	38.75
INT					
RAL	4	3	19	11*	19.00
N.W.	1	1	4	4*	-
B&H	2	1	35	27*	35.00

CAREER: BATTING

	I.	N. O.	R.	H. S.	AV.
TEST					
1ST	79	26	776	50*	14.64
INT					
RAL	17	9	73	13	9.12
N.W.	7	4	11	4*	3.66
B&H	8	2	64	27*	10.66

LAST SEASON: BOWLING

	O.	M.	R.	W.	AV.
TEST					
1ST	671.1	157	1827	67	27.26
INT					
RAL	76.2	3	316	18	17.55
N.W.	24	3	79	2	39.50
B&H	51.5	9	237	9	26.33

CAREER: BOWLING

	O.	M.	R.	W.	AV.
TEST					
1ST	2446.2	592	6810	258	26.39
INT					
RAL	373.2	17	1506	53	28.41
N.W.	149	20	484	17	28.47
B&H	128.5	20	510	23	22.17

BISHOP, I. R.

Name: Ian Raphael Bishop
Role: Right-hand bat, right-arm fast bowler
Born: 24 October 1967, Port of Spain, Trinidad, West Indies
Height: 6ft 5 1/2in **Weight:** 15st 10lbs
Nickname: Bish
County debut: 1989
Test debut: 1988–89
Tests: 8
One-Day Internationals: 26
50 wickets in a season: 1
1st-Class 100s scored: 1
1st-Class 5 w. in innings: 13
1st-class 10 w. in match: 1
Place in batting averages: 181st av. 27.75 (1989 262nd av. 10.00)
Place in bowling averages: 1st av. 19.05 (1989 26th av. 22.43)
Strike rate: 41.44 (career 44.63)
1st-Class catches: 2 (career 13)
Parents: Randolph and Recalda
Marital status: Single
Family links with cricket: Uncle played for Young West Indies against England U–20 in the Caribbean 1984–85
Education: Belmont Primary and Belmont Secondary Schools
Qualifications: 2 O-levels

LAST SEASON: BATTING

	I.	N. O.	R.	H. S.	AV.
TEST					
1ST	16	4	333	103*	27.75
INT					
RAL					
N.W.					
B&H					

LAST SEASON: BOWLING

	O.	M.	R.	W.	AV.
TEST					
1ST	407.3	92	1124	59	19.05
INT					
RAL					
N.W.					
B&H					

CAREER: BATTING

	I.	N. O.	R.	H. S.	AV.
TEST	12	6	124	30*	20.66
1ST	74	23	785	103*	15.39
INT	11	7	73	33*	18.25
RAL	1	1	16	16*	-
N.W.					
B&H					

CAREER: BOWLING

	O.	M.	R.	W.	AV.
TEST	299.1	75	790	37	21.35
1ST	1463.5	308	4254	200	21.27
INT	223.1	15	858	46	18.65
RAL	8	0	51	1	51.00
N.W.					
B&H					

Off-season: Touring Pakistan with West Indies
Overseas tours: West Indies to England 1988; Australia 1988–89; India for Nehru Cup 1989–90; Pakistan 1990–91
Overseas teams played for: Trinidad & Tobago
Cricketers particularly admired: Malcolm Marshall, Michael Holding, Gordon Greenidge
Other sports followed: Athletics, soccer, basketball
Relaxations: Watching television, reading sports magazines and theological books
Extras: Played for Northumberland club Tynedale in 1987. Top of 1990 bowling averages. 'I am a born-again Christian.'
Opinions on cricket: 'I think wickets at county level should be well-prepared to encourage bowlers and batters to learn their trade thoroughly. The present fining for slow over-rates is ridiculous.'
Best batting: 103* Derbyshire v Yorkshire, Scarborough 1990
Best bowling: 6–39 West Indians v Kent, Canterbury 1988

BLAKEY, R. J. Yorkshire

Name: Richard John Blakey
Role: Right-hand bat, wicket-keeper
Born: 15 January 1967, Huddersfield
Height: 5ft 10in **Weight:** 11st 3lbs
Nickname: Dick, Mutley, Warren
County debut: 1985
County cap: 1987
1000 runs in a season: 3
1st-Class 50s scored: 26
1st-Class 100s scored: 6
1st-Class 200s scored: 2
One-Day 50s: 16
One-Day 100s: 1
Place in batting averages: 164th av. 30.38 (1989 85th av. 32.19)
Parents: Brian and Pauline
Marital status: Single
Family links with cricket: Father played local cricket
Education: Woodhouse Primary; Rastrick Grammar School
Qualifications: 4 O-levels, NCA coaching certificate
Off-season: Touring Pakistan with England A
Overseas tours: Young England to West Indies 1985; England A to Zimbabwe and Kenya 1989–90 and Pakistan 1990–91

Cricketers particularly admired: 'Any successful cricketers.'
Other sports followed: 'Watch Leeds United FC and follow most sports but not ice skating.'
Relaxations: Eating out, holidays abroad, music
Extras: Established himself in Huddersfield League. Made record 2nd XI score – 273* v Northamptonshire 1986. Yorkshire's Young Player of the Year 1989
Opinions on cricket: 'In favour of coloured clothing for Sunday League matches; 16 four-day matches to create a fairer Championship and to allow a day in between games for travelling.'
Best batting: 221 England A v Zimbabwe, Bulawayo 1989–90
Best bowling: 1–68 Yorkshire v Nottinghamshire, Sheffield 1986

LAST SEASON: BATTING

	I.	N. O.	R.	H. S.	AV.
TEST					
1ST	43	9	1033	111	30.38
INT					
RAL	15	2	609	100*	46.84
N.W.	1	0	21	21	21.00
B&H	4	0	212	79	53.00

LAST SEASON: WICKET-KEEPING

	CT	ST		
TEST				
1ST	45	9		
INT				
RAL	12	2		
N.W.	7	1		
B&H	2	0		

CAREER: BATTING

	I.	N. O.	R.	H. S.	AV.
TEST					
1ST	179	23	5092	221	32.64
INT					
RAL	37	8	1359	100*	46.86
N.W.	6	1	78	22	15.60
B&H	15	2	457	79	35.15

CAREER: WICKET-KEEPING

	CT	ST		
TEST				
1ST	162	13		
INT				
RAL	21	2		
N.W.	13	1		
B&H	5	0		

10. Which county bowler had the best strike rate last season, and what was it?

11. What was the name of John Arlott's autobiography, published last season?

12. Who played for Hampshire from 1905 to 1936?

Name: Timothy James Boon
Role: Right-hand bat, right-arm medium bowler
Born: 1 November 1961, Doncaster, South Yorkshire
Height: 5ft 11 1/2in **Weight:** 12st 3lbs
Nickname: Ted Moon, Cod
County debut: 1980
County cap: 1986
1000 runs in a season: 5
1st-Class 50s scored: 42
1st-Class 100s scored: 8
One-Day 50s: 9
Place in batting averages: 123rd av. 37.53 (1989 93rd av. 30.73)
1st-Class catches: 13 (career 80)
Parents: Jeffrey and Elizabeth
Marital status: Single
Family links with cricket: Father played club cricket
Education: Mill Lane Primary; Edlington Comprehensive. Three months at Doncaster Art School
Qualifications: 1 A-level, 6 O-levels. Coaching qualifications
Overseas tours: England YCs to West Indies 1980
Cricketers particularly admired: 'Those who make the most of their ability.'
Other sports followed: 'Enjoy playing and watching all sports.'
Relaxations: Sleeping, barbecue in garden, dining out
Extras: Captain England YCs v West Indies 1980 and v India 1981; missed 1985

LAST SEASON: BATTING

	I.	N. O.	R.	H. S.	AV.
TEST					
1ST	45	4	1539	138	37.53
INT					
RAL	16	0	545	97	34.06
N.W.	1	0	19	19	19.00
B&H	3	0	127	84	42.33

LAST SEASON: BOWLING

	O.	M.	R.	W.	AV.
TEST					
1ST	6.5	0	39	0	-
INT					
RAL					
N.W.					
B&H					

CAREER: BATTING

	I.	N. O.	R.	H. S.	AV.
TEST					
1ST	269	34	7484	144	31.84
INT					
RAL	74	10	1470	97	22.96
N.W.	8	3	115	24	23.00
B&H	18	5	445	84	34.23

CAREER: BOWLING

	O.	M.	R.	W.	AV.
TEST					
1ST	64.1	7	329	6	54.83
INT					
RAL	2	0	14	0	-
N.W.	1	0	2	0	-
B&H					

season due to broken leg sustained in a car crash in South Africa the previous winter
Best batting: 144 Leicestershire v Gloucestershire, Leicester 1984
Best bowling: 3–40 Leicestershire v Yorkshire, Leicester 1986

BOOTH, P. A.   Warwickshire

Name: Paul Anthony Booth
Role: Left-hand bat, left-arm spin bowler
Born: 5 September 1965, Huddersfield
Height: 6ft **Weight:** 11st 7lbs
Nickname: Boot, Spike
County debut: 1982 (Yorks),
1990 (Warwicks)
1st-Class 50s scored: 2
1st-Class 5 w. in innings: 1
Place in batting averages: 238th av.
17.14
Place in bowling averages: 127th av.
48.92
Strike rate: 115.76 (career 112.95)
1st-Class catches: 3 (career 10)
Parents: Colin and Margaret
Wife and date of marriage: Beverley,
13 October 1990
Family links with cricket: Father
played local cricket for thirty years
Education: Meltham Church of England; Honley High School
Qualifications: 2 O-levels; coaching certificate

LAST SEASON: BATTING

	I.	N. O.	R.	H. S.	AV.
TEST					
1ST	16	2	240	60	17.14
INT					
RAL	-	-	-	-	-
N.W.					
B&H	2	1	18	13*	18.00

LAST SEASON: BOWLING

	O.	M.	R.	W.	AV.
TEST					
1ST	250.5	75	636	13	46.00
INT					
RAL	13	0	79	2	39.50
N.W.					
B&H	15	1	72	2	36.00

CAREER: BATTING

	I.	N. O.	R.	H. S.	AV.
TEST					
1ST	45	11	433	60	12.73
INT					
RAL	-	-	-	-	-
N.W.	1	1	6	6*	-
B&H	3	1	19	13*	9.50

CAREER: BOWLING

	O.	M.	R.	W.	AV.
TEST					
1ST	903.4	291	2153	48	44.85
INT					
RAL	24	0	146	3	48.66
N.W.	11	2	33	0	-
B&H	27	1	119	4	29.75

Career outside cricket: 'Postman through the winter for last four years.'
Overseas tours: England YC to the West Indies 1985
Cricketers particularly admired: Ray Illingworth, Keith Piper
Other sports followed: Football (Leeds United) and golf
Injuries: Side strain – out for two weeks in May; abscess to the base of right foot – out for eight weeks in June and July
Relaxations: Listening to tapes and records; rounds of golf; playing football
Extras: Made debut for Yorkshire when 17 years 3 days. Released by Yorkshire at end of 1989 season
Opinions on cricket: 'Cricket should be like American football and have specialist positions, e. g. bowlers only have to be on the field when bowling.'
Best batting: 60 Warwickshire v Somerset, Edgbaston 1990
Best bowling: 5–98 Yorkshire v Lancashire, Old Trafford 1988

BOTHAM, I. T. Worcestershire

Name: Ian Terrence Botham
Role: Right-hand bat, right-arm fast-medium bowler, slip fielder
Born: 24 November 1955, Heswall, Cheshire
Height: 6ft 2in **Weight:** 15st 5lbs
Nickname: Guy, Both, Beefy
County debut: 1974 (Somerset), 1987 (Worcs)
County cap: 1976 (Somerset), 1987 (Worcs)
Benefit: 1984 (90,822)
Test debut: 1977
Tests: 97
One-Day Internationals: 98
1000 runs in a season: 4
50 wickets in a season: 7
1st-Class 50s scored: 88
1st-Class 100s scored: 34
1st-Class 200s scored: 2
1st-Class 5 w. in innings: 56
1st-Class 10 w. in match: 8
One-Day 50s: 34
One-Day 100s: 7
Place in batting averages: 131st av. 35.00 (1989 198th av. 18.21)
Place in bowling averages: 28th av. 29.23 (1989 42nd av. 25.30)
Strike rate: 55.42 (career 53.66)
1st-Class catches: 7 (career 324)

Parents: Les and Marie

Wife and date of marriage: Kathryn, 31 January 1976

Children: Liam James, 26 August 1977; Sarah Lianne, 3 February 1979; Rebecca Kate, 13 November 1985

Family links with cricket: Father played for Navy and Fleet Air Arm; mother played for VAD nursing staff; son Liam already a very promising all-rounder

Education: Millford Junior School; Buckler's Mead Secondary School, Yeovil

Overseas tours: England to Pakistan and New Zealand 1977–78; Australia 1978–79; Australia and India 1979–80; West Indies 1980–81; India 1981–82; Australia and New Zealand 1982–83; West Indies 1985–86; Australia 1986–87

Cricketers particularly admired: Viv Richards, David Gower, Allan Border, Andy Roberts ('the fastest bowler I ever faced')

Off-season: Appearing in pantomine. Captain of celebrity team in the BBC quiz show 'A Question of Sport'

Other sports followed: Rugby, football, American sports, 'virtually anything'

Injuries: Various injuries badly disrupted 1990 season

Relaxations: Golf, shooting, fishing (salmon and trout), flying

Extras: England captain for twelve Tests between 1980 and 1981. Played for Somerset 2nd XI 1971. On MCC staff 1972–73. Took five Australian wickets on his first day in Test cricket aged 21. One of *Wisden's* Five Cricketers of the Year, 1977. Best man at Viv Richards's wedding in Antigua in March 1981. Subject of 'This is Your Life' television programme in November 1981 and voted BBC TV Sports Review Sporting Personality of 1981 following his exploits against Australia – and he even outdid the Americans with a baseball bat. Scored 200 in 272 minutes for England v India at The Oval in 1982, third fastest Test double century by an Englishman, after Walter Hammond and Denis Compton. Crashed two 12,000 sports cars at 100 mph in same afternoon in May 1982. His published books include *High, Wide and Handsome*, an account of his record-breaking 1985 season; *It Sort of Clicks*, in collaboration with Peter Roebuck, and *Cricket My Way* with Jack Bannister. First cricketer since W. G. Grace to have painting commissioned by National Portrait Gallery. Captain of Somerset 1984–85. Holds record for having scored 1000 runs and taken 100 wickets in fewest Test matches. First player to score a century and take eight wickets in an innings in a Test match, v Pakistan at Lord's in 1978. Most sixes in a first-class season in 1985. Left Somerset at the beginning of 1987 to join Worcestershire after Somerset had decided not to renew the contracts of Richards and Garner. Missed nearly all 1988 season with back injury. Appeared on 'Desert Island Discs' in November 1989, when his choice of music ranged from Elton John and the Beatles, to Beethoven and 'Land of Hope and Glory'. The one book he wanted was an encyclopedia of fish, and his luxury was a fishing rod. Raised over £1,000,000 for Leukaemia Research with a series of fund-raising walks

Opinions on cricket: 'The Comprehensive (school) system is a disgrace. How can we bring our youngsters on when there are 3000 kids in one school, and no facilities for cricket. When I was a lad we would stay on after school, being taught how to play by an experienced cricket master. Now the kids are just not being given the chance.'

Best batting: 228 Somerset v Gloucestershire, Taunton 1980

Best bowling: 8–34 England v Pakistan, Lord's 1978

LAST SEASON: BATTING

	I.	N. O.	R.	H. S.	AV.
TEST					
1ST	18	1	595	113	35.00
INT					
RAL	12	1	257	45	23.36
N.W.	2	2	86	86*	-
B&H	4	1	235	138*	78.33

LAST SEASON: BOWLING

	O.	M.	R.	W.	AV.
TEST					
1ST	194.4	38	614	21	29.23
INT					
RAL	67	1	346	15	23.06
N.W.	31.1	2	151	6	25.16
B&H	50	7	209	7	29.85

CAREER: BATTING

	I.	N. O.	R.	H. S.	AV.
TEST	154	5	5119	208	34.35
1ST	397	34	12317	228	33.93
INT	89	12	1730	72	22.46
RAL	160	23	4333	175*	31.62
N.W.	33	8	1065	101	42.60
B&H	63	8	1434	138*	26.07

CAREER: BOWLING

	O.	M.	R.	W.	AV.
TEST	3546.5	762	10633	376	28.27
1ST	6131.2	1957	18378	706	26.03
INT	878.1	96	3511	118	29.75
RAL	1128.5	65	5067	222	22.82
N.W.	419.4	67	1499	59	25.40
B&H	710.4	129	2470	119	20.75

BOWLER, P. D.   Derbyshire

Name: Peter Duncan Bowler
Role: Right-hand opening bat,
off-spinner, part-time wicket-keeper
Born: 30 July 1963, Plymouth,
Australia
Height: 6ft 2in **Weight:** 13st
Nickname: Skippy
County debut: 1986 (Leics), 1988
(Derbys)
1000 runs in a season: 3
1st-Class 50s scored: 27
1st-Class 100s scored: 10
1st-Class 200s scored: 1
One-Day 50s: 16
One-Day 100s: 1
Place in batting averages: 96th av.
42.00 (1989 103rd av. 29.71)
1st-Class catches: 17 (career 54 &
1 stumping)
Parents: Peter and Etta
Marital status: Single
Education: Daramalan College, Canberra, Australia
Qualifications: Australian Yr 12 certificate
Cricketers particularly admired: Greg Chappell, Richard Hadlee, Dennis Lillee

Relaxations: Music, reading, newspapers. Playing sports other than cricket. Relaxing with family

Extras: First Leicestershire player to score a first-class hundred on debut (100 not out v Hampshire 1986). Moved to Derbyshire at end of 1987 season and scored a hundred on his debut v Cambridge University in 1988

Best batting: 210 Derbyshire v Kent, Chesterfield 1990

Best bowling: 2–1 Derbyshire v Leicestershire, Derby 1989

LAST SEASON: BATTING

	I.	N. O.	R.	H. S.	AV.
TEST					
1ST	39	5	1428	210	42.00
INT					
RAL	16	1	539	59	35.93
N.W.	2	0	16	14	8.00
B&H	4	0	263	109	65.75

LAST SEASON: BOWLING

	O.	M.	R.	W.	AV.
TEST					
1ST	11	0	81	1	81.00
INT					
RAL					
N.W.					
B&H					

CAREER: BATTING

	I.	N. O.	R.	H. S.	AV.
TEST					
1ST	141	12	4754	210	36.85
INT					
RAL	56	4	1470	71	28.26
N.W.	7	0	98	46	14.00
B&H	14	0	496	109	35.42

CAREER: BOWLING

	O.	M.	R.	W.	AV.
TEST					
1ST	243.3	43	893	11	81.18
INT					
RAL	32	1	185	4	46.25
N.W.	3	0	14	0	-
B&H	41	7	125	4	31.25

13. Who has taken most Test wickets, and how many?

14. Who topped the batting averages in the English 1990 season?

15. What did Mark Waugh and David Ward have in common last season?

BRAMHALL, S.   Lancashire

Name: Stephen Bramhall
Role: Right-hand bat, wicket-keeper
Born: 26 November 1967, Warrington
Height: 6ft **Weight:** 12st 7lbs
Nickname: Bram, Bush
County debut: 1990
Parents: Harry and Dorothy
Marital status: Single
Education: Stockton Heath County
High School, Warrington; Newcastle-
upon-Tyne University
Qualifications: 8 O-levels, 3 A-levels
Off-season: Playing in Canberra,
Australia
Cricketers particularly admired: Alan
Knott, Viv Richards, Gordon Greenidge,
Jack Russell
Other sports followed: Football
Injuries: Sore hands and damaged
fingers
Relaxations: Listening to music,
playing snooker
Extras: 'I am a non-contracted player at Lancashire and play for Cheshire in the
Minor Counties Championship.'
Best batting: 1* Lancashire v Sri Lanka, Old Trafford 1990

LAST SEASON / CAREER: BATTING

	I.	N. O.	R.	H. S.	AV.
TEST					
1ST	3	2	1	1*	1.00
INT					
RAL					
N.W.					
B&H					

LAST SEASON / CAREER: WICKET-KEEPING

	CT	ST			
TEST					
1ST	1	2			
INT					
RAL					
N.W.					
B&H					

BRIERS, N. E. Leicestershire

Name: Nigel Edwin Briers
Role: Right-hand bat, right-arm medium bowler, county captain
Born: 15 January 1955, Leicester
Height: 6ft **Weight:** 12st 5lbs
Nickname: Kudu
County debut: 1971 (aged 16 yrs 104 days)
County cap: 1981
Benefit: 1990
1000 runs in a season: 7
1st-Class 50s scored: 68
1st-Class 100s scored: 19
1st-Class 200s scored: 1
One-Day 50s: 32
One-Day 100s: 3
Place in batting averages: 50th av. 49.90 (1989 132nd av. 25.87)
1st-Class catches: 7 (career 113)
Parents: Leonard Arthur Roger and Eveline
Wife and date of marriage: Suzanne Mary Tudor, 3 September 1977
Children: Michael Edward Tudor, 25 March 1983; Andrew James Tudor, 30 June 1986
Family links with cricket: Father was captain and wicket-keeper of Narborough and Littlethorpe CC in the Leics League for fifteen years and mother was scorer. Father was also captain of South Leicestershire Representative XI and played for the Royal Marines in the same team as Trevor Bailey. Cousin, Norman Briers, played

LAST SEASON: BATTING

	I.	N. O.	R.	H. S.	AV.
TEST					
1ST	44	4	1996	176	49.90
INT					
RAL	16	1	424	90*	28.26
N.W.	1	0	8	8	8.00
B&H	3	1	110	93*	55.00

LAST SEASON: BOWLING

	O.	M.	R.	W.	AV.
TEST					
1ST					
INT					
RAL					
N.W.					
B&H					

CAREER: BATTING

	I.	N. O.	R.	H. S.	AV.
TEST					
1ST	462	44	13120	201*	31.38
INT					
RAL	167	23	4637	119*	32.20
N.W.	26	2	441	59	18.37
B&H	39	3	676	93*	18.77

CAREER: BOWLING

	O.	M.	R.	W.	AV.
TEST					
1ST	341.1	70	988	32	30.87
INT					
RAL	80.2	5	384	10	38.40
N.W.	14	0	75	6	12.50
B&H	55	3	266	3	88.66

for Leicestershire once in 1967
Education: Lutterworth Grammar School; Borough Road College
Qualifications: Qualified teacher (Certificate of Education), BEd Hons, MCC advanced coach
Career outside cricket: Teacher (History and PE)
Off-season: Working on benefit and teaching at Ludgrove School
Extras: Vice-captain of Leicestershire 1988 and 1989. Appointed captain before the 1990 season
Best batting: 201* Leicestershire v Warwickshire, Edgbaston 1983
Best bowling: 4–29 Leicestershire v Derbyshire, Leicester 1985

BROAD, B. C.   Nottinghamshire

Name: Brian Christopher Broad
Role: Left-hand bat, right-arm medium bowler
Born: 29 September 1957, Bristol
Height: 6ft 4in **Weight:** 14st 7lbs
Nickname: Walter, Broadie
County debut: 1979 (Gloucs), 1984 (Notts)
County cap: 1981 (Gloucs), 1984 (Notts)
Test debut: 1984
Tests: 25
One-Day Internationals: 34
1000 runs in a season: 8
1st-Class 50s scored: 88
1st-Class 100s scored: 37
1st-class 200s scored: 1
One-Day 50s: 5
One-Day 100s: 7
Place in batting averages: 37th av. 54.29 (1989 44th av. 38.76)
1st-Class catches: 7 (career 158)
Parents: Nancy and Kenneth
Wife and date of marriage: Carole Ann, 14 July 1979
Children: Gemma Joanne, 14 January 1984; Stuart Christopher John, 24 June 1986
Family links with cricket: Father and grandfather both played local cricket. Father member of Gloucestershire Committee until retired
Education: Colston's School, Bristol; St Paul's College, Cheltenham
Qualifications: 5 O-levels, NCA advanced coach
Career outside cricket: Runs his own furniture import business
Off-season: Running business and watching rugby

Overseas tours: English Counties to Zimbabwe 1985; England to Australia 1986–87; Pakistan, Australia and New Zealand 1987–88; Unofficial English team to South Africa 1989–90
Overseas teams played for: Orange Free State 1985–86 (captain)
Cricketers particularly admired: Graham Gooch, Richard Hadlee, Clive Rice
Other sports followed: Rugby
Relaxations: 'Playing any sport, spending time with my family.'
Extras: Struck down by osteomyelitis at age 15. First played adult cricket for Downend CC, where W. G. Grace learnt to play; played with Allan Border in Gloucestershire 2nd XI. Published autobiography *Home Thoughts from Abroad* in 1987 after he had hit three centuries in a row in Test series v Australia, 1986–87. Banned from Test cricket for five years for joining tour to South Africa. Passed 2000 runs in a season for the first time and made his first double hundred in 1990
Opinions on cricket: 'I would have loved playing as an amateur. I am an unashamed traditionalist.'
Best batting: 227* Nottinghamshire v Kent, Tunbridge Wells 1990
Best bowling: 2–14 Gloucestershire v West Indians, Bristol 1980

LAST SEASON: BATTING

	I.	N. O.	R.	H. S.	AV.
TEST					
1ST	43	2	2226	227*	54.29
INT					
RAL	17	1	586	106*	36.62
N.W.	2	0	128	115	64.00
B&H	6	0	163	49	27.16

LAST SEASON: BOWLING

	O.	M.	R.	W.	AV.
TEST					
1ST					
INT					
RAL					
N.W.					
B&H					

CAREER: BATTING

	I.	N. O.	R.	H. S.	AV.
TEST	44	2	1661	162	39.54
1ST	448	30	15707	227*	37.57
INT	34	0	1361	106	40.02
RAL	138	7	4351	106*	33.21
N.W.	27	0	1015	115	37.59
B&H	52	2	1542	122	30.84

CAREER: BOWLING

	O.	M.	R.	W.	AV.
TEST	1	0	4	0	-
1ST	269.5	60	1032	16	64.50
INT	1	0	6	0	-
RAL	11.3	4	602	19	31.68
N.W.					
B&H	58	2	308	6	51.33

BROWN, A. M.   Derbyshire

Name: Andrew Mark Brown
Role: Left-hand bat, right-arm medium bowler
Born: 6 November 1964, Heanor, Derbyshire
Height: 5ft 9in **Weight:** 10st 7lbs
Nickname: Brownie
County debut: 1985
1st-Class 50s scored: 3
1st-Class 100s scored: 1
1st-Class catches: 7 (career 12)
Parents: John and Marion
Marital status: Single
Family links with cricket: 'Father is Youth Coaching Organiser for Derbyshire; brother Stephen played for Derbyshire youth teams; sister Helen played junior club cricket.'

Education: Langley Mill Junior School; Aldercar Comprehensive School; South-East Derbyshire College of PE
Qualifications: 8 O-levels, 1 A-level; coaching certificate
Off-season: 'Trying to find someone to employ me in the Derby area.'
Cricketers particularly admired: John Wright, Bob Taylor
Other sports followed: Football (Nottingham Forest)
Injuries: Forced to retire hurt with a shattered left index finger after completing his maiden 100 on 9 August and didn't play again for the season
Relaxations: 'Lying on beaches and attempting to surf.'
Extras: 'Born 100 yards away from where where I made my first senior appearance for Derbyshire.'
Opinions on cricket: 'Players should be allowed to coach in South Africa without penalty.'
Best batting: 139* Derbyshire v Northamptonshire, Chesterfield 1990

LAST SEASON: BATTING

	I.	N. O.	R.	H. S.	AV.
TEST					
1ST	12	2	413	139*	41.30
INT					
RAL					
N.W.					
B&H					

CAREER: BATTING

	I.	N. O.	R.	H. S.	AV.
TEST					
1ST	22	3	668	139*	35.15
INT					
RAL	1	1	2	2*	-
N.W.					
B&H					

BROWN, K. R. Middlesex

Name: Keith Robert Brown
Role: Right-hand bat, wicket-keeper
Born: 18 March 1963, Edmonton
Height: 5ft 11in **Weight:** 13st 7lbs
Nickname: Browny, Gloves, Scarface
County debut: 1984
County cap: 1990
1000 runs in a season: 1
1st-Class 50s scored: 22
1st-Class 100s scored: 8
1st-class 200s scored: 1
One-Day 50s: 5
One-Day 100s: 2
Place in batting averages: 39th av.
53.75 (1989 5th av. 58.00)
1st-Class catches: 30 (career 105)
Parents: Kenneth William and Margaret
Sonia
Wife and date of marriage: Marie,
3 November 1984
Children: Zachary, 24 February 1987; Rosa 18 December 1989
Family links with cricket: Brother Gary was on Middlesex staff for three years and now plays for Durham. Father is qualified umpire
Education: Chace Comprehensive School, Enfield
Qualifications: French O-level; senior cricket coach
Jobs outside cricket: Plasterer, PE instructor
Cricketers particularly admired: Clive Radley
Other sports followed: Rugby, soccer, most other sports apart from motor racing
Relaxations: 'Enjoy relaxing with family, walking pet dog and finishing with a couple of pints in local.'
Extras: Had promising boxing career but gave it up in order to concentrate on cricket. Picked to play rugby for Essex
Opinions on cricket: 'Four-day cricket produces more results, but batsmen get into a more negative state of mind. Short-leg fielders should be paid danger money.'

LAST SEASON: BATTING

	I.	N. O.	R.	H. S.	AV.
TEST					
1ST	36	8	1505	200*	53.75
INT					
RAL	15	4	406	68	36.90
N.W.	3	1	120	103*	60.00
B&H	5	0	141	56	28.20

CAREER: BATTING

	I.	N. O.	R.	H. S.	AV.
TEST					
1ST	134	23	4099	200*	36.92
INT					
RAL	45	10	956	102	27.31
N.W.	7	2	212	103*	42.40
B&H	10	1	226	56	25.11

Best batting: 200* Middlesex v Nottinghamshire, Lord's 1990
Best bowling: 2–7 Middlesex v Gloucestershire, Bristol 1987

BROWN, S. J. Northamptonshire

Name: Simon John Brown
Role: Right-hand bat, left-arm medium
pace bowler, gully fielder
Born: 29 June 1969, Cleadon Village,
Sunderland
Height: 6ft 3in **Weight:** 13st
Nickname: Chubby, Biffa
County debut: 1987
1st-Class catches: 2 (career 5)
Parents: Ernie and Doreen
Marital status: Single
Education: Boldon Comprehensive,
Tyne & Wear
Qualifications: 5 O-levels, 5 CSEs
Career outside cricket: Electrician
Overseas tours: England YCs to Sri
Lanka 1987; Australia for Youth World
Cup 1988
Cricketers particularly admired: John
Lever, Dennis Lillee, Richard Hadlee,
Ian Botham
Other sports followed: Basketball, golf and football
Relaxations: Listening to U2, renovating old cars
Extras: Offered basketball scholarship in America. Also professional terms with

LAST SEASON: BATTING

	I.	N. O.	R.	H. S.	AV.
TEST					
1ST	2	1	6	4*	6.00
INT					
RAL	2	1	3	3*	3.00
N.W.					
B&H					

LAST SEASON: BOWLING

	O.	M.	R.	W.	AV.
TEST					
1ST	73	17	250	6	41.66
INT					
RAL	39	0	226	5	45.20
N.W.					
B&H					

CAREER: BATTING

	I.	N. O.	R.	H. S.	AV.
TEST					
1ST	14	6	70	25*	8.75
INT					
RAL	3	1	4	3*	2.00
N.W.					
B&H	-	-	-	-	-

CAREER: BOWLING

	O.	M.	R.	W.	AV.
TEST					
1ST	288.0	80	814	25	32.56
INT					
RAL	83.3	1	467	13	35.92
N.W.					
B&H	7	0	33	0	-

Sunderland FC
Opinions on cricket: 'Too much cricket is played during the season. Players should be rested more often.'
Best batting: 25* Northamptonshire v Gloucestershire, Northampton 1988
Best bowling: 3–20 Northamptonshire v Oxford University, The Parks 1988

BUNTING, R. A. Sussex

Name: Rodney Alan Bunting
Role: Right-hand bat, right-arm
fast-medium bowler
Born: 25 April 1965, King's Lynn
Height: 6ft 5in **Weight:** 13st 10lbs
Nickname: Tiddler
County debut: 1988
1st-Class 50s scored: 1
1st-Class 5 w. in innings: 3
Place in batting averages: 273rd av.
10.62
Place in bowling averages: 131st av.
50.53
Strike rate: 83.07 (career 66.33)
1st-Class catches: 2 (career 4)
Parents: Geoffrey Thomas and Frances
Wife and date of marriage: Christine
Antoinette, 7 March 1986
Children: Jonathan Charles, 16
September 1986
Family links with cricket: Two

LAST SEASON: BATTING

	I.	N.O.	R.	H.S.	AV.
TEST					
1ST	13	5	85	24*	10.62
INT					
RAL	-	-	-	-	-
N.W.					
B&H					

LAST SEASON: BOWLING

	O.	M.	R.	W.	AV.
TEST					
1ST	360	61	1314	26	50.53
INT					
RAL	1	0	12	0	-
N.W.					
B&H					

CAREER: BATTING

	I.	N.O.	R.	H.S.	AV.
TEST					
1ST	36	11	260	73	10.40
INT					
RAL	1	1	5	5*	-
N.W.	1	0	6	6	6.00
B&H	2	1	0	0*	0.00

CAREER: BOWLING

	O.	M.	R.	W.	AV.
TEST					
1ST	796	80	2787	72	38.70
INT					
RAL	9	1	61	2	30.50
N.W.	5	0	30	1	30.00
B&H	56	0	255	7	36.42

elder brothers played county schools cricket. Parents very interested in cricket
Education: King Edward VII Grammar School
Qualifications: 6 O-levels
Off-season: Coaching in South Africa
Cricketers particularly admired: Bob Willis, Mike Hendrick
Other sports followed: Soccer, American football, golf
Relaxations: 'Crosswords, enjoying being with my family, making collections for Ian Gould's benefit.'
Extras: 'After six years in the game, won first title with Sussex 2nd XI in 1990.'
Opinions on cricket: 'If bowlers have to bowl with a reduced-seam ball, why not reduce the width of the batsman's bat? Fair's fair!'
Best batting: 73 Sussex v Warwickshire, Hove 1989
Best bowling: 5–44 Sussex v Warwickshire, Hove 1988

BURNS, N. D. Somerset

Name: Neil David Burns
Role: Left-hand bat, wicket-keeper
Born: 19 September 1965, Chelmsford
Height: 5ft 10in **Weight:** 11st 7lbs
Nickname: Burnsie, Ernie, George
County debut: 1986 (Essex), 1987 (Somerset)
County cap: 1987 (Somerset)
1st-Class 50s scored: 16
1st-Class 100s scored: 3
One-Day 50s: 2
Place in batting averages: 109th av. 39.62 (1989 98th av. 30.29)
Parents: Roy and Marie
Wife and date of marriage: Susan, 26 September 1987
Family links with cricket: Father Roy played club cricket for Finchley CC; brother Ian captained Essex U–19s

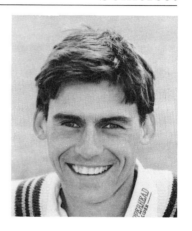

and plays for Woodford Wells and MCC
Education: Mildmay Junior and Moulsham High School
Qualifications: 6 O-levels, advanced cricket coach
Career outside cricket: Director of NBC Ltd, a sports promotion and management company; cricket coach
Off-season: 'Working for NBC Ltd; training and practising in Australia; raising money for the National Holiday Fund for sick and disabled children.'
Overseas tours: England YC to West Indies 1985
Overseas teams played for: Western Province B 1985–86

Cricketers particularly admired: Alan Knott, Bob Taylor, Rod Marsh, Graham Gooch, Martin Crowe, John Lever, Steve Waugh, Peter Roebuck

Other sports followed: Most sports particularly soccer ('I'm an ardent fan of West Ham United.')

Relaxations: 'Relaxing at home with my wife, music, theatre, watching and playing sport, TV, dining at home, training in off-season.'

Extras: Former schoolboy footballer with Tottenham Hotspur FC and Orient FC. Joined Somerset in 1987 after spending four years at Essex. Signed further four-year contract in 1989. Once took eight stumpings in match v Kent 2nd XI at Dartford in 1984. Once took a hat-trick of stumpings off Nasser Hussain's leg-breaks for Essex U–11s v Berkshire U–11s. Scored maiden first-class 100 against old county at Chelmsford in 1988

Opinions on cricket: 'Championship should be 16 four-day games. Sunday cricket should be more commercially exploited to attract more revenue: for example, coloured clothing, white balls, the substitute rule innovated in South Africa etc. Pitches in the Championship in 1990 were excellent but some one-day wickets were not conducive to run-making. If the quality of pitches remains the same, please can we have the 1989 ball back? It was great to see the media's suppport of England last year, let's just hope their loyalty extends to days when results are not so good. I am in favour of the 25-point deduction for under-prepared pitches, but not for well-grassed ones: at Taunton the grass adds to the pace and bounce which is even because the surface below the grass is so good.'

Best batting: 166 Somerset v Gloucestershire, Taunton 1990

LAST SEASON: BATTING

	I.	N. O.	R.	H. S.	AV.
TEST					
1ST	34	10	951	166	39.62
INT					
RAL	12	1	202	58	18.36
N.W.	1	1	25	25*	-
B&H	4	1	60	21	20.00

LAST SEASON: WICKET-KEEPING

	CT	ST			
TEST					
1ST	42	1			
INT					
RAL	13	1			
N.W.	2	0			
B&H	4	1			

CAREER: BATTING

	I.	N. O.	R.	H. S.	AV.
TEST					
1ST	144	30	3290	166	28.86
INT					
RAL	48	11	609	58	16.45
N.W.	5	2	64	25*	21.33
B&H	14	5	231	51	25.66

CAREER: WICKET-KEEPING

	CT	ST			
TEST					
1ST	201	17			
INT					
RAL	60	10			
N.W.	6	3			
B&H	21	4			

BUTCHER, A. R. Glamorgan

Name: Alan Raymond Butcher
Role: Left-hand bat, slow left-arm
or medium pace bowler, county captain
Born: 7 January 1954, Croydon
Height: 5ft 8in **Weight:** 11st 7lbs
Nickname: Butch, Budgie
County debut: 1972 (Surrey), 1987
(Glamorgan)
County cap: 1975 (Surrey), 1987
(Glamorgan)
Benefit: 1985 (Surrey)
Test debut: 1979
Tests: 1
One-Day Internationals: 1
1000 runs in a season: 11
1st-Class 50s scored: 108
1st-Class 100s scored: 42
1st-Class 200s scored: 1
1st-Class 5 w. in innings: 1
One-Day 50s: 49
One-Day 100s: 5
Place in batting averages: 24th av. 58.77 (1989 18th av. 46.62)
1st-Class catches: 8 (career 169)
Parents: Raymond and Jackie
Wife and date of marriage: Elaine, 27 September 1972
Children: Mark, Gary, Lisa
Family links with cricket: Brother Martin played for MCC Young Professionals.
Brother Ian plays for Gloucestershire CC. Son Mark made his Surrey 2nd XI debut

LAST SEASON: BATTING

	I.	N. O.	R.	H. S.	AV.
TEST					
1ST	41	5	2116	151*	58.77
INT					
RAL	15	2	345	52	26.53
N.W.	3	1	175	104*	87.50
B&H	5	0	185	95	37.00

LAST SEASON: BOWLING

	O.	M.	R.	W.	AV.
TEST					
1ST	25.3	2	153	1	153.00
INT					
RAL	4	0	20	1	20.00
N.W.					
B&H					

CAREER: BATTING

	I.	N. O.	R.	H. S.	AV.
TEST	2	0	34	20	17.00
1ST	636	57	20739	216*	35.81
INT	1	0	14	14	14.00
RAL	212	25	5149	113*	27.53
N.W.	33	4	996	104*	34.34
B&H	70	4	1703	95	25.80

CAREER: BOWLING

	O.	M.	R.	W.	AV.
TEST	2	0	9	0	-
1ST	1660	335	5379	139	38.69
INT					
RAL	340.2	22	1520	38	40.00
N.W.	67.2	10	249	5	49.80
B&H	184.3	32	587	27	21.74

in 1989; Gary captained Croydon Schools U–15s v London Schools
Education: Heath Clark Grammar School
Qualifications: 5 O-levels, 1 A-level
Other sports followed: Football
Relaxations: Most sport, rock music, reading
Extras: Released by Surrey at end of 1986 season. Joined Glamorgan in 1987. First Englishman to score 1000 runs in both 1989 and 1990. Appointed captain of Glamorgan during 1989 after Hugh Morris resigned in mid-season
Best batting: 216* Surrey v Cambridge University, Fenner's 1980
Best bowling: 6–48 Surrey v Hampshire, Guildford 1972

BUTCHER, I. P. Gloucestershire

Name: Ian Paul Butcher
Role: Right-hand bat, slip fielder
Born: 1 July 1962, Farnborough, Kent
Height: 6ft **Weight:** 14st
Nickname: Butch-Dog, Buster
County debut: 1980 (Leics), 1988 (Gloucs)
County cap: 1984 (Leics)
1000 runs in a season: 2
1st-Class 50s scored: 24
1st-Class 100s scored: 11
One-Day 50s: 8
One-Day 100s: 2
Place in batting averages: 135th av. 34.20 (1989 165th av. 21.85)
1st-Class catches: 4 (career 87)
Parents: Raymond and Jackie
Wife and date of marriage: Marie, 12 March 1983
Family links with cricket: Brother Alan captains Glamorgan CCC; brother Martin on MCC ground staff and captains club side

Education: John Ruskin High School
Qualifications: Preliminary coaching certificate
Overseas tours: England Young Cricketers to West Indies 1980
Cricketers particularly admired: Brian Davison, Graham Gooch, David Gower
Other sports folllowed: Football, golf
Relaxations: Sleeping, good beer, good food, music, TV
Extras: Scored century on Championship debut for Leicestershire at Grace Road in 1980. Moved to Gloucestershire in 1988, but missed most of season through injury

Best batting: 139 Leicestershire v Nottinghamshire, Leicester 1983
Best bowling: 1–2 Leicestershire v Essex, Chelmsford 1983

LAST SEASON: BATTING	I.	N. O.	R.	H. S.	AV.
TEST					
1ST	19	4	513	102	34.20
INT					
RAL	1	0	13	13	13.00
N.W.					
B&H					

CAREER: BATTING	I.	N. O.	R.	H. S.	AV.
TEST					
1ST	201	16	5480	139	29.62
INT					
RAL	55	3	984	71	18.92
N.W.	9	0	245	81	27.22
B&H	18	1	647	103*	38.05

BYAS, D.   Yorkshire

Name: David Byas
Role: Left-hand bat, right-arm
medium bowler
Born: 26 August 1963, Kilham
Height: 6ft 4in **Weight:** 14st 7lbs
Nickname: Bingo, Gadgett
County debut: 1986
1st-Class 50s scored: 14
1st-Class 100s scored: 2
One-Day 50s: 2
Place in batting averages: 176th av.
28.16 (1989 123rd av. 26.90)
1st-Class catches: 21 (career 48)
Parents: Richard and Anne
Wife and date of marriage: Rachael
Elizabeth, 27 October 1990
Family links with cricket: Father plays
in local league
Education: Scarborough College

Qualifications: 1 O-level (Engineering)
Career outside cricket: Working on
family farm
Cricketers particularly admired: David Gower, Viv Richards, Ian Botham
Other sports followed: Hockey, squash
Relaxations: 'Playing hockey, gardening, watching motor sport, game shooting.'
Best batting: 117 Yorkshire v Kent, Scarborough 1989
Best bowling: 3–55 Yorkshire v Derbyshire, Chesterfield 1990

LAST SEASON: BATTING

	I.	N.O.	R.	H.S.	AV.
TEST					
1ST	29	4	704	83	28.16
INT					
RAL	13	4	212	35*	23.55
N.W.	1	0	4	4	4.00
B&H	1	0	36	36	36.00

LAST SEASON: BOWLING

	O.	M.	R.	W.	AV.
TEST					
1ST	96	19	358	4	89.50
INT					
RAL	36	0	183	8	22.87
N.W.	3	0	23	1	23.00
B&H	13	1	50	1	50.00

CAREER: BATTING

	I.	N.O.	R.	H.S.	AV.
TEST					
1ST	88	7	2140	117	26.42
INT					
RAL	41	9	763	69*	23.84
N.W.	3	0	75	54	25.00
B&H	6	1	92	36	18.40

CAREER: BOWLING

	O.	M.	R.	W.	AV.
TEST					
1ST	149	29	598	10	59.80
INT					
RAL	87.1	1	445	19	23.42
N.W.	3	0	23	1	23.00
B&H	47.1	5	155	5	31.00

CANN, M. J.   Glamorgan

Name: Michael James Cann
Role: Left-hand bat, off-break bowler
Born: 4 July 1965, Cardiff
Height: 5ft 9in **Weight:** 11st 7lbs
Nickname: Tin, Canny
County debut: 1986
1st-Class 50s scored: 7
1st-Class 100s scored: 3
Place in batting averages: 218th av.
20.60 (1989 116th av. 27.97)
1st-Class catches: 2 (career 15)
Parents: Leslie and Catherine
Marital status: Single
Family links with cricket: 'Mother
bought me my first bat.'
Education: St Illtyds College, Cardiff;
Swansea University
Qualifications: 10 O-levels, 3 A-levels,
Degree in Biochemistry, senior NCA
coach
Career outside cricket: 'Researching Indian restaurants.'
Off-season: Playing for Griqualand West in South Africa
Overseas teams played for: Orange Free State B 1989–90; Griqualand W.1990–91
Cricketers particularly admired: 'Everyone who can put up with the
psychological ups and downs of this game.'
Other sports followed: Football (Cardiff City)
Relaxations: General socialising
Extras: Represented Combined Universities in B & H Cup 1987

Opinions on cricket: 'Practice facilities are of such a low standard that practice and attitudes towards it suffer greatly. People connected with the game should realise it is a professional sport and should forget any remnants of the amateur philosophies which still pervade some aspects of county cricket.'
Best batting: 138 Orange Free State B v Griqualand West, Virginia 1989–90
Best bowling: 3–30 Glamorgan v Middlesex, Abergavenny 1989

LAST SEASON: BATTING

	I.	N. O.	R.	H. S.	AV.
TEST					
1ST	10	0	206	64	20.60
INT					
RAL					
N.W.					
B&H					

LAST SEASON: BOWLING

	O.	M.	R.	W.	AV.
TEST					
1ST	35	3	162	1	162.00
INT					
RAL					
N.W.					
B&H					

CAREER: BATTING

	I.	N. O.	R.	H. S.	AV.
TEST					
1ST	62	5	1578	138	27.68
INT					
RAL	3	0	6	5	2.00
N.W.	2	1	4	2*	4.00
B&H	6	2	97	46	24.25

CAREER: BOWLING

	O.	M.	R.	W.	AV.
TEST					
1ST	236.5	17	920	14	65.71
INT					
RAL					
N.W.	11	2	40	3	13.33
B&H	27	0	127	2	63.50

CAPEL, D. J.   Northamptonshire

Name: David John Capel
Role: Right-hand bat, right-arm fast-medium bowler, all-rounder
Born: 6 July 1963, Northampton
Height: 6ft **Weight:** 12st 4lbs
Nickname: Capes, Fiery
County debut: 1981
County cap: 1986
Test debut: 1987
Tests: 15
One-Day Internationals: 23
1000 runs in a season: 3
50 wickets in a season: 3
1st-Class 50s scored: 50
1st-Class 100s scored: 10
1st-Class 5 w. in innings: 11
One-Day 50s: 15
One-Day 100s: 3
Place in batting averages: 63rd av. 47.47 (1989 56th av. 36.41)

Place in bowling averages: 21st av. 28.44 (1989 65th av. 29.70)

Strike rate: 56.16 (career 61.21)

1st-Class catches: 16 (career 100)

Parents: John and Angela Janet

Wife and date of marriage: Debbie, 21 September 1985

Children: Jenny, 21 October 1987

Family links with cricket: Father played in local league and brother Andrew in County League

Education: Roade Primary and Roade Comprehensive School

Qualifications: 3 O-levels, 4 CSEs, NCA coaching certificate

Off-season: 'Now self-employed in promotions and coaching cricket, whilst training to regain full fitness.'

Overseas tours: England to Sharjah 1986; Pakistan, New Zealand and Australia 1987–88; India for Nehru Cup and West Indies 1989–90

Overseas teams played for: Eastern Province 1985–87

Cricketers particularly admired: 'Numerous, for various reasons: Sobers, Richards and Botham (ability), Gooch and Wessels (professionalism), Clive Lloyd and Geoff Cook (gentlemen), Lillee (bowling, character, great man), Rice and Hadlee (great all-rounders), Boycott (dedication and knowledge).'

Other sports followed: 'Golf, local rugby and soccer teams.'

Injuries: 'Back, ankle, knee and broken little finger (luckily had them all in one season and six months' rest from bowling might help cure them).'

Relaxations: 'I enjoy swimming, watching TV – good comedy programmes – and listening to most kinds of music; spending time with my daughter Jenny.'

Extras: Only second Northampton-born man to play for England

Opinions on cricket: 'The contest between bat and ball should be as even as possible and, ideally, variety is essential. Flat batting pitches make for plenty of runs and attractive strokes, but the game could get a bit stereotyped with the same brown pitches producing record-breaking run-feasts. It would be a more interesting proposition going from a turning pitch to a seamer and then to a flat one, etc., each game bringing a fresh set of circumstances to work out and to test the technique of

LAST SEASON: BATTING

	I.	N.O.	R.	H.S.	AV.
TEST					
1ST	29	6	1092	123	47.47
INT					
RAL	15	2	543	121	41.76
N.W.	4	0	233	101	58.25
B&H	3	0	45	33	15.00

LAST SEASON: BOWLING

	O.	M.	R.	W.	AV.
TEST					
1ST	234	51	711	25	28.44
INT					
RAL	72.5	3	383	7	54.71
N.W.	39	1	205	2	102.50
B&H	28	1	91	3	30.33

CAREER: BATTING

	I.	N.O.	R.	H.S.	AV.
TEST	25	1	374	98	15.58
1ST	302	51	8010	134	31.91
INT	19	2	327	50*	19.23
RAL	99	21	2336	121	29.94
N.W.	21	7	703	101	50.21
B&H	29	5	509	97	21.20

CAREER: BOWLING

	O.	M.	R.	W.	AV.
TEST	333.2	50	1064	21	50.66
1ST	3370.1	65	10945	342	32.00
INT	173	12	805	17	47.35
RAL	522.3	18	2446	74	33.05
N.W.	163.1	18	662	18	36.77
B&H	263	27	929	40	23.22

individual players and the strength in depth of sides. As long as pitches are not dangerous for the batsmen, and pace and bounce are even, lateral movement is what makes for a test of skill – whether it is spin, seam or swing – and is where, I believe, the art of the game lies. Demands on county cricketers are high: 16 or 17 four-day games and 2 rather than 3 one-day competitions (50-overs a side) would give players more time to build up for and wind down from games and to train properly. This would make for far better first-class cricket and more keenly contested one-day matches – to the benefit of both players and spectators.'

Best batting: 134 Eastern Province v Western Province, Port Elizabeth 1986–87
Best bowling: 7–46 Northamptonshire v Yorkshire, Northampton 1987

CARRICK, P. Yorkshire

Name: Phillip Carrick
Role: Right-hand bat, slow left-arm bowler
Born: 16 July 1952, Leeds
Height: 6ft **Weight:** 14st
Nickname: Fergie
County debut: 1970
County cap: 1976
Benefit: 1985
50 wickets in a season: 10
1st-Class 50s scored: 37
1st-Class 100s scored: 3
1st-Class 5 w. in innings: 43
1st-Class 10 w. in match: 5
One-Day 50s: 2
Place in batting averages: 193rd av. 25.75 (1989 207th av. 17.25)
Place in bowling averages: 52nd av. 34.13 (1989 57th av. 28.12)
Strike rate: 78.39 (career 72.22)
1st-Class catches: 7 (career 186)
Parents: Arthur (deceased) and Ivy
Wife and date of marriage: Elspeth, 2 April 1977
Children: Emma Elizabeth, 6 May 1980; Philippa Louise, 11 January 1982
Family links with cricket: Father and brother useful league players
Education: Bramley CS, Intake CS, Park Lane College of Further Education
Qualifications: 2 O-levels, 8 CSEs, NCA coaching certificate
Jobs outside cricket: Company Director in own promotional business
Off-season: 'Running my own business.'

Overseas teams played for: Eastern Province 1976–77; Northern Transvaal 1982–83
Cricketers particularly admired: Graeme Pollock, Gary Sobers, Geoff Boycott, Malcolm Marshall
Other sports followed: Rugby League and football
Injuries: Hamstring pull and knee problems
Relaxations: Golf. 'Watching my daughters with their ponies.'
Extras: Yorkshire captain 1987–1989. Won B & H Cup in first season
Best batting: 131* Yorkshire v Northamptonshire, Northampton 1980
Best bowling: 8–33 Yorkshire v Cambridge University, Fenner's 1973

LAST SEASON: BATTING

	I.	N. O.	R.	H. S.	AV.
TEST					
1ST	22	2	515	64	25.75
INT					
RAL	9	2	106	30	15.14
N.W.	1	0	14	14	14.00
B&H	2	0	11	8	5.50

LAST SEASON: BOWLING

	O.	M.	R.	W.	AV.
TEST					
1ST	601	170	1570	46	34.13
INT					
RAL	97	5	443	20	22.15
N.W.	36	9	68	7	9.71
B&H	22	1	71	1	71.00

CAREER: BATTING

	I.	N. O.	R.	H. S.	AV.
TEST					
1ST	509	88	9325	131*	22.15
INT					
RAL	130	36	1366	48*	14.53
N.W.	21	3	308	54	17.11
B&H	32	5	297	53	11.00

CAREER: BOWLING

	O.	M.	R.	W.	AV.
TEST					
1ST	11592.1	3705	28878	963	29.98
INT					
RAL	958	45	4346	140	31.04
N.W.	247	55	658	23	28.60
B&H	420.3	55	1372	35	39.20

16. What was Angus Fraser's highest score last season?

17. Who headed the Derbyshire batting averages last season?

18. Who headed the Hampshire batting averages last season?

CHAPMAN, C. A. Yorkshire

Name: Colin Anthony Chapman
Role: Right-hand bat, wicket-keeper
Born: 8 June 1971, Bradford
Height: 5ft 8in **Weight:** 11 st
Nickname: Humpy, Chappers
County debut: 1990
1st-Class catches: 2 (career 2)
Parents: Mick and Joyce
Marital status: Single
Education: Nabwood Middle;
Beckfoot Grammar; Bradford & Ilkley
Community College
Qualifications: 5 O-levels; BTec
Diploma in Graphic Design
Career outside cricket: Printing/
graphics
Off-season: 'Going to New Zealand.'
Cricketers particularly admired: Phil
Carrick, Alan Knott
Other sports followed: 'Anything.'
Injuries: Back injury
Relaxations: 'Socialising after matches.'
Best batting: 20 Yorkshire v Middlesex, Uxbridge 1990

LAST SEASON / CAREER: BATTING

	I.	N. O.	R.	H.S.	AV.
TEST					
1ST	4	0	47	20	11.75
INT					
RAL	1	1	36	36*	-
N.W.					
B&H					

LAST SEASON / CAREER: BOWLING

	O.	M.	R.	W.	AV.
TEST					
1ST					
INT					
RAL					
N.W.					
B&H					

Name: John Henry Childs
Role: Left-hand bat, slow left-arm bowler
Born: 15 August 1951, Plymouth
Height: 6ft **Weight:** 12st 6lbs
Nickname: Charlie
County debut: 1975 (Gloucs), 1985 (Essex)
County cap: 1977 (Gloucs), 1986 (Essex)
Testimonial: 1985
Test debut: 1988
Tests: 2
50 wickets in a season: 5
1st-Class 5 w. in innings: 38
1st-Class 10 w. in match: 8
Place in batting averages: 269th av. 11.18
Place in bowling averages: 140th av. 58.88 (1989 29th av. 22.70)
Strike rate: 145.74 (career 70.11)
1st-Class catches: 7 (career 92)
Parents: Sydney and Barbara (both deceased)
Wife and date of marriage: Jane Anne, 11 November 1978
Children: Lee Robert, 28 November 1980; Scott Alexander, 21 August 1984
Education: Audley Park Secondary Modern, Torquay
Qualifications: Advanced cricket coach
Off-season: Working for Essex CCC marketing department

LAST SEASON: BATTING

	I.	N. O.	R.	H. S.	AV.
TEST					
1ST	16	5	123	26	11.18
INT					
RAL	5	4	15	5*	15.00
N.W.	-	-	-	-	-
B&H	-	-	-	-	-

LAST SEASON: BOWLING

	O.	M.	R.	W.	AV.
TEST					
1ST	655.5	211	1590	27	58.88
INT					
RAL	86	6	412	6	68.66
N.W.	24	1	104	1	104.00
B&H	38	3	144	5	28.80

CAREER: BATTING

	I.	N. O.	R.	H. S.	AV.
TEST	4	4	2	2*	-
1ST	254	117	1159	34*	8.45
INT					
RAL	27	16	103	16*	9.36
N.W.	4	3	22	14*	22.00
B&H	7	5	25	10	12.50

CAREER: BOWLING

	O.	M.	R.	W.	AV.
TEST	86	29	183	3	61.00
1ST	8187.5	2510	21183	705	30.04
INT					
RAL	459.1	25	2075	53	39.15
N.W.	84	13	284	8	35.50
B&H	205	38	656	21	31.23

Cricketers particularly admired: Gary Sobers, Mike Procter

Relaxations: 'Watching rugby, decorating at home, walking on moors and beaches, enjoying my family.'

Extras: Played for Devon 1973–74. Released by Gloucestershire at end of 1984 and joined Essex. One of *Wisden's* Five Cricketers of the Year, 1986. Selected for England's cancelled tour to India 1988–89

Best batting: 34* Gloucestershire v Nottinghamshire, Cheltenham 1982

Best bowling: 9–56 Gloucestershire v Somerset, Bristol 1981

CLINTON, G. S. Surrey

Name: Grahame Selvey Clinton

Role: Left-hand bat, right-arm medium bowler

Born: 5 May 1953, Sidcup

Height: 5ft 6in

Nickname: Clint, Grimbo

County debut: 1974 (Kent), 1979 (Surrey)

County cap: 1980 (Surrey)

Benefit: 1989 (83,000)

1000 runs in a season: 7

1st-Class 50s scored: 73

1st-Class 100s scored: 20

One-Day 50s: 32

One-Day 100s: 4

Place in batting averages: 67th av. 46.14 (1989 148th av. 23.51)

1st-Class catches: 6 (career 96)

Wife: Cathy

Children: Richard, Peter and Robert

Family links with cricket: Father captained Kemnal Manor CC. Younger brothers Neil and Tony regular members of Blackheath CC

Education: Chislehurst and Sidcup Grammar School

Overseas tours: England YC to West Indies 1972

Extras: Left Kent to join Surrey at end of 1978 season. Renowned as a dressing-room

LAST SEASON: BATTING

	I.	N. O.	R.	H. S.	AV.
TEST					
1ST	32	4	1292	146	46.14
INT					
RAL	4	0	139	45	34.75
N.W.	2	0	83	50	41.50
B&H	5	0	217	77	43.40

CAREER: BATTING

	I.	N. O.	R.	H. S.	AV.
TEST					
1ST	450	53	13118	192	33.04
INT					
RAL	89	9	2682	105*	33.52
N.W.	28	2	780	146	30.00
B&H	50	2	1710	121*	35.62

wit and as being one of the most injury-prone cricketers. Claims to have seen the inside of the casualty departments in 15 out of 17 counties. Scored his first first-class century for Surrey in his first match against his old county. Top scorer for Surrey, with 6, when they were dismissed for 14 by Essex at Chelmsford in 1983. Played for London Colts in 1968 with Emburey and Gooch and topped the batting averages. Retired at end of 1990 season

Best batting: 192 Surrey v Yorkshire, The Oval 1984
Best bowling: 2–8 Kent v Pakistan, Canterbury 1978

CONNOR, C. A. Hampshire

Name: Cardigan Adolphus Connor
Role: Right-hand bat, right-arm fast-medium bowler
Born: 24 March 1961, Anguilla
Height: 5ft 10in **Weight:** 11st 4lbs
Nickname: Cardi, CC
County debut: 1984
County cap: 1988
50 wickets in a season: 3
1st-Class 5 w. in innings: 9
1st-Class 10 w. in match: 1
Place in batting averages: 200th av. 24.66 (1989 256th av. 10.75)
Place in bowling averages: 80th av. 38.06 (1989 17th av. 21.27)
Strike rate: 65.12 (career 61.90)
1st-Class catches: 10 (career 39)
Parents: Ethleen Snagg

LAST SEASON: BATTING

	I.	N.O.	R.	H.S.	AV.
TEST					
1ST	10	4	148	46	24.66
INT					
RAL	3	1	11	4*	5.50
N.W.	2	1	20	13	20.00
B&H	1	0	3	3	3.00

LAST SEASON: BOWLING

	O.	M.	R.	W.	AV.
TEST					
1ST	510.1	88	1789	47	38.06
INT					
RAL	86.1	5	426	14	30.42
N.W.	42	4	203	7	29.00
B&H	34	1	162	6	27.00

CAREER: BATTING

	I.	N.O.	R.	H.S.	AV.
TEST					
1ST	100	33	614	46	9.16
INT					
RAL	21	11	92	19	9.20
N.W.	4	2	28	13	14.00
B&H	6	4	16	5*	8.00

CAREER: BOWLING

	O.	M.	R.	W.	AV.
TEST					
1ST	3497.4	735	10634	339	31.36
INT					
RAL	692.1	50	3036	122	24.88
N.W.	183.3	25	700	26	26.92
B&H	251.4	28	980	42	23.33

Marital status: Single
Education: The Valley Secondary
School, Anguilla; Langley College
Qualifications: Engineer
Off-season: Playing club cricket in Newcastle, Australia
Cricketers particularly admired: Viv Richards, Richard Hadlee
Other sports followed: American football, athletics and most others
Relaxations: Keeping fit and playing golf
Extras: Played for Buckinghamshire in Minor Counties before joining Hampshire.
First Anguillan-born player to appear in the County Championship
Best batting: 46 Hampshire v Derbyshire, Portsmouth 1990
Best bowling: 7–31 Hampshire v Gloucestershire, Portsmouth 1989

COOK, G. Northamptonshire

Name: Geoffrey Cook
Role: Right-hand bat, slow left-arm
bowler
Born: 9 October 1951, Middlesbrough,
Yorkshire
Height: 6ft **Weight:** 12st 10lbs
Nickname: Geoff
County debut: 1971
County cap: 1975
Benefit: 1985
Test debut: 1981–82
Tests: 7
One-Day Internationals: 6
1000 runs in a season: 12
1st-Class 50s scored: 112
1st-Class 100s scored: 37
1st-Class 200s scored: 1
One-Day 50s: 51
One-Day 100s: 4
Place in batting averages: 191st av.
26.09 (1989 63rd av. 35.57)
1st-Class catches: 2 (career 419 & 3 stumpings)
Parents: Harry and Helen
Wife and date of marriage: Judith, 22 November 1975
Children: Anna, 21 May 1980
Family links with cricket: Father and brother David very keen club cricketers.
Father very involved in running cricket in Middlesbrough
Education: Middlesbrough High School
Qualifications: 6 O-levels, 1 A-level

Off-season: New job promoting Durham's claims to become a first-class county
Overseas tours: England to India and Sri Lanka 1981–82, Australia 1982–83
Overseas teams played for: Eastern Province 1978–81
Cricketers particularly admired: Clive Rice
Relaxations: Walking, reading, crosswords
Extras: 'Great believer in organised recreation for young people. Would enjoy time and scope to carry my beliefs through.' Northants captain from 1981 to 1988. Secretary of Cricketers' Association. Retired at end of 1990 season and has taken up new job promoting Durham's claims to join the County Championship
Best batting: 203 Northamptonshire v Yorkshire, Scarborough 1988
Best bowling: 3–47 England XI v South Australia, Adelaide 1982–83

LAST SEASON: BATTING

	I.	N. O.	R.	H. S.	AV.
TEST					
1ST	12	1	287	87	26.09
INT					
RAL	1	0	16	16	16.00
N.W.					
B&H	3	0	40	28	13.33

LAST SEASON: BOWLING

	O.	M.	R.	W.	AV.
TEST					
1ST					
INT					
RAL					
N.W.					
B&H					

CAREER: BATTING

	I.	N. O.	R.	H. S.	AV.
TEST	13	0	203	66	15.61
1ST	780	65	23074	203	32.27
INT	6	0	106	32	17.66
RAL	221	20	4783	98	23.79
N.W.	42	2	1520	130	38.00
B&H	71	6	1915	108	29.46

CAREER: BOWLING

	O.	M.	R.	W.	AV.
TEST	7	3	27	0	-
1ST	199.2	40	779	15	51.93
INT					
RAL	2	0	10	0	-
N.W.					
B&H					

COOK, N. G. B.　　Northamptonshire

Name: Nicholas Grant Billson Cook
Role: Right-hand bat, slow
left-arm bowler
Born: 17 June 1956, Leicester
Height: 6ft **Weight:** 12st 8lbs
Nickname: Beast, Rag'ead
County debut: 1978 (Leics), 1986
(Northants)
County cap: 1982 (Leics), 1987
(Northants)
Test debut: 1983
Tests: 15
One-Day Internationals: 3
50 wickets in a season: 8
1st-Class 50s scored: 4
1st-Class 5 w. in innings: 30
1st-Class 10 w. in match: 3
Place in batting averages: 260th av.
13.00
Place in bowling averages: 50th av.
34.10 (1989 21st av. 21.77)
Strike rate: 79.07 (career 73.17)
1st-Class catches: 10 (career 179)
Parents: Peter and Cynthia
Marital status: Divorced
Family links with cricket: Father
played club cricket

Education: Stokes Croft Junior; Lutterworth High; Lutterworth Upper
Qualifications: 7 O-levels, 1 A-level, advanced cricket coach
Off-season: Working for Northants, watching soccer and National Hunt horse racing. MCC tour to USA
Overseas tours: England to New Zealand and Pakistan 1983–84; Pakistan 1987–88; India for Nehru Trophy 1989–90; English Counties XI to Zimbabwe 1984–85; England B to Sri Lanka 1985–86
Other sports followed: Soccer (especially Leicester City), rugby, horse racing
Relaxations: Crosswords, reading (especially Wilbur Smith), good comedy programmes, good food
Extras: Played for ESCA 1975. Played for Young England v Young West Indies 1975. Left Leicestershire to join Northamptonshire in 1986
Opinions on cricket: 'The edict of a colour chart for pitches was completely wrong as each square has its own peculiarities. The ball should have a 12-strand seam, because at the moment bat definitely outweighs ball. A more realistic over-rate, i. e. 17 per hour, should be introduced.'

Best batting: 75 Leicestershire v Somerset, Taunton 1980
Best bowling: 7–63 Leicestershire v Somerset, Taunton 1982

LAST SEASON: BATTING

	I.	N. O.	R.	H. S.	AV.
TEST					
1ST	19	8	143	30	13.00
INT					
RAL	6	3	14	7*	4.66
N.W.	3	1	16	9	8.00
B&H	-	-	-	-	-

LAST SEASON: BOWLING

	O.	M.	R.	W.	AV.
TEST					
1ST	527.1	167	1364	40	34.10
INT					
RAL	93	4	533	12	44.41
N.W.	58.4	12	209	7	29.85
B&H	11	1	45	0	-

CAREER: BATTING

	I.	N. O.	R.	H. S.	AV.
TEST	25	4	179	31	8.52
1ST	293	79	2578	75	12.04
INT	-	-	-	-	-
RAL	38	18	185	13*	9.25
N.W.	7	2	42	13	8.40
B&H	13	5	127	23	15.87

CAREER: BOWLING

	O.	M.	R.	W.	AV.
TEST	695.2	226	1689	52	32.48
1ST	8914.3	2636	20758	736	28.20
INT	24	1	95	5	19.00
RAL	613.5	40	2746	89	30.85
N.W.	206.4	36	691	21	32.90
B&H	258.1	30	935	20	46.75

COOK, S. J. Somerset

Name: Stephen James Cook
Role: Right-hand bat
Born: 31 July 1953, Johannesburg
Height: 6ft 3in **Weight:** 14st
Nickname: Mutley
County debut: 1989
County cap: 1989
1000 runs in a season: 2
1st-Class 50s scored: 69
1st-Class 100s scored: 43
1st-Class 200s scored: 2
One-Day 50s: 11
One-Day 100s: 7
Place in batting averages: 7th av. 76.70 (1989 3rd av. 60.56)
1st-Class catches: 11 (career 109)
Parents: Denzil Chesney and Nancy Harding
Wife and date of marriage: Linsey, 11 April 1981
Children: Stephen Craig, 29 November 1982; Ryan Lyall, 2 October 1985
Family links with cricket: Father played local club cricket
Education: Rosebank Primary and Hyde Park High Schools; Wits University;

Johannesburg College of Education
Qualifications: Matric Pass; TTHD from Johannesburg College of Education
Career outside cricket: School teacher; Manager of Cricket Affairs at Rand Afrikaans University
Off-season: Playing for Transvaal
Overseas teams played for: Transvaal 1972–1990; South Africa 1982–1990
Cricketers particularly admired: Barry Richards, Clive Rice, Vince van der Bijl, Graeme Pollock, Kevin McKenzie, Henry Fotheringham
Other sports followed: Golf, football, rugby, tennis, athletics
Relaxations: Quiet meal and a glass of wine with family and friends
Extras: 'Scored 114 against England on my debut in unofficial Tests in 1981–82.' Captain of South African team v Mike Gatting's English team in 1989–90. First batsman to reach 1000 first-class runs in both 1989 and 1990. One of *Wisden's* Five Cricketers of the Year, 1990. His 313* is the highest score by a South African in county cricket. Highest run aggregate (902) for a Sunday League season in 1990. Came to England as manager of South African Schools side in 1983, 1988. Has signed to play for a third season in 1991
Opinions on cricket: 'I would like to see more four-day cricket. Players should be able to play against whomever they wish without government interference.'
Best batting: 313* Somerset v Glamorgan, Cardiff 1990
Best bowling: 2–25 Somerset v Derbyshire, Chesterfield 1990

LAST SEASON: BATTING

	I.	N. O.	R.	H. S.	AV.
TEST					
1ST	41	7	2608	313*	76.70
INT					
RAL	16	2	902	136*	64.42
N.W.	2	0	87	45	43.50
B&H	6	0	329	177	54.83

CAREER: BATTING

	I.	N. O.	R.	H. S.	AV.
TEST					
1ST	359	40	15394	313*	48.25
INT					
RAL	32	3	1458	136*	50.27
N.W.	4	0	121	45	30.25
B&H	12	0	641	177	53.41

COOPER, K. E. Nottinghamshire

Name: Kevin Edwin Cooper
Role: Left-hand bat, right-arm
fast-medium bowler
Born: 27 December 1957, Sutton-in-
Ashfield
Height: 6ft **Weight:** 12st 4lbs
Nickname: Henry
County debut: 1976
County cap: 1980
Benefit: 1990
50 wickets in a season: 8
1st-Class 5 w. in innings: 25
1st-Class 10 w. in match: 1
Place in batting averages: 266th av.
11.35 (1989 246th av. 11.95)
Place in bowling averages: 103rd av.
40.79 (1989 40th av. 26.36)
Strike rate: 78.18 (career 60.60)
1st-Class catches: 9 (career 85)
Parents: Gerald Edwin and Margaret
Wife and date of marriage: Linda Carol, 14 February 1981
Children: Kelly Louise, 8 April 1982; Tara Amy, 22 November 1984
Family links with cricket: Father played local cricket
Cricketers particularly admired: John Snow
Relaxations: Golf, clay pigeon shooting
Extras: In 1974, playing for Hucknall Ramblers CC, took 10 wickets for 6 runs in one innings against Sutton College in the Mansfield and District League. First bowler to reach 50 first-class wickets in 1988 season

LAST SEASON: BATTING

	I.	N. O.	R.	H. S.	AV.
TEST					
1ST	26	6	227	35*	11.35
INT					
RAL	6	1	37	21	7.40
N.W.	2	0	10	10	5.00
B&H	2	2	19	11*	-

LAST SEASON: BOWLING

	O.	M.	R.	W.	AV.
TEST					
1ST	703.4	153	2203	54	40.79
INT					
RAL	126	8	571	10	57.10
N.W.	20	3	65	4	16.25
B&H	64.2	11	199	7	28.42

CAREER: BATTING

	I.	N. O.	R.	H. S.	AV.
TEST					
1ST	279	67	2139	46	10.09
INT					
RAL	53	16	246	31	6.64
N.W.	8	1	45	11	6.42
B&H	21	13	118	25*	14.75

CAREER: BOWLING

	O.	M.	R.	W.	AV.
TEST					
1ST	7110.4	1929	19215	704	27.29
INT					
RAL	1077.4	69	4725	135	35.00
N.W.	261.2	58	717	34	21.08
B&H	178.5	109	574	24	23.91

Best batting: 46 Nottinghamshire v Middlesex, Trent Bridge 1985
Best bowling: 8–44 Nottinghamshire v Middlesex, Lord's 1984

CORK, D. G.   Derbyshire

Name: Dominic Gerald Cork
Role: Right-hand bat, right-arm
medium-fast bowler
Born: 7 August 1971, Newcastle-under-
Lyme, Staffordshire
Height: 6ft 2in
County debut: 1990
Marital status: Single
Education: St Joseph's College, Stoke-
on-Trent
Overseas tours: England YCs to
Australia 1989–90
Extras: Played for England YCs v
New Zealand 1989 and Pakistan 1990,
making a hundred in the third match v
Pakistan at Taunton. Took a wicket in
first over in first-class cricket v New
Zealand at Derby. First played cricket for
Betley CC in the North Staffordshire and
South Cheshire League. Played Minor
Counties cricket for Staffordshire in 1989
and 1990
Best batting: 7 Derbyshire v Leicestershire, Derby 1990
Best bowling: 1–4 Derbyshire v New Zealand, Derby 1990

LAST SEASON / CAREER: BATTING

	I.	N. O.	R.	H. S.	AV.
TEST					
1ST	2	1	9	7	9.00
INT					
RAL					
N.W.					
B&H					

LAST SEASON / CAREER: BOWLING

	O.	M.	R.	W.	AV.
TEST					
1ST	39	8	123	2	61.50
INT					
RAL					
N.W.					
B&H					

COTTEY, P. A.   Glamorgan

Name: Phillip Anthony Cottey
Role: Right-hand opening bat, cover fielder
Born: 2 June 1966, Swansea
Height: 5ft 5in **Weight:** 9st 10lbs
County debut: 1986
Nickname: Cotts
1000 runs in season: 1
1st-Class 50s scored: 9
1st-Class 100s scored: 3
One-Day 50s: 2
Place in batting averages: 143rd av. 33.36
1st-Class catches: 12 (career 22)
Parents: Bernard John and Ruth
Family links with cricket: Father played for Swansea CC
Education: Bishopston Comprehensive School, Swansea
Qualifications: 9 O-levels
Cricketers particularly admired: Alan Jones, Ian Botham, Viv Richards, Geoff Boycott
Other sports followed: Soccer, golf, squash
Relaxations: Anything revolving around sport. Watching videos, listening to music
Extras: Left school at 16 to play for Swansea City FC for three years as a professional. Captained Welsh Youth Soccer XI (3 caps)
Opinions on cricket: 'I think that 16 four-day games would make for a fairer Championship. I do not think that sport and politics should mix. It baffles me that young cricketers are encouraged not to go to South Africa, and yet in the Championship all nationalities play with South Africans. South African-born players even play for England. There is a double standard somewhere.'
Best batting: 156 Glamorgan v Oxford University, The Parks 1990
Best bowling: 1–49 Glamorgan v Warwickshire, Swansea 1990

LAST SEASON: BATTING

	I.	N.O.	R.	H.S.	AV.
TEST					
1ST	35	5	1001	156	33.36
INT					
RAL	5	1	150	50*	37.50
N.W.	2	1	29	27	29.00
B&H	1	0	2	2	2.00

CAREER: BATTING

	I.	N.O.	R.	H.S.	AV.
TEST					
1ST	79	10	1845	156	26.73
INT					
RAL	15	2	236	50*	18.15
N.W.	2	1	29	27	29.00
B&H	7	0	107	68	15.28

COWANS, N. G.   Middlesex

Name: Norman George Cowans
Role: Right-hand bat, right-arm
fast bowler
Born: 17 April 1961, Enfield St Mary,
Jamaica
Height: 6ft 3in **Weight:** 14st 7lbs
Nickname: Flash, George, Seed
County debut: 1980
County cap: 1984
Test debut: 1982–83
Tests: 19
One-Day Internationals: 23
50 wickets in a season: 6
1st-Class 50s scored: 1
1st-Class 5 w. in innings: 23
1st-Class 10 w. in match: 1
Place in batting averages: 261st av.
12.70
Place in bowling averages: 38th av.
31.97 (1989 18th av. 21.30)
Strike rate: 70.76 (career 47.12)
1st-Class catches: 3 (career 54)
Parents: Gloria and Ivan
Children: Kimberley, 27 December 1983
Education: Park High Secondary, Stanmore, Middlesex
Qualifications: Qualified coach
Overseas tours: England YCs to Australia 1979; England to Australia and New

LAST SEASON: BATTING

	I.	N. O.	R.	H. S.	AV.
TEST					
1ST	17	7	127	46*	12.70
INT					
RAL	4	1	27	27	9.00
N.W.	-	-	-	-	-
B&H	3	1	23	12	11.50

LAST SEASON: BOWLING

	O.	M.	R.	W.	AV.
TEST					
1ST	460	124	1247	39	31.97
INT					
RAL	87	6	456	13	35.07
N.W.	45	8	158	6	26.33
B&H	44	5	171	4	42.75

CAREER: BATTING

	I.	N. O.	R.	H. S.	AV.
TEST	29	7	175	36	7.95
1ST	170	43	1170	66	9.21
INT	8	3	13	4*	2.60
RAL	27	10	146	27	8.58
N.W.	10	2	33	12*	4.12
B&H	13	5	45	12	5.62

CAREER: BOWLING

	O.	M.	R.	W.	AV.
TEST	575.2	113	2003	51	39.27
1ST	3948.5	874	11729	525	22.34
INT	213.4	17	913	23	39.69
RAL	565.2	57	2257	84	26.86
N.W.	292.4	50	957	42	22.78
B&H	277.1	39	897	39	23.00

Zealand 1982–83; New Zealand and Pakistan 1983–84; India and Australia 1984–85 England B to Sri Lanka 1985–86
Cricketers particularly admired: Viv Richards, Malcolm Marshall
Other sports followed: Football (Arsenal FC), athletics, boxing
Relaxations: Fishing, photography, travelling, being with friends, listening to reggae and soul music
Extras: Played for England YC. Won athletics championships in sprinting and javelin throwing and was a squash and real tennis professional. Played thirteen Tests for England before being awarded his Middlesex cap
Opinions on cricket: 'The county programme is far too intense, and I think that 16 four-day games would be a much better system for producing quality players.'
Best batting: 66 Middlesex v Surrey, Lord's 1984
Best bowling: 6–31 Middlesex v Leicestershire, Leicester 1985

COWDREY, C. S. Kent

Name: Christopher Stuart Cowdrey
Role: Right-hand bat, right-arm medium bowler
Born: 20 October 1957, Farnborough, Kent
Height: 6ft **Weight:** 14st
Nickname: Cow, Woody
County debut: 1977
County cap: 1979
Benefit: 1989 (146,287)
Test debut: 1984–85
Tests: 6
One-Day Internationals: 3
1000 runs in a season: 4
1st-Class 50s scored: 56
1st-Class 100s scored: 21
1st-Class 5 w. in innings: 2
One-Day 50s: 40
One-Day 100s: 2
Place in batting averages: 104th av. 40.72 (1989 43rd av. 38.96)
1st-Class catches: 9 (career 288)
Parents: Michael Colin and Penelope Susan
Wife and date of marriage: Christel, 1 January 1989
Family links with cricket: Grandfather, Stuart Chiesman, on Kent Committee, twelve years as Chairman. Pavilion on Kent's ground at Canterbury named after him. Father played for Kent and England, brother Graham made Kent debut 1984

Education: Wellesley House, Broadstairs; Tonbridge School
Career outside cricket: Director of Ten Tenths Travel. Consultant to Stuart Canvas Products
Overseas tours: Captained England YC to West Indies 1976; England to India and Australia 1984–85; Unofficial English XI to South Africa 1989–90
Cricketers particularly admired: David Gower
Other sports followed: All sports
Extras: Played for Kent 2nd XI at age 15. County vice-captain 1984 and appointed captain in 1985. Captained England for one Test v West Indies in 1988; injury kept him out of next Test and was not selected again. Banned from Test cricket for joining tour to South Africa in 1989–90. Resigned from Kent captaincy at end of 1990 season. David Gower was best man at his wedding. Published autobiography, *Good Enough?*, 1986
Best batting: 159 Kent v Surrey, Canterbury 1985
Best bowling: 5–46 Kent v Hampshire, Canterbury 1986

LAST SEASON: BATTING

	I.	N. O.	R.	H. S.	AV.
TEST					
1ST	24	6	733	107*	40.72
INT					
RAL	14	2	277	46	23.08
N.W.	2	0	11	6	5.50
B&H	4	1	172	67*	57.33

LAST SEASON: BOWLING

	O.	M.	R.	W.	AV.
TEST					
1ST	61	12	192	4	48.00
INT					
RAL	52	0	306	12	25.50
N.W.	5	0	29	0	
B&H	22	2	100	8	12.50

CAREER: BATTING

	I.	N. O.	R.	H. S.	AV.
TEST	8	1	101	38	14.42
1ST	439	67	11947	159	32.11
INT	3	1	51	46*	25.50
RAL	179	28	3949	95	26.15
N.W.	30	6	841	122*	35.04
B&H	58	9	1477	114	30.14

CAREER: BOWLING

	O.	M.	R.	W.	AV.
TEST	66.5	2	309	4	77.25
1ST	2354.1	450	7653	196	39.04
INT	8.4	0	55	2	27.50
RAL	670.2	9	3317	117	28.35
N.W.	171	17	628	22	28.54
B&H	342.4	19	1473	45	32.73

COWDREY, G. R. Kent

Name: Graham Robert Cowdrey
Role: Right-hand bat, right-arm
medium bowler, cover fielder
Born: 27 June 1964, Farnborough, Kent
Height: 5ft 10in **Weight:** 13st 7lbs
Nickname: Van, Cow
County debut: 1984
County cap: 1988
1000 runs in season: 1
1st-Class 50s scored: 21
1st-Class 100s scored: 5
One-Day 50s: 7
One-Day 100s: 1
Place in batting averages: 61st av.
47.75 (1989 122nd av. 27.11)
1st-Class catches: 9 (career 43)
Parents: Michael Colin and Penelope
Susan
Marital status: Single
Family links with cricket: 'Father
had a couple of knocks with England, and brother likewise.'
Education: Wellesley House, Broadstairs; Tonbridge School; Durham University
Qualifications: 8 O-levels, 3 A-levels, University entrance
Off-season: 'Working for Zenith Sporting Company and following Van Morrison
on his UK tour.'
Cricketers particularly admired: Chris Cowdrey, Steve Marsh, John Inverarity,
Justin Bairmian
Other sports followed: Rugby Union, horse racing, golf

LAST SEASON: BATTING

	I.	N. O.	R.	H. S.	AV.
TEST					
1ST	39	6	1576	135	47.75
INT					
RAL	14	3	347	70*	31.54
N.W.	2	0	40	37	20.00
B&H	2	0	12	12	6.00

LAST SEASON: BOWLING

	O.	M.	R.	W.	AV.
TEST					
1ST	6.3	1	44	0	-
INT					
RAL					
N.W.	2.3	0	13	1	13.00
B&H	5	0	23	0	-

CAREER: BATTING

	I.	N. O.	R.	H. S.	AV.
TEST					
1ST	128	17	3543	145	31.91
INT					
RAL	59	12	1204	102*	25.61
N.W.	7	2	148	37	29.60
B&H	18	2	474	69	29.62

CAREER: BOWLING

	O.	M.	R.	W.	AV.
TEST					
1ST	131.1	24	530	9	58.88
INT					
RAL	96	3	441	21	21.00
N.W.	40.5	11	107	6	17.83
B&H	18.4	4	62	2	31.00

Relaxations: Reading, theatre, and music. 'I have seen Van Morrison 70 times in concert. A wonderful musician – truly a genius.'

Extras: Played for England YC. Made 1000 runs for Kent 2nd XI first season on staff, and broke 2nd XI record with 1300 runs in 26 innings in 1985. Enjoyed his most successful season in the first team in 1990

Opinions on cricket: 'I do not enjoy the travel and the constant checking into hotels. I would like to see cricketers having time for another career in the summer – more like Sheffield Shield players in Australia.'

Best batting: 145 Kent v Essex, Chelmsford 1988

Best bowling: 1–5 Kent v Warwickshire, Edgbaston 1988

COWLEY, N. G. Glamorgan

Name: Nigel Geoffrey Cowley
Role: Right-hand bat, off-break bowler
Born: 1 March 1953, Shaftesbury, Dorset
Height: 5ft 7in **Weight:** 12st 5lbs
Nickname: Dougal
County debut: 1974 (Hampshire), 1990 (Glamorgan)
County cap: 1978 (Hampshire)
Benefit: 1988 (88,274)
1000 runs in a season: 1
50 wickets in a season: 2
1st-Class 50s scored: 36
1st-Class 100s scored: 2
1st-Class 5 w. in innings: 5
One-Day 50s: 5
Place in batting averages: 101st av. 41.23
Place in bowling averages: 155th av. 75.00
Strike rate: 158.25 (career 74.74)
1st-Class catches: 9 (career 105)
Parents: Geoffrey and Betty
Wife: Susan
Children: Mark and Darren
Family links with cricket: Father played good club cricket; son Mark played for Hampshire Schools U–16, and son Darren captained Hampshire Schools U–12
Education: Mere Dutchy Manor, Mere, Wiltshire
Off-season: Coaching in South Africa
Injuries: Pelvic injury – out of cricket from 6 August. Operation in September
Extras: Left Hampshire at end of 1989 season and signed two-year contract with

Glamorgan
Best batting: 109* Hampshire v Somerset, Taunton 1977
Best bowling: 6–48 Hampshire v Leicestershire, Southampton 1982

LAST SEASON: BATTING

	I.	N. O.	R.	H. S.	AV.
TEST					
1ST	17	4	536	76	41.23
INT					
RAL	7	2	37	17	7.40
N.W.	2	1	37	32*	37.00
B&H	5	0	35	19	7.00

LAST SEASON: BOWLING

	O.	M.	R.	W.	AV.
TEST					
1ST	316.3	64	900	12	75.00
INT					
RAL	54	3	286	9	31.77
N.W.	32	3	135	2	67.50
B&H	53	2	173	4	43.25

CAREER: BATTING

	I.	N. O.	R.	H. S.	AV.
TEST					
1ST	359	58	6786	109*	22.54
INT					
RAL	151	33	2086	74	17.67
N.W.	27	7	379	63*	18.95
B&H	48	5	557	59	12.95

CAREER: BOWLING

	O.	M.	R.	W.	AV.
TEST					
1ST	5443.4	1402	14879	437	34.04
INT					
RAL	1100	56	5305	178	29.80
N.W.	325.1	40	1041	31	33.58
B&H	502.3	68	1595	35	45.57

COX, R. M. F.   Hampshire

Name: Rupert Michael Fiennes Cox
Role: Left-hand bat, off-break bowler,
cover fielder
Born: 20 August 1967, Guildford
Height: 5ft 8in **Weight:** 11st 3lbs
Nickname: Coxy, Ucca and MC
Hammer
County debut: 1990
1st-Class 100s scored: 1
1st-Class catches: 3 (career 3)
Parents: Mike and Jo
Marital status: Single
Family links with cricket: Father
played for MCC and Hampshire Hogs
Education: Cheam Prep School and
Bradfield School
Qualifications: 8 O-levels, 2 A-levels
Career outside cricket: School sports
master and kitchen furnisher
Off-season: 'Half spent away from
cricket, half overseas preparing for 1991 season.'
Cricketers particularly admired: Geoffrey Boycott

Other sports followed: Golf and football
Injuries: 'A couple of finger dislocations.'
Relaxations: 'Music, partying and then sleeping.'
Extras: Scored century in second first-class match
Opinions on cricket: 'Improve the marketing of the game; play and enjoy cricket positively; lift the disgraceful ban on South African cricket.'
Best batting: 104* Hampshire v Worcestershire, Worcester 1990

LAST SEASON / CAREER: BATTING					
	I.	N. O.	R.	H. S.	AV.
TEST					
1ST	7	2	220	104*	44.00
INT					
RAL	1	1	2	2*	-
N.W.					
B&H					

LAST SEASON / CAREER: BOWLING					
	O.	M.	R.	W.	AV.
TEST					
1ST	1	0	1	0	-
INT					
RAL					
N.W.					
B&H					

CRAWLEY, J. P.   Lancashire

Name: John Paul Crawley
Role: Right-hand bat, occasional wicket-keeper
Born: 21 September 1971, Malden, Essex
Height: 6ft 1in **Weight:** 13st
Nickname: Creeps, Jonty, Flid
County debut: 1990
1st-Class 50s scored: 1
1st-Class catches: 1 (career 1)
Parents: Frank and Jean
Marital status: Single
Family links with cricket: Father played in Manchester Association; brother Mark plays for Lancashire and Oxford U; other brother Peter plays for Warrington CC, Cheshire and Scottish Universities; godfather umpires in Manchester Association
Education: Manchester Grammar School and Trinity College, Cambridge
Qualifications: 10 O-levels, 3 A-levels, 2 S-levels
Off-season: 'At University; captaining England YCs tour to New Zealand.'
Overseas tours: England YCs to Australia 1989–90; New Zealand 1990–91
Cricketers particularly admired: Michael Atherton, Neil Fairbrother, Graeme

103

Hick, Graham Gooch, Robin Smith, Allan Lamb
Other sports followed: Soccer (Man Utd), golf
Relaxations: 'Golf, soccer, squash, listening to music, any sports really.'
Extras: Played for England YCs v New Zealand 1989, Pakistan 1990
Opinions on cricket: 'Tea-break not long enough; cricket is not commercial enough; not enough money in cricket; there is too much played at a high level.'
Best batting: 76* Lancashire v Zimbabwe, Old Trafford, 1990

LAST SEASON / CAREER: BATTING

	I.	N. O.	R.	H. S.	AV.
TEST					
1ST	3	1	103	76*	51.50
INT					
RAL					
N.W.					
B&H					

LAST SEASON / CAREER: BOWLING

	O.	M.	R.	W.	AV.
TEST					
1ST					
INT					
RAL					
N.W.					
B&H					

CROFT, R. D. B. Glamorgan

Name: Robert Damien Bale Croft
Role: Right-hand bat, off-spinner
Born: 25 May 1970, Swansea
Height: 5ft 11in **Weight:** 11st 5lbs
Nickname: Crofty
County debut: 1989
1st-Class 50s scored: 4
Place in batting averages: 80th av. 44.80 (1989 168th av. 21.50)
Place in bowling averages: 121st av. 47.67
Strike rate: 85.10 (career 101.62)
1st-Class catches: 2 (career 3)
Parents: Malcolm and Susan
Family links with cricket: Father played local league cricket
Education: St John Lloyd Comprehensive, West Glamorgan Institute of Higher Education
Qualifications: 9 O-levels; OND Business Studies; HND Business Studies; NCA senior coaching certificate
Other sports followed: Rugby, soccer
Relaxations: Shooting, fishing
Extras: Captained England South to victory in International Youth Tournament 1989; also voted Player of Tournament

Best batting: 91* Glamorgan v Worcestershire, Abergavenny 1990
Best bowling: 3–10 Glamorgan v Derbyshire, Cardiff 1990

LAST SEASON: BATTING

	I.	N.O.	R.	H.S.	AV.
TEST					
1ST	26	11	672	91*	44.80
INT					
RAL	3	0	50	31	16.66
N.W.	1	0	26	26	26.00
B&H					

LAST SEASON: BOWLING

	O.	M.	R.	W.	AV.
TEST					
1ST	397.1	83	1335	28	47.67
INT					
RAL	24	0	131	1	131.00
N.W.	10	0	44	0	-
B&H					

CAREER: BATTING

	I.	N.O.	R.	H.S.	AV.
TEST					
1ST	34	13	801	91*	38.14
INT					
RAL	4	1	53	31	17.66
N.W.	1	0	26	26	26.00
B&H					

CAREER: BOWLING

	O.	M.	R.	W.	AV.
TEST					
1ST	491.1	104	1647	29	56.79
INT					
RAL	29	0	159	1	159.00
N.W.	10	0	44	0	-
B&H					

CURRAN, K. M.   Northamptonshire

Name: Kevin Malcolm Curran
Role: Right-hand bat, right-arm fast-medium bowler
Born: 7 September 1959, Rusape, Rhodesia
Height: 6ft 2in **Weight:** 13st 8lbs
Nickname: KC
County debut: 1985 (Gloucs)
County cap: 1985 (Gloucs)
One-Day Internationals: 11
1000 runs in a season: 5
50 wickets in a season: 3
1st-Class 50s scored: 31
1st-Class 100s scored: 18
1st-Class 5 w. in innings: 10
1st-Class 10 w. in match: 4
One-Day 50s: 20
Place in batting averages: 47th av. 50.68 (1989 67th av. 35.31)
Place in bowling averages: 32nd av. 30.64 (1989 46th av. 26.76)
Strike rate: 56.10 (career 47.74)
1st-Class catches: 15 (career 96)
Parents: Kevin Patrick and Sylvia
Marital status: Single

Family links with cricket: Father played for Rhodesia 1947–54. Cousin Patrick Curran played for Rhodesia 1975
Education: Marandellas High School, Zimbabwe
Qualifications: 6 O-levels, 2 M-levels
Career outside cricket: Tobacco buyer/farmer
Off-season: Playing for Natal
Overseas tours: Zimbabwe to Sri Lanka 1982 and 1984; England 1982 and for World Cup 1983; Pakistan and India for World Cup 1987
Overseas teams played for: Zimbabwe and Natal 1988–90
Other sports followed: Rugby Union
Relaxations: 'Game fishing, especially along the North Natal coast, the Mozambique coast, and Magaruque Island.'
Extras: First player to take a Sunday League hat-trick, and score a 50 in the same match, Gloucestershire v Warwickshire, Edgbaston 1989. Released by Gloucestershire at end of 1990 after he had completed the season's double of 1000 runs and 50 wickets. Chose to join Northamptonshire for the 1991 season after he had been approached by several counties
Opinions on cricket: 'Too much cricket is played in an English county season. Players need time to prepare themselves and rest minor injuries, to obtain better results. Games need to be made more a spectacle than an everyday occurrence. Marketing of cricket in England is below par. More money needs to be injected into the game, as well as the players' pockets. Wages need to be reviewed to secure the futures of those players who cannot obtain winter employment.'
Best batting: 144* Gloucestershire v Sussex, Bristol 1990
Best bowling: 7–54 Natal v Transvaal, Johannesburg 1988–89

LAST SEASON: BATTING

	I.	N.O.	R.	H.S.	AV.
TEST					
1ST	33	8	1267	144*	50.68
INT					
RAL	15	3	465	92	38.75
N.W.	3	0	4	2	1.33
B&H	3	0	69	55	23.00

LAST SEASON: BOWLING

	O.	M.	R.	W.	AV.
TEST					
1ST	598.3	111	1961	64	30.64
INT					
RAL	113	2	518	14	37.00
N.W.	32	7	104	2	52.00
B&H	32	2	141	7	20.14

CAREER: BATTING

	I.	N.O.	R.	H.S.	AV.
TEST					
1ST	259	45	7883	144*	36.83
INT	11	0	287	73	26.09
RAL	85	16	2139	92	31.00
N.W.	16	2	371	58*	26.50
B&H	22	6	541	57	33.81

CAREER: BOWLING

	O.	M.	R.	W.	AV.
TEST					
1ST	2474.5	514	8009	311	25.75
INT	84.2	3	398	9	44.22
RAL	405.1	15	1910	81	23.58
N.W.	128.5	25	405	14	28.92
B&H	209.1	23	777	35	22.20

CURTIS, T. S.   Worcestershire

Name: Timothy Stephen Curtis
Role: Right-hand bat, leg-break bowler
Born: 15 January 1960, Chislehurst, Kent
Height: 5ft 11in **Weight:** 12st 5lbs
Nickname: TC, Duracell, Professor
County debut: 1979
County cap: 1984
Test debut: 1988
Tests: 5
1000 runs in a season: 7
1st-Class 50s scored: 65
1st-Class 100s: 20
One-Day 50s: 44
One-Day 100s: 4
Place in batting averages: 32nd av. 55.83 (1989 27th av. 43.33)
1st-Class catches: 13 (career 109)
Parents: Bruce and Betty
Wife and date of marriage: Philippa, 21 September 1985
Family links with cricket: Father played good club cricket in Bristol and Stafford
Education: The Royal Grammar School, Worcester; Durham University; Cambridge University
Qualifications: 12 O-levels, 4 A-levels, BA (Hons) English, PCGE in English and Games
Off-season: Teaching at Royal Grammar School, Worcester

LAST SEASON: BATTING

	I.	N. O.	R.	H. S.	AV.
TEST					
1ST	39	8	1731	197*	55.83
INT					
RAL	15	2	784	124	60.30
N.W.	3	0	158	112	52.66
B&H	7	1	299	97	49.83

LAST SEASON: BOWLING

	O.	M.	R.	W.	AV.
TEST					
1ST	5.3	1	43	0	-
INT					
RAL					
N.W.					
B&H					

CAREER: BATTING

	I.	N. O.	R.	H. S.	AV.
TEST	9	0	140	41	15.55
1ST	379	54	13421	197*	41.29
INT					
RAL	105	15	3598	124	39.97
N.W.	25	3	1124	120	51.09
B&H	34	3	1015	97	32.74

CAREER: BOWLING

	O.	M.	R.	W.	AV.
TEST	3	0	7	0	-
1ST	98.2	13	417	7	59.57
INT					
RAL					
N.W.	4	1	15	2	7.50
B&H	0.2	0	4	0	-

Overseas tours: NCA U–19 tour of Canada 1979

Other sports followed: Rugby, tennis, squash, golf

Extras: Captained Durham University to UAU Championship. Chairman of the Cricketers' Association

Opinions on cricket: '16 four-day matches would seem to be the best combination for Championship cricket, with one-day competitions taking place at the weekends. This would reduce the amount of cricket played and place a greater emphasis on the quality.'

Best batting: 197* Worcestershire v Warwickshire, Worcester 1990

Best bowling: 2–58 Cambridge University v Nottinghamshire, Fenner's 1983

DALE, A.   Glamorgan

Name: Adrian Dale

Role: Right-hand bat, right-arm medium bowler

Born: 24 October 1968

Height: 6ft **Weight:** 11st 8lbs

Nickname: Arthur, Emma

County debut: 1989

1st-Class 50s scored: 1

One-Day 50s: 1

Place in batting averages: 245th av. 16.35 (1989 190th av. 19.14)

1st-Class catches: 7 (career 7)

Parents: John and Maureen

Marital status: Single

Family links with cricket: Father played for Glamorgan 2nd XI and Chepstow CC

Education: Pembroke Primary, Chepstow Comprehensive and Swansea University

Qualifications: 9 O-levels, 3 A-levels, BA (Hons) Economics

Off-season: Playing club cricket and coaching in Harare, Zimbabwe

Overseas tours: Combined Universities to Barbados 1989

Cricketers particularly admired: Ian Botham, Michael Holding, Viv Richards, Malcolm Marshall, Graeme Hick

Other sports followed: Football (Arsenal FC) and squash

Relaxations: 'Eating out or a good video and a bottle of wine.'

Extras: Played in successful Combined Universities sides of 1989 and 1990

Opinions on cricket: 'Too much cricket, together with the travelling, makes it difficult to prepare mentally and physically for each game – 16 four-day matches seems reasonable. Better practice facilities along with video cameras to help players

to see their own faults and work on them.'
Best batting: 92 Glamorgan v Essex, Southend 1990
Best bowling: 3–21 Glamorgan v Indians, Swansea 1990

LAST SEASON: BATTING

	I.	N. O.	R.	H. S.	AV.
TEST					
1ST	14	0	229	92	16.35
INT					
RAL	7	1	113	42	18.83
N.W.	2	1	7	4*	7.00
B&H	4	0	60	40	15.00

LAST SEASON: BOWLING

	O.	M.	R.	W.	AV.
TEST					
1ST	90	13	338	7	48.28
INT					
RAL	43	0	241	8	30.12
N.W.	9	1	42	1	42.00
B&H	21	2	93	1	93.00

CAREER: BATTING

	I.	N. O.	R.	H. S.	AV.
TEST					
1ST	22	1	363	92	17.28
INT					
RAL	14	3	252	67*	22.90
N.W.	3	1	17	10	8.50
B&H	8	1	105	40	15.00

CAREER: BOWLING

	O.	M.	R.	W.	AV.
TEST					
1ST	129	23	467	9	51.88
INT					
RAL	92	1	540	14	38.57
N.W.	28.4	2	112	4	28.00
B&H	68	6	261	9	29.00

DAVIS, R. P.   Kent

Name: Richard Peter Davis
Role: Right-hand bat, slow left-arm bowler
Born: 18 March 1966, Westgate
Height: 6ft 4in **Weight:** 14st 4 lbs
Nickname: Dicky
County debut: 1986
50 wickets in season: 1
1st-Class 50s scored: 3
1st-Class 5 w. in innings: 6
1st-Class 10 w. in match: 1
Place in batting averages: 236th av. 17.37 (1989 219th av. 15.47)
Place in bowling averages: 88th av. 38.95 (1989 117th av. 48.16)
Strike rate: 74.64 (career 85.23)
1st-Class catches: 27 (career 60)
Parents: Brian and Silvia
Wife and date of marriage: Sam, 3 March 1990
Family links with cricket: Father played league cricket; brother-in-law Raj Sharma (ex-Kent and Derbyshire); father-in-law Colin Tomlin assists England team with their fitness

109

Education: King Ethelbert's School, Birchington; Thanet Technical College, Broadstairs
Qualifications: 8 CSEs; NCA coaching certificate
Career outside cricket: Carpentry
Off-season: 'Keeping fit and working at my game.'
Cricketers particularly admired: Derek Underwood, Graham Gooch, Angus Fraser, Don Wilson
Other sports followed: Football, badminton, tennis, local athletics
Relaxations: 'Having a bottle of wine in front of the TV with my wife.'
Extras: 'Enjoyed the experience of training with the England squads before their tours in 1989–90. Here I enjoyed the help and encouragement of Don Wilson and the hospitality of the Lord's and East Molesey Indoor School staffs.' Kent's leading wicket-taker in 1990 and third best in country
Opinions on cricket: 'I would like to see better practice facilities at all first-class grounds and more specialist coaches on hand to give advice.'
Best batting: 67 Kent v Hampshire, Southampton 1989
Best bowling: 6–40 Kent v Cambridge University, Fenner's 1990

LAST SEASON: BATTING

	I.	N. O.	R.	H. S.	AV.
TEST					
1ST	32	3	504	59	17.37
INT					
RAL	5	3	16	14	8.00
N.W.	1	0	12	12	12.00
B&H	1	1	0	0*	-

LAST SEASON: BOWLING

	O.	M.	R.	W.	AV.
TEST					
1ST	908.1	221	2844	73	38.95
INT					
RAL	84	1	395	16	24.68
N.W.	21	3	60	2	30.00
B&H	30	1	121	3	40.33

CAREER: BATTING

	I.	N. O.	R.	H. S.	AV.
TEST					
1ST	86	22	925	67	14.45
INT					
RAL	15	5	58	16	5.80
N.W.	3	1	13	12	6.50
B&H	2	2	0	0*	-

CAREER: BOWLING

	O.	M.	R.	W.	AV.
TEST					
1ST	2400.4	554	6870	169	40.65
INT					
RAL	283.2	11	1294	51	25.37
N.W.	73.5	13	210	6	35.00
B&H	76.5	3	313	8	39.12

DAVIS, W. W.   Northamptonshire

Name: Winston Walter Davis
Role: Right-hand bat, right-arm fast bowler
Born: 18 September 1958, St Vincent, Windward Islands
Height: 6ft 2in **Weight:** 12st
Nickname: Davo
County debut: 1982 (Glamorgan), 1987 (Northants)
County cap: 1987 (Northants)
Test debut: 1982–83
Tests: 15
One-Day Internationals: 35
50 wickets in a season: 5
1st-Class 50s scored: 4
1st-Class 5 w. in innings: 28
1st-Class 10 w. in match: 7
Place in batting averages: 240th av. 16.83 (1989 254th av. 11.06)
Place in bowling averages: 143rd av. 62.46 (1989 52nd av. 27.76)
Strike rate: 109.76 (career 53.19)
1st-Class catches: 2 (career 57)
Overseas tours: Young West Indies to Zimbabwe 1981–82; West Indies to India and Australia 1983–84; England 1984; Australia 1984–85; India 1987–88
Overseas teams played for: Windward and Combined Islands; Tasmania 1985–86
Cricketers particularly admired: 'I like watching Viv Richards bat and Malcolm Marshall bowl.'

LAST SEASON: BATTING

	I.	N. O.	R.	H. S.	AV.
TEST					
1ST	7	1	101	47	16.83
INT					
RAL	9	1	97	24	12.12
N.W.					
B&H					

LAST SEASON: BOWLING

	O.	M.	R.	W.	AV.
TEST					
1ST	237.5	27	812	13	62.46
INT					
RAL	77.5	5	393	6	65.50
N.W.					
B&H					

CAREER: BATTING

	I.	N. O.	R.	H. S.	AV.
TEST	17	4	202	77	15.53
1ST	198	54	2009	60	13.95
INT	5	3	28	10	14.00
RAL	21	5	188	34	11.75
N.W.	6	3	24	14*	8.00
B&H	9	3	64	15*	10.66

CAREER: BOWLING

	O.	M.	R.	W.	AV.
TEST	462.1	53	1472	45	32.71
1ST	4697.4	884	15141	537	28.19
INT	320.3	31	1302	39	33.38
RAL	331.3	24	1455	51	28.52
N.W.	91.5	13	303	10	30.30
B&H	163.2	16	644	22	29.27

Other sports followed: Soccer, athletics, tennis
Extras: Released by Northamptonshire at end of 1990 season
Relaxations: 'Reading, watching television, playing with my children.'
Opinions on cricket: 'I should like to see the leg-bye rule changed for all one-day matches. No runs should be allowed for a ball coming off the batsman's pads. Cricket is a game very true to life, and because of that I believe it helps those who play it to understand and to cope with life's ups and downs better.'
Best batting: 77 West Indies v England, Old Trafford 1984
Best bowling: 7–52 Northamptonshire v Sussex, Northampton 1988

DEFREITAS, P. A. J.   Lancashire

Name: Phillip Anthony Jason DeFreitas
Role: Right-hand bat, right-arm fast-medium bowler, 'all-rounder, come drinks boy'
Born: 18 February 1966, Dominica
Height: 5ft 11in **Weight:** 12st 7lbs
Nickname: Daffy, Denzil
County debut: 1985 (Leics), 1989 (Lancs)
County cap: 1986 (Leics)
Test debut: 1986–87
Tests: 17
One-Day Internationals: 52
50 wickets in a season: 4
1st-Class 50s scored: 15
1st-Class 100s scored: 4
1st-Class 5 w. in innings: 23
1st-Class 10 w. in match: 2
One-Day 50s: 3
Place in batting averages: 112th av. 38.82 (1989 161st av. 22.30)
Place in bowling averages: 63rd av. 36.00 (1989 45th av. 26.73)
Strike rate: 73.42 (career 55.42)
1st-Class catches: 7 (career 40)
Parents: Sybil and Martin
Marital status: Single
Family links with cricket: Father played in the Windward Islands. All six brothers play
Education: Willesden High School
Qualifications: 2 CSEs
Off-season: Touring with England A to Pakistan
Overseas tours: Young England to West Indies 1985; England to Australia

1986–87; Pakistan, Australia and New Zealand 1987–88; India and West Indies 1989–90; England A to Pakistan 1990–91
Cricketers particularly admired: Ian Botham, Ken Higgs, Geoff Arnold
Other sports followed: Football
Injuries: Broken big toe, sinusitis
Relaxations: 'Listening to music, watching Man. United and Man. City, the odd round of golf.'
Extras: Left Leicestershire and joined Lancashire at end of 1988 season. Originally agreed to join unofficial English tour of South Africa 1989–90, but withdrew under pressure. Man of the match in 1990 NatWest Trophy final
Opinions on cricket: 'Sunday League cricket should be more commercial – coloured clothing encouraging youngsters to buy team's kit to show their support and interest (as in football). Second XI wickets ought to be much better.'
Best batting: 113 Leicestershire v Nottinghamshire, Worksop 1988
Best bowling: 7–21 Lancashire v Middlesex, Lord's 1989

LAST SEASON: BATTING

	I.	N. O.	R.	H. S.	AV.
TEST	2	0	52	38	26.00
1ST	18	3	608	102	40.53
INT	3	1	13	11	6.50
RAL	8	2	124	35*	20.66
N.W.	2	1	3	2*	3.00
B&H	6	1	145	75*	29.00

LAST SEASON: BOWLING

	O.	M.	R.	W.	AV.
TEST	59.4	9	175	6	29.16
1ST	429.5	100	1265	34	37.20
INT	42.5	2	216	2	108.00
RAL	102.3	2	531	20	26.55
N.W.	50	12	156	10	15.60
B&H	65	5	242	11	22.00

CAREER: BATTING

	I.	N. O.	R.	H. S.	AV.
TEST	25	1	301	40	12.54
1ST	147	18	3022	113	23.42
INT	36	14	355	33	16.13
RAL	50	8	521	37	12.40
N.W.	10	2	169	69	21.12
B&H	17	4	315	75*	24.23

CAREER: BOWLING

	O.	M.	R.	W.	AV.
TEST	591.4	117	1713	38	45.07
1ST	4223.5	673	9538	375	25.43
INT	490.4	62	1923	60	32.05
RAL	461.4	19	2176	85	25.60
N.W.	164.2	34	489	29	16.86
B&H	234.5	29	781	35	22.31

DENNIS, S. J.   Glamorgan

Name: Simon John Dennis
Role: Right-hand bat, left-arm
fast-medium bowler
Born: 18 October 1960, Scarborough
Height: 6ft 1in **Weight:** 14st
Nickname: Donkey
County debut: 1980 (Yorks), 1989
(Glamorgan)
County cap: 1983 (Yorks)
50 wickets in a season: 1
1st-Class 50s scored: 1
1st-Class 5 w. in innings: 7
Place in bowling averages: 125th av.
48.68 (1989 88th av. 34.17)
Strike rate: 87.81 (career 63.04)
1st-Class catches: 3 (career 26)
Parents: Margaret and Geoff
Marital status: Single
Family links with cricket: Father
captained Scarborough for many years.
Uncle, Frank Dennis, played for Yorkshire 1928–33. Uncle, Sir Leonard Hutton,
played for Yorkshire and England
Education: Northstead County Primary School; Scarborough College
Qualifications: 7 O-levels, 1 A-level, City and Guilds Computer Literacy
Off-season: 'Trying to get some experience in a job I can do after cricket.'
Overseas tours: ESCA to India 1978–79; England YC to Australia 1980
Overseas teams played for: Orange Free State 1982–83
Cricketers particularly admired: Dennis Lillee, John Lever

LAST SEASON: BATTING

	I.	N. O.	R.	H. S.	AV.
TEST					
1ST	8	1	23	6	3.28
INT					
RAL	6	1	30	14	6.00
N.W.	-	-	-	-	-
B&H	3	1	5	2*	2.50

LAST SEASON: BOWLING

	O.	M.	R.	W.	AV.
TEST					
1ST	322	61	1071	22	48.68
INT					
RAL	99.4	1	527	6	87.83
N.W.	19	0	99	0	-
B&H	25	3	95	2	47.50

CAREER: BATTING

	I.	N. O.	R.	H. S.	AV.
TEST					
1ST	98	29	666	53*	9.65
INT					
RAL	31	13	140	16*	7.77
N.W.	3	0	15	14	5.00
B&H	8	1	16	10	2.28

CAREER: BOWLING

	O.	M.	R.	W.	AV.
TEST					
1ST	2637.3	547	8328	251	33.17
INT					
RAL	450.5	18	2174	44	49.40
N.W.	89.2	14	357	6	59.50
B&H	148	23	526	11	47.81

Relaxations: Car maintenance, wine-and beer-making. Photography and real ale. Home computer, video games. 'Also terrible snooker player.'
Extras: Sunil Gavaskar was first first-class wicket. Left Yorkshire at end of 1988 season
Opinions on cricket: 'I think that to bring money into the game we should play a 60-over league on Saturdays, a 40-over league on Sundays and 16 four-day games in the week.'
Best batting: 53* Yorkshire v Nottinghamshire, Trent Bridge 1984
Best bowling: 5–35 Yorkshire v Somerset, Sheffield 1981

DE VILLIERS, P. S.   Kent

Name: Petrus Stephanus De Villiers
Role: Right-hand bat, right-arm medium-fast bowler
Born: 13 October 1964, Vereenigining, Transvaal, South Africa
Height: 6ft 2in **Weight:** 13st 7lbs
Nickname: Fanie
County debut: 1990
1st-Class 5 w. in innings: 7
Place in batting averages: 212nd av. 22.00
Place in bowling averages: 95th av. 39.68
Strike rate: 73.16 (career 50.08)
1st-Class catches: 6 (career 24)
Parents: Braan and Hanna
Marital status: Single
Family links with cricket: Brother plays in South Africa
Education: Pretoria College of Education
Qualifications: High Teaching Diploma
Off-season: Playing for Northern Transvaal
Overseas teams played for: Northern Transvaal since 1985–86; South African XI v English XI 1989–90
Cricketers particularly admired: Vernon Du Preez 'a very hard-worker', 'suppleness of West Indians.'
Other sports followed: Tennis, golf, rugby and athletics
Injuries: Injured right foot in foot-hole
Relaxations: 'Company of Kent players and trying to drive a golf ball further than

Alan Igglesden.'
Extras: Released by Kent at end of 1990 season
Opinions on cricket: 'Cricket as a profession is hard enough as it is without admin-istrators making it harder for the players, i. e. ball, pitches, some rules. Too much cricket is played in England – it lowers the standard of the game.'
Best batting: 46* Northern Transvaal v Orange Free State, Verwoerdburg 1988–89
Best bowling: 6–47 Northern Transvaal v Western Province, Cape Town 1988–89

LAST SEASON: BATTING

	I.	N. O.	R.	H. S.	AV.
TEST					
1ST	15	3	264	37	22.00
INT					
RAL	4	0	21	10	5.25
N.W.	2	0	24	14	12.00
B&H	1	0	0	0	0.00

LAST SEASON: BOWLING

	O.	M.	R.	W.	AV.
TEST					
1ST	304.5	58	992	25	39.68
INT					
RAL	28	4	121	3	40.33
N.W.	16	4	57	1	57.00
B&H	10	0	37	2	18.50

CAREER: BATTING

	I.	N. O.	R.	H. S.	AV.
TEST					
1ST	59	20	672	46*	17.23
INT					
RAL	4	0	21	10	5.25
N.W.	2	0	24	14	12.00
B&H	1	0	0	0	0.00

CAREER: BOWLING

	O.	M.	R.	W.	AV.
TEST					
1ST	1252.1	276	3771	150	25.14
INT					
RAL	28	4	121	3	40.33
N.W.	16	4	57	1	57.00
B&H	10	0	37	2	18.50

DILLEY, G. R. Worcestershire

Name: Graham Roy Dilley
Role: Left-hand bat, right-arm
fast bowler
Born: 18 May 1959, Dartford
Height: 6ft 4in **Weight:** 15st
Nickname: Picca
County debut: 1977 (Kent), 1987
(Worcs)
County cap: 1980 (Kent), 1987
(Worcs)
Test debut: 1979–80
Tests: 41
One-Day Internationals: 36
50 wickets in a season: 3
1st-Class 50s scored: 4
1st-Class 5 w. in innings: 33
1st-Class 10 w. in match: 3
Place in bowling averages: 49th av.

116

46.25 (1989 36th av. 23.96)
Strike rate: 56.06 (career 53.09)
1st-Class catches: 2 (career 72)
Parents: Geoff and Jean
Wife and date of marriage: Helen, 6 November 1980
Children: Paul and Christopher
Family links with cricket: Father and grandfather both played local cricket. Wife is sister of former Kent colleague Graham Johnson
Education: Dartford West Secondary School
Qualifications: 3 O-levels
Overseas tours: With England to Australia and India 1979–80; West Indies 1980–81; India and Sri Lanka 1981–82; New Zealand and Pakistan 1983–84; Australia 1986–87; Pakistan, New Zealand and Australia 1987–88; unofficial English team to South Africa 1989–90
Overseas teams played for: Natal 1985–86
Injuries: Knee injuries allowed him to play in only ten Championship matches
Relaxations: Music; playing golf
Extras: Cricket Writers' Club Young Cricketer of the Year 1980. Missed 1984 season after suffering back injury on 1983–84 tour. Joined Worcestershire in 1987. Banned from Test cricket for joining tour to South Africa in 1989–90. Autobiography *Swings and Roundabouts*, 1988
Opinions on cricket: 'For years counties have held almost a feudal grip on their players. Unhappy employees have been forced to show a false sense of loyalty with the hope of a lucrative benefit. The system had one merit in that a player around the age of 30 to 35 was given the chance to make enough money in a year to make himself financially secure for life. But it failed to take into account others less fortunate who might have been forced out of the game at a younger age without any lump sum, or any formal training.'
Best batting: 81 Kent v Northamptonshire, Northampton 1979
Best bowling: 7–63 Natal v Transvaal, Johannesburg 1985–86

LAST SEASON: BATTING

	I.	N. O.	R.	H. S.	AV.
TEST					
1ST	8	4	185	45*	46.25
INT					
RAL					
N.W.					
B&H	1	1	5	5*	–

LAST SEASON: BOWLING

	O.	M.	R.	W.	AV.
TEST					
1ST	224.2	30	818	24	34.08
INT					
RAL					
N.W.					
B&H	50.5	4	211	11	19.18

CAREER: BATTING

	I.	N. O.	R.	H. S.	AV.
TEST	58	19	521	56	13.35
1ST	180	68	1720	81	15.36
INT	18	8	114	31*	11.40
RAL	27	8	252	33	13.26
N.W.	13	4	105	25	11.66
B&H	27	9	159	37*	8.83

CAREER: BOWLING

	O.	M.	R.	W.	AV.
TEST	1365.2	281	4107	138	29.76
1ST	4041.2	826	12408	473	26.23
INT	340.3	33	1291	48	26.89
RAL	494.2	35	2017	77	26.19
N.W.	214.4	40	669	35	19.11
B&H	453.1	57	1533	77	19.90

DOBSON, M. C.   Kent

Name: Mark Christopher Dobson
Role: Right-hand opening bat, slow
left-arm bowler
Born: 24 October 1967, Canterbury
Height: 5ft 10in **Weight:** 12st 9lbs
Nickname: Dobbo, Jack
County debut: 1989
1st-Class 50s scored: 1
Parents: Bryan and Yvonne
Marital status: Single
Family links with cricket: 'Father
claims to have been top club cricketer.'
Education: Simon Langton Grammar
School for Boys, Canterbury
Qualifications: 8 O-levels, 2
A-levels; qualified coach
Off-season: 'Getting fit and working
locally, then playing and coaching in
Cape Town.'
Cricketers particularly admired: Roy
Pienaar and Chris Penn. 'Learnt most
from Dad, Hartley Alleyne, Mark Benson and Colin Page.'
Other sports followed: 'Football. Play Sunday mornings and six-a-side indoor.
Support Chelsea and follow QPR since grandfather played for them in the 1930s.'
Relaxations: 'Listening to music, reading, walking along beaches in temperatures
of 80F, spending money.'
Opinions on cricket: 'Too much cricket is played. Continue with four-day cricket
with each county playing each other once. Too many 2nd XI venues are unsuitable.'

LAST SEASON: BATTING

	I.	N. O.	R.	H. S.	AV.
TEST					
1ST	2	0	6	6	3.00
INT					
RAL					
N.W.					
B&H					

LAST SEASON: BOWLING

	O.	M.	R.	W.	AV.
TEST					
1ST	3.1	1	7	0	-
INT					
RAL					
N.W.					
B&H					

CAREER: BATTING

	I.	N. O.	R.	H. S.	AV.
TEST					
1ST	12	1	143	52	13.00
INT					
RAL	1	0	21	21	21.00
N.W.					
B&H					

CAREER: BOWLING

	O.	M.	R.	W.	AV.
TEST					
1ST	121.4	23	424	8	53.00
INT					
RAL					
N.W.					
B&H					

Best batting: 52 Kent v Glamorgan, Canterbury 1989
Best bowling: 2–20 Kent v Glamorgan, Canterbury 1989

DODEMAIDE, A. I. C.   Sussex

Name: Anthony Ian Christopher
Dodemaide
Role: Right-hand bat, right-arm
fast-medium bowler
Born: 5 October 1963, Williamstown,
Victoria, Australia
Height: 6ft 2in **Weight:** 13st 7lbs
Nickname: Dodders
County debut: 1989
Test debut: 1987–88
Tests: 8
One-Day Internationals: 12
1000 runs in a season: 1
50 wickets in a season: 2
1st-Class 50s scored: 21
1st-class 100s scored: 2
1st-Class 5 w. in innings: 8
Place in batting averages: 144th av.
33.36 (1989 82nd av. 32.52)
Place in bowling averages: 99th av.
40.27 (1989 67th av. 30.32)
Strike rate: 75.06 (career 72.17)
1st-Class catches: 9 (career 61)
Parents: Ian and Irene
Wife and date of marriage: Danielle, 7 April 1989
Family links with cricket: 'Brother Alan plays district cricket in Melbourne.
Brother Warren and several uncles were keen club cricketers around home town
Footscray.'
Education: St Johns & Chisholm College, Braybrook, Footscray; Chisholm Institute
of Technology, Melbourne
Qualifications: Higher School Certificate, Bachelor of Applied Science (Physics)
Off-season: Playing for Victoria in Sheffield Shield
Overseas tours: Australia U–19 to England 1983; Australia U–25 to Zimbabwe
1985; Australia to Pakistan 1988–89
Cricketers particularly admired: Sunil Gavaskar, Imran Khan, Richard Hadlee,
Terry Alderman
Other sports followed: 'Will watch most sports.'
Relaxations: Watching movies (particularly old ones), reading, listening to music,
playing golf and 'social tennis'

Extras: Played for Sussex 2nd XI on Esso Scholarship Scheme in 1985. Completed double of 1000 runs and 50 wickets in 1990. Returned career best bowling figures on his Test debut v New Zealand in 1987–88

Opinions on cricket: 'Too much emphasis in the English season on the one-day game (40, 55 and 60 overs) compared to Championship cricket which could adversely affect the development of young players.'

Best batting: 112 Sussex v Somerset, Hove 1990
Best bowling: 6–58 Australia v New Zealand, Melbourne 1987–88

LAST SEASON: BATTING

	I.	N. O.	R.	H. S.	AV.
TEST					
1ST	38	8	1001	112	33.36
INT					
RAL	14	6	280	31*	35.00
N.W.	1	0	1	1	1.00
B&H	1	0	32	32	32.00

LAST SEASON: BOWLING

	O.	M.	R.	W.	AV.
TEST					
1ST	763.1	130	2457	61	40.27
INT					
RAL	109	7	484	19	25.47
N.W.	23	8	79	8	9.87
B&H	44	4	193	5	38.60

CAREER: BATTING

	I.	N. O.	R.	H. S.	AV.
TEST	12	3	171	50	19.00
1ST	168	39	3871	112	30.00
INT	8	5	84	30	28.00
RAL	26	11	476	40*	31.73
N.W.	3	0	9	7	3.00
B&H	5	1	139	38	34.75

CAREER: BOWLING

	O.	M.	R.	W.	AV.
TEST	310.1	77	803	28	28.67
1ST	3527.1	725	10093	291	34.68
INT	109.1	11	360	20	18.00
RAL	213.4	14	897	35	25.62
N.W.	57.4	13	181	12	15.08
B&H	86	10	316	12	26.33

19. Who headed the Gloucestershire batting averages last season?

20. What was unusual about the players who topped the Kent batting and Middlesex bowling averages?

21. Who headed the bowling averages for Nottinghamshire last season?

D'OLIVEIRA, D. B.　Worcestershire

Name: Damian Basil D'Oliveira
Role: Right-hand bat, off-break
bowler, slip or boundary fielder
Born: 19 October 1960, Cape Town,
South Africa
Height: 5ft 8in **Weight:** 11st 10lbs
Nickname: Dolly
County debut: 1982
County cap: 1985
1000 runs in a season: 4
1st-Class 50s scored: 37
1st-Class 100s scored: 8
One-Day 50s: 15
One-Day 100s: 1
Place in batting averages: 116th
av. 38.27 (1989 169th av. 21.27)
1st-Class catches: 33 (career 153)
Parents: Basil and Naomi
Wife and date of marriage: Tracey
Michele, 26 September 1983
Children: Marcus Damian, 27 April
1986; Dominic James, 29 April 1988
Family links with cricket: Father played for Worcestershire and England
Education: St George's RC Primary School; Blessed Edward Oldcorne Secondary
School
Qualifications: 3 O-levels, 5 CSEs
Overseas tours: English Counties XI to Zimbabwe 1985
Cricketers particularly admired: Greg Chappell, Viv Richards, Dennis Lillee,

LAST SEASON: BATTING

	I.	N. O.	R.	H. S.	AV.
TEST					
1ST	35	2	1263	155	38.27
INT					
RAL	14	1	266	58	20.46
N.W.	3	2	86	51*	86.00
B&H	6	1	104	57	20.80

LAST SEASON: BOWLING

	O.	M.	R.	W.	AV.
TEST					
1ST	11.3	1	80	2	40.00
INT					
RAL					
N.W.	5	0	17	2	8.50
B&H					

CAREER: BATTING

	I.	N. O.	R.	H. S.	AV.
TEST					
1ST	287	19	7465	155	27.85
INT					
RAL	110	10	2303	103	23.03
N.W.	19	3	445	99	27.81
B&H	34	4	697	66	23.23

CAREER: BOWLING

	O.	M.	R.	W.	AV.
TEST					
1ST	268.4	50	1003	25	40.12
INT					
RAL	39	2	232	7	33.14
N.W.	43	5	151	8	18.87
B&H	38	4	148	5	29.60

Malcolm Marshall, Richard Hadlee
Other sports followed: 'Most others, but not horse racing.'
Relaxations: 'Watching films, TV, eating out, and playing with the kids.'
Best batting: 155 Worcestershire v Lancashire, Old Trafford 1990
Best bowling: 2–17 Worcestershire v Gloucestershire, Cheltenham 1986

DONALD, A. A. Warwickshire

Name: Allan Anthony Donald
Role: Right-hand bat, right-arm
fast bowler
Born: 20 October 1966, Bloemfontein,
South Africa
Height: 6ft 3in **Weight:** 13st 7lbs
County debut: 1987
County cap: 1989
50 wickets in a season: 1
1st-Class 5 w. in innings: 15
1st-Class 10 w. in match: 1
Place in bowling averages: 76th av.
37.55 (1989 2nd av. 16.25)
Strike rate: 80.89 (career 48.98)
1st-Class catches: 0 (career 19)
Parents: Stuart and Francina
Marital status: Single
Education: Grey College High School
and Technical High School,
Bloemfontein
Qualifications: Matriculation
Off-season: Playing cricket in South
Africa
Overseas teams played for: Orange Free State, South Africa 1985–90
Cricketers particularly admired: Ian Botham, Imran Khan
Other sports followed: Rugby, football
Relaxations: Playing tennis, listening to music
Extras: Played for South African XI v Australian XI in 1986–87 and v English XI
in 1989–90. Retained by Warwickshire for 1991 season ahead of Tom Moody
Opinions on cricket: 'There should not be politics in world sport.'
Best batting: 40 Warwickshire v Yorkshire, Edgbaston 1989
Best bowling: 8–37 Orange Free State v Transvaal, Johannesburg 1986–87

	I.	N.O.	R.	H.S.	AV.
TEST					
1ST	22	6	148	25*	9.25
INT					
RAL					
N.W.					
B&H	-	-	-	-	-

LAST SEASON: BOWLING

	O.	M.	R.	W.	AV.
TEST					
1ST	391	89	1089	29	37.55
INT					
RAL					
N.W.					
B&H	11	1	42	1	42.00

CAREER: BATTING

	I.	N.O.	R.	H.S.	AV.
TEST					
1ST	120	43	843	40	10.94
INT					
RAL	14	6	111	18*	13.87
N.W.	1	0	0	0	0.00
B&H	4	3	30	23*	30.00

CAREER: BOWLING

	O.	M.	R.	W.	AV.
TEST					
1ST	2759.4	547	8007	338	23.68
INT					
RAL	155	14	638	26	24.53
N.W.	77	9	225	24	9.37
B&H	77.1	10	289	10	28.90

DONELAN, B. T. P.   Sussex

Name: Bradleigh Thomas Peter Donelan
Role: Right-hand bat, off-spin bowler
Born: 3 January 1968, Middlesex
Height: 6ft 2in **Weight:** 12st 7lbs
Nickname: Rooster, Freddie, Claw
County debut: 1989
1st-Class 50s: 1
Place in batting averages: 165th av.
30.14
Place in bowling averages: 130th av.
50.00 (1989 111th av. 45.21)
Strike rate: 104.00 (career 87.82)
1st-Class catches: 4 (career 8)
Parents: Terry and Patricia
Marital status: Single
Education: Our Lady of Grace Junior
School, Finchley Catholic High School
Qualifications: 8 CSEs
Cricketers particularly admired:
Martin Crowe and Paul Parker for their
dedication to the game
Other sports followed: Football, golf
Relaxations: Listening to music, sleeping
Extras: A late starter at the age of 13; was a product of the MCC ground staff
Opinions on cricket: 'Would like to see 16 four-day games which would give you
a day off a week. In favour of better pitches although wicket-taking is not so easy.'
Best batting: 53 Sussex v Warwickshire, Eastbourne 1990
Best bowling: 3–51 Sussex v Worcestershire, Hove 1989

LAST SEASON: BATTING

	I.	N. O.	R.	H. S.	AV.
TEST					
1ST	13	6	211	53	30.14
INT					
RAL	1	0	4	4	4.00
N.W.					
B&H					

LAST SEASON: BOWLING

	O.	M.	R.	W.	AV.
TEST					
1ST	304.4	56	1000	20	50.00
INT					
RAL	22	2	103	2	51.50
N.W.					
B&H					

CAREER: BATTING

	I.	N. O.	R.	H. S.	AV.
TEST					
1ST	22	9	252	53	19.38
INT					
RAL	1	0	4	4	4.00
N.W.					
B&H					

CAREER: BOWLING

	O.	M.	R.	W.	AV.
TEST					
1ST	497.4	98	1633	34	48.02
INT					
RAL	23	2	117	2	58.50
N.W.					
B&H					

DOWNTON, P. R.   *Middlesex*

Name: Paul Rupert Downton
Role: Right-hand bat, wicket-keeper
Born: 4 April 1957, Farnborough, Kent
Height: 5ft 10in **Weight:** 12st 4lbs
Nickname: Nobby
County debut: 1977 (Kent), 1980 (Middlesex)
County cap: 1979 (Kent), 1981 (Middlesex)
Benefit: 1990
Test debut: 1980–81
Tests: 30
One-Day Internationals: 28
1000 runs in a season: 1
1st-Class 50s scored: 42
1st-Class 100s scored: 6
One-Day 50s: 8
Place in batting averages: 189th av. 26.68 (1989 198th av. 18.45)
Parents: George Charles and Jill Elizabeth
Wife and date of marriage: Alison, 19 October 1985
Children: Phoebe Alice, 16 December 1987; Jonathan George, 20 September 1989
Family links with cricket: Father kept wicket for Kent 1948–49
Education: Sevenoaks School; Exeter University
Qualifications: 9 O-levels, 3 A-levels; Law degree (LLB); NCA coaching certificate

Career outside cricket: Stockbroker
Off-season: Working for James Capel, city stockbrokers
Overseas tours: England YC to West Indies 1976; England to Pakistan and New Zealand 1977–78; West Indies 1980–81; India and Australia 1984–85; West Indies 1985–86
Cricketers particularly admired: Alan Knott, Rod Marsh
Other sports followed: Golf and rugby (England U19 and Exeter U 1st XV)
Injuries: 'Hit in the eye by a bail – six weeks out of the game and still have blurred vision in left eye.'
Relaxations: Reading, playing golf
Opinions on cricket: 'I can't understand why the game clings on to the past. Uncovering wickets is simply an excuse to prolong the three-day game, whereas I'm convinced four-day cricket is the way forward. It has been proven that groundsmen can produce wickets that last given reasonable weather: they certainly will be able to if you reduce the number of wickets they have to prepare. Quality not quantity must be right.'
Best batting: 126* Middlesex v Oxford University, The Parks 1986
Best bowling: 1–4 Middlesex v Surrey, The Oval 1990

LAST SEASON: BATTING

	I.	N. O.	R.	H. S.	AV.
TEST					
1ST	24	2	587	63	26.68
INT					
RAL	7	2	124	34*	24.80
N.W.	1	1	4	4*	-
B&H	5	2	102	40	34.00

LAST SEASON: WICKET-KEEPING

	CT	ST		
TEST				
1ST	42	3		
INT				
RAL	5	5		
N.W.	2	0		
B&H	9	0		

CAREER: BATTING

	I.	N. O.	R.	H. S.	AV.
TEST	48	8	785	74	19.62
1ST	351	66	7296	126*	25.60
INT	20	5	242	44*	16.13
RAL	111	34	1661	70	21.57
N.W.	28	7	556	69	26.47
B&H	40	14	647	80*	24.88

CAREER: WICKET-KEEPING

	CT	ST		
TEST	70	5		
1ST	609	83		
INT	26	3		
RAL	135	41		
N.W.	54	7		
B&H	55	9		

EALHAM, M. A. Kent

Name: Mark Alan Ealham
Role: Right-hand bat, right-arm medium bowler
Born: 27 August 1969, Ashford
Height: 5ft 10in **Weight:** 13st 7lbs
Nickname: Ealy, Burger
County debut: 1989
Parents: Alan George Ernest and Sue
Marital status: Single
Family links with cricket: 'My father played county cricket for Kent.'
Education: Stour Valley Secondary School
Qualifications: 9 CSEs
Off-season: Working in family business
Cricketers particularly admired: Ian Botham, Viv Richards, Malcolm Marshall, Robin Smith
Other sports followed: Football, golf, snooker, darts
Relaxations: Playing golf, watching films, music
Extras: 'Enjoyed playing for Ashford CC since the age of 11.'
Opinions on cricket: 'Pitches should still be covered, so good, flat wickets are produced, but the seam on the ball should be increased.'
Best batting: 45 Kent v Lancashire, Old Trafford 1989
Best bowling: 2–33 Kent v Middlesex, Lord's 1990

LAST SEASON: BATTING

	I.	N. O.	R.	H. S.	AV.
TEST					
1ST	2	1	13	13*	13.00
INT					
RAL	4	1	59	29*	19.66
N.W.					
B&H	3	1	22	17*	11.00

LAST SEASON: BOWLING

	O.	M.	R.	W.	AV.
TEST					
1ST	34.2	5	120	3	40.00
INT					
RAL	53	1	287	3	95.66
N.W.					
B&H	30	1	141	8	17.62

CAREER: BATTING

	I.	N. O.	R.	H. S.	AV.
TEST					
1ST	5	2	69	45	23.00
INT					
RAL	11	4	104	29*	14.85
N.W.					
B&H	3	1	22	17*	11.00

CAREER: BOWLING

	O.	M.	R.	W.	AV.
TEST					
1ST	63.2	10	238	4	59.50
INT					
RAL	103	5	509	14	36.35
N.W.					
B&H	30	1	141	8	17.62

ELLISON, R. M. Kent

Name: Richard Mark Ellison
Role: Left-hand bat, right-arm medium bowler
Born: 21 September 1959, Ashford, Kent
Height: 6ft 3in **Weight:** 14st 7lbs
Nickname: Elly
County debut: 1981
County cap: 1983
Test debut: 1984
Tests: 11
One-Day Internationals: 14
50 wickets in a season: 4
1st-Class 50s scored: 16
1st-Class 100s scored: 1
1st-Class 5 w. in innings: 14
1st-Class 10 w. in match: 2
One-Day 50s: 4
Place in batting averages: 110th av. 39.41 (1989 192nd av. 18.85)
Place in bowling averages: 132nd av. 50.68 (1989 38th av. 25.93)
Strike rate: 97.52 (career 61.93)
1st-Class catches: 6 (career 62)
Parents: Peter Richard Maxwell (deceased) and Bridget Mary
Wife and date of marriage: Fiona, 28 September 1985
Family links with cricket: Brother Charles Christopher gained blue at Cambridge University 1981–86. Grandfather played with Grace brothers and was secretary of Derby CCC in about 1915
Education: Friars Preparatory School, Great Chart, Ashford; Tonbridge School; St Luke's College; Exeter University
Qualifications: 8 O-levels, 2 A-levels; Degree B. Ed. ; Teacher
Overseas tours: With England to India and Australia 1984–85; Sharjah 1984–85; West Indies 1985–86; unofficial English tour to South Africa 1989–90
Cricketers particularly admired: Malcolm Marshall, Richard Hadlee, Chris Tavare, Terry Alderman
Other sports followed: Anything but horse racing and greyhounds
Relaxations: Social drinking, good food, music: Chris Rea, Dire Straits, New Order
Extras: Did not play at all in 1987 due to back injury. One of *Wisden's* Five Cricketers of the Year, 1985. Debut for Canterbury Amateur Operatic Society in April 1989, in 'Fiddler on the Roof'. Banned from Test cricket after touring South Africa in 1989–90
Opinions on cricket: 'We should not be dictated to in the way in which we select the England teams. Manner in which people qualify for English registration is a joke.

127

Why should we be prevented from going to South Africa?'
Best batting: 108 Kent v Oxford University, The Parks 1984
Best bowling: 7–75 Kent v Nottinghamshire, Dartford 1988

LAST SEASON: BATTING

	I.	N.O.	R.	H.S.	AV.
TEST					
1ST	19	7	473	81	39.41
INT					
RAL	8	3	83	43	16.60
N.W.	1	1	27	27*	-
B&H	1	0	12	12	12.00

LAST SEASON: BOWLING

	O.	M.	R.	W.	AV.
TEST					
1ST	308.5	51	963	19	50.68
INT					
RAL	52	0	239	6	39.83
N.W.	12	6	18	1	18.00
B&H	6	2	14	0	-

CAREER: BATTING

	I.	N.O.	R.	H.S.	AV.
TEST	16	1	202	41	13.46
1ST	216	55	4014	108	24.93
INT	12	4	86	24	10.75
RAL	66	28	981	84	25.81
N.W.	16	7	302	49*	33.55
B&H	24	6	410	72	22.77

CAREER: BOWLING

	O.	M.	R.	W.	AV.
TEST	377.2	90	1048	35	29.94
1ST	3700.2	920	9872	360	27.42
INT	116	9	510	12	42.50
RAL	536	28	2406	88	27.34
N.W.	200.3	39	620	29	21.37
B&H	281.1	5	930	40	23.25

EMBUREY, J. E.   Middlesex

Name: John Ernest Emburey
Role: Right-hand bat, off-break bowler
Born: 20 August 1952, Peckham
Height: 6ft 2in **Weight:** 14st
Nickname: Embers, Ernie
County debut: 1973
County cap: 1977
Benefit: 1986
Test debut: 1978
Tests: 60
One-Day Internationals: 58
50 wickets in a season: 12
1st-Class 50s scored: 39
1st-Class 100s scored: 4
1st-Class 5 w. in innings: 58
1st-Class 10 w. in match: 9
One-Day 50s: 2
Place in batting averages: 177th av. 28.08 (1989 197th av. 18.56)
Place in bowling averages: 39th av. 32.08 (1989 66th av. 30.14)
Strike rate: 92.70 (career 70.52)
1st-Class catches: 33 (career 357)

Parents: John and Rose
Wife and date of marriage: Susie, 20 September 1980
Children: Clare, 1 March 1983; Chloe, 31 October 1985
Education: Peckham Manor Secondary School
Qualifications: O-levels, advanced cricket coaching certificate
Overseas tours: With England to Australia 1978–79; Australia and India 1979–80; West Indies 1980–81; India 1981–82; West Indies 1985–86; Australia 1986–87; Pakistan, Australia and New Zealand 1987–88; unofficial English tours to South Africa 1981–82 and 1989–90
Overseas teams played for: Western Province 1982–83 and 1983–84
Cricketers particularly admired: Ken Barrington, Graham Gooch, Paul Downton
Relaxations: Reading, gardening, going to the theatre, playing golf
Extras: Played for Surrey Young Cricketers 1969–70. Phil Edmonds of Middlesex and England was the best man at his wedding. Middlesex vice-captain since 1983. One of *Wisden's* Five Cricketers of the Year, 1983. Captain of England v West Indies for two Tests in 1988. Banned from Test cricket for three years for touring South Africa in 1981–82, and for five more for touring in 1989–90. Published autobiography *Emburey* in 1988
Opinions on cricket: 'I don't believe that anybody who plays cricket for a living should have his livelihood jeopardised or restricted (by bans on going to South Africa)... It can't be right to discriminate against a youngster who is prepared to pay his own fare to coach or play abroad to supplement his income or widen his experience.'
Best batting: 133 Middlesex v Essex, Chelmsford 1983
Best bowling: 7–27 Middlesex v Gloucestershire, Cheltenham 1989

LAST SEASON: BATTING

	I.	N.O.	R.	H.S.	AV.
TEST					
1ST	32	7	702	111*	28.08
INT					
RAL	11	5	126	32	21.00
N.W.	2	2	19	15*	-
B&H	5	2	23	12	7.66

LAST SEASON: BOWLING

	O.	M.	R.	W.	AV.
TEST					
1ST	942.3	275	1957	61	32.08
INT					
RAL	129.1	12	664	34	19.52
N.W.	46	7	174	4	43.50
B&H	51.2	3	198	7	28.28

CAREER: BATTING

	I.	N.O.	R.	H.S.	AV.
TEST	89	18	1540	75	21.69
1ST	413	84	7592	133	23.07
INT	43	10	471	34	14.27
RAL	137	45	1506	50	16.37
N.W.	29	11	449	36*	24.94
B&H	45	14	536	50	17.29

CAREER: BOWLING

	O.	M.	R.	W.	AV.
TEST	2371.1	735	5105	138	36.99
1ST	11934.4	3618	26255	1079	24.33
INT	546.5	38	2226	75	29.68
RAL	1368	111	5954	275	21.65
N.W.	524.5	99	1441	49	29.40
B&H	532	86	1613	57	28.29

EVANS, K. P.   Nottinghamshire

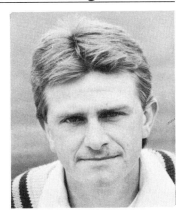

Name: Kevin Paul Evans
Role: Right-hand bat, right-arm medium
bowler, slip fielder
Born: 10 September 1963, Calverton,
Nottingham
Height: 6ft 2in **Weight:** 13st
Nickname: Ghost
County debut: 1984
1st-Class 50s scored: 8
1st-Class 100s scored: 1
One-Day 50s: 1
Place in batting averages: 68th av.
46.12 (1989 129th av. 26.33)
Place in bowling averages: 65th av.
36.23 (1989 47th av. 26.93)
Strike rate: 62.32 (career 65.90)
1st-Class catches: 13 (career 51)
Parents: Eric and Eileen
Wife and date of marriage: Sandra,
19 March 1988
Family links with cricket: Brother Russell played for Nottinghamshire. Father
played local cricket
Education: William Lee Primary; Colonel Frank Seely Comprehensive, Calverton
Qualifications: 10 O-levels, 3 A-levels. Qualified coach
Cricketers particularly admired: Richard Hadlee
Other sports followed: Football, tennis, squash
Relaxations: Listening to music, reading, DIY, gardening
Extras: With brother Russell, first brothers to bat together for Nottinghamshire in

LAST SEASON: BATTING

	I.	N. O.	R.	H. S.	AV.
TEST					
1ST	25	9	738	100*	46.12
INT					
RAL	7	4	139	55*	46.33
N.W.	1	0	0	0	0.00
B&H					

LAST SEASON: BOWLING

	O.	M.	R.	W.	AV.
TEST					
1ST	356	78	1232	34	36.23
INT					
RAL	87.4	1	514	12	42.83
N.W.	12	3	53	2	26.50
B&H					

CAREER: BATTING

	I.	N. O.	R.	H. S.	AV.
TEST					
1ST	81	19	1647	100*	26.56
INT					
RAL	34	13	368	55*	17.52
N.W.	6	1	27	10	5.40
B&H	9	2	124	31*	17.71

CAREER: BOWLING

	O.	M.	R.	W.	AV.
TEST					
1ST	1032.3	212	3404	94	36.21
INT					
RAL	351.2	8	1808	55	32.87
N.W.	95	16	311	11	28.27
B&H	105.2	7	418	15	27.86

first-class cricket for fifty years
Opinions on cricket: 'We should play 16 four-day matches, but change the bonus point system, so that the batsman can concentrate on hitting the bad ball rather than improvising on the good ones.'
Best batting: 100* Nottinghamshire v Somerset, Weston 1990
Best bowling: 4–50 Nottinghamshire v Cambridge University, Fenner's 1990

EVANS, R. J.   Nottinghamshire

Name: Russell John Evans
Role: Right-hand bat, right-arm medium bowler
Born: 1 October 1965, Calverton
Height: 6ft **Weight:** 12st 8lbs
Nickname: Boggle, Brains, Rubber Hand
County debut: 1985 (one-day), 1987 (1st-class)
1st-Class 50s scored: 1
1st-Class catches: 1 (career 4)
Parents: Eric and Eileen
Wife and date of marriage: Alison, 6 October 1990
Family links with cricket: Father played local league cricket and brother Kevin plays for Nottinghamshire
Education: Colonel Frank Seely Comprehensive School, Calverton
Qualifications: 8 O-levels, 3 A-levels, NCA senior coach
Off-season: 'Hopefully working towards a professional qualification and career.'
Cricketers particularly admired: Clive Rice, Geoff Boycott, Barry Richards
Other sports followed: Golf, football
Relaxations: 'Home improvements and social drinking.'
Best batting: 50* Nottinghamshire v Sri Lanka, Trent Bridge 1988
Best bowling: 3–40 Nottinghamshire v Oxford University, The Parks 1988

LAST SEASON: BATTING

	I.	N. O.	R.	H. S.	AV.
TEST					
1ST	5	2	37	21*	12.33
INT					
RAL					
N.W.					
B&H					

CAREER: BATTING

	I.	N. O.	R.	H. S.	AV.
TEST					
1ST	9	3	112	50*	18.66
INT					
RAL	5	1	55	20	13.75
N.W.					
B&H					

FAIRBROTHER, N. H.   Lancashire

Name: Neil Harvey Fairbrother
Role: Left-hand bat, left-arm medium
bowler
Born: 9 September 1963, Warrington,
Cheshire
Height: 5ft 8in **Weight:** 11st
Nickname: Harvey
County debut: 1982
County cap: 1985
Test debut: 1987
Tests: 7
One-Day Internationals: 11
1000 runs in a season: 7
1st-Class 50s scored: 60
1st-Class 100s scored: 20
1st-Class 200s scored: 2
One-Day 50s: 32
One-Day 100s: 5
Place in batting averages: 11th av.
69.60 (1989 29th av. 42.88)
1st-Class catches: 20 (career 111)
Parents: Leslie Robert and Barbara
Wife and date of marriage: Audrey, 23 September 1988
Family links with cricket: Father and two uncles played local league cricket
Education: St Margaret's Church of England School, Oxford; Lymn Grammar
School
Qualifications: 5 O-levels
Off-season: Vice-captain of England A in Pakistan

LAST SEASON: BATTING

	I.	N. O.	R.	H. S.	AV.
TEST	5	1	59	33*	14.75
1ST	27	6	1681	366	80.04
INT					
RAL	13	1	441	86*	36.75
N.W.	5	1	304	86	76.00
B&H	7	2	290	95*	58.00

LAST SEASON: BOWLING

	O.	M.	R.	W.	AV.
TEST					
1ST	7	0	29	0	-
INT					
RAL					
N.W.					
B&H					

CAREER: BATTING

	I.	N. O.	R.	H. S.	AV.
TEST	9	1	64	33*	8.00
1ST	281	40	10162	366	42.16
INT	11	2	232	54	25.77
RAL	100	20	2944	116*	36.80
N.W.	20	4	901	93*	56.31
B&H	31	9	967	116*	43.95

CAREER: BOWLING

	O.	M.	R.	W.	AV.
TEST	2	0	9	0	-
1ST	107.2	22	414	5	82.80
INT					
RAL	2	0	15	0	-
N.W.	3	0	16	0	-
B&H					

Overseas tours: England to Sharjah 1986–87; World Cup, Pakistan, Australia and New Zealand 1987–88; England A to Pakistan 1990–91

Cricketers particularly admired: Clive Lloyd, Allan Border

Other sports followed: Football, Rugby Union, Rugby League

Relaxations: Music and playing sport

Extras: 'I was named after the Australian cricketer Neil Harvey, who was my mum's favourite cricketer.' England YC v Australia 1983. His innings of 366 was the third highest score ever made in the County Championship, the second highest first-class score by a Lancashire batsman and the best at The Oval

Best batting: 366 Lancashire v Surrey, The Oval 1990

Best bowling: 2–91 Lancashire v Nottinghamshire, Old Trafford 1987

FARBRACE, P. Middlesex

Name: Paul Farbrace

Role: Right-hand bat, wicket-keeper

Born: 7 July 1967, Ash, nr Canterbury

Height: 5ft 10in **Weight:** 12st

Nickname: Farby, Biggles

County debut: 1987 (Kent), 1990 (Middlesex)

1st-Class 50s scored: 2

Place in batting averages: 217th av. 20.66

Parents: David and Betty

Wife and date of marriage: Elizabeth Jane, 27 July 1985

Children: Jemma, 30 March 1985; Eleanor, 3 September 1988

Family links with cricket: 'Father played village cricket, as do my two brothers. Dad and eldest brother both wicket-keepers.'

Education: Ash CE Primary School; Geoffrey Chaucer School, Canterbury

Qualifications: 2 O-levels, 6 CSEs, NCA coaching certificate and senior award – 'taking advanced course in October 1990.'

Off-season: 'Coaching football and cricket at Hampton School. Sports Reporter for BBC Radio Kent.'

Cricketers particularly admired: Alan Knott, Derek Underwood. 'Indebted to Steve Marsh and Paul Downton for their superb help; Clive Radley and Don Bennett for their patience with my batting.'

Other sports followed: All sports except horse racing and show-jumping

Relaxations: 'Sport, reading and spending as much time with my wife and daughters

133

as possible.'

Extras: Played County Schools football, had England Schools U–18 trial, attracted attention from Notts County and Coventry City. Captained Kent v Essex in a five-a-side cricket game in Dartford Tunnel in February 1989 to raise money for Children in Need

Opinions on cricket: 'County clubs should do more to encourage families into cricket grounds. Make Sunday League cricket into a batsman's game, with coloured clothes and all 10 fielders to bowl four overs a side – free entrance for children.'

Best batting: 79 Middlesex v Cambridge University, Fenner's 1990

LAST SEASON: BATTING

	I.	N. O.	R.	H. S.	AV.		
TEST							
1ST	8	2	124	79	20.66		
INT							
RAL	3	0	5	3	1.66		
N.W.	1	0	17	17	17.00		
B&H							

LAST SEASON: WICKET-KEEPING

	CT	ST				
TEST						
1ST	17	2				
INT						
RAL	2	4				
N.W.	4	0				
B&H						

CAREER: BATTING

	I.	N. O.	R.	H. S.	AV.		
TEST							
1ST	11	2	168	79	18.66		
INT							
RAL	4	1	6	3	2.00		
N.W.	2	0	21	17	10.50		
B&H							

CAREER: WICKET-KEEPING

	CT	ST				
TEST						
1ST	22	4				
INT						
RAL	2	4				
N.W.	7	0				
B&H						

FELTHAM, M. A. Surrey

Name: Mark Andrew Feltham
Role: Right-hand bat, right-arm
fast-medium bowler
Born: 26 June 1963, London
Height: 6ft 2in **Weight:** 14st
Nickname: Felts, Felpsy, Boff or
Douglas
County debut: 1983
50 wickets in a season: 1
1st-Class 50s scored: 5
1st-Class 100s scored: 1
One-day 50s: 2
1st-Class 5 w. in innings: 6
Place in batting averages: 171st av.
29.15 (1989 191st av. 19.00)
Place in bowling averages: 24th av.
28.75 (1989 77th av. 31.22)
Strike rate: 52.45 (career 58.93)
1st-Class catches: 11 (career 41)
Parents: Leonard William and Patricia
Louise

Wife and date of marriage: Debi, 22 September 1990
Family links with cricket: 'Mum responsible for fund-raising to build new development at Foster's Oval.'
Education: Roehampton Church School; Tiffin Boys' School
Qualifications: 7 O-levels; advanced cricket coach
Career outside cricket: Marketing and sales
Off-season: Working for Simba Security Systems
Cricketers particularly admired: Ian Botham, Gordon Greenidge and Desmond Haynes
Other sports followed: Football, golf and most others
Injuries: Injured left knee
Relaxations: Music, particularly Luther Vandross; Woody Allen films
Extras: 'I write a weekly column in local newspaper, *The Wandsworth Borough News*. Currently I am the most experienced and oldest uncapped player in the country!!'
Opinions on cricket: 'Keep pitches the same, go back to the 1989 ball. Scrap over-rate fines: having to bowl 110 overs in a day is penalty enough. There is too much Championship cricket; 16 four-day matches is fairer and must produce better equipped Test players. When are we going to follow the rest of the world and play night cricket under floodlights. The commercial possibilities are endless. Wake up Lord's.'
Best batting: 101 Surrey v Middlesex, The Oval 1990

Best bowling: 6–53 Surrey v Leicestershire, The Oval 1990

LAST SEASON: BATTING

	I.	N. O.	R.	H. S.	AV.
TEST					
1ST	16	3	379	101	29.15
INT					
RAL	13	2	293	61	26.63
N.W.	1	0	5	5	5.00
B&H	1	0	4	4	4.00

LAST SEASON: BOWLING

	O.	M.	R.	W.	AV.
TEST					
1ST	349.4	61	1150	40	28.75
INT					
RAL	76	2	369	10	36.90
N.W.	11.4	0	65	1	65.00
B&H	9	0	52	0	-

CAREER: BATTING

	I.	N. O.	R.	H. S.	AV.
TEST					
1ST	105	27	1714	101	21.97
INT					
RAL	52	14	684	61	18.00
N.W.	9	3	72	19*	12.00
B&H	14	3	137	29	12.45

CAREER: BOWLING

	O.	M.	R.	W.	AV.
TEST					
1ST	2278.5	480	7066	232	30.45
INT					
RAL	478.5	15	2470	69	35.79
N.W.	121.1	15	541	12	45.08
B&H	202.2	19	817	30	27.23

FELTON, N. A.   Northamptonshire

Name: Nigel Alfred Felton
Role: Left-hand bat
Born: 24 October 1960, Guildford
Height: 5ft 7in **Weight:** 10st 7lbs
Nickname: Will, Twiglets
County debut: 1982 (Somerset), 1989
(Northants)
County cap: 1986 (Somerset)
1000 runs in a season: 3
1st-Class 50s scored: 41
1st-Class 100s scored: 12
One-Day 50s: 11
Place in batting averages: 99th av.
41.56 (1989 136th av. 25.17)
1st-Class catches: 19 (career 76)
Parents: Ralph and Enid
Marital status: Single
Family links with cricket: Father
played club cricket
Education: Hawes Down Secondary
School, Kent; Millfield School, Somerset; Loughborough University
Qualifications: 6 O-levels, 2 A-levels, BSc (Hons), Cert of Education PE/Sports
Sciences, qualified teacher
Overseas tours: England YC to Australia 1978
Other sports followed: Most ball games

Relaxations: Music, reading, relaxing at home
Extras: Played a season for Kent in 1980 after leaving Millfield and joined Somerset at end of first year at Loughborough. Released by Somerset at end of 1988 season
Opinions on cricket: 'I'm in favour of four-day cricket.'
Best batting: 173* Somerset v Kent, Taunton 1983
Best bowling: 1–48 Northamptonshire v Derbyshire, Northampton 1990

LAST SEASON: BATTING

	I.	N. O.	R.	H. S.	AV.
TEST					
1ST	39	2	1538	122	41.56
INT					
RAL	10	1	239	64	26.55
N.W.	5	0	149	70	29.80
B&H	1	0	16	16	16.00

CAREER: BATTING

	I.	N. O.	R.	H. S.	AV.
TEST					
1ST	245	12	7104	173*	28.10
INT					
RAL	58	9	1192	96	24.32
N.W.	16	2	522	87	37.28
B&H	12	0	162	50	13.50

FERRIS, G. J. F. — Leicestershire

Name: George John Fitzgerald Ferris
Role: Right-hand and left-hand bat, right-arm fast bowler
Born: 18 October 1964, Urlings Village, Antigua
Height: 6ft 3in **Weight:** 14st 7lbs
Nickname: Ferro, Slugo
County debut: 1983
County cap: 1988
50 wickets in a season: 3
1st-Class 5 w. in innings: 9
1st-Class 10 w. in match: 1
Place in batting averages: 237th av. 17.33 (1989 236th av. 13.33)
Place in bowling averages: 98th av. 40.16
Strike rate: 69.16 (career 47.29)
1st-Class catches: 1 (career 13)
Parents: Leslie and Verona
Wife and date of marriage: Janet, 25 March 1989
Children: Imran
Education: Jenning's Secondary
Career outside cricket: Physical education teacher
Off-season: Playing cricket in West Indies
Overseas tours: With Young West Indies to England 1982; Young West Indies to Zimbabwe 1983 and 1986

Overseas teams played for: Leeward Islands 1982–90
Cricketers particularly admired: Michael Holding
Other sports followed: Motor sports, boxing, wrestling, tennis
Relaxations: Listening to gospel music
Extras: Released by Leicestershire at end of 1990 season. Has dual US nationality
Best batting: 36* Leicestershire v Hampshire, Leicester 1988
Best bowling: 7–42 Leicestershire v Glamorgan, Hinckley 1983

LAST SEASON: BATTING

	I.	N. O.	R.	H. S.	AV.
TEST					
1ST	6	0	104	35	17.33
INT					
RAL	1	0	6	6	6.00
N.W.					
B&H					

LAST SEASON: BOWLING

	O.	M.	R.	W.	AV.
TEST					
1ST	138.2	29	482	12	40.16
INT					
RAL	13	1	55	2	27.50
N.W.					
B&H					

CAREER: BATTING

	I.	N. O.	R.	H. S.	AV.
TEST					
1ST	105	44	745	36*	12.21
INT					
RAL	13	7	49	13*	8.16
N.W.	3	2	3	2*	3.00
B&H	2	2	1	1*	-

CAREER: BOWLING

	O.	M.	R.	W.	AV.
TEST					
1ST	2254.3	429	7355	286	25.71
INT					
RAL	188.3	10	808	33	24.48
N.W.	52	5	238	5	47.60
B&H	82	8	347	15	23.13

22. Who headed the batting averages for Sussex last season?

23. Who headed the batting averages for Yorkshire last season?

24. Which county captain published his autobiography, *Double Life*, last season?

FIELD-BUSS, M. G. Nottinghamshire

Name: Michael Gwyn Field-Buss
Role: Right-hand bat, off-break
bowler
Born: 23 September 1964, Malta
Height: 5ft 10in **Weight:** 11st
Nickname: Mouse
County debut: 1987 (Essex), 1989
(Notts)
1st-Class catches: 0 (career 1)
Parents: Gwyn and Monica
Marital status: Engaged to Paula
Family links with cricket: Father
played local cricket with Ilford RAFA
Education: Wanstead High School
Qualifications: Qualified coach
Off-season: Working for local
council
Cricketers particularly admired:
'Bill Morris (coach at Ilford Cricket
School) during my early years, Ray
East and David Acfield at Essex, Eddie Hemmings at Notts.'
Other sports followed: 'Watching Leyton Orient FC (although really support
Arsenal). Into most sports except motor racing.'
Injuries: 'Spent two months in plaster with fractured right wrist.'
Relaxations: 'Spending time with family and girlfriend, listening to music at every
available moment, playing football.'
Opinions on cricket: 'Please bring back the old ball and bring 2nd XI wickets up
to the standard of first-class.'

LAST SEASON: BATTING

	I.	N. O.	R.	H. S.	AV.
TEST					
1ST	2	0	0	0	0.00
INT					
RAL					
N.W.					
B&H					

LAST SEASON: BOWLING

	O.	M.	R.	W.	AV.
TEST					
1ST	48.5	16	99	3	33.00
INT					
RAL					
N.W.					
B&H					

CAREER: BATTING

	I.	N. O.	R.	H. S.	AV.
TEST					
1ST	9	2	68	34*	9.71
INT					
RAL	2	0	5	5	2.50
N.W.					
B&H					

CAREER: BOWLING

	O.	M.	R.	W.	AV.
TEST					
1ST	96.5	31	227	10	22.70
INT					
RAL	9	2	54	0	-
N.W.					
B&H					

Best batting: 34* Essex v Middlesex, Lord's 1987
Best bowling: 4–33 Nottinghamshire v Somerset, Trent Bridge 1989

FITTON, J. D. — Lancashire

Name: John Dexter Fitton
Role: Left-hand bat, off-break bowler
Born: 24 August 1965, Rochdale
Height: 5ft 10in **Weight:** 12st 7lbs
Nickname: Jo, Ted, Philbert, Lord
County debut: 1987
1st-Class 5 w. in innings: 3
Place in batting averages: 242nd av. 16.62 (1989 201st av. 17.68)
Place in bowling averages: 157th av. 103.35 (1989 108th av. 42.14)
Strike rate: 194.85 (career 104.22)
1st-Class catches: 3 (career 10)
Parents: Derek and Jean
Marital status: Single
Family links with cricket: Father dedicated cricketer for 20 years with Littleborough in Central Lancashire League and Robinsons in North Manchester League
Education: Redbrook High School and Ounder Hill Upper School
Qualifications: 4 O-levels, Diploma in Business Studies
Career outside cricket: 'Changes from winter to winter.'

LAST SEASON: BATTING

	I.	N. O.	R.	H. S.	AV.
TEST					
1ST	13	5	133	25*	16.62
INT					
RAL	-	-	-	-	-
N.W.					
B&H					

LAST SEASON: BOWLING

	O.	M.	R.	W.	AV.
TEST					
1ST	454.4	91	1447	14	103.35
INT					
RAL	8	0	53	1	53.00
N.W.					
B&H					

CAREER: BATTING

	I.	N. O.	R.	H. S.	AV.
TEST					
1ST	41	12	519	44	17.89
INT					
RAL	1	0	0	0	0.00
N.W.					
B&H					

CAREER: BOWLING

	O.	M.	R.	W.	AV.
TEST					
1ST	990.1	210	3065	57	53.77
INT					
RAL	16	0	78	2	39.00
N.W.					
B&H					

Off-season: Playing for Sydenham CC in Christchurch, New Zealand
Cricketers particularly admired: 'Everyone at Old Trafford, especially Fairbrother and Lloyd; Nick Speak for earning a 2nd XI benefit; Clive Lloyd and David Gower.'
Other sports followed: 'Watch Manchester City FC and Rochdale Hornets, golf, own a couple of greyhounds.'
Injuries: Fluid on the left knee, chipped bone in right knee
Relaxations: Listening to music, watching comedy films and shows, playing golf
Extras: Youngest player to take 50 wickets and score 500 runs for Rochdale in the Central Lancashire League. Scored 1000 runs a season for three seasons running in the same league. Captained Lancashire U–19s, North of England, and NAYC in 1984
Opinions on cricket: 'All 2nd XI games should be played on county grounds. Tea should be 30 minutes. We should play 16 four-day games.'
Best batting: 44 Lancashire v Australians, Old Trafford 1989
Best bowling: 6–59 Lancashire v Yorkshire, Old Trafford 1988

FLEMING, M. V. Kent

Name: Matthew Valentine Fleming
Role: Right-hand bat, right-arm medium bowler
Born: 12 December 1964, Macclesfield
Height: 6ft **Weight:** 12st 4lbs
Nickname: Jazz
County debut: 1988
1st-class 50s: 5
1st-class 100s: 1
Place in batting averages: 121st av. 37.69 (1989 157th av. 22.66)
Place in bowling averages: 126th av. 48.72 (1989 126th av. 74.16)
Strike rate: 107.68 (career 114.60)
1st-Class catches: 6 (career 7)
Parents: Valentine and Elizabeth
Wife and date of marriage: Caroline, 23 September 1989
Family links with cricket: 'Great-grandfather Mr Leslie played for England and apparently hit an all-run 7 at Lord's.'
Education: St Aubyns School, Rottingdean; Eton College
Qualifications: 8 O-levels, 3 A-levels
Career outside cricket: Stockbroker
Cricketers particularly admired: 'Mark Benson and everyone else who hits the ball as hard as they can as often as they can.'

Other sports followed: Shooting, fishing, football, squash, fives, toboganning

Relaxations: 'Tai-chi', Arsenal FC

Extras: Ex-army officer – Royal Green Jackets. First two scoring shots in Championship cricket were sixes

Opinions on cricket: 'Three-day cricket is a waste of time, more often than not finishing in a contrived one-day game. Trust House Forte should build a hotel next to every first-class venue and sort out their room service!'

Best batting: 102 Kent v Nottinghamshire, Tunbridge Wells 1990

Best bowling: 3–65 Kent v Sussex, Hove 1990

LAST SEASON: BATTING

	I.	N. O.	R.	H. S.	AV.
TEST					
1ST	32	6	980	102	37.69
INT					
RAL	13	4	172	29*	19.11
N.W.	1	0	7	7	7.00
B&H	2	0	6	6	3.00

LAST SEASON: BOWLING

	O.	M.	R.	W.	AV.
TEST					
1ST	394.5	94	1072	22	48.72
INT					
RAL	104	2	502	17	29.52
N.W.	3	1	4	2	2.00
B&H	15	2	41	1	41.00

CAREER: BATTING

	I.	N. O.	R.	H. S.	AV.
TEST					
1ST	44	9	1184	102	33.82
INT					
RAL	25	7	351	37	19.50
N.W.	2	0	19	12	9.50
B&H	6	0	85	28	14.16

CAREER: BOWLING

	O.	M.	R.	W.	AV.
TEST					
1ST	534.5	124	1517	28	54.17
INT					
RAL	174	4	858	29	29.58
N.W.	15	4	41	3	13.66
B&H	55	7	184	5	36.80

FLETCHER, S. D.   Yorkshire

Name: Stuart David Fletcher
Role: Right-hand bat, right-arm
medium bowler
Born: 8 June 1964, Keighley
Height: 5ft 10in **Weight:** 12st
Nickname: Fletch, Godber, Norman
Stanley, Dr Death, Ghostie
County debut: 1983
County cap: 1988
50 wickets in a season: 1
1st-Class 5 w. in innings: 4
Place in bowling averages: 59th av.
35.69 (1989 118th av. 51.46)
Strike rate: 60.58 (career 55.56)
1st-Class catches: 3 (career 20)
Parents: Brough and Norma Hilda
Wife and date of marriage: Katharine,
4 October 1986

Children: Craig, 26 July 1989
Family links with cricket: Father
played league cricket
Education: Woodhouse Primary; Reins Wood Secondary
Qualifications: O-level English and Woodwork; City and Guilds in coachbuilding
Off-season: 'Working in an engineers shop, playing football and getting fit.'
Cricketers particularly admired: Ian Botham, Arnie Sidebottom
Other sports followed: Watches Leeds United FC

LAST SEASON: BATTING

	I.	N. O.	R.	H. S.	AV.
TEST					
1ST	13	3	39	19	3.90
INT					
RAL	3	1	9	6	4.50
N.W.	1	1	6	6*	-
B&H	1	1	15	15*	-

LAST SEASON: BOWLING

	O.	M.	R.	W.	AV.
TEST					
1ST	292.5	60	1035	29	35.69
INT					
RAL	78.1	2	416	11	37.81
N.W.	24	1	109	2	54.50
B&H	41.5	4	162	5	32.40

CAREER: BATTING

	I.	N. O.	R.	H. S.	AV.
TEST					
1ST	80	29	366	28*	7.17
INT					
RAL	15	9	34	8	5.66
N.W.	6	4	27	16*	13.50
B&H	4	2	17	15*	8.50

CAREER: BOWLING

	O.	M.	R.	W.	AV.
TEST					
1ST	1981.5	390	7201	214	33.65
INT					
RAL	525.2	15	2709	96	28.21
N.W.	147.1	15	561	15	37.40
B&H	184.5	12	766	27	28.37

Relaxations: Watching TV, snooker and golf
Best batting: 28* Yorkshire v Kent, Tunbridge Wells 1984
Best bowling: 8–58 Yorkshire v Essex, Sheffield 1988

FORDHAM, A.   Northamptonshire

Name: Alan Fordham
Role: Right-hand bat, occasional
right-arm medium pace bowler
Born: 9 November 1964, Bedford
Height: 6ft 1in **Weight:** 13st
Nickname: Fordy
County debut: 1986
1st-Class 50s scored: 16
1st-Class 100s scored: 6
1st-Class 200s scored: 1
One-day 50s: 7
One-day 100s: 1
Place in batting averages: 85th av.
44.17 (1989 83rd av. 32.35)
1st-Class catches: 22 (career 43)
Parents: Clifford and Ruth
Marital status: Single
Family links with cricket: Brother
John played school and college cricket
Education: Bedford Modern School;
Durham University
Qualifications: 9 O-levels, 3 A-levels, BSc Honours Degree in Chemistry, NCA
senior coaching award
Career outside cricket: 'As yet unexplored.'
Off-season: Teaching
Cricketers particularly admired: Allan Lamb, Bob Willis, Mike Brearley
Other sports followed: Rugby Union
Relaxations: Music, squash, 'the odd round of golf.'
Extras: Has appeared for Bedfordshire in Minor Counties Championship. Played
for Combined Universities in B & H Cup 1987. Shared county record stand of 393

LAST SEASON: BATTING

	I.	N. O.	R.	H. S.	AV.
TEST					
1ST	42	2	1767	206*	44.17
INT					
RAL	15	1	481	74	34.35
N.W.	5	0	255	130	51.00
B&H	3	0	76	67	25.33

CAREER: BATTING

	I.	N. O.	R.	H. S.	AV.
TEST					
1ST	97	11	3077	206*	35.77
INT					
RAL	25	1	640	74	26.66
N.W.	5	0	255	130	51.00
B&H	5	0	109	67	21.80

with Allan Lamb v Yorkshire at Headingley in 1990

Opinions on cricket: 'It is odd that each team in the County Championship plays ten others once and six others twice. This must favour certain teams depending on the luck of the draw and thus cannot be fair. However, I am yet to be convinced that a Championship of 16 four-day games is the answer.'

Best batting: 206* Northamptonshire v Yorkshire, Headingley 1990
Best bowling: 1–25 Northamptonshire v Yorkshire, Northampton 1990

FOSTER, N. A.   Essex

Name: Neil Alan Foster
Role: Right-hand bat, right-arm fast-medium bowler, outfielder
Born: 6 May 1962, Colchester
Height: 6ft 4in **Weight:** 13st
Nickname: Fozzy, Nibbler
County debut: 1980
County cap: 1983
Test debut: 1983
Tests: 28
One-Day Internationals: 48
50 wickets in a season: 8
1st-Class 50s scored: 8
1st-Class 100s scored: 1
1st-Class 5 w. in innings: 42
1st-Class 10 w. in match: 7
Place in batting averages: 190th av. 26.50 (1989 159th av. 22.36)
Place in bowling averages: 11th av. 26.61 (1989 20th av. 21.60)
Strike rate: 52.29 (career 49.61)
1st-Class catches: 13 (career 92)
Parents: Jean and Alan
Wife and date of marriage: Romany, 21 September 1985
Family links with cricket: Father and brother both play local cricket
Education: Broomgrove Infant & Junior Schools; Philip Morant Comprehensive, Colchester
Qualifications: 8 O-levels, 1 A-level, NCA coaching award. Has consumer credit licence for Financial Consultancy
Overseas tours: Young England YC to West Indies 1980; England to New Zealand and Pakistan 1983–84; India and Australia 1984–85; West Indies 1985–86; Australia 1986–87; Pakistan, Australia and New Zealand 1987–88; unofficial English team to South Africa 1989–90
Other sports followed: Nearly any sport. Has had football trials with Colchester

and Ipswich. Golf, tennis. 'Nothing horsey.'

Relaxations: 'My Boxer dog – Bertie; kennel name: Tropical Burlington Bertie. Playing golf. Mowing the lawn.'

Extras: Was summoned from school at short notice to play for Essex v Kent at Ilford. First ball went for 4 wides, but he finished with figures of 3 for 51. Played for England YC v India 1981. Banned from Test cricket for touring South Africa in 1989–90. Leading first-class wicket-taker in 1990 season

Opinions on cricket: 'It's about time our Championship consisted of playing each other only once, whether it be in three-or four-day matches.'

Best batting: 101 Essex v Leicestershire, Chelmsford 1990
Best bowling: 8–107 England v Pakistan, Headingley 1987

LAST SEASON: BATTING

	I.	N. O.	R.	H. S.	AV.
TEST					
1ST	22	2	530	101	26.50
INT					
RAL	11	4	106	39*	15.14
N.W.	1	0	0	0	0.00
B&H	1	0	8	8	8.00

LAST SEASON: BOWLING

	O.	M.	R.	W.	AV.
TEST					
1ST	819.2	175	2502	94	26.61
INT					
RAL	96.3	3	467	19	24.57
N.W.	24	8	61	4	15.25
B&H	43	6	145	6	24.16

CAREER: BATTING

	I.	N. O.	R.	H. S.	AV.
TEST	43	7	410	39	11.38
1ST	178	45	2859	101	21.49
INT	25	12	150	24	11.53
RAL	36	12	404	44	16.83
N.W.	10	1	119	26	13.22
B&H	14	7	145	37*	20.71

CAREER: BOWLING

	O.	M.	R.	W.	AV.
TEST	1013.3	232	2797	88	31.78
1ST	5328.3	1177	15732	679	23.16
INT	437.5	28	1836	59	31.11
RAL	485.2	30	2123	93	22.82
N.W.	185.2	35	552	34	16.23
B&H	383.4	45	1387	66	21.01

FOWLER, G. Lancashire

Name: Graeme Fowler
Role: Left-hand opening bat, occasional
wicket-keeper, 1st slip, 'slow right-hand
declaration bowler'
Born: 20 April 1957, Accrington
Height: 5ft 9in **Weight:** 'Near 11st'
Nickname: Fow, Foxy
County debut: 1979
County cap: 1981
Benefit: 1991
Test debut: 1982
Tests: 21

One-Day Internationals: 26
1000 runs in a season: 8
1st-Class 50s scored: 72
1st-Class 100s scored: 32
1st-Class 200s scored: 2
One-Day 50s: 41
One-Day 100s: 7
Place in batting averages: 154th av.
32.34 (1989 51st av.37.02)
1st-Class catches: 15 (career 136 & 5 stumpings)
Marital status: Single
Education: Accrington Grammar School; Bede College, Durham University
Qualifications: Certificate of Education, advanced cricket coach
Career outside cricket: 'Some radio and TV work.'
Off-season: 'Preparing for Benefit year in 1991.'
Overseas tours: England to Australia and New Zealand 1982–83; New Zealand and
Pakistan 1983–84; India and Australia 1984–85
Overseas teams played for: Tasmania 1981–82
Cricketers particularly admired: David Lloyd and Paul Allott
Other sports folowed: 'Bits of everything.'
Injuries: 'Plastic surgery on my top lip. Ball came off wicket-keeper's elbow into
my face at first slip. Couldn't laugh without pain for two weeks.'
Relaxations: Music, gardening, playing drums
Extras: Played for Accrington and Rawtenshall in Lancashire League: at 15 he was
the youngest opener in the League. Played for England YC in 1976. Published *Fox
on the Run*, a cricketing diary from 1984 to 1986, which won Channel 4's Sports
Book of the Year Award. First Englishman to score a double century in India
Opinions on cricket: 'Good game isn't it!'
Best batting: 226 Lancashire v Kent, Maidstone 1984
Best bowling: 2–34 Lancashire v Warwickshire, Old Trafford 1986

	I.	N. O.	R.	H. S.	AV.
TEST					
1ST	35	6	938	126	32.34
INT					
RAL	16	1	793	108	52.86
N.W.	4	0	98	52	24.50
B&H	7	0	185	96	26.42

LAST SEASON: BOWLING

	O.	M.	R.	W.	AV.
TEST					
1ST	4.1	2	33	1	33.00
INT					
RAL					
N.W.					
B&H					

CAREER: BATTING

	I.	N. O.	R.	H. S.	AV.
TEST	37	0	1307	201	35.32
1ST	374	23	12920	226	36.80
INT	26	2	744	81*	31.00
RAL	140	9	4137	112	31.58
N.W.	26	0	731	122	28.11
B&H	50	1	1311	97	26.75

CAREER: BOWLING

	O.	M.	R.	W.	AV.
TEST	3	1	11	0	-
1ST	52.5	8	254	8	31.75
INT					
RAL	1	0	1	0	-
N.W.					
B&H					

FRASER, A. R. C.   Middlesex

Name: Angus Robert Charles Fraser
Role: Right-hand bat, right-arm fast-medium bowler, outfielder
Born: 8 August 1965, Billinge, Lancashire
Height: 6ft 6in **Weight:** 15st 3lbs
Nickname: Gus, Lard
County debut: 1984
County cap: 1988
Test debut: 1989
Tests: 8
One-day Internationals: 13
50 wickets in a season: 3
1st-class 50s scored: 1
1st-Class 5 w. in innings: 15
1st-Class 10 w. in match: 2
Place in batting averages: 226th av. 19.45 (1989 244th av. 12.57)
Place in bowling averages: 13th av. 26.89 (1989 13th av. 20.22)
Strike rate: 62.73 (career 60.47)
1st-Class catches: 3 (career 13)
Parents: Don and Irene
Marital status: Single
Family links with cricket: Father played and is now keen follower of cricket; brother Alastair on Essex staff. 'Mum is a nervous watcher!'
Education: Gayton High School, Harrow; Orange High School, Edgware

Qualifications: 7 O-levels, qualified cricket coach
Off-season: Touring Australia with England
Overseas tours: England to India and West Indies 1989–90; Australia 1990–91
Cricketers particularly admired: Dennis Lillee, Richard Hadlee, Allan Border, 'any bowler who gives 110% every time he walks onto the field.'
Other sports followed: 'Rugby, football, golf, most except horse racing.'
Injuries: Missed Fourth and Fifth Test matches v West Indies and the whole series v New Zealand after suffering a torn rib cartilage; 'dodgy hamstring for quite a while at end of season.'
Relaxations: 'Watching Liverpool FC when possible or rugby internationals if I can get tickets – cricket seems to take up too large a part of cricketers' lives for us to have too many outside interests.'
Extras: Sponsored by local Benskins pub, 'The Seven Balls' – one pint for first-class wickets, two pints for Test wickets
Opinions on cricket: 'If one looks at the figures for 1989, one finds that the batsmen did not have as bad a deal as it seemed compared to years gone by. Batsmen's averages have increased markedly since the 1950s, and bowlers averages have also gone up. 1989 fitted in with that trend and did not stand out – unlike 1990 when 50 batsmen averaged over 50 compared to 10 in 1989 and 10 bowlers averaged under 25 compared to 35 in 1989. I agree that wickets had to improve but I think it may have gone too far – the ball should return to 1989 standard and the pitches stay the same.'
Best batting: 92 Middlesex v Surrey, The Oval 1990
Best bowling: 7–77 Middlesex v Kent, Canterbury 1989

LAST SEASON: BATTING

	I.	N. O.	R.	H. S.	AV.
TEST	2	0	1	1	0.50
1ST	11	2	213	92	23.66
INT	2	2	4	4*	-
RAL	2	1	10	6	10.00
N.W.	-	-	-	-	-
B&H					

LAST SEASON: BOWLING

	O.	M.	R.	W.	AV.
TEST	159.1	41	460	16	28.75
1ST	436.5	103	1073	41	26.17
INT	22	4	75	1	75.00
RAL	71	7	292	11	26.54
N.W.	47.5	3	171	7	24.42
B&H					

CAREER: BATTING

	I.	N. O.	R.	H. S.	AV.
TEST	9	1	61	29	7.62
1ST	95	25	901	92	12.87
INT	3	3	7	4*	-
RAL	27	12	156	30*	10.40
N.W.	3	2	27	19	27.00
B&H	8	3	36	13*	7.20

CAREER: BOWLING

	O.	M.	R.	W.	AV.
TEST	374.4	99	944	36	26.22
1ST	2740	699	6472	273	23.70
INT	118.4	16	457	10	45.70
RAL	446.1	37	1734	62	27.96
N.W.	117.3	35	529	28	18.89
B&H	152.1	20	517	15	34.46

FRENCH, B. N. Nottinghamshire

Name: Bruce Nicholas French
Role: Right-hand bat, wicket-keeper
Born: 13 August 1959, Warsop,
Nottinghamshire
Height: 5ft 8in **Weight:** 10st
Nickname: Frog
County debut: 1976
County cap: 1980
Benefit: 1991
Test debut: 1986
Tests: 16
One-Day Internationals: 13
1st-Class 50s scored: 11
1st-class 100s scored: 1
Place in batting averages: 220th av.
20.24

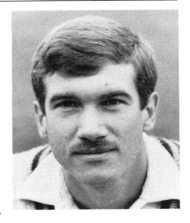

Parents: Maurice and Betty
Wife and date of marriage: Ellen Rose,
9 March 1978
Children: Charles Daniel, 31 August
1978; Catherine Ellen, 28 December 1980
Family links with cricket: Brothers, Neil, David, Charlie, Joe, play for Welbeck
CC and father is Treasurer. Neil also plays for Lincolnshire
Education: Meden School, Warsop
Qualifications: O-level and CSE
Overseas tours: England to India and Sri Lanka 1984–85; West Indies 1985–86;
Australia 1986–87; World Cup, Pakistan, Australia and New Zealand 1987–88;
unofficial English team to South Africa 1989–90
Cricketers particularly admired: Bob Taylor
Other sports followed: Rock climbing, fell walking and all aspects of
mountaineering
Injuries: Missed most of 1988 season following operations in May on index finger
of left hand, and in 1989 broke the same finger again, missing end of season.
Previously, French was bitten by a dog whilst jogging in the Caribbean in 1985–86;
had to be carried off the field with a cut head and concussion after being struck by
a short-pitched delivery from Richard Hadlee; contracted a chest infection after being
hit in the chest by a ball in Australia in 186–87; in Pakistan in 1987–88, he needed
stitches in a cut eye and on the way to hospital a car struck his legs
Relaxations: Reading, pipe smoking and drinking Theakston's Ale
Extras: Youngest player to play for Nottinghamshire, aged 16 years 10 months.
Equalled Nottinghamshire record for dismissals in match with 10 (7ct, 3st), and in
innings with 6 catches; also set new county record for dismissals in a season with 87
(75ct, 12st). Banned from Test cricket for touring South Africa in 1989–90. Made

his maiden first-class 100 in 1990 in 15th season of county cricket
Best batting: 105* Nottinghamshire v Derbyshire, Derby 1990

LAST SEASON: BATTING

	I.	N. O.	R.	H. S.	AV.		
TEST							
1ST	34	9	506	105*	20.24		
INT							
RAL	9	3	96	34*	16.00		
N.W.	2	0	42	35	21.00		
B&H	4	1	67	25	22.33		

LAST SEASON: WICKET-KEEPING

	CT	ST		
TEST				
1ST	46	11		
INT				
RAL	12	3		
N.W.	5	0		
B&H	5	2		

CAREER: BATTING

	I.	N. O.	R.	H. S.	AV.		
TEST	21	4	308	59	18.11		
1ST	379	76	5838	105*	19.26		
INT	8	3	34	9*	6.80		
RAL	83	25	796	37	13.72		
N.W.	21	5	338	49	21.12		
B&H	39	11	364	48*	13.00		

CAREER: WICKET-KEEPING

	CT	ST		
TEST	38	1		
1ST	639	82		
INT	13	3		
RAL	104	16		
N.W.	38	4		
B&H	55	11		

FROST, M. Glamorgan

Name: Mark Frost
Role: Right-hand bat, right-arm
medium-fast bowler
Born: 21 October 1962, Barking
Height: 6ft 2in **Weight:** 14st
Nickname: Harold, Frosty, Jack
County debut: 1988 (Surrey), 1990
(Glamorgan)
50 wickets in a season: 1
1st-Class 5 w. in innings: 3
1st-class 10 w. in match: 1
Place in bowling averages: 54th av.
34.69 (1989 112nd av. 45.26)
Strike rate: 56.66 (career 60.16)
1st-Class catches: 2 (career 4)
Parents: George and Joyce
Marital status: Engaged to Janet
Family links with cricket: All three
brothers play
Education: Alexandra High, Tipton;
St Peters, Wolverhampton; University
of Durham
Qualifications: 10 O-levels, 4 A-levels, Hons Degree in Geography
Off-season: Tour to India with Christians in Sport, then working as sales

representative for SCS Business Systems

Cricketers particularly admired: Jack Breakwell, Andy Webster, Ron Headley, Chris Derham, Nick Peters, Geoff Arnold, Pete Frost

Other sports followed: Soccer, rugby, tennis, athletics

Injuries: Back strain, knuckle bruising

Relaxations: Hill walking, climbing, listening to compact discs, theatre going. 'Climbing snowy mountains in Scotland with Janet. Converting Tony Cottey.'

Extras: Member of Christians in Sport. Played for Old Hill CC, winners of Cockspur Cup in 1987 and for Staffordshire before joining Surrey. Released by Surrey at end of 1989 season and joined Glamorgan

Opinions on cricket: 'The cricket ball should be standardised so that they all deteriorate, shine, or go soft in the same way. There should be no declarations so that batsmen have to give up their wickets to tired seamers!'

Best batting: 12 Glamorgan v Warwickshire, Edgbaston 1990

Best bowling: 5–40 Surrey v Leicestershire, Leicester 1989; Glamorgan v Gloucestershire, Bristol 1990

LAST SEASON: BATTING

	I.	N. O.	R.	H. S.	AV.
TEST					
1ST	18	8	42	12	4.20
INT					
RAL	3	2	9	6	9.00
N.W.	-	-	-	-	-
B&H	2	1	4	3	4.00

LAST SEASON: BOWLING

	O.	M.	R.	W.	AV.
TEST					
1ST	557.1	74	2047	59	34.69
INT					
RAL	92.4	3	505	16	31.56
N.W.	31	5	123	3	41.00
B&H	39.2	8	146	9	16.22

CAREER: BATTING

	I.	N. O.	R.	H. S.	AV.
TEST					
1ST	31	9	64	12	2.90
INT					
RAL	3	2	9	6	9.00
N.W.	-	-	-	-	-
B&H	2	1	4	3	4.00

CAREER: BOWLING

	O.	M.	R.	W.	AV.
TEST					
1ST	842.2	133	3052	84	36.33
INT					
RAL	92.4	3	505	16	31.56
N.W.	31	5	123	3	41.00
B&H	39.2	8	146	9	16.22

GARNHAM, M. A. Essex

Name: Michael Anthony Garnham
Role: Right-hand bat, wicket-keeper
Born: 20 August 1960, Johannesburg, South Africa
Height: 5ft 10 3/4in **Weight:** 12st
Nickname: Bones, Fred
County debut: 1979 (Gloucs), 1980 (Leics), 1989 (Essex)
County cap: 1989 (Essex)
1st-Class 50s scored: 17
1st-Class 100s scored: 1
One-Day 50s: 2
One-Day 100s: 1
Place in batting averages: 170th av. 29.28 (1989 97th av. 30.56)
Parents: Pauline Anne and Robert Arthur
Wife and date of marriage: Lorraine, 15 September 1984
Children: Laura Clare, 3 November 1988
Family links with cricket: Father was a club cricketer in Essex. He lost the sight of an eye keeping wicket
Education: Camberwell Grammar, Melbourne, Australia; Scotch College, Perth, Australia; Park School, Barnstaple, North Devon; North Devon College; University of East Anglia (for one year)
Qualifications: 10 O-levels, 2 A-levels
Overseas tours: England Schools to India 1977–78; England YC to Australia 1979
Cricketers particularly admired: Bob Taylor

LAST SEASON: BATTING

	I.	N. O.	R.	H. S.	AV.
TEST					
1ST	28	7	615	84*	29.28
INT					
RAL	11	4	161	40*	23.00
N.W.	1	1	1	1*	-
B&H	3	2	38	21*	38.00

LAST SEASON: WICKET-KEEPING

	CT	ST			
TEST					
1ST	49	2			
INT					
RAL	11	1			
N.W.	1	0			
B&H	5	1			

CAREER: BATTING

	I.	N. O.	R.	H. S.	AV.
TEST					
1ST	164	34	3401	100	26.16
INT					
RAL	83	18	1107	79*	17.03
N.W.	14	4	297	110	29.70
B&H	30	11	440	55	23.15

CAREER: WICKET-KEEPING

	CT	ST			
TEST					
1ST	259	28			
INT					
RAL	100	14			
N.W.	10	2			
B&H	38	4			

Other sports followed: Athletics
Relaxations: Carpentry – 'I make reproduction antique furniture', DIY, music, reading, walking
Extras: Moved to England in 1975 after living in Australia for ten years and in South Africa for four years. Played for Devon in 1976 and 1977 before joining Gloucestershire. Signed for Leicestershire in 1980 and was banned by the registration committee from competitive first-team cricket for a month for breach of registration regulations. Retired at end of 1985, but returned for five one-day games in 1988 following injury to Phil Whitticase. Signed for Essex in 1989, having been playing for Cambridgeshire. 'Having run a business making keeping gloves, I wear gloves I have made myself.'
Best batting: 100 Leicestershire v Oxford University, The Parks 1985

GATTING, M. W.   Middlesex

Name: Michael William Gatting
Role: Right-hand bat, right-arm medium bowler, slip fielder
Born: 6 June 1957, Kingsbury, Middlesex
Height: 5ft 10in **Weight:** 14st 7lbs
Nickname: Gatt, Jabba
County debut: 1975
County cap: 1977
Benefit: 1988 (205,000)
Test debut: 1977–78
Tests: 68
One-Day Internationals: 85
1000 runs in a season: 12
1st-Class 50s scored: 128
1st-Class 100s scored: 58
1st-Class 200s scored: 4
1st-Class 5 w. in innings: 2
One-Day 50s: 61
One-Day 100s: 9
Place in batting averages: 31st av. 56.80 (1989 9th av. 55.66)
1st-Class catches: 20 (career 346)
Parents: Bill and Vera
Wife and date of marriage: Elaine, September 1980
Children: Andrew, 21 January 1983; James, 11 July 1986
Family links with cricket: Father used to play club cricket. Brother Steve played for Middlesex 2nd XI
Education: Wykeham Primary School; John Kelly Boys' High School
Qualifications: 4 O-levels

Off-season: In Australia

Overseas tours: England to New Zealand and Pakistan 1977–78; West Indies 1980–81; India and Sri Lanka 1981–82; New Zealand and Pakistan 1983–84; India 1984–85; West Indies 1985–86; Australia 1986–87; World Cup, Pakistan, Australia and New Zealand 1987–88; unofficial English team to South Africa 1989–90

Cricketers particularly admired: Sir Gary Sobers, Sir Leonard Hutton

Other sports followed: Football, tennis, swimming, golf, squash

Injuries: Hamstring, Achilles tendon, ankle, bruised arm

Relaxations: Reading science fiction thrillers, 'hooked on Tolkien' and a great fan of 'Dr Who'; music, 'the only music I dislike is punk rock and heavy metal.'

Extras: Awarded OBE in Queen's Birthday Honours for services to cricket. Captain of Middlesex since 1983. Captain of England from 1986 to 1988. Published autobiography *Leading From the Front* in 1988. Won a bronze medal for ballroom dancing at the Neasden Ritz. Played football for Edgware Town as a teenager. Started as a goalkeeper, but also played centre-half for Middlesex Schools. Was recommended to West Ham, had a trial with QPR and offered an apprenticeship by Watford. His brother Steve has had a successful football career with Arsenal and Brighton. Mike started his cricket career as wicket-keeper for his school team. He toured West Indies with England Young Cricketers in 1976 and 'to my immense pleasure (and to most other people's total disbelief) I was given the job of opening the bowling in the 'Test' matches.' One of *Wisden's* Five Cricketers of the Year, 1983. His finest achievement was as captain of England on victorious tour of Australia, 1986–87, when they won the Ashes, the Perth Challenge Cup and World Series Cup. Was relieved of England captaincy after the First Test against West Indies in 1988. Captain of unofficial English team in South Africa in 1989–90 and has been banned from Test cricket for five years. Captained Middlesex to Championship title in 1990

Opinions on cricket: 'There seems to be far too much cricket compressed into our domestic season and with all the travelling involved, it leaves most of us rather jaded by the time September comes.'

Best batting: 258 Middlesex v Somerset, Bath 1984

LAST SEASON: BATTING

	I.	N.O.	R.	H.S.	AV.
TEST					
1ST	37	7	1704	170*	56.80
INT					
RAL	14	3	435	124*	39.54
N.W.	4	2	205	79*	102.50
B&H	4	0	142	66	35.50

LAST SEASON: BOWLING

	O.	M.	R.	W.	AV.
TEST					
1ST	56	21	138	7	19.71
INT					
RAL	53	1	304	6	50.66
N.W.	8	0	51	1	51.00
B&H	33	1	158	4	39.50

CAREER: BATTING

	I.	N.O.	R.	H.S.	AV.
TEST	117	14	3870	207	37.57
1ST	484	76	20585	258	50.45
INT	82	17	2049	115*	31.52
RAL	162	21	4406	124*	31.24
N.W.	50	13	1744	132*	47.13
B&H	64	17	2275	143*	48.40

CAREER: BOWLING

	O.	M.	R.	W.	AV.
TEST	125.2	29	317	4	79.25
1ST	1429.3	358	4012	150	26.74
INT	64.2	4	334	10	33.40
RAL	488.5	14	2468	83	29.73
N.W.	166.2	23	635	18	35.27
B&H	230.2	17	940	41	22.92

Best bowling: 5–34 Middlesex v Glamorgan, Swansea 1982

GIDLEY, M. I.   Leicestershire

Name: Martyn Ian Gidley
Role: Left-hand bat, off-spin bowler
Born: 30 September 1968, Leicester
Height: 6ft 1in **Weight:** 12st
Nickname: Gidders
County debut: 1989
1st-class 50s scored: 1
1st-Class catches: 2 (career 3)
Parents: Barry and Susan
Marital status: Single
Family links with cricket: Father was
club cricketer with Loughborough
Town, now chairman
Education: Loughborough Grammar
School
Qualifications: 7 O-levels, 3 A-levels
Off-season: Playing and coaching in
Orange Free State
Cricketers particularly admired:
David Gower, John Emburey. 'Have
learnt a lot from Bobby Simpson, Leicestershire's cricket manager.'
Other sports followed: Football, keen pool player
Relaxations: Listen to most types of chart music
Extras: Leicestershire Young Cricketer 1987, England Schools U–19 1987
Opinions on cricket: 'Players should be allowed to play where they want to during
close season. Four-day cricket should be encouraged more as it encourages spin
bowlers. There is too much cricket played.'
Best batting: 73 Leicestershire v Glamorgan, Cardiff 1990
Best bowling: 1–23 Leicestershire v Nottinghamshire, Trent Bridge 1989

LAST SEASON: BATTING

	I.	N. O.	R.	H. S.	AV.
TEST					
1ST	5	1	113	73	28.25
INT					
RAL	5	4	37	14*	37.00
N.W.					
B&H	1	1	20	20*	-

CAREER: BATTING

	I.	N. O.	R.	H. S.	AV.
TEST					
1ST	6	1	128	73	25.60
INT					
RAL	5	4	37	14*	37.00
N.W.					
B&H	1	1	20	20*	-

GOLDSMITH, S. C. Derbyshire

Name: Steven Clive Goldsmith
Role: Right-hand bat, right-arm
medium / slow bowler
Born: 19 December 1964, Ashford, Kent
Height: 5ft 10 1/2in **Weight:** 12st 7lbs
Nickname: Goldy, Nagger
County debut: 1987 (Kent), 1988
(Derbys)
1000 runs in a season: 1
1st-Class 50s scored: 9
One-Day 50s: 2
Place in batting averages: 241st av.
16.68 (1989 193rd av. 18.80)
1st-Class catches: 9 (career 32)
Parents: Tony and Daphne
Wife and date of marriage: Joanne,
10 March 1990
Family links with cricket: Father played
club cricket in Kent and Surrey
Education: Simon Langton Grammar
School, Canterbury
Qualifications: 8 O-levels, NCA coaching award
Career outside cricket: 'I want to get into car sales, particularly classic cars.'
Off-season: Coaching in South Africa for Natal CA
Cricketers particularly admired: Chris Tavare, David Gower, Chris Adams
Other sports followed: Motor sport, hockey, football and any other TV sports
Relaxations: Cars, golf, sleeping
Injuries: 'The usual back problems.'

LAST SEASON: BATTING

	I.	N. O.	R.	H. S.	AV.
TEST					
1ST	17	1	267	51	16.68
INT					
RAL	9	5	104	50	26.00
N.W.	1	0	21	21	21.00
B&H	2	1	49	45*	49.00

LAST SEASON: BOWLING

	O.	M.	R.	W.	AV.
TEST					
1ST	128	22	383	7	54.71
INT					
RAL	15	0	97	0	-
N.W.	10.2	0	43	1	43.00
B&H	10	0	38	3	12.66

CAREER: BATTING

	I.	N. O.	R.	H. S.	AV.
TEST					
1ST	81	6	1763	89	23.50
INT					
RAL	30	8	567	61	25.77
N.W.	4	0	42	21	10.50
B&H	10	3	159	45*	22.71

CAREER: BOWLING

	O.	M.	R.	W.	AV.
TEST					
1ST	177	30	545	8	68.12
INT					
RAL	17	0	120	0	-
N.W.	10.2	0	43	1	43.00
B&H	10	0	38	3	12.66

Extras: Spent four years on Kent staff until released at end of the 1987 season. Derbyshire's Cricketers' Association rep.

Cricketing opinions: 'Four-day cricket is the only way forward in cricket today to produce the best Test players and raise the standard of county cricket. The sooner Lord's stop messing around with the game, i. e. pitches, balls, over-rates, the sooner the players can get on with their jobs.'

Best batting: 89 Derbyshire v Kent, Chesterfield 1988

Best bowling: 2–105 Derbyshire v Essex, Derby 1990

GOOCH, G. A. Essex

Name: Graham Alan Gooch
Role: Right-hand bat,
right-arm medium bowler
Born: 23 July 1953, Leytonstone
Height: 6ft **Weight:** 13st
Nickname: Zap, Goochie
County debut: 1973
County cap: 1975
Benefit: 1985 (153,906)
Test debut: 1975
Tests: 79
One-Day Internationals: 85
1000 runs in a season: 14
1st-Class 50s scored: 159
1st-Class 100s scored: 82
1st-Class 200s scored: 8
1st-Class 5 w. in innings: 3
One-Day 50s: 97
One-Day 100s: 32
Place in batting averages: 1st av. 101.70 (1989 37th av. 41.86)
1st-Class catches: 15 (career 426)
Parents: Alfred and Rose
Wife and date of marriage: Brenda, 23 October 1976
Children: Hannah; Megan and Sally (twins)
Family links with cricket: Father played local cricket for East Ham Corinthians. Second cousin, Graham Saville, played for Essex CCC and is now England YC team manager
Education: Cannhall School and Norlington Junior High School, Leytonstone; Redbridge Technical College
Qualifications: 6 CSEs; four-year apprenticeship in toolmaking
Off-season: Captaining England in Australia
Overseas tours: England YC to West Indies 1972; England to Australia 1978–79;

Australia and India 1979–80; West Indies 1980–81; India and Sri Lanka 1981–82; World Cup and Pakistan 1987–88; India and West Indies 1989–90; Australia 1990–91; unofficial English team to South Africa 1981–82

Overseas teams played for: Western Province, South Africa 1982–84

Cricketers particularly admired: Bob Taylor, a model sportsman; Mike Procter for his enthusiasm; Barry Richards for his ability

Other sports followed: Squash, soccer, golf. Has trained with West Ham United FC

Injuries: Suffered broken hand during Port of Spain Test and missed last two Tests of the series with West Indies; broke thumb in Essex's penultimate match of the 1990 season and then required an operation after suffering an infected hand at the start of England's tour of Australia

Relaxations: 'Relaxing at home.'

Extras: One of *Wisden's* Five Cricketers of the Year, 1979. Captained English rebel team in South Africa in 1982 and was banned from Test cricket for three years. Hit a hole in one at Tollygunge Golf Club during England's tour in India, 1981–82. Appointed Essex captain 1986, but resigned captaincy at end of 1987; reappointed in 1989 following retirement of Keith Fletcher. Captain of England for last two Tests of 1988 season against West Indies and Sri Lanka in 1988 and chosen to captain England on the cancelled tour of India in 1988–89. Reappointed captain for the tour to India and West Indies in 1989–90, and led England to their first Test victory over West Indies for sixteen years. His 333 in the Lord's Test against India was the third highest score ever by an English batsman in a Test match, and by also hitting 123 in the second innings he created a record Test aggregate of 456 runs and became the first man to hit a triple century and a century in the same first-class match. His aggregate for the season (2746 runs at 101.70) was the best since 1961 and he was only the fourth batsman to finish an English season with an average better than 100. When he first joined Essex, he was a wicket-keeper and batted at number 11 in his first match. He went on a Young England tour to the West Indies as second wicket-keeper to Andy Stovold of Gloucestershire. Autobiography *Out of the Wilderness* published in 1988; *Test of Fire,* an account of the West Indies tour,

LAST SEASON: BATTING

	I.	N. O.	R.	H. S.	AV.
TEST	11	0	1058	333	96.18
1ST	19	3	1688	215	105.50
INT	4	1	219	112*	73.00
RAL	10	0	386	136	38.60
N.W.	2	1	247	144	247.00
B&H	4	1	285	102	95.00

LAST SEASON: BOWLING

	O.	M.	R.	W.	AV.
TEST	31	11	95	1	95.00
1ST	35	8	125	0	-
INT	4	0	23	2	11.50
RAL	37	0	231	2	115.50
N.W.					
B&H	28	3	122	2	61.00

CAREER: BATTING

	I.	N. O.	R.	H. S.	AV.
TEST	147	5	5910	333	41.62
1ST	585	52	25453	275	47.75
INT	83	5	3305	142	42.37
RAL	208	19	6366	176	33.68
N.W.	38	2	1820	144	50.55
B&H	86	10	3954	198*	52.02

CAREER: BOWLING

	O.	M.	R.	W.	AV.
TEST	300.3	88	717	15	47.80
1ST	2421	597	6622	198	33.44
INT	266.2	23	1203	31	38.80
RAL	866.2	41	3945	135	29.22
N.W.	246.1	34	741	25	29.64
B&H	537.5	58	1844	60	30.73

published in 1990

Opinions on cricket: Regarding four-day cricket: 'We have had some excellent four-day games, and purely in cricketing terms I believe it is worth trying, as long as it is scheduled so that Test cricketers are available for almost all the games.'

Best batting: 333 England v India, Lord's 1990

Best bowling: 7–14 Essex v Worcestershire, Ilford 1982

GOUGH, D.   Yorkshire

Name: Darren Gough
Role: Right-hand bat, right-arm fast-medium bowler, all-rounder
Born: 18 September 1970, Barnsley
Height: 5ft 11in **Weight:** 12st 7lbs
Nickname: Roland, Gazza
County debut: 1989
Place in batting averages: 270th av. 11.18
Place in bowling averages: 71st av. 37.03
Strike rate: 59.92 (career 60.76)
1st-class catches: 1 (career 1)
Parents: Trevor and Christine
Marital status: Single
Family links with cricket: Younger brother Adrian plays in local league for Monk Bretton CC
Education: St Helens Primary; Priory Comprehensive School
Qualifications: 7 CSEs, BTec Leisure Certificate, NCA coaching certificate
Off-season: Playing cricket in New Zealand for East Shirley CC in Christchurch
Overseas tours: England YC to Australia 1989–90
Cricketers particularly admired: Ian Botham, Richard Hadlee
Other sports followed: Football
Relaxations: Watching videos, playing golf
Extras: Played football for Barnsley and had trials with Rotherham United
Best batting: 24 Yorkshire v Leicestershire, Sheffield 1990
Best bowling: 4–68 Yorkshire v Middlesex, Headingley 1990

LAST SEASON: BATTING

	I.	N. O.	R.	H. S.	AV.
TEST					
1ST	17	6	123	24	11.18
INT					
RAL	2	1	21	17*	21.00
N.W.	-	-	-	-	-
B&H	-	-	-	-	-

LAST SEASON: BOWLING

	O.	M.	R.	W.	AV.
TEST					
1ST	279.4	49	1037	28	37.03
INT					
RAL	26	0	146	2	73.00
N.W.	19	3	67	4	16.75
B&H	6	0	27	0	-

CAREER: BATTING

	I.	N. O.	R.	H. S.	AV.
TEST					
1ST	19	7	134	24	11.16
INT					
RAL	2	1	21	17*	21.00
N.W.	-	-	-	-	-
B&H	-	-	-	-	-

CAREER: BOWLING

	O.	M.	R.	W.	AV.
TEST					
1ST	344.2	62	1210	34	35.58
INT					
RAL	26	0	146	2	73.00
N.W.	19	3	67	4	16.75
B&H	6	0	27	0	

GOULD, I. J.   Sussex

Name: Ian James Gould
Role: Left-hand bat, wicket-keeper
Born: 19 August 1957, Taplow, Bucks
Height: 5ft 8in **Weight:** 12st
Nickname: Gunner
County debut: 1975 (Middlesex), 1981 (Sussex)
County cap: 1977 (Middlesex), 1981 (Sussex)
Benefit: 1990
One-Day Internationals: 18
1st-Class 50s scored: 47
1st-Class 100s scored: 4
One-Day 50s: 20
Place in batting averages: 205th av. 23.50 (1989 100th av. 30.00)
1st-Class catches: 8 (career 536 & 67 stumpings)
Parents: Doreen and George
Wife and date of marriage: Joanne, 25 September 1986
Children: Gemma Louise, Michael
Family links with cricket: 'Brothers tried!'
Education: Westgate School
Overseas tours: England YC to West Indies 1976; England to Australia and New Zealand 1982–83
Overseas teams played for: Auckland 1979–80
Cricketers particularly admired: Richard Hadlee, David Smith

Other sports followed: Soccer – played as an amateur for Slough Town
Relaxations: 'Spending time with the family. Drinking in pubs with the best lager.'
Extras: Captain of Sussex in 1986 and 1987
Best batting: 128 Middlesex v Worcestershire, Worcester 1978
Best bowling: 3–10 Sussex v Surrey, The Oval 1989

LAST SEASON: BATTING

	I.	N.O.	R.	H.S.	AV.
TEST					
1ST	12	2	235	73	23.50
INT					
RAL	11	0	260	68	23.63
N.W.	1	0	26	26	26.00
B&H	4	2	41	16*	20.50

LAST SEASON: BOWLING

	O.	M.	R.	W.	AV.
TEST					
1ST	5.4	0	19	0	-
INT					
RAL					
N.W.					
B&H	3	0	16	0	-

CAREER: BATTING

	I.	N.O.	R.	H.S.	AV.
TEST					
1ST	399	63	8756	128	26.06
INT	14	2	155	42	12.91
RAL	169	27	2886	84*	20.32
N.W.	24	2	443	88	20.13
B&H	54	9	761	72	16.91

CAREER: BOWLING

	O.	M.	R.	W.	AV.
TEST					
1ST	79.4	5	365	7	52.14
INT					
RAL					
N.W.					
B&H	3.2	0	16	1	16.00

GOVAN, J. W. Northamptonshire

Name: James Walter Govan
Role: Off-spin bowler, right-hand bat
Born: 6 May 1966, Dunfermline
Height: 5ft 6in **Weight:** 12st
Nickname: Haggis, Elmur
County debut: 1989
1st-Class 5 w. in innings: 1
1st-Class catches: 0 (career 4)
Parents: James and Robertha
Marital status: Single
Family links with cricket: Dad played club cricket
Education: Dunfermline High School, Napier College
Qualifications: 8 O-grades, 4 M-grades, B. Eng Honours Degree
Cricketers particularly admired: Omar Henry, Richard Swan, Allan Lamb, Wayne Larkins, Ian Botham
Other sports followed: Football, supports Heart of Midlothian

Relaxations: Listening and playing music, reading
Extras: Played for Scottish Colleges and Scottish Students at rugby. Played first-class cricket for Scotland 1987–89. Released by Northamptonshire at end of 1990
Best batting: 17 Scotland v Ireland, Dublin 1989; Northamptonshire v Derbyshire, Northampton 1990 & Northamptonshire v Nottinghamshire, Trent Bridge 1990
Best bowling: 5–54 Scotland v Ireland, Dumfries 1988

LAST SEASON: BATTING

	I.	N. O.	R.	H. S.	AV.
TEST					
1ST	4	0	41	17	10.25
INT					
RAL	2	1	14	9*	14.00
N.W.					
B&H	3	0	42	30	14.00

LAST SEASON: BOWLING

	O.	M.	R.	W.	AV.
TEST					
1ST	47	14	142	5	28.40
INT					
RAL	15	0	78	1	78.00
N.W.					
B&H	23	4	85	1	85.00

CAREER: BATTING

	I.	N. O.	R.	H. S.	AV.
TEST					
1ST	11	1	80	17	8.00
INT					
RAL	3	2	23	9*	23.00
N.W.	1	0	0	0	0.00
B&H	6	1	98	38*	19.60

CAREER: BOWLING

	O.	M.	R.	W.	AV.
TEST					
1ST	243.1	75	614	25	24.56
INT					
RAL	23	2	101	4	25.25
N.W.	12	3	29	2	14.50
B&H	47	7	178	1	178.00

25. For which county has England soccer captain Gary Lineker played cricket?

26. What was the nickname of England and Lancashire fast bowler Brian Statham?

27. Who hit the most first-class sixes in the England 1990 season, and how many?

GOWER, D. I.   Hampshire

Name: David Ivon Gower
Role: Left-hand bat, off-break
bowler
Born: 1 April 1957, Tunbridge Wells
Height: 6ft **Weight:** 11st 11lbs
Nickname: Lubo
County debut: 1975 (Leics), 1990
(Hampshire)
County cap: 1977 (Leics)
Benefit: 1987 (121,546)
Test debut: 1978
Tests: 109
One-Day Internationals: 109
1000 runs in a season: 10
1st-Class 50s scored: 112
1st-Class 100s scored: 46
1st-Class 200s scored: 2
One-Day 50s: 50
One-Day 100s: 18
Place in batting averages: 66th av.
46.77 (1989 47th av. 38.00)
1st-Class catches: 17 (career 239 & 1 stumping)
Parents: Richard Hallam and Sylvia Mary
Marital status: Single
Family links with cricket: Father was club cricketer
Education: Marlborough House School; King's School, Canterbury; University
College, London (did not complete law course)
Qualifications: 8 O-levels, 3 A-levels
Career outside cricket: 'Offers considered.'
Off-season: England tour of Australia
Overseas tours: English Schools XI to South Africa 1974–75; England YC to West
Indies 1976; England to Australia 1978–79; Australia and India 1979–80; West
Indies 1980–81; India and Sri Lanka 1981–82; Australia and New Zealand 1982–83;
New Zealand and Pakistan 1983–84; India and Australia 1984–85; West Indies
1985–86; Australia 1986–87; Australia 1990–91
Cricketers particularly admired: Graeme Pollock and many others
Other sports followed: Rugby, bob-sledding
Relaxations: 'Photography – particularly wildlife, good wine, music.'
Extras: Played for King's Canterbury 1st XI for three years. One of *Wisden's* Five
Cricketers of the Year, 1978. Books include *Anyone for Cricket* (1979), *With Time
to Spare* (1980), *Heroes and Contemporaries* (1983), *A Right Ambition* (1986), and
he writes regular column for *Wisden Cricket Monthly*. England and Leicestershire
captain 1984–86. Declared himself not available for England tour 1987–88.

Reappointed Leicestershire captain for 1988 and reappointed captain of England v Australia in 1989. Sacked as captain and player after losing the Ashes to Allan Border's team. Resigned the Leicestershire captaincy at the end of the season and decided to join Hampshire. Surprisingly not selected for England's winter tours to either India or West Indies, but when in the Caribbean writing for *The Times*, he was called into the England side for their match v Barbados. Made sure of a fifth tour to Australia with 157* v India at The Oval when he became England's second highest Test run-maker

Best batting: 228 Leicestershire v Glamorgan, Leicester 1989
Best bowling: 3–47 Leicestershire v Essex, Leicester 1977

LAST SEASON: BATTING

	I.	N. O.	R.	H. S.	AV.
TEST	6	2	291	157*	72.75
1ST	26	3	972	145	42.26
INT	4	0	80	50	20.00
RAL	12	2	340	66*	34.00
N.W.	4	0	159	86	39.75
B&H	3	1	50	44*	25.00

CAREER: BATTING

	I.	N. O.	R.	H. S.	AV.
TEST	189	15	7674	215	44.10
1ST	420	41	14584	228	38.48
INT	106	8	3110	158	31.73
RAL	150	23	4589	135*	36.13
N.W.	37	5	1675	156	52.34
B&H	55	7	1270	114*	26.45

GRAVENEY, D. A.   Gloucestershire

Name: David Anthony Graveney
Role: Right-hand bat, slow
left-arm bowler
Born: 2 January 1953, Bristol
Height: 6ft 4in **Weight:** 14st
Nickname: Gravity, Grav
County debut: 1972
County cap: 1976
Benefit: 1986
50 wickets in a season: 6
1st-Class 50s scored: 15
1st-Class 100s scored: 2
1st-Class 5 w. in innings: 36
1st-Class 10 w. in match: 7
One-Day 50s: 1
Place in batting averages: 265th av. 11.88 (1989 251st av. 11.71)
Place in bowling averages: 82nd av. 38.35 (1989 56th av. 28.07)
Strike rate: 94.00 (career 68.45)
1st-Class catches: 7 (career 201)
Parents: Ken and Jeanne (deceased)
Wife and date of marriage: Julie, 23 September 1978

Children: Adam, 13 October 1982
Family links with cricket: Son of J. K. Graveney, captain of Gloucestershire, who took 10 wickets for 66 runs v Derbyshire at Chesterfield in 1949, and nephew of Tom Graveney of Gloucestershire, Worcestershire and England. Brother, John, selected for English Public Schools v English Schools at Lord's
Education: Millfield School, Somerset
Career outside cricket: Company director. Accountant
Overseas tours: Unofficial England tour to South Africa 1989–90
Other sports followed: Golf, soccer, squash
Relaxations: 'Playing sport, TV and cinema. Relaxing at a good pub.'
Extras: Treasurer of Cricketers' Association. Captain of Gloucestershire, 1981 to 1988. Third member of the Graveney family to be dismissed by Gloucester CCC – Uncle Tom as captain in 1960 and father Ken as chairman in 1982 – when he was sacked as captain. Player-manager of unofficial tour to South Africa 1989–90. Left Gloucestershire at end of 1990 season, and has been approached by Somerset
Best batting: 119 Gloucestershire v Oxford University, The Parks 1980
Best bowling: 8–85 Gloucestershire v Nottinghamshire, Cheltenham 1974

LAST SEASON: BATTING

	I.	N. O.	R.	H. S.	AV.
TEST					
1ST	13	4	107	46*	11.88
INT					
RAL	-	-	-	-	-
N.W.	-	-	-	-	-
B&H	1	1	12	12*	-

CAREER: BATTING

	I.	N. O.	R.	H. S.	AV.
TEST					
1ST	487	142	6109	119	17.70
INT					
RAL	131	49	1272	56*	15.51
N.W.	25	9	292	44	18.25
B&H	42	15	422	49*	15.63

LAST SEASON: BOWLING

	O.	M.	R.	W.	AV.
TEST					
1ST	485.4	137	1189	31	38.35
INT					
RAL	16	1	62	1	62.00
N.W.	18.5	0	47	2	23.50
B&H	22	1	95	1	95.00

CAREER: BOWLING

	O.	M.	R.	W.	AV.
TEST					
1ST	9458.5	2835	23953	829	28.89
INT					
RAL	955.1	53	4431	131	33.82
N.W.	351.4	51	1133	48	23.60
B&H	458.2	43	1682	51	32.98

GRAY, A. H. — Surrey

Name: Anthony Hollis Gray
Role: Right-hand bat, right-arm fast-medium bowler
Born: 23 April 1963, Port of Spain
Height: 6ft 6in **Weight:** 15st
Nickname: Big Man
County debut: 1985
County cap: 1985
Test debut: 1986–87
Tests: 5
One-Day Internationals: 21
50 wickets in a season: 1
1st-Class 50s scored: 1
1st-Class 5 w. in innings: 18
1st-class 10 w. in match: 4
Place in bowling averages: 56th av. 35.05
Strike rate: 75.73 (career 43.40)
1st-Class catches: 7 (career 41)
Parents: Anthony and Merle
Education: Marlick Ser. Comprehensive; St Augustine Ser. Comprehensive
Qualifications: 3 O-levels
Off-season: Playing in West Indies
Overseas tours: West Indies to Pakistan and New Zealand 1986–87; World Cup in India and Pakistan 1987–88; Young West Indies to Zimbabwe 1989–90
Overeas teams played for: Trinidad & Tobago
Cricketers particularly admired: Viv Richards, Michael Holding

LAST SEASON: BATTING

	I.	N. O.	R.	H. S.	AV.
TEST					
1ST	2	0	22	11	11.00
INT					
RAL					
N.W.					
B&H	-	-	-	-	-

LAST SEASON: BOWLING

	O.	M.	R.	W.	AV.
TEST					
1ST	239.5	43	666	19	35.05
INT					
RAL					
N.W.					
B&H	21	2	72	0	-

CAREER: BATTING

	I.	N. O.	R.	H. S.	AV.
TEST	8	2	48	12*	8.00
1ST	86	13	861	54*	11.79
INT	8	4	43	10*	10.75
RAL	11	6	115	24*	23.00
N.W.	1	0	3	3	3.00
B&H	-	-	-	-	-

CAREER: BOWLING

	O.	M.	R.	W.	AV.
TEST	148	37	377	22	17.13
1ST	2810	450	7511	337	22.28
INT	174.4	18	629	36	17.47
RAL	173	5	768	39	19.69
N.W.	23	3	89	5	17.80
B&H	33-	3	105	0	-

Other sports followed: Football
Relaxations: Watching sport and movies
Extras: Surrey's player of the year 1985; released by Surrey 1988; re-signed for 1990 season; released again at end of season
Best batting: 54* Trinidad & Tobago v Leeward Islands, Basseterre 1985–86
Best bowling: 8–40 Surrey v Yorkshire, Sheffield 1985

GRAYSON, A. P. Yorkshire

Name: Adrian Paul Grayson
Role: Right-hand bat, slow left-arm bowler
Born: 31 March 1971, Ripon
Height: 6ft 1in
Nickname: PG
County debut: 1990
1st-Class catches: 2 (career 2)
Parents: Adrian and Carol
Marital status: Single
Family links with cricket: 'Dad played good league cricket and is also an NCA staff coach; brother also plays.'
Education: Bedale Comprehensive School
Qualifications: 8 CSEs, BTec in Leisure, NCA coaching certificate
Career outside cricket: 'Joined Yorkshire Cricket School on 2-year YTS after leaving school.'
Off-season: 'Coaching at the Indoor School, getting fit.'
Overseas tours: England YCs to Australia 1989–90
Cricketers particularly admired: Graham Gooch, Martyn Moxon, Phil Carrick, Steve Oldham
Other sports followed: Keen supporter of Leeds United
Injuries: 'Missed start of season with groin injury.'
Relaxations: 'Listening to music, watching sport.'

LAST SEASON / CAREER: BATTING

	I.	N. O.	R.	H. S.	AV.
TEST					
1ST	8	4	145	44*	36.25
INT					
RAL					
N.W.					
B&H					

LAST SEASON /CAREER: BOWLING

	O.	M.	R.	W.	AV.
TEST					
1ST	80	19	270	1	270.00
INT					
RAL					
N.W.					
B&H					

Extras: Brother Simon is a professional footballer with Leeds United. Played for England YCs v New Zealand 1989 and Pakistan 1990. Turned down an offer by Middlesex

Opinions on cricket: 'In favour of four-day cricket. Politics should not interfere with cricket.'

Best batting: 44* Yorkshire v Somerset, Scarborough 1990

Best bowling: 1–55 Yorkshire v Nottinghamshire, Trent Bridge 1990

GREENFIELD, K.   Sussex

Name: Keith Greenfield
Role: Right-hand bat, right-arm medium or off-break bowler
Born: 6 December 1968, Brighton
Height: 6ft **Weight:** 12st 10lbs
Nickname: Grubby
County debut: 1987
1st-class 50s scored: 1
1st-class 100s scored: 1
1st-Class catches: 1 (career 67)
Parents: Leslie Ernest and Sheila
Marital status: Single
Education: Coldgan Primary and Middle Schools, Falmer High School
Qualifications: O-level Art and Technical Drawing, BTec Leisure Centre Management certificate, junior and senior coaching certificates
Off-season: Coaching at Sussex CCC
Cricketers particularly admired: Derek Randall, Ian Botham, Norman Gifford
Other sports followed: Golf, football, tennis, swimming, motor racing
Injuries: Strained groin and hip
Relaxations: 'Listening to UB40, going to good restaurants with friends, pubs, watching concerts, playing sport, seeing my girlfriend.'

LAST SEASON: BATTING

	I.	N. O.	R.	H. S.	AV.
TEST					
1ST	6	2	230	102*	57.50
INT					
RAL					
N.W.					
B&H					

CAREER: BATTING

	I.	N. O.	R.	H. S.	AV.
TEST					
1ST	18	2	396	102*	24.75
INT					
RAL	5	1	48	22	12.00
N.W.					
B&H	1	0	0	0	0.00

Extras: 'First person taken on Youth Training Scheme to become a professional cricketer at Sussex.'

Opinions on cricket: 'Club should be responsible for employing players during the winter on a salary on which they can live. Second XI Bain Dawes Trophy should be a national one-day competition played the day before Championship matches.'

Best batting: 102* Sussex v Cambridge University, Hove 1990

GREIG, I. A. Surrey

Name: Ian Alexander Greig
Role: Right-hand bat, right-arm medium bowler, slip fielder
Born: 8 December 1955, Queenstown, South Africa
Height: 5ft 11 3/4in **Weight:** 12st
Nickname: Wash, Greigy
County debut: 1980 (Sussex), 1987 (Surrey)
County cap: 1981 (Sussex), 1987 (Surrey)
Test debut: 1982
Tests: 2
1000 runs in a season: 2
50 wickets in a season: 3
1st-Class 50s scored: 37
1st-Class 100s scored: 8
1st-class 200s scored: 1
1st-Class 5 w. in innings: 10
1st-Class 10 w. in match: 2
One-Day 50s: 5
Place in batting averages: 35th av. 54.73 (1989 33rd av. 42.20)
Place in bowling averages: 151st av. 66.00 (1989 120th av. 54.18)
Strike rate: 99.76 (career 58.70)
1st-Class catches: 16 (career 145)
Parents: Sandy and Joyce
Wife and date of marriage: Cheryl, 8 January 1983
Children: Michelle, 17 December 1984; Andrew, 20 January 1987
Family links with cricket: Brother of Tony, former captain of Sussex and England; brother-in-law Phillip Hodson played for Cambridge University and Yorkshire
Education: Queens College, Queenstown; Downing College, Cambridge
Qualifications: MA Law (Cantab)
Off-season: Marketing / cricket activities at Surrey CCC
Overseas teams played for: Border, South Africa 1974–75, 1979–80; Griqualand West, South Africa 1975–76

170

Cricketers particularly admired: Garth le Roux, Richard Hadlee
Other sports followed: Rugby
Relaxations: Relaxing with family, barbecues, fly-fishing
Opinions on cricket: 'We must move to 16 four-day matches as soon as possible, played on the best possible surfaces, and reducing the amount of cricket played. A mixture of limited-overs cricket to be carefully restored around the four-day game.'
Best batting: 291 Surrey v Lancashire, The Oval 1990
Best bowling: 7–43 Sussex v Cambridge University, Fenner's 1981

LAST SEASON: BATTING

	I.	N. O.	R.	H. S	AV.
TEST					
1ST	29	6	1259	291	54.73
INT					
RAL	14	7	217	43	31.00
N.W.	-	-	-	-	-
B&H	4	1	34	15	11.33

LAST SEASON: BOWLING

	O.	M.	R.	W.	AV.
TEST					
1ST	216.1	21	858	13	66.00
INT					
RAL	12	0	75	1	75.00
N.W.					
B&H	36.2	0	176	3	58.66

CAREER: BATTING

	I.	N. O.	R.	H. S.	AV.
TEST	4	0	26	14	6.50
1ST	304	46	7665	291	29.70
INT					
RAL	111	33	1834	61*	23.51
N.W.	17	2	355	82	23.66
B&H	48	4	592	51	13.45

CAREER: BOWLING

	O.	M.	R.	W.	AV.
TEST	31.2	6	114	4	28.50
1ST	3970.4	801	12483	405	30.82
INT					
RAL	687	21	3496	120	29.13
N.W.	161.4	17	579	22	26.31
B&H	424.3	38	1604	57	28.14

28. Who took most first-class wickets in England in 1990, and how many?

29. Who scored the most first-class runs in the 1990 English season?

30. How many runs in all matches did G.A.Gooch score in the English 1990 season – 2746, 3821, 4005?

GRIFFITH, F. A.   Derbyshire

Name: Frank Alexander Griffith
Role: Right-hand bat, right-arm medium bowler
Born: 15 August 1968, Leyton
Height: 6ft **Weight:** 12st
Nickname: Sir Learie
County debut: 1988
1st-Class catches: 0 (career 6)
Parents: Alex and Daisy
Marital status: Single
Education: William Morris High School, Walthamstow
Qualifications: Food and nutrition and art O-levels; NCA coaching certificate
Cricketers particularly admired: Collis King, Franklyn Stephenson
Other sports followed: Table tennis, basketball, football
Relaxations: Listening to music
Extras: Attended Haringey Cricket College
Opinions on cricket: 'We must play more four-day games in order to get more results.'
Best batting: 37 Derbyshire v Northamptonshire, Northampton 1988
Best bowling: 4–47 Derbyshire v Lancashire, Old Trafford 1988

LAST SEASON: BATTING

	I.	N. O.	R.	H. S.	AV.
TEST					
1ST	1	0	1	1	1.00
INT					
RAL					
N.W.					
B&H					

LAST SEASON: BOWLING

	O.	M.	R.	W.	AV.
TEST					
1ST	11	2	20	1	20.00
INT					
RAL					
N.W.					
B&H					

CAREER: BATTING

	I.	N. O.	R.	H. S.	AV.
TEST					
1ST	17	1	297	37*	12.93
INT					
RAL	9	1	36	9	4.50
N.W.					
B&H	1	0	10	10	10.00

CAREER: BOWLING

	O.	M.	R.	W.	AV.
TEST					
1ST	151.3	28	519	16	32.43
INT					
RAL	55	4	282	9	31.33
N.W.					
B&H					

HALL, J. W.   Sussex

Name: James William Hall
Role: Right-hand opening batsman,
cover fielder
Born: 30 March 1968, Chichester
Height: 6ft 2in **Weight:** 13st 7lbs
Nickname: Gud, Hally
County debut: 1990
1000 runs in a season: 1
1st-Class 50s scored: 5
1st-Class 100s scored: 2
Place in batting averages: 152nd av.
32.57
1st-Class catches: 6 (career 6)
Parents: Maurice and Marlene (deceased)
Marital status: Single
Family links with cricket: 'Father
played club cricket for Chichester Priory
Park and brother David is Chichester's
number one supporter.'
Education: Chichester High School for
boys 'where father is a teacher.'
Qualifications: 9 GCSE O-levels
Off-season: 'Recharging my batteries.'
Cricketers particularly admired: Alan Wells, David Smith, Norman Gifford,
Allan Green, Murray Lee-Smith
Other sports followed: Football (Brighton & Hove Albion – 'only because the
tickets are free' – and Carlisle United)
Relaxations: 'Eating out, music, spending time with Emma.'
Extras: Scored 53 on first XI debut v Zimbabwe and scored maiden first-class 100
in same week (120* v New Zealand). Over 1000 runs in debut season of first-class
cricket. Run out without facing a ball on NatWest debut v Glamorgan ('thanks Neil')
Opinions on cricket: 'Players should have more time off between games to prevent
staleness and to reduce the amount of travelling needed at the end of matches to play
again the following day. Reducing overseas players to one per county will allow
more English players to play county cricket but will deny 2nd XI players the chance

LAST SEASON / CAREER: BATTING

	I.	N. O.	R.	H. S.	AV.
TEST					
1ST	37	2	1140	125	32.57
INT					
RAL					
N.W.	1	0	0	0	0.00
B&H					

LAST SEASON / CAREER: BOWLING

	O.	M.	R.	W.	AV.
TEST					
1ST					
INT					
RAL					
N.W.					
B&H					

to play against top-class batsmen or bowlers, so making the step from 2nd team to first-class cricket even greater. Counties should do more for players in the off-season.'
Best batting: 125 Sussex v Nottinghamshire, Trent Bridge 1990

HALLETT, J. C.   Somerset

Name: Jeremy Charles Hallett
Role: Right-hand bat, right-arm medium-fast bowler
Born: 18 October 1970, Yeovil
Height: 6ft 2in **Weight:** 12st
Nickname: Chicks, Pikey
County debut: 1990
Parents: Glyn and Rosemarie
Marital status: Single
Family links with cricket: Father plays Somerset League cricket
Education: Wells Cathedral Junior School; Millfield School
Qualifications: 10 O-levels, 3 A-levels
Off-season: 'Starting at Durham University.'
Overseas tours: England YCs to Australia 1989–90
Cricketers particularly admired: Viv Richards, Richard Hadlee, Terry Alderman, Malcolm Marshall, Martin Crowe, Jimmy Cook
Other sports followed: Soccer (Yeovil Town), golf, rugby, 'all sports really'
Relaxations: 'Reading, playing golf, a good pub.'
Extras: Player of the series, England YCs v Australia 1989–90. Also played v New Zealand 1989 and Pakistan 1990
Best bowling: 2–40 Somerset v Kent, Canterbury 1990

LAST SEASON / CAREER: BATTING

	I.	N. O.	R.	H. S.	AV.
TEST					
1ST	1	0	0	0	0.00
INT					
RAL	3	3	7	4*	-
N.W.					
B&H	-	-	-	-	-

LAST SEASON / CAREER: BOWLING

	O.	M.	R.	W.	AV.
TEST					
1ST	65.5	9	238	6	39.66
INT					
RAL	45.3	2	246	7	35.14
N.W.					
B&H	11	0	70	1	70.00

Name: Robin Hanley
Role: Middle-order right-hand bat,
close fielder
Born: 5 January 1968, Tunbridge, Kent
Height: 6ft 2in **Weight:** 14st
Nickname: Ninj, Ninja
County debut: 1990
Parents: Peter and Janet
Marital status: Single
Education: Willingdon School;
Eastbourne VIth Form College
Qualifications: 6 O-levels
Off-season: Playing grade cricket in
Tasmania
Cricketers particularly admired:
Graham Gooch, David Smith, Dean
Jones, Allan Border, Robin Smith
Other sports followed: Rugby Union,
football
Injuries: Crack on helmet at short leg
– four days off
Relaxations: Studying the martial arts
Extras: 'Played a season of Central Lancashire League cricket for Rochdale in 1989
and scored 1000 runs – very good competition.'
Opinions on cricket: 'One Championship game of four days per week (Tues-Fri);
60-over competition in first two months of season (on Saturdays – final in
September); remainder of Saturdays for 40-over competition. Pitches should stay the
same, but balls should be of the 1989 variety.'
Best batting: 28 Sussex v Warwickshire, Eastbourne 1990

LAST SEASON / CAREER: BATTING

	I.	N. O.	R.	H. S.	AV.
TEST					
1ST	4	0	32	28	8.00
INT					
RAL	1	0	11	11	11.00
N.W.					
B&H					

LAST SEASON / CAREER: BOWLING

	O.	M.	R.	W.	AV.
TEST					
1ST					
INT					
RAL					
N.W.					
B&H					

HANSFORD, A. R. Sussex

Name: Alan Roderick Hansford
Role: Right-hand bat, right-arm
medium-fast bowler
Born: 1 October 1968, Burgess Hill,
West Sussex
Height: 6ft **Weight:** 13st 7lbs
Nickname: Skater
County debut: 1989
1st-Class 5 w. in innings: 1
1st-Class catches: 1 (career 3)
Parents: John and Muriel
Marital status: Single
Family links with cricket: Father
played club cricket primarily in Dorset.
Four brothers all play or played county
youth and club cricket
Education: Oakmeeds Community
School, Burgess Hill; Haywards Heath
VIth Form College, Haywards Heath;
University of Surrey, Guildford
Qualifications: 10 O-levels, 3 A-levels, presently studying for BSc (Hons) Degree
in Maths and Statistics
Off-season: 'At university finishing my degree and getting fit!'
Cricketers particularly admired: Ian Botham, Viv Richards, Malcolm Marshall,
Sylvester Clarke, Phil Edmonds
Injuries: 'Out for fourteen weeks with broken left forearm which re-fractured –
broken by Malcolm Marshall after making career best score.'
Relaxations: Eating out, statistics, crosswords

LAST SEASON: BATTING

	I.	N. O.	R.	H. S.	AV.
TEST					
1ST	6	1	55	29	11.00
INT					
RAL	2	1	7	5*	7.00
N.W.					
B&H	1	1	2	2*	-

LAST SEASON: BOWLING

	O.	M.	R.	W.	AV.
TEST					
1ST	123.5	21	425	7	60.71
INT					
RAL	36	1	240	6	40.00
N.W.					
B&H	44	0	265	2	132.50

CAREER: BATTING

	I.	N. O.	R.	H. S.	AV.
TEST					
1ST	10	3	108	29	15.42
INT					
RAL	4	2	10	5*	5.00
N.W.	1	1	5	5*	-
B&H	4	3	12	8*	12.00

CAREER: BOWLING

	O.	M.	R.	W.	AV.
TEST					
1ST	291.1	60	910	27	33.70
INT					
RAL	88	3	460	17	27.05
N.W.	12	0	48	2	24.00
B&H	79.2	12	432	7	61.71

Extras: Took wicket with 4th ball in first-class cricket. Was member of 1989 Combined Universities side. First seven county matches were all four-day games
Opinions on cricket: 'The lunch and tea intervals should be lengthened to one hour and half-an-hour respectively. Coaches should generally become less rigid re unorthodox and individual bowling and batting techniques. All Championship cricket should be four-day, but bring back the bigger seam.'
Best batting: 29 Sussex v Hampshire, Southampton 1990
Best bowling: 5–79 Sussex v Hampshire, Hove 1989

HARDEN, R. J.   Somerset

Name: Richard John Harden
Role: Right-hand bat, left-arm medium bowler
Born: 16 August 1965, Bridgwater
Height: 5ft 11in **Weight:** 13st 7lbs
Nickname: Sumo, Curtis
County debut: 1985
1000 runs in a season: 2
1st-Class 50s scored: 27
1st-Class 100s scored: 9
One-Day 50s: 8
Place in batting averages: 23rd av. 60.83 (1989 71st av. 34.60)
1st-Class catches: 18 (career 65)
Parents: Chris and Ann
Marital status: Single
Family links with cricket: Grandfather played club cricket for Bridgwater
Education: Kings College, Taunton
Qualifications: 8 O-levels, 2 A-levels. Coaching award
Off-season: Playing and coaching in New Zealand
Overseas teams: Central Districts
Cricketers particularly admired: Viv Richards, Jimmy Cook
Other sports followed: Squash, golf, rugby
Relaxations: 'Love my domestic duties (dusting, hoovering, etc) rather than golf. Good food and the odd drink.'
Opinions on cricket: 'We should play 16 four-day games, but must be played on decent pitches.'
Best batting: 115* Somerset v Northamptonshire, Luton 1989
Best bowling: 2–7 Central Districts v Canterbury, Blenheim 1987–88

LAST SEASON: BATTING

	I.	N. O.	R.	H. S.	AV.
TEST					
1ST	31	7	1460	104*	60.83
INT					
RAL	16	7	397	53	44.11
N.W.	1	0	12	12	12.00
B&H	6	2	115	53*	28.75

LAST SEASON: BOWLING

	O.	M.	R.	W.	AV.
TEST					
1ST	67	6	276	6	46.00
INT					
RAL					
N.W.					
B&H					

CAREER: BATTING

	I.	N. O.	R.	H. S.	AV.
TEST					
1ST	173	28	5160	115*	35.58
INT					
RAL	67	14	1514	73	28.56
N.W.	4	0	43	17	10.75
B&H	23	3	394	53*	19.70

CAREER: BOWLING

	O.	M.	R.	W.	AV.
TEST					
1ST	206	24	799	16	49.93
INT					
RAL	0.1	0	0	0	-
N.W.					
B&H					

HARDIE, B. R.　　　Essex

Name: Brian Ross Hardie
Role: Right-hand bat, right-arm medium bowler, bat/pad fielder
Born: 14 January 1950, Stenhousemuir
Height: 5ft 10in **Weight:** 12st 7lbs
Nickname: Lager, Bert
County debut: 1973
County cap: 1974
Benefit: 1983 (48,486)
1000 runs in a season: 11
1st-Class 50s scored: 89
1st-Class 100s scored: 27
One-Day 50s: 51
One-Day 100s: 6
Place in batting averages: 8th av. 72.80 (1989 90th av. 31.68)
1st-Class catches: 11 (career 349)
Parents: James Millar (deceased) and Elspet
Wife and date of marriage: Fiona, 28 October 1977
Family links with cricket: Father and brother, Keith, played for Scotland
Education: Stenhousemuir Primary School; Larbert High School
Qualifications: 7 O-levels, 3 H-levels, NCA advanced cricket coach
Off-season: Taking up new job as sports master at Brentwood School
Other sports followed: Football, golf
Relaxations: Sport
Extras: Played for Stenhousemuir in East of Scotland League. Debut for Scotland

1970. Man of the Match in 1985 NatWest Final. Retired from county cricket at end of 1990 season
Best batting: 162 Essex v Warwickshire, Edgbaston 1975 & Essex v Somerset, Southend 1985
Best bowling: 2–39 Essex v Glamorgan, Ilford 1979

LAST SEASON: BATTING

	I.	N. O.	R.	H. S.	AV.
TEST					
1ST	17	7	728	125	72.80
INT					
RAL	13	1	392	76	32.66
N.W.	1	0	31	31	31.00
B&H	4	0	81	34	20.25

CAREER: BATTING

	I.	N. O.	R.	H. S.	AV.
TEST					
1ST	608	79	18103	162	34.22
INT					
RAL	221	21	5657	109	28.23
N.W.	34	1	1143	110	34.63
B&H	80	16	1943	119*	30.35

HARDY, J. J. E. Gloucestershire

Name: Jonathan James Ean Hardy
Role: Left-hand bat
Born: 2 October 1960, Nakuru, Kenya
Height: 6ft 3in **Weight:** 13st 7lbs
Nickname: JJ
County debut: 1984 (Hampshire), 1986 (Somerset)
County cap: 1987 (Somerset)
1000 runs in a season: 1
1st-Class 50s scored: 35
1st-Class 100s scored: 4
One-Day 50s: 7
One-Day 100s: 2
Place in batting averages: 148th av. 32.81 (1989 154th av. 22.89)
1st-Class catches: 6 (career 79)
Parents: Ray and Petasue
Wife and date of marriage: Janet, 25 September 1987
Family links with cricket: Father played for Yorkshire Schools
Education: Pembroke House, Gilgil, Kenya; Canford School, Dorset
Qualifications: 10 O-levels, 3 A-levels (English, Economics, Geography)
Off-season: 'Playing for Western Province and organising the shipment of Cape wines to the UK.'
Overseas teams played for: Western Province 1987–90
Cricketers particularly admired: Graeme Pollock, Greg Chappell, Malcolm Marshall

Other sports followed: Hockey (captain Dorset U–19), rugby, squash
Injuries: 'A disc problem which ended my season in June.'
Relaxations: Photography, walking
Extras: Suffered from bilharzia, a tropical parasitic disease, from 1980 to February 1986. Released by Somerset at end of 1990 season and has joined Gloucestershire
Opinions on cricket: 'A balance must be found where a fair contest can be fought between bat and ball – where a team's average completed innings is 300 – not 150 or 700! Less cricket would make games more competitive from start to finish and more suitable to the demands of the modern spectator.'
Best batting: 119 Somerset v Gloucestershire, Taunton 1987

LAST SEASON: BATTING

	I.	N. O.	R.	H. S.	AV.
TEST					
1ST	16	5	361	91	32.81
INT					
RAL					
N.W.					
B&H	2	0	128	109	64.00

CAREER: BATTING

	I.	N. O.	R.	H. S.	AV.
TEST					
1ST	217	29	5828	119	31.16
INT					
RAL	48	7	890	94*	21.70
N.W.	8	1	191	100	27.28
B&H	19	1	494	109	27.44

HARTLEY, P. J.   Yorkshire

Name: Peter John Hartley
Role: Right-hand bat, right-arm fast-medium bowler
Born: 18 April 1960, Keighley
Height: 6ft **Weight:** 13st 3lbs
Nickname: Daisy, Jack
County debut: 1982 (Warwicks), 1985 (Yorks)
County cap: 1987 (Yorks)
50 wickets in a season: 1
1st-Class 50s scored: 5
1st-Class 100s scored: 1
1st-Class 5 w. in innings: 6
Place in batting averages: 249th av. 15.57
Place in bowling averages: 53rd av. 34.25
Strike rate: 56.65 (career 67.48)
1st-Class catches: 8 (career 32)

Parents: Thomas and Molly
Wife and date of marriage: Sharon, 12 March 1988
Family links with cricket: Father played local league cricket
Education: Greenhead Grammar School; Bradford College
Qualifications: City & Guilds in Textiles and design
Off-season: 'Trying to find employment and working on my golf swing.'
Cricketers particularly admired: Dennis Lillee, Malcolm Marshall
Other sports followed: Golf (4 handicap), football (Bradford City and Chelsea)
Injuries: 'Usual bowling strains.'
Relaxations: Music, golf
Opinions on cricket: 'Should return to uncovered pitches for Championship matches.'
Best batting: 127* Yorkshire v Lancashire, Old Trafford 1988
Best bowling: 6–57 Yorkshire v Warwickshire, Sheffield 1990

LAST SEASON: BATTING

	I.	N. O.	R.	H. S.	AV.
TEST					
1ST	15	1	218	75	15.57
INT					
RAL	10	3	143	51	20.42
N.W.	1	0	52	52	52.00
B&H	2	0	1	1	0.50

LAST SEASON: BOWLING

	O.	M.	R.	W.	AV.
TEST					
1ST	491	80	1781	52	34.25
INT					
RAL	83.5	4	405	18	22.50
N.W.	32.5	3	136	10	13.60
B&H	20	3	63	3	21.00

CAREER: BATTING

	I.	N. O.	R.	H. S.	AV.
TEST					
1ST	91	22	1572	127*	22.78
INT					
RAL	33	12	291	51	13.85
N.W.	5	2	98	52	32.66
B&H	8	3	51	29*	10.20

CAREER: BOWLING

	O.	M.	R.	W.	AV.
TEST					
1ST	2339.2	304	7332	208	35.25
INT					
RAL	327.3	11	1582	59	26.81
N.W.	91.5	7	342	24	14.25
B&H	160	15	649	29	22.37

31. Which counties did Jon Hardy of Gloucestershire previously play for?

32. What do I.D.Austin, M.W.Alleyne and J.A.Afford have in common?

33. What do Viv Richards, David Gower and Ian Bishop have in common?

HAWKES, C. J. Leicestershire

Name: Christopher James Hawkes
Role: Left-hand bat, slow left-arm
bowler
Born: 14 July 1972, Loughborough
Height: 6ft 3in **Weight:** 13st 6lbs
Nickname: Hawkeye, Hawksey
County debut: 1990
1st-Class catches: 1 (career 1)
Parents: Richard and Mavis
Marital status: Single
Education: Loughborough Grammar
School; Durham University
Qualifications: 10 GCSEs and 4
A-levels
Off-season: 'Student at Durham
University.'
Overseas tours: England YCs to New
Zealand 1990–91
Cricketers particularly admired: Chris
Lewis, Justin Benson, Graeme Hick,
Greg Matthews, Phil Edmonds and Nigel Briers
Other sports followed: Rugby Union, wrestling, football, golf
Relaxations: 'All sports, TV and cinema, theatre, socialising.'
Extras: Youngest player on Leicestershire staff in 1990 and made
first-class debut in last match of season
Opinions on cricket: 'I would like to see the introduction of day / night games to
increase attendances and the return of uncovered pitches. Players should be allowed
to exercise their freedom of individual right and be able to play in South Africa
without punishment.'
Best batting: 3 Leicestershire v Derbyshire, Derby 1990

LAST SEASON / CAREER: BATTING

	I.	N. O.	R.	H. S.	AV.
TEST					
1ST	2	1	5	3	5.00
INT					
RAL					
N.W.					
B&H					

LAST SEASON / CAREER: BOWLING

	O.	M.	R.	W.	AV.
TEST					
1ST	14	3	40	0	-
INT					
RAL					
N.W.					
B&H					

HAYHURST, A. N.　　　Somerset

Name: Andrew Neil Hayhurst
Role: Right-hand bat, right-arm
medium bowler
Born: 23 November 1962, Davyhulme,
Manchester
Height: 6ft **Weight:** 13st
Nickname: Bull
County debut: 1985 (Lancs),
1990 (Somerset)
1000 runs in a season: 1
1st-Class 50s scored: 12
1st-Class 100s scored: 5
One-Day 50s: 6
Place in batting averages: 27th av.
57.74 (1989 181st av. 19.84)
Place in bowling averages: 147th av.
63.94
Strike rate: 113.41 (career 75.18)
1st-Class catches: 9 (career 20)

Parents: William and Margaret
Marital status: Single
Family links with cricket: Father played club cricket
Education: St Mark's Primary School; Worsley Wardley High; Eccles College;
Carnegie PE College, Leeds
Qualifications: 8 O-levels, 3 A-levels, BA (Hons) Human Movement
Off-season: Teaching and coaching in Somerset
Cricketers particularly admired: Viv Richards, Clive Lloyd, Richard Hadlee,
Chris Tavare and Jimmy Cook
Other sports followed: Football, Rugby League (Salford)
Relaxations: All sport, good food
Extras: Scored a record 197 runs whilst playing for North of England v South,
Southampton 1982. Holds record for number of runs in Manchester & District
Cricket Association League, whilst playing for Worsley CC in 1984: 1193 runs (av.
70.17). Represented Greater Manchester U–19s at football. Released by Lancashire
at the end of 1989 season and joined Somerset on a three-year contract, 1990. Made
a century on his first-class debut for Somerset
Opinions on cricket: 'Four-day cricket, now that pitches are of an excellent
standard, is the best game, but we still play too much. We should play one-day games
in coloured clothing.'
Best batting: 170 Somerset v Sussex, Taunton 1990 & Somerset v Yorkshire,
Scarborough 1990
Best bowling: 4–27 Lancashire v Middlesex, Old Trafford 1987

	I.	N. O.	R.	H. S.	AV.
TEST					
1ST	35	8	1559	170	57.74
INT					
RAL	11	1	192	70*	19.20
N.W.	2	0	97	51	48.50
B&H	5	1	119	76	29.75

LAST SEASON: BOWLING

	O.	M.	R.	W.	AV.
TEST					
1ST	321.2	50	1087	17	63.94
INT					
RAL	86	1	453	15	30.20
N.W.	2	0	14	0	-
B&H	42	0	176	6	29.33

CAREER: BATTING

	I.	N. O.	R.	H. S.	AV.
TEST					
1ST	98	14	2744	170	32.66
INT					
RAL	43	6	914	84	24.70
N.W.	8	1	245	51	35.00
B&H	12	1	155	76	14.09

CAREER: BOWLING

	O.	M.	R.	W.	AV.
TEST					
1ST	827	143	2731	66	41.37
INT					
RAL	292.3	8	1512	38	39.78
N.W.	73.5	6	279	9	31.00
B&H	88.5	6	353	13	27.15

HAYNES, D. L.   Middlesex

Name: Desmond Leo Haynes
Role: Right-hand bat, right-arm bowler
Born: 15 February 1956, St James, Barbados, West Indies
County debut: 1989
County cap: 1989
Test debut: 1977–78
Tests: 89
One-Day Internationals: 174
1000 runs in a season: 2
1st-Class 50s scored: 95
1st-Class 100s scored: 38
1st-Class 200s scored: 3
One-Day 50s: 53
One-Day 100s: 19
Place in batting averages: 14th av. 69.00 (1989 21st av. 45.18)
1st-Class catches: 9 (career 145 & 1 stumping)
Education: Federal HS, Barbados
Off-season: Captaining West Indies in Pakistan
Overseas teams played for: Barbados 1976–90
Overseas tours: World Series Cricket (Kerry Packer) 1978–79; West Indies to Australia 1979–80, 1981–82, 1984–85, 1988–89; New Zealand 1979–80, 1986–87; England 1980, 1984, 1988; Pakistan 1980–81, 1986–87, 1990–91; India 1983–84, 1987–88, 1989–90; West Indies B to Zimbabwe 1981
Extras: Played for Scotland in the B & H Cup. Captained West Indies v England, Port of Spain in 1989–90 and on tour of Pakistan 1990–91. Britannic Assurance

Player of the Year 1990
Best batting: 255* Middlesex v Sussex, Lord's 1990
Best bowling: 1–2 West Indies v Pakistan, Lahore 1980–81

LAST SEASON: BATTING

	I.	N. O.	R.	H. S.	AV.
TEST					
1ST	39	5	2346	255*	69.00
INT					
RAL	17	2	753	107*	50.20
N.W.	4	2	274	149*	137.00
B&H	5	0	326	131	65.20

LAST SEASON: BOWLING

	O.	M.	R.	W.	AV.
TEST					
1ST	35	7	113	2	56.50
INT					
RAL	50.2	1	281	4	70.25
N.W.	20	3	59	1	59.00
B&H	12	0	57	1	57.00

CAREER: BATTING

	I.	N. O.	R.	H. S.	AV.
TEST	153	17	5711	184	41.99
1ST	268	29	11415	255*	47.71
INT	173	23	6471	152*	43.14
RAL	27	2	951	107*	38.04
N.W.	9	2	575	149*	82.14
B&H	9	0	457	131	50.77

CAREER: BOWLING

	O.	M.	R.	W.	AV.
TEST	3	0	8	1	8.00
1ST	63.4	11	188	5	37.60
INT	5	0	24	0	-
RAL	53.2	1	300	4	75.00
N.W.	20	3	59	1	59.00
B&H	30	4	89	2	44.50

HEGG, W. K. Lancashire

Name: Warren Kevin Hegg
Role: Right-hand bat, wicket-keeper
Born: 23 February 1968, Radcliffe,
Lancashire
Height: 5ft 8in **Weight:** 12st
Nickname: Chucky, Chutch, Boss
County debut: 1986
1st-Class 50s scored: 9
1st-Class 100s scored: 2
Place in batting averages: 95th av.
42.12 (1989 184th av. 19.82)
Parents: Kevin and Glenda
Marital status: Single
Family links with cricket: Father
and brother played in local leagues
Education: Unsworth High School;
Stand College, Whitefield
Qualifications: 5 O-levels, 7 CSEs;
qualified coach
Off-season: England A tour to Pakistan
and Sri Lanka; holidaying and playing golf
Overseas tours: England YCs to Sri Lanka 1986–87; Youth World Cup in Australia
1988; England A to Pakistan and Sri Lanka 1990–91

Cricketers particularly admired: Ian Botham, Alan Knott, Bob Taylor
Other sports followed: Football, golf, Australian rules
Relaxations: Watching movies, sleeping, fishing
Extras: First player to make County debut from Lytham CC. Youngest player to score a 100 for Lancashire for thirty years, 130 v Northamptonshire in fourth first-class game. Eleven victims in match v Derbyshire – to equal world record
Opinions on cricket: 'Players should be given more time to prepare for games. There should always be a travelling day for long journeys.'
Best batting: 130 Lancashire v Northamptonshire, Northampton 1987

LAST SEASON: BATTING

	I.	N. O.	R.	H. S.	AV.
TEST					
1ST	22	6	674	100*	42.12
INT					
RAL	7	5	66	24*	33.00
N.W.	1	1	13	13*	-
B&H	2	2	41	31*	-

LAST SEASON: WICKET-KEEPING

	CT	ST		
TEST				
1ST	49	2		
INT				
RAL	8	2		
N.W.	8	0		
B&H	13	1		

CAREER: BATTING

	I.	N. O.	R.	H. S.	AV.
TEST					
1ST	122	19	2272	130	22.05
INT					
RAL	24	11	127	24*	9.76
N.W.	6	1	104	29	20.80
B&H	7	3	81	31*	20.25

CAREER: WICKET-KEEPING

	CT	ST		
TEST				
1ST	208	26		
INT				
RAL	56	8		
N.W.	10	0		
B&H	27	1		

HEMMINGS, E. E.　Nottinghamshire

Name: Edward Ernest Hemmings
Role: Right-hand bat, off-break bowler
Born: 20 February 1949, Leamington Spa, Warwickshire
Height: 5ft 10in **Weight:** 13st
Nickname: Eddie, Whale, Fossil 'with many thanks to Angus Fraser for the last of my nicknames'
County debut: 1966 (Warwicks), 1979 (Notts)
County cap: 1974 (Warwicks), 1980 (Notts)
Benefit: 1987
Test debut: 1982
Tests: 15

One-Day Internationals: 28
50 wickets in a season: 14
1st-Class 50s scored: 26
1st-Class 100s scored: 1
1st-Class 5 w. in innings: 64
1st-Class 10 w. in match: 14
One-Day 50s: 1
Place in batting averages: 210th av. 22.20 (1989 178th av. 20.20)
Place in bowling averages: 64th av. 36.15 (1989 64th av. 29.65)
Strike rate: 80.98 (career 66.12)
1st-Class catches: 2 (career 188)
Parents: Edward and Dorothy Phyliss
Wife and date of marriage: Christine Mary, 23 October 1971
Children: Thomas Edward, 26 July 1977; James Oliver, 9 September 1979
Family links with cricket: Father and father's father played Minor Counties and League cricket
Education: Campion School, Leamington Spa
Off-season: Touring Australia with England
Overseas tours: England to Australia and New Zealand 1982–83; World Cup, Pakistan, Australia and New Zealand 1987–88; India and West Indies 1989–90; Australia 1990–91
Cricketers particularly admired: Tim Robinson, Clive Rice, John Jameson
Other sports followed: Golf, football
Relaxations: 'Watching football at any level – especially junior. Dining out with my wife. Golf, real ale – and sleeping it off!'
Extras: Took a hat-trick for Warwickshire in 1977; hit first century – 127* for Nottinghamshire v Yorkshire at Worksop, July 1982 – after sixteen years in

187

first-class game

Opinions on cricket: 'I think this year has gone to prove the old motto, "never give up trying".'

Best batting: 127* Nottinghamshire v Yorkshire, Worksop 1982

Best bowling: 10–175 International XI v West Indies XI, Kingston 1982–83

LAST SEASON: BATTING

	I.	N.O.	R.	H.S.	AV.
TEST	6	1	103	51	20.60
1ST	14	4	230	83	23.00
INT	2	0	3	3	1.50
RAL	6	3	91	32*	30.33
N.W.	2	0	3	3	1.50
B&H	3	1	23	12*	11.50

LAST SEASON: BOWLING

	O.	M.	R.	W.	AV.
TEST	244.5	70	669	21	31.85
1ST	443.3	127	1175	30	39.16
INT	44	3	174	2	87.00
RAL	81	3	377	18	20.94
N.W.	19.3	4	95	4	23.75
B&H	54	8	182	4	45.50

CAREER: BATTING

	I.	N.O.	R.	H.S.	AV.
TEST	20	4	383	95	23.93
1ST	575	133	8620	127*	19.50
INT	8	4	15	4*	3.75
RAL	165	51	1606	44*	14.08
N.W.	28	9	233	31*	12.26
B&H	50	16	487	61*	14.32

CAREER: BOWLING

	O.	M.	R.	W.	AV.
TEST	666.3	190	1626	37	43.94
1ST	13936	3943	37121	1288	28.82
INT	244	15	1045	32	32.65
RAL	1626	104	7498	259	28.95
N.W.	432.4	74	1456	44	33.09
B&H	803.1	106	2515	72	34.93

HEPWORTH, P. N. Leicestershire

Name: Peter Nash Hepworth

Role: Right-hand bat, off-break bowler 'when given the chance'

Born: 4 May 1967, Ackworth, West Yorkshire

Height: 6ft 1in **Weight:** 12st 7lbs

Nickname: Nash, Heppers

County debut: 1988

1st-Class 50s scored: 2

Place in batting averages: 159th av. 30.83

1st-Class catches: 1 (career 4)

Parents: George and Zena

Marital status: Single

Family links with cricket: Father and uncle played cricket for Ackworth

Education: Ackworth Junior/Middle Schools, Hemsworth High School

Qualifications: 8 CSEs, MCC Part 1

coaching certificate. 'Almost passed my bricklaying exams but played cricket on days of the exams.'

Off-season: Coaching, working, relaxing
Cricketers particularly admired: David Gower, Geoff Boycott, Don Wilson – for his attitude with young players
Other sports followed: 'Watch football, rugby and most other sports. Follow Featherstone Rovers at Rugby League.'
Injuries: Bad left wrist – 'played with a tight bandage for four weeks which impaired my batting a lot.'
Relaxations: Watching sport, music, videos, going to the cinema
Extras: Started playing for Ackworth Cricket Club following the likes of Neil Lloyd, Graham Stevenson, Geoff Boycott
Opinions on cricket: 'The pitches have been a lot better this year, resulting in the big scores we've seen. The new seam on the ball also made a big difference.'
Best batting: 55* Leicestershire v Derbyshire, Derby 1990

LAST SEASON: BATTING

	I.	N. O.	R.	H. S.	AV.
TEST					
1ST	8	2	185	55*	30.83
INT					
RAL					
N.W.					
B&H					

CAREER: BATTING

	I.	N. O.	R.	H. S.	AV.
TEST					
1ST	22	2	380	55*	19.00
INT					
RAL	4	1	89	38	29.66
N.W.					
B&H					

34. What is the prize money for the winner of the Refuge Assurance League – £15,000, £24,000 or £36,000?

35. What was unusual about Jonathan Lewis's debut in Essex?

36. How many times have Middlesex won the County Championship in the last hundred years – 7, 9 or 14 times?

HICK, G. A. Worcestershire

Name: Graeme Ashley Hick
Role: Right-hand bat, off-break bowler
Born: 23 May 1966, Salisbury, Rhodesia
Height: 6ft 3in **Weight:** 14st 7lbs
Nickname: Hicky, Ash
County debut: 1984
County cap: 1986
1000 runs in a season: 6
1st-Class 50s scored: 54
1st-Class 100s scored: 56
1st-Class 200s scored: 7
1st-Class 5 w. in innings: 3
1st-Class 10 w. in match: 1
One-Day 50s: 36
One-Day 100s: 8
Place in batting averages: 2nd av. 90.26 (1989 7th av. 57.00)
Place in bowling averages: 40th av. 32.25 (1989 12th av. 19.96)
Strike rate: 62.65 (career 71.09)
1st-Class catches: 26 (career 189)
Parents: John and Eve
Marital status: Single

Family links with cricket: Father served on Zimbabwe Cricket Union Board of Control since 1984; also played representative cricket in Zimbabwe
Education: Banket Primary; Prince Edward Boys' High School, Zimbabwe
Qualifications: 4 O-levels, NCA coaching award
Off-season: Playing for Queensland in Australia
Overseas tours: Zimbabwe to England for 1983 World Cup; Sri Lanka 1983–84; England 1985
Overseas teams played for: Old Hararians in Zimbabwe 1982–90; Northern Districts 1987–89; Queensland 1990–91
Cricketers particularly admired: Duncan Fletcher (Zimbabwe captain) for approach and understanding of the game, David Houghton, Basil D'Oliveira
Other sports followed: Follows Liverpool FC, golf, tennis, squash, hockey
Injuries: Broke finger during Worcestershire's match with New Zealand
Relaxations: 'Watching Gordon Lord preparing to dive to save the ball on the boundary. Leaning against Steve Rhodes at first-slip.'
Extras: Made first 100 aged 6 for school team; youngest player participating in 1983 Prudential World Cup (aged 17); youngest player to represent Zimbabwe. Scored 1234 runs in Birmingham League and played for Worcestershire 2nd XI in 1984 – hitting six successive 100s. In 1986, at age 20, he became the youngest player to

score 2000 runs in an English season. One of *Wisden's* Five Cricketers of the Year, 1986. In 1988 he made 405* v Somerset, the highest individual score in England since 1895, and scored 1000 first-class runs by end of May 1988, hitting a record 410 runs in April. In 1990 became youngest batsman ever to make 50 first-class 100s and scored 645 runs without being dismissed – a record for English cricket. Qualifies as an English player in 1991. Published *Hick'n Dilley Circus* and *A Champion's Diary*. Also played hockey for Zimbabwe

Opinions on cricket: 'What a great game.'

Best batting: 405* Worcestershire v Somerset, Taunton 1988

Best bowling: 5–37 Worcestershire v Gloucestershire, Worcester 1990

LAST SEASON: BATTING

	I.	N. O.	R.	H. S.	AV.
TEST					
1ST	35	9	2347	252*	90.26
INT					
RAL	13	3	751	114*	75.10
N.W.	3	1	129	78*	64.50
B&H	6	1	165	64	33.00

LAST SEASON: BOWLING

	O.	M.	R.	W.	AV.
TEST					
1ST	208.5	41	645	20	32.25
INT					
RAL	33.5	1	222	6	37.00
N.W.	32	2	118	0	-
B&H	30	0	125	4	31.25

CAREER: BATTING

	I.	N. O.	R.	H. S.	AV.
TEST					
1ST	269	34	15080	405*	64.17
INT					
RAL	85	15	3085	114*	44.07
N.W.	18	5	917	172*	70.53
B&H	25	4	1032	109	49.14

CAREER: BOWLING

	O.	M.	R.	W.	AV.
TEST					
1ST	1374.3	312	4192	116	36.13
INT					
RAL	183	2	1021	33	30.93
N.W.	98.3	6	343	9	38.11
B&H	63	1	260	7	37.14

HINKS, S. G.

Kent

Name: Simon Graham Hinks
Role: Left-hand opening bat
Born: 12 October 1960, Northfleet, Kent
Height: 6ft 2in **Weight:** 12st 10lbs
Nickname: Hinksey
County debut: 1982
County cap: 1985
1000 runs in a season: 3
1st-Class 50s scored: 33
1st-Class 100s scored: 11
1st-Class 200s scored: 1
One-Day 50s: 21
Place in batting averages: 124th av.
36.93 (1989 87th av. 32.12)
1st-Class catches: 8 (career 90)
Parents: Mary and Graham
Wife and date of marriage: Victoria,
September 1990
Family links with cricket: Father
captained Gravesend CC and is now
chairman. Brother Jonathan captains Gravesend and has played for Kent U–19s
Education: Dover Road Infant and Junior Schools, Northfleet; St George's C of E
School, Gravesend
Qualifications: 5 O-levels, 1 A-level; senior cricket coach
Career outside cricket: Sales rep for Reed Corrugated Cases
Cricketers particularly admired: 'Admired Clive Lloyd's style and power and
anyone who has proved themselves over a long period.'

LAST SEASON: BATTING

	I.	N. O.	R.	H. S.	AV.
TEST					
1ST	43	0	1588	234	36.93
INT					
RAL	15	0	562	89	37.46
N.W.	2	0	58	43	29.00
B&H	4	0	7	3	1.75

LAST SEASON: BOWLING

	O.	M.	R.	W.	AV.
TEST					
1ST	15	2	60	2	30.00
INT					
RAL					
N.W.	3	0	23	0	-
B&H					

CAREER: BATTING

	I.	N. O.	R.	H. S.	AV.
TEST					
1ST	253	13	7294	234	30.39
INT					
RAL	86	6	1985	99	24.81
N.W.	10	2	380	95	47.50
B&H	31	1	708	85	23.60

CAREER: BOWLING

	O.	M.	R.	W.	AV.
TEST					
1ST	96.5	11	367	8	45.87
INT					
RAL	25	1	139	4	34.75
N.W.	3	0	23	0	-
B&H	41	0	198	5	39.60

Other sports followed: All sports
Relaxations: Sport, TV, DIY, gardening
Opinions on cricket: 'Young players are still very dependent on going abroad during the winter months as counties still do very little, if anything, to find them winter employment. Players, particularly bowlers, therefore do not have time to recover from injury or rest sufficiently. Six-month wages also make it very difficult to afford mortgages and to settle down.'
Best batting: 234 Kent v Middlesex, Canterbury 1990
Best bowling: 2–18 Kent v Nottinghamshire, Trent Bridge 1989

HODGSON, G. D.   Gloucestershire

Name: Geoffrey Dean Hodgson
Role: Right-hand bat
Born: 22 October 1966, Carlisle
Height: 6ft 1in **Weight:** 12st 7lbs
Nickname: Deano, Ocko
County debut: 1987 (Warwicks), 1989 (Gloucs)
1000 runs in a season: 1
1st-Class 50s scored: 10
1st-class 100s scored: 2
One-Day 50s: 1
Place in batting averages: 125th av. 36.66
Parents: John Geoffrey and Dorothy Elizabeth
Marital status: Single
Education: Nelson Thomlinson Comprehensive, Wigton; Loughborough University
Qualifications: 11 O-levels, 4 A-levels, BSc (Hons) Human Biological Sciences, NCA qualified cricket coach, PFA qualified football coach, LTA qualified tennis coach
Off-season: Playing for Western Suburbs in Brisbane, Australia
Cricketers particularly admired: Dennis Amiss, Barry Richards, Sunil Gavaskar. 'I learnt a lot from Graham Wiltshire, Eddie Barlow, Neal Abberley and Alan Ormrod, and all the Gloucestershire players have been very helpful.'
Other sports followed: Football, international rugby, golf, tennis, skiing
Relaxations: Listening to music ('all types depending on mood'), reading thrillers and autobiographies, watching comedies and thrillers, going to wine bars
Extras: Played Minor County Cricket for Cumberland 1982–88; also played for Lancashire and Worcestershire 2nd XIs; first-class debut for Gloucestershire in 1989
Opinions on cricket: 'Play 17 four-day Championship matches (including Durham)

on good covered wickets. Less one-day cricket: both B&H Cup and NatWest Trophy should be knockouts; Sunday League divided into two (North and South) with play-offs for top two in each division. Better fixture arrangement to reduce travelling. Increased awareness of players needs in the winter by county clubs or all-year-round contracts.'

Best batting: 126 Gloucestershire v Zimbabwe, Bristol 1990

LAST SEASON: BATTING

	I.	N. O.	R.	H. S.	AV.
TEST					
1ST	40	4	1320	126	36.66
INT					
RAL	8	2	113	28	18.83
N.W.	3	0	133	52	44.33
B&H	1	0	1	1	1.00

CAREER: BATTING

	I.	N. O.	R.	H. S.	AV.
TEST					
1ST	44	4	1380	126	34.50
INT					
RAL	11	2	176	39	19.55
N.W.	4	0	168	52	42.00
B&H	1	0	1	1	1.00

HOLMES, G. C. Glamorgan

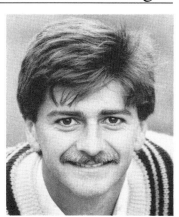

Name: Geoffrey Clark Holmes
Role: Right-hand bat, right-arm medium bowler
Born: 16 September 1958, Newcastle-on-Tyne
Height: 5ft 10in **Weight:** 11st 2lbs
County debut: 1978
County cap: 1985
Benefit: 1991
1000 runs in a season: 3
1st-Class 50s scored: 36
1st-Class 100s scored: 11
1st-Class 5 w. in innings: 2
One-Day 50s: 16
Place in batting averages: 94th av. 42.27 (1989 194th av. 18.72)
1st-Class catches: 2 (career 82)
Parents: George and Rita
Wife: Christine
Children: Victoria
Family links with cricket: Father played in the Northumberland League
Education: West Denton High School
Qualifications: 6 O-levels, 2 A-levels; advanced cricket coach
Off-season: Preparing for Benefit season in 1991
Overseas teams played for: Border, South Africa 1989–90
Cricketers particularly admired: Geoff Boycott, John Snow

Other sports followed: Soccer, and most others
Injuries: Two broken fingers
Relaxations: Reading (especially cricket books), TV, sport, 3-card brag
Opinions on cricket: 'I think we play too much county cricket and would like to see 16 Championship matches per season. I would like to see one of the one-day competitions played as day/night matches, under floodlights.'
Best batting: 182 Border v Western Province B, East London 1989–90
Best bowling: 5–38 Glamorgan v Essex, Colchester 1988

LAST SEASON: BATTING

	I.	N. O.	R.	H. S.	AV.
TEST					
1ST	15	4	465	125*	42.27
INT					
RAL	5	2	150	57	50.00
N.W.					
B&H	5	0	109	62	21.80

LAST SEASON: BOWLING

	O.	M.	R.	W.	AV.
TEST					
1ST	42	10	132	4	33.00
INT					
RAL	7	0	50	1	50.00
N.W.					
B&H	19	0	92	3	30.66

CAREER: BATTING

	I.	N. O.	R.	H. S.	AV.
TEST					
1ST	327	50	7956	182	28.72
INT					
RAL	110	20	2198	73	24.42
N.W.	14	0	280	57	20.00
B&H	28	6	652	70	29.63

CAREER: BOWLING

	O.	M.	R.	W.	AV.
TEST					
1ST	1155.2	223	3963	88	45.03
INT					
RAL	460.1	13	2495	97	25.72
N.W.	82	15	220	11	20.00
B&H	156.2	14	650	25	26.00

37. What first-class record does M.A.Robinson of Northants hold?

38. Who won the Minor Counties Eastern and Western championships, respectively?

39. Who topped the Minor Counties batting averages in 1990?

Name: Ian James Houseman
Role: Right-hand bat, right-arm
fast-medium bowler
Born: 12 October 1969, Harrogate,
North Yorkshire
Height: 5ft 10in **Weight:** 11st 7lbs
Nickname: Acid, Eddie
County debut: 1989
Parents: Eric and Jennifer
Marital status: Single
Family links with cricket: Father
is a Yorkshire committee man; sister
Fiona played for Yorkshire Ladies
U–19s
Education: Harrogate Grammar School,
Loughborough University
Qualifications: 10 O-levels, 5 A-levels
Off-season: Working in family business
Cricketers particularly admired:
Michael Holding, Fred Trueman,
Richard Hadlee, Dennis Lillee
Other sports followed: Golf, Rugby League, boxing
Injuries: Tendonitis in elbow – missed last fortnight of season
Relaxations: 1960s/70s music – Lou Reed
Extras: Played for England YCs v New Zealand 1989
Opinions on cricket: 'It should be more difficult to qualify for England. Reduce the
amount of professional cricket played. Greater efforts should be made to encourage
cricket in the schools.'
Best batting: 18 Yorkshire v Sussex, Middlesbrough 1989
Best bowling: 2–26 Yorkshire v Indians, Headingley 1990

LAST SEASON: BATTING

	I.	N. O.	R.	H. S.	AV.
TEST					
1ST	1	1	0	0*	-
INT					
RAL					
N.W.					
B&H					

CAREER: BATTING

	I.	N. O.	R.	H. S.	AV.
TEST					
1ST	2	1	18	18	18.00
INT					
RAL					
N.W.					
B&H					

HUGHES, D. P.   Lancashire

Name: David Paul Hughes
Role: Right-hand bat, slow
left-arm bowler
Born: 13 May 1947, Newton-le-Willows
Height: 5ft 11in **Weight:** 12st
Nickname: Yozzer
County debut: 1967
County cap: 1970
Benefit: 1981
1000 runs in a season: 2
50 wickets in a season: 4
1st-Class 50s scored: 44
1st-Class 100s scored: 8
1st-Class 5 w. in innings: 20
1st-Class 10 w. in match: 2
One-Day 50s: 10
Place in batting averages: 204th av.
23.70 (1989 166th av. 21.73)
Place in bowling averages: 81st av.
38.25 (1989 41st av. 25.25)
Strike rate: 70.16 (career 66.07)
1st-Class catches: 13 (career 321)
Parents: Both deceased
Wife and date of marriage: Christine,
March 1973
Children: James, July 1975
Family links with cricket: Father, Lloyd, a professional with Bolton League club
Walkden, before and after Second World War
Education: Newton-le-Willows Grammar School
Qualifications: NCA coaching certificate
Overseas tours: England Counties side to West Indies 1974–75
Overseas teams played for: Tasmania while coaching there 1975–77
Cricketers particularly admired: 'At the start of my career I spoke to all the leading
left-arm spin bowlers in the game for help.'
Relaxations: Golf
Extras: Hit 24 runs off John Mortimer v Gloucestershire in penultimate over in
Gillette Cup semi-final in 1972. Hit 26 runs off last over of innings v
Northamptonshire in Gillette Final at Lord's, 1976. Bowled 13 consecutive maiden
overs v Gloucestershire at Bristol, 1980. Appointed Lancashire captain 1987. One
of *Wisden's* Five Cricketers of the Year, 1987. Led Lancashire to B & H and NatWest
double in 1990 – the first time any county has won both knockout competitions in
the same year. He has now played in nine Lord's finals
Best batting: 153 Lancashire v Glamorgan, Old Trafford 1983

Best bowling: 7–24 Lancashire v Oxford University, The Parks 1970

LAST SEASON: BATTING

	I.	N. O.	R.	H. S.	AV.
TEST					
1ST	17	7	237	57	23.70
INT					
RAL	3	3	29	21*	-
N.W.	-	-	-	-	-
B&H	1	1	1	1*	-

LAST SEASON: BOWLING

	O.	M.	R.	W.	AV.
TEST					
1ST	280.4	61	918	24	38.25
INT					
RAL	18	0	113	3	37.66
N.W.	3	0	19	0	-
B&H					

CAREER: BATTING

	I.	N. O.	R.	H. S.	AV.
TEST					
1ST	578	106	10308	153	21.83
INT					
RAL	220	51	3045	92	18.01
N.W.	40	16	810	71	33.75
B&H	58	15	978	52	22.74

CAREER: BOWLING

	O.	M.	R.	W.	AV.
TEST					
1ST	7158.1	2181	19613	650	30.17
INT					
RAL	827.1	62	3681	172	21.40
N.W.	303.2	29	1185	44	26.93
B&H	237.2	40	754	29	26.00

HUGHES, J. G. Northamptonshire

Name: John Gareth Hughes
Role: Right-hand bat, right-arm medium bowler
Born: 3 May 1971, Wellingborough
Height: 6ft 1in
County debut: 1990
Marital status: Single
Education: Sir Christopher Hatton School, Wellingborough; Sheffield City Polytechnic
Off-season: Studying at Polytechnic
Other sports followed: Football
Extras: Played for ESCA and made 2nd XI debut in 1987. Played football for Northamptonshire U19s – grandfather played for Wales and father for Scotland youth team

LAST SEASON / CAREER: BATTING

	I.	N. O.	R.	H. S.	AV.
TEST					
1ST	7	0	4	2	0.57
INT					
RAL	1	1	1	1*	-
N.W.					
B&H					

LAST SEASON / CAREER: BOWLING

	O.	M.	R.	W.	AV.
TEST					
1ST	66	12	293	3	97.66
INT					
RAL	4	0	16	0	-
N.W.					
B&H					

Best batting: 2 Northamptonshire v Hampshire, Bournemouth 1990
Best bowling: 2–57 Northamptonshire v Derbyshire, Chesterfield 1990

HUGHES, S. P.   Middlesex

Name: Simon Peter Hughes
Role: Right-hand bat, right-arm
fast-medium bowler
Born: 20 December 1959, Kingston,
Surrey
Height: 5ft 10in **Weight:** 11st 7lbs
Nickname: Yozzer, Spam, Yule
County debut: 1980
County cap: 1981
Benefit: 1991
50 wickets in a season: 2
1st-Class 50s scored: 1
1st-Class 5 w. in innings: 9
Place in bowling averages: 89th av.
39.00 (1989 19th av. 21.41)
Strike rate: 70.24 (career 56.88)
1st-Class catches: 3 (career 41)
Parents: Peter and Erica
Wife and date of marriage: Jan, 31
March 1990
Family links with cricket: Father very keen coach and player who owned indoor
cricket school. 'Uncle once hit a ball over the school pavilion!'
Education: Latymer Upper School, Hammersmith; Durham University
Qualifications: 10 O-levels, 4 A-levels, BA General Studies
Career outside cricket: 'Write column for *The Independent* newspaper and
broadcast on radio and TV.'
Off-season: 'On the phone getting people to my benefit functions.'
Overseas teams played for: Colts CC, Colombo, Sri Lanka, and Sri Lanka Board
President's XI; Northern Transvaal 1982–83
Cricketers particularly admired: John Emburey, Clive Radley, Malcolm
Marshall, Richard Hadlee
Other sports followed: Soccer, rugby, tennis, golf
Relaxations: Travelling, slapstick films, jazz and blues piano, eating curry,
broadcasting and journalism
Extras: Took 4–82 v Kent on Championship debut, and played in County
Championship and Gillette Cup winning sides in first season in 1980. Awarded cap
after only 20 matches. Middlesex/Austin Reed Player of the Year 1986
Opinions on cricket: 'Too much of it.'
Best batting: 53 Middlesex v Cambridge University, Fenner's 1988

Best bowling: 7–35 Middlesex v Surrey, The Oval 1986

LAST SEASON: BATTING

	I.	N.O.	R.	H.S.	AV.
TEST					
1ST	18	5	111	23*	8.53
INT					
RAL	1	0	14	14	14.00
N.W.	-	-	-	-	-
B&H	2	0	24	22	12.00

LAST SEASON: BOWLING

	O.	M.	R.	W.	AV.
TEST					
1ST	386.2	73	1287	33	39.00
INT					
RAL	67.5	3	393	12	32.75
N.W.	12	0	68	2	34.00
B&H	43.5	0	187	6	31.16

CAREER: BATTING

	I.	N.O.	R.	H.S.	AV.
TEST					
1ST	188	61	1498	53	11.79
INT					
RAL	36	18	255	22*	14.16
N.W.	12	7	45	11	9.00
B&H	15	7	71	22	8.87

CAREER: BOWLING

	O.	M.	R.	W.	AV.
TEST					
1ST	3962.4	784	12527	418	29.96
INT					
RAL	636.2	17	3180	115	27.65
N.W.	234.2	28	880	39	22.56
B&H	199	14	807	35	23.05

HUMPAGE, G. W.   Warwickshire

Name: Geoffrey William Humpage
Role: Right-hand bat, wicket-keeper, right-arm medium bowler
Born: 24 April 1954, Birmingham
Height: 5ft 9in **Weight:** 12st 7lbs
Nickname: Farsley
County debut: 1974
County cap: 1976
Benefit: 1987
One-Day Internationals: 3
1000 runs in a season: 11
1st-Class 50s scored: 97
1st-Class 100s scored: 29
1st-Class 200s scored: 2
One-Day 50s: 35
One-Day 100s: 3
Place in batting averages: 132nd av. 34.88 (1989 45th av. 38.55)
Parents: Ernest and Mabel
Wife and date of marriage: Valerie Anne, 14 September 1983 (2nd marriage)
Children: Philip Andrew Guy, 16 November 1977
Education: Golden Hillock Comprehensive School, Birmingham
Career outside cricket: Former police cadet, then police constable, Birmingham

City Police
Overseas tours: Toured South Africa with unofficial English team 1981–82
Overseas teams played for: Orange Free State 1981–82
Other sports followed: Soccer, squash, tennis, swimming, golf, snooker, table tennis
Relaxations: Reading, listening to E. L. O.
Extras: Good impressionist, particularly of Frankie Howerd. Took part in record English first-class 4th wicket partnership of 470 v Lancashire at Southport, July 1982, with Alvin Kallicharran (230*). Humpage made 254 including 13 sixes. Joined England Rebels in South Africa in 1981–82. One of *Wisden's* Five Cricketers of the Year, 1984. Released by Warwickshire at the end of 1990 season
Best batting: 254 Warwickshire v Lancashire, Southport 1982
Best bowling: 2–13 Warwickshire v Gloucestershire, Edgbaston 1980

LAST SEASON: BATTING

	I.	N. O.	R.	H. S.	AV.
TEST					
1ST	22	4	628	74	34.88
INT					
RAL	9	3	151	40*	25.16
N.W.	2	0	45	43	22.50
B&H	4	1	52	30*	17.33

LAST SEASON: WICKET-KEEPING

	CT	ST		
TEST				
1ST	30	0		
INT				
RAL	5	0		
N.W.	0	1		
B&H	8	0		

CAREER: BATTING

	I.	N. O.	R.	H. S.	AV.
TEST					
1ST	574	76	18098	254	36.34
INT	2	0	11	6	5.50
RAL	190	27	4064	109*	24.93
N.W.	38	4	953	77	28.02
B&H	62	8	1398	100*	25.88

CAREER: WICKET-KEEPING

	CT	ST		
TEST				
1ST	671	72		
INT	2	0		
RAL	128	20		
N.W.	39	9		
B&H	80	3		

HUSSAIN, N.   Essex

Name: Nasser Hussain
Role: Right-hand bat
Born: 28 March 1968, Madras, India
Height: 6ft 1in
Nickname: Bunny
County debut: 1987
Test debut: 1989–90
Tests: 3
One-Day Internationals: 2
1st-Class 50s scored: 8
1st-Class 100s scored: 5
One-Day 50s: 5
One-day 100s: 1
Place in batting averages: 122nd av.
37.60 (1989 17th av. 47.14)
1st-Class catches: 16 (career 48)
Parents: Jainad and Shireen
Marital status: Single
Family links with cricket: Father
played for Madras in Ranji Trophy
1966–67. Uncle played for

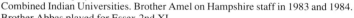

Combined Indian Universities. Brother Amel on Hampshire staff in 1983 and 1984.
Brother Abbas played for Essex 2nd XI
Education: Forest School; Durham University
Qualifications: 9 O-levels, 3 A-levels; BSc (Hons) in Geology; NCA cricket
coaching award
Off-season: Touring with England A to Pakistan and Sri Lanka
Overseas tours: England YC to Sri Lanka 1987 and Australia for Youth World Cup
1988; England to India and West Indies 1990; England A to Pakistan and Sri Lanka
1990–91
Overseas teams played for: Madras 1986–87
Cricketers particularly admired: 'They are all in the Essex dressing room, plus
David Gower.'
Other sports followed: Golf, football, American football
Relaxations: Music, TV
Injuries: Broke wrist playing tennis in Guyana and missed first half of English
season after an operation
Extras: Played for England Schools U–15 for two years (one as captain). Youngest
player to play for Essex Schools U–11 at the age of 8 and U–15 at the age of 12. At
15, was considered the best young leg-spin bowler in the country. Cricket Writers'
Club Young Cricketer of the Year, 1989
Best batting: 197 Essex v Surrey, The Oval 1990

	I.	N. O.	R.	H. S.	AV.
TEST					
1ST	23	3	752	197	37.60
INT					
RAL	7	3	161	66*	40.25
N.W.	1	1	2	2*	-
B&H					

CAREER: BATTING

	I.	N. O.	R.	H. S.	AV.
TEST	5	0	100	35	20.00
1ST	73	10	2520	197	40.00
INT	2	1	17	15*	17.00
RAL	26	6	557	66*	27.85
N.W.	2	1	26	24	26.00
B&H	12	2	450	118	45.00

IGGLESDEN, A. P.   Kent

Name: Alan Paul Igglesden
Role: Right-hand bat, right-arm fast-medium bowler, outfielder
Born: 8 October 1964, Farnborough, Kent
Height: 6ft 6in **Weight:** 14st 8lbs
Nickname: Iggy, Norman
County debut: 1986
Test debut: 1989
Tests: 1
50 wickets in a season: 2
1st-Class 5 w. in innings: 10
1st-Class 10 w. in match: 2
Place in batting averages: 259th av. 13.12
Place in bowling averages: 61st av. 35.93 (1989 90th av. 34.87)
Strike rate: 61.12 (career 51.25)
1st-Class catches: 5 (career 20)
Parents: Alan Trevor and Gillian Catharine
Wife and date of marriage: Hilary Moira, 20 January 1990
Family links with cricket: Brother Kevin plays for Holmesdale in the Kent League
Education: St Mary's Primary School; Hosey School; Churchill Secondary School, Westerham
Qualifications: 9 CSEs, coaching certificate
Off-season: Coaching at Kent; Fred Rumsey tour to Barbados
Overseas tours: With England A to Zimbabwe and Kenya 1989–90
Overseas teams played for: Western Province 1987–89
Cricketers particularly admired: Terry Alderman, Dennis Lillee, Chris Penn, Mark Benson, Roy Pienaar, Fanie De Villiers ('I don't know how he's still alive!')
Other sports followed: 'Very keen Crystal Palace supporter – present at Wembley for the FA Cup final replay v Man United in 1990
Injuries: Stress fracture of the right leg, salmonella food poisoning, torn side muscle, broken finger

Relaxations: 'Listening to music, golf, crosswords, watching movies at home with my wife.'

Extras: 'I didn't play any schools representative cricket.'

Opinions on cricket: 'After a year like this it would be very easy for me to complain bitterly about a bowler's lot. I am sure the administrators had the game's best interests at heart, but as the statistics for 1990 have shown, the balance has been tipped too heavily in the batsman's favour. I just hope something is done to redress the situation for the sake of all bowlers. After speaking to many members, spectators and friends, the majority said they did not enjoy the season any more than the one before, so who are the administrators trying to please? It's still the best game in the world though.'

Best batting: 41 Kent v Surrey, Canterbury 1988

Best bowling: 6–34 Kent v Surrey, Canterbury 1988

LAST SEASON: BATTING

	I.	N. O.	R.	H. S.	AV.
TEST					
1ST	17	9	105	24	13.12
INT					
RAL	4	2	4	3*	2.00
N.W.	2	2	14	12*	-
B&H	1	1	0	0*	-

LAST SEASON: BOWLING

	O.	M.	R.	W.	AV.
TEST					
1ST	326	47	1150	32	35.93
INT					
RAL	52.5	2	236	6	39.33
N.W.	14	1	47	2	23.50
B&H	5	0	31	0	-

CAREER: BATTING

	I.	N. O.	R.	H. S.	AV.
TEST	1	1	2	2*	-
1ST	75	27	500	41	10.41
INT					
RAL	12	6	31	13*	5.16
N.W.	3	2	16	12*	16.00
B&H	4	3	8	5*	8.00

CAREER: BOWLING

	O.	M.	R.	W.	AV.
TEST	37	3	146	3	48.66
1ST	1944.5	336	6365	229	27.79
INT					
RAL	203.4	10	800	38	21.05
N.W.	50	2	174	8	21.75
B&H	90	6	366	11	33.27

ILLINGWORTH, R. K. Worcestershire

Name: Richard Keith Illingworth
Role: Right-hand bat, slow
left-arm bowler
Born: 23 August 1963, Bradford
Height: 6ft **Weight:** 13st
Nickname: Lucy, Harry
County debut: 1982
County cap: 1986
50 wickets in a season: 3
1st-Class 50s scored: 9
1st-Class 100s scored: 3
1st-Class 5 w. in innings: 15
1st-Class 10 w. in match: 4
Place in batting averages: 146th av.
33.25 (1989 230th av. 13.87)
Place in bowling averages: 20th av.
28.29 (1989 22nd av. 21.78)
Strike rate: 70.06 (career 68.53)
1st-Class catches: 7 (career 87)
Parents: Keith and Margaret
Wife and date of marriage: Anne, 20 September 1985
Children: Miles, 28 August 1987; Thomas, 20 April 1989
Family links with cricket: Father played Bradford League cricket
Education: Wrose Brow Middle; Salts Grammar School ('same school as the late Jim Laker')
Qualifications: 6 O-levels, senior coaching award holder
Career outside cricket: Buyer for Golding Pipeworks
Off-season: Touring Pakistan and Sri Lanka with England A

LAST SEASON: BATTING

	I.	N. O.	R.	H. S.	AV.
TEST					
1ST	22	6	532	117	33.25
INT					
RAL	5	1	35	16*	8.75
N.W.	1	0	7	7	7.00
B&H	4	1	63	36*	21.00

LAST SEASON: BOWLING

	O.	M.	R.	W.	AV.
TEST					
1ST	875.5	280	2122	75	28.29
INT					
RAL	80	3	311	14	22.21
N.W.	36	9	92	2	46.00
B&H	46	1	182	2	91.00

CAREER: BATTING

	I.	N. O.	R.	H. S.	AV.
TEST					
1ST	208	54	3186	120*	20.68
INT					
RAL	46	21	221	22	8.84
N.W.	8	2	55	22	9.16
B&H	15	8	141	36*	20.14

CAREER: BOWLING

	O.	M.	R.	W.	AV.
TEST					
1ST	4877.4	1672	13509	427	31.63
INT					
RAL	572.4	28	2568	117	21.94
N.W.	186.1	30	552	17	32.47
B&H	211	22	780	22	35.45

Overseas tours: England A to Zimbabwe and Kenya 1989–90; Pakistan and Sri Lanka 1990–91
Overseas teams played for: Natal 1988–89
Other sports followed: Football (follows Leeds United, Bradford City), golf
Injuries: Broken right thumb – missed three weeks
Relaxations: 'Listening to music. Playing with Miles and Thomas.'
Extras: Took 11 for 108 on South African first-class debut for Natal B v Boland 1988. Scored 120 not out as a night-watchman for Worcestershire v Warwickshire 1988 and 106 for England A v Zimbabwe 1989–90
Best batting: 120* Worcestershire v Warwickshire, Worcester 1987
Best bowling: 7–50 Worcestershire v Oxford University, The Parks 1985

ILOTT, M. C. Essex

Name: Mark Christopher Ilott
Role: Left-hand bat, left-arm fast bowler
Born: 27 August 1970, Watford
Height: 6ft 2in **Weight:** 12st
Nickname: Bambi, Chook, Headless
County debut: 1988
1st-Class 5 w. in innings: 2
Place in batting averages: 251st av. 15.37
Place in bowling averages: 47th av. 33.41 (1989 95th av. 36.50)
Strike rate: 62.35 (career 65.47)
1st-Class catches: 1 (career 2)
Parents: John and Glenys
Marital status: Single
Family links with cricket: 'Brother plays for Hertfordshire CCC, Grandad played for years as a swing bowler and dad has done everything.'
Education: Francis Combe School
Qualifications: 6 O-levels, 2 A/O-levels, 2 A-levels
Off-season: 'Three months working for my dad, three months overseas.'
Cricketers particularly admired: John Lever, Graham Gooch, Malcolm Marshall, Richard Hadlee
Other sports followed: Tennis, football, snooker
Injuries: Broken finger – out for four weeks
Relaxations: Swimming, reading
Opinions on cricket: 'Haven't been in the game long enough.'

Best batting: 42* Essex v Kent, Chelmsford 1990
Best bowling: 5–34 Essex v Derbyshire, Derby 1990

LAST SEASON: BATTING

	I.	N. O.	R.	H. S.	AV.
TEST					
1ST	10	2	123	42*	15.37
INT					
RAL	3	1	10	6	5.00
N.W.	-	-	-	-	-
B&H	-	-	-	-	-

LAST SEASON: BOWLING

	O.	M.	R.	W.	AV.
TEST					
1ST	322.1	65	1036	31	33.41
INT					
RAL	70	3	304	9	33.77
N.W.	9	0	45	1	45.00
B&H	9	1	39	0	-

CAREER: BATTING

	I.	N. O.	R.	H. S.	AV.
TEST					
1ST	15	6	151	42*	16.77
INT					
RAL	4	1	14	6	4.66
N.W.	-	-	-	-	-
B&H	-	-	-	-	-

CAREER: BOWLING

	O.	M.	R.	W.	AV.
TEST					
1ST	480.1	102	1512	44	34.36
INT					
RAL	78	3	331	9	36.77
N.W.	9	0	45	1	45.00
B&H	9	1	39	0	

JAMES, K. D. — Hampshire

Name: Kevan David James
Role: Left-hand bat, left-arm medium bowler
Born: 18 March 1961, Lambeth, South London
Height: 6ft 1/2in **Weight:** 12st 6lbs
Nickname: Jambo, Jaimo
County debut: 1980 (Middlesex), 1985 (Hampshire)
County cap: 1989
1st-Class 50s scored: 10
1st-Class 100s scored: 5
1st-Class 5 w. in innings: 7
One-Day 50s: 2
1st-Class catches: 0 (career 28)
Parents: David and Helen
Wife and date of marriage: Debbie, October 1987
Family links with cricket: Late father played club cricket in North London
Education: Edmonton County High School
Qualifications: 5 O-levels; qualified coach

207

Off-season: 'Recovering from surgery on my lower back and setting up wholesale wine company.'
Overseas tours: England YC tour of Australia 1978–79; West Indies 1979–80
Overseas teams played for: Wellington, New Zealand 1982–83
Other sports followed: Watches American football, follows Spurs
Injuries: Back injury – 'only managed 10 days of cricket.'
Relaxations: DIY and making money
Extras: Released by Middlesex at end of 1984 season and joined Hampshire
Best batting: 162 Hampshire v Glamorgan, Cardiff 1989
Best bowling: 6–22 Hampshire v Australia, Southampton 1985

LAST SEASON: BATTING

	I.	N.O.	R.	H.S.	AV.
TEST					
1ST	2	1	154	104*	154.00
INT					
RAL	1	0	4	4	4.00
N.W.					
B&H	2	0	4	2	2.00

LAST SEASON: BOWLING

	O.	M.	R.	W.	AV.
TEST					
1ST	28	8	74	1	74.00
INT					
RAL	8	0	33	1	33.00
N.W.					
B&H	16	3	70	2	35.00

CAREER: BATTING

	I.	N.O.	R.	H.S.	AV.
TEST					
1ST	121	23	2802	162	28.59
INT					
RAL	45	18	712	66	26.37
N.W.	8	2	132	42	22.00
B&H	17	2	256	45	17.06

CAREER: BOWLING

	O.	M.	R.	W.	AV.
TEST					
1ST	1710.5	403	5019	163	30.79
INT					
RAL	511.1	29	2142	64	33.46
N.W.	113.4	12	472	16	29.50
B&H	215.1	24	822	24	34.25

40. Name the players awarded their Yorkshire county caps in 1990?

41. Who took the most wickets in Minor County cricket?

42. Whose bowling figures of 8 for 58 were the best in the 1990 County Championship?

JAMES, S. P.   Glamorgan

Name: Stephen Peter James
Role: Right-hand bat
Born: 7 September 1967, Lydney
Height: 6ft **Weight:** 12st
Nickname: Jamer, Douggie, Pedro,
Sid, The Doc
County debut: 1985
1000 runs in a season: 1
1st-Class 50s scored: 8
1st-Class 100s scored: 7
One-Day 50s: 3
Place in batting averages: 134th
av. 34.48 (1989 66th av. 35.46)
1st-Class catches: 11 (career 25)
Parents: Peter and Margaret
Marital status: Single
Family links with cricket: Father
played for Gloucestershire 2nd XI
Education: Monmouth School;
University College, Swansea; Cambridge
University
Qualifications: BA (Hons) Classics; BA (Hons) Land Economy
Off-season: Playing and coaching in Zimbabwe
Cricketers particularly admired: Geoff Boycott, Michael Atherton, Graham
Gooch
Other sports followed: All sports, especially Rugby Union
Injuries: 'Injured shoulder tendons at start; strained ligaments in left knee in
mid-season.'
Relaxations: Music, films and videos. 'Like to keep myself fit.'
Extras: Scored maiden century in only second first-class game. Played rugby for
Lydney and Gloucestershire and Cambridge University and was on the substitutes
bench for 1988 and 1989 Varsity matches
Best batting: 151* Cambridge University v Warwickshire, Fenner's 1989

LAST SEASON: BATTING

	I.	N. O.	R.	H. S.	AV.
TEST					
1ST	31	2	1000	131*	34.48
INT					
RAL					
N.W.					
B&H	4	0	168	63	42.00

CAREER: BATTING

	I.	N. O.	R.	H. S.	AV.
TEST					
1ST	71	4	2168	151*	32.35
INT					
RAL	3	0	30	13	10.00
N.W.	2	0	32	26	16.00
B&H	8	0	273	65	34.12

JARVIS, K. B. S.　　Gloucestershire

Name: Kevin Bertram Sidney Jarvis
Role: Right-hand bat, right-arm
fast-medium bowler
Born: 23 April 1953, Dartford,
Kent
Height: 6ft 3in **Weight:** 13st
Nickname: Jarvo, Ferret, KJ
County debut: 1975 (Kent), 1988
(Gloucs)
County cap: 1977 (Kent)
Benefit: 1987 (48,485)
50 wickets in a season: 7
1st-Class 5 w. in innings: 20
1st-Class 10 w. in match: 3
1st-Class catches: 0 (career 59)
Parents: Herbert John and Margaret
Elsie
Wife and date of marriage: Margaret
Anne, 16 September 1978
Children: Simon Martin, 16 April 1985;
Laura Emily, 6 January 1988
Family links with cricket: Son very keen; father played club cricket; Simon Hinks
is a distant relative
Education: Springhead School, Northfleet, Kent; Thames Polytechnic
Qualifications: 6 O-levels, 3 A-levels, NCA coach, ISMA, MAMSA
Cricketers particularly admired: Richard Hadlee, Dennis Lillee
Other sports followed: 'Watch everything except synchronised swimming.'
Extras: Released by Kent at end of 1987 season. Joined Gloucestershire on a

LAST SEASON: BATTING

	I.	N. O.	R.	H. S.	AV.
TEST					
1ST	2	2	1	1*	-
INT					
RAL	-	-	-	-	-
N.W.					
B&H	-	-	-	-	-

LAST SEASON: BOWLING

	O.	M.	R.	W.	AV.
TEST					
1ST	34	3	142	3	47.33
INT					
RAL	14	1	75	0	-
N.W.					
B&H	17	1	87	1	87.00

CAREER: BATTING

	I.	N. O.	R.	H. S.	AV.
TEST					
1ST	199	87	403	32	3.59
INT					
RAL	54	31	82	11	3.56
N.W.	11	5	16	5*	2.66
B&H	24	15	16	4*	1.77

CAREER: BOWLING

	O.	M.	R.	W.	AV.
TEST					
1ST	6324.4	1381	19998	674	29.67
INT					
RAL	1192.3	98	5048	204	24.74
N.W.	259.3	31	931	45	20.68
B&H	549.2	79	1972	87	22.66

two-year contract in 1988. 'Surpassed my previous highest score in 1989 – an achievement thought by many to be the equivalent of running a three-minute mile.' Retired at end of 1990 season

Opinions on cricket: 'There are too many people with too many opinions on cricket.'

Best batting: 32 Gloucestershire v Hampshire, Portsmouth 1989

Best bowling: 8–97 Kent v Worcestershire, Worcester 1978

JARVIS, P. W. Yorkshire

Name: Paul William Jarvis
Role: Right-hand bat, right-arm fast-medium bowler
Born: 29 June 1965, Redcar, North Yorkshire
Height: 5ft 11in **Weight:** 12st 5lbs
Nickname: Jarv, Beaver, Gnasher
County debut: 1981
County cap: 1986
Test debut: 1987–88
Tests: 6
One-Day Internationals: 5
50 wickets in a season: 3
1st-Class 50s scored: 1
1st-Class 5 w. in innings: 18
1st-Class 10 w. in match: 3
Place in batting averages: 234th av. 17.66 (1989 249th av. 11.80)
Place in bowling averages: 78th av. 37.64 (1989 33rd av. 25.31)

Strike rate: 65.72 (career 59.51)
1st-Class catches: 2 (career 34)
Parents: Malcolm and Marjorie
Wife: Wendy
Children: Alexander Michael, 13 July 1989
Family links with cricket: Father has played league cricket for thirty years with Marske CC; brother Andrew played for English Schools U–15s, and also had trials for Northamptonshire and Derbyshire
Education: Bydales Comprehensive School, Marske
Qualifications: 4 O-levels
Overseas tours: England to World Cup, Pakistan, Australia and New Zealand 1987–88; unofficial English team to South Africa 1989–90
Cricketers particularly admired: Dennis Lillee, Richard Hadlee
Other sports followed: Most sports

Injuries: Stress fracture of the shin

Relaxations: Fishing, music, golf, keeping fit

Extras: Youngest player ever to play for Yorkshire in County Championship (16 years, 2 months, 13 days) and youngest player to take hat-trick in JPL and Championship. Played for England YCs v West Indies 1982 and Australia 1983. Banned from Test cricket for joining tour of South Africa

Opinions on cricket: 'Only people actually born in England should be permitted to play for England. County cricket should be divided into two divisions, with 10 teams in each division and promotion and relegation. The Refuge League would also be played in two divisions with the winners and runners up in each division then playing off for the overall champions cup. This system would make the cricket much more interesting for more teams – nearly every team rather than just a few at the end of a season will have something to play for – encouraging better cricket and making it more exciting for the spectators. Four-day cricket should be scrapped.' Regarding the 1989–90 tour of South Africa: 'I would have to play in every Test match at home and away for the next six years to earn as much as 80,000 after tax. As a fast bowler with a history of injuries, I did not think that was possible.'

Best batting: 59* Yorkshire v Nottinghamshire, Trent Bridge 1989

Best bowling: 7–55 Yorkshire v Surrey, Headingley 1986

LAST SEASON: BATTING

	I.	N. O.	R.	H. S.	AV.
TEST					
1ST	16	4	212	43*	17.66
INT					
RAL	5	1	42	28*	10.50
N.W.	1	0	6	6	6.00
B&H	2	1	44	42	44.00

LAST SEASON: BOWLING

	O.	M.	R.	W.	AV.
TEST					
1ST	405.2	68	1393	37	37.64
INT					
RAL	80.5	4	317	19	16.68
N.W.	12	1	58	0	-
B&H	43	3	186	5	37.20

CAREER: BATTING

	I.	N. O.	R.	H. S.	AV.
TEST	9	2	109	29*	15.57
1ST	134	43	1299	59*	14.27
INT	2	1	5	5*	5.00
RAL	36	17	199	29*	10.47
N.W.	7	2	62	16	12.40
B&H	9	2	88	42	12.57

CAREER: BOWLING

	O.	M.	R.	W.	AV.
TEST	224.3	41	708	14	50.57
1ST	3253	657	10464	391	26.76
INT	47.5	4	187	6	31.16
RAL	556	40	2396	117	20.47
N.W.	141.1	16	520	16	32.50
B&H	229	38	776	39	19.89

JEAN-JACQUES, M. Derbyshire

Name: Martin Jean-Jacques
Role: Right-hand bat, right-arm
fast-medium pace bowler
Born: 2 August 1960,
Soufriere, Dominica
Height: 5ft 11in **Weight:** 12st 7lbs
Nickname: JJ
County debut: 1986
1st-Class 50s scored: 1
1st-Class 5 w. in innings: 2
1st-Class 10 w. in match: 1
Place in batting averages: 257th av.
13.37
Place in bowling averages: 112th
av. 44.24
Strike rate: 72.00 (career 59.72)
1st-Class catches: 2 (career 11)
Education: Scotts Head Primary,
Dominica; Aylestone High, London
Career outside cricket: Electrician
Cricketers particularly admired: Michael Holding
Other sports followed: Football
Relaxations: Listening to music – reggae and soul
Extras: Played Minor Counties cricket for Buckinghamshire. On debut for
Derbyshire (v Yorkshire) put on a record 132 with Alan Hill for the 10th wicket
Best batting: 73 Derbyshire v Yorkshire, Sheffield 1986
Best bowling: 8–77 Derbyshire v Kent, Derby 1986

LAST SEASON: BATTING

	I.	N. O.	R.	H. S.	AV.
TEST					
1ST	13	5	107	25	13.37
INT					
RAL	-	-	-	-	-
N.W.					
B&H					

LAST SEASON: BOWLING

	O.	M.	R.	W.	AV.
TEST					
1ST	300	42	1106	25	44.24
INT					
RAL	30	0	180	5	36.00
N.W.					
B&H					

CAREER: BATTING

	I.	N. O.	R.	H. S.	AV.
TEST					
1ST	57	13	546	73	12.40
INT					
RAL	12	1	69	15	6.27
N.W.	5	3	28	16	14.00
B&H	2	1	4	2*	4.00

CAREER: BOWLING

	O.	M.	R.	W.	AV.
TEST					
1ST	975.5	144	3460	98	35.30
INT					
RAL	161	2	896	25	35.84
N.W.	74	7	310	12	25.83
B&H	30	0	164	5	32.80

JESTY, T. E. Lancashire

Name: Trevor Edward Jesty
Role: Right-hand bat, right-arm medium bowler
Born: 2 June 1948, Gosport, Hampshire
Height: 5ft 9in **Weight:** 11st 10lbs
Nickname: Jets
County debut: 1966 (Hampshire), 1985 (Surrey), 1988 (Lancs)
County cap: 1971 (Hampshire), 1985 (Surrey)
Benefit: 1982
One-Day Internationals: 10
1000 runs in a season: 10
50 wickets in a season: 2
1st-Class 50s scored: 110
1st-Class 100s scored: 34
1st-Class 200s scored: 2
1st-Class 5 w. in innings: 19
One-Day 50s: 44
One-Day 100s: 7
Place in batting averages: 90th av. 43.61 (1989 52nd av. 36.78)
1st-Class catches: 6 (career 265 & 1 stumping)
Parents: Aubrey Edward and Sophia
Wife and date of marriage: Jacqueline, 12 September 1970
Children: Graeme Barry, 27 September 1972; Lorna Samantha, 7 November 1976
Family links with cricket: Brother Aubrey, a wicket-keeper and left-hand bat, could have joined Hampshire staff, but decided to continue with his apprenticeship
Education: Privet County Secondary Modern, Gosport

LAST SEASON: BATTING

	I.	N. O.	R.	H. S.	AV.
TEST					
1ST	24	6	785	98	43.61
INT					
RAL	7	1	124	25	20.66
N.W.					
B&H					

LAST SEASON: BOWLING

	O.	M.	R.	W.	AV.
TEST					
1ST	8	3	27	1	27.00
INT					
RAL	4	0	25	1	25.00
N.W.					
B&H					

CAREER: BATTING

	I.	N. O.	R.	H. S.	AV.
TEST					
1ST	775	105	21790	248	32.52
INT	10	4	127	52*	21.16
RAL	268	37	5737	166*	24.83
N.W.	35	2	976	118	29.57
B&H	71	11	2150	105	35.83

CAREER: BOWLING

	O.	M.	R.	W.	AV.
TEST					
1ST	6143	1637	16075	585	27.47
INT	17	0	93	1	93.00
RAL	1304.3	76	6151	249	24.70
N.W.	314	52	1038	39	26.61
B&H	519.4	64	1797	74	24.28

Overseas tours: England to Australia and New Zealand 1982–83
Overseas teams played for: Border 1973–74, and Griqualand West in1974–75 and 1975–76 in South Africa; Canterbury, New Zealand 1979–80
Cricketers particularly admired: Barry Richards
Relaxations: Watching soccer, gardening, golf
Extras: Took him ten years to score maiden first-class century. Missed most of 1980 season through injury. Considered to be most unlucky not to be chosen for England tour of Australia 1982–83, then was called in as a replacement. One of *Wisden's* Five Cricketers of the Year, 1982. Left Hampshire at end of 1984 when not appointed captain. Captaincy of Surrey 1985. Released by Surrey at end of 1987 season and joined Lancashire 1988
Best batting: 248 Hampshire v Cambridge University, Fenner's 1984
Best bowling: 7–75 Hampshire v Worcestershire, Southampton 1976

JOHNSON, P.   Nottinghamshire

Name: Paul Johnson
Role: Right-hand bat, right-arm occasional bowler
Born: 24 April 1965, Newark
Height: 5ft 8in **Weight:** 12st
Nickname: Johno, Dwarf, Gus, Midge
County debut: 1982
County cap: 1986
1000 runs in a season: 4
1st-Class 50s scored: 44
1st-Class 100s scored: 17
One-Day 50s: 14
One-Day 100s: 5
Place in batting averages: 118th av. 37.95 (1989 112th av. 28.75)
1st-Class catches: 14 (career 119 & 1 stumping)
Parents: Donald Edward and Joyce
Marital status: Separated
Family links with cricket: Father played local cricket and is a qualified coach

Education: Grove Comprehensive School, Newark
Qualifications: 9 CSEs, senior coaching certificate
Career outside cricket: 'Varies!'
Off-season: 'Coaching and looking for a job which might be beneficial after my cricket career.'
Cricketers particularly admired: 'Clive Rice and Jimmy Cook – both great players

who always have time to talk to players and the public.'

Other sports followed: Watches ice-hockey (Nottingham Panthers), football (Forest and County), golf

Injuries: Broken right thumb – missed end of season, strained hamstring

Relaxations: 'Listening to music, crosswords and reading autobiographies.'

Extras: Played for English Schools in 1980–81 and England YC 1982 and 1983. Youngest player ever to join the Nottinghamshire CCC staff. Made 235 for Notting-hamshire 2nd XI, July 1982, aged 17. Won Man of Match award in first NatWest game (101* v Staffordshire); missed 1985 final due to appendicitis

Opinions on cricket: 'Who would take any notice?'

Best batting: 165* Nottinghamshire v Northamptonshire, Trent Bridge 1990

Best bowling: 1–9 Nottinghamshire v Oxford University, Trent Bridge 1984

LAST SEASON: BATTING

	I.	N. O.	R.	H. S.	AV.
TEST					
1ST	43	3	1518	165*	37.95
INT					
RAL	17	1	668	114	41.75
N.W.	2	0	62	48	31.00
B&H	6	1	258	104*	51.60

CAREER: BATTING

	I.	N. O.	R.	H. S.	AV.
TEST					
1ST	280	26	8645	165*	34.03
INT					
RAL	96	11	2172	114	25.55
N.W.	17	2	395	101*	26.33
B&H	27	3	568	104*	23.66

JONES, A. N. Sussex

Name: Adrian Nicholas Jones
Role: Left-hand bat, right-arm fast bowler, outfielder
Born: 22 July 1961, Woking
Height: 6ft 2in **Weight:** 14st
Nickname: Quincy, Jonah, Billy
County debut: 1981 (Sussex), 1987 (Somerset)
County cap: 1986 (Sussex), 1987 (Somerset)
50 wickets in a season: 4
1st-Class 5 w. in innings: 10
1st-Class 10 w. in match: 1
Place in bowling averages: 68th av. 36.69 (1989 58th av. 28.36)
Strike rate: 61.35 (career 53.74)
1st-Class catches: 6 (career 40)
Parents: William Albert and Emily Doris

Wife and date of marriage: Elizabeth Antoinette, 1 October 1988

Children: Amy Elizabeth, 2 May 1990
Family links with cricket: Father and brother, Glynne, both fine club cricketers
Education: Forest Grange Preparatory School; Seaford College
Qualifications: 8 O-levels, 2 A-levels, NCA coaching qualification, financial planning and advising qualifications
Career outside cricket: Financial consultant/adviser
Off-season: 'Working for Jarvis-Allen Ltd.'
Overseas teams played for: Border 1981–82; Orange Free State 1986
Cricketers particularly admired: Imran Khan, Geoff Arnold, Garth le Roux, Jimmy Cook, Chris Tavare, Tony Pigott
Other sports followed: 'Play golf badly; hockey slightly better; rugby like an animal.'
Injuries: 'Thigh injury after colliding with boundary board.'
Relaxations: 'UB40, watching Laurel and Hardy films, walking, eating, good wine and port.'
Extras: Played for England YC in 1981. Left Sussex to join Somerset at end of 1986 season, but returned for start of 1991 season
Opinions on cricket: 'There should be an alternative system for the awarding of a benefit rather than the present haphazard method. Perhaps an endowment scheme taken out when the player is capped. Too much notice is taken of averages.'
Best batting: 43* Somerset v Leicestershire, Taunton 1989
Best bowling: 7–30 Somerset v Hampshire, Southampton 1988

LAST SEASON: BATTING

	I.	N. O.	R.	H. S.	AV.
TEST					
1ST	9	5	100	41	25.00
INT					
RAL	3	0	12	10	4.00
N.W.	-	-	-	-	-
B&H	3	1	11	7	5.50

LAST SEASON: BOWLING

	O.	M.	R.	W.	AV.
TEST					
1ST	572.4	92	2055	56	36.69
INT					
RAL	50	1	254	8	31.75
N.W.	16	1	84	1	84.00
B&H	46.5	3	223	9	24.77

CAREER: BATTING

	I.	N. O.	R.	H. S.	AV.
TEST					
1ST	120	51	814	43*	11.79
INT					
RAL	25	16	150	37	16.66
N.W.	4	2	13	7	6.50
B&H	13	5	78	25	9.75

CAREER: BOWLING

	O.	M.	R.	W.	AV.
TEST					
1ST	3045.5	518	10480	340	30.82
INT					
RAL	498.1	28	2498	117	21.35
N.W.	105.5	14	442	14	31.57
B&H	224	24	966	50	19.32

JOSEPH, L. A.   Hampshire

Name: Linden Anthony Joseph
Role: Right-hand bat, right-arm
fast-medium bowler
Born: 8 January 1969, Georgetown,
Guyana
Height: 6ft 1in
County debut: 1990
1st-Class 50s scored: 2
1st-Class catches: 1 (career 7)
Education: St Ambers School,
Georgetown
Off-season: Playing cricket in
West Indies
Overseas tours: Young West
Indies to Zimbabwe 1989–90
Overseas teams played for: Guyana
and Berbice (debut 1985–86)
Extras: Signed for 1990 on one-year
contract on recommendation of
Malcolm Marshall. Released at end of
season

Best batting: 69* Hampshire v Oxford University, The Parks 1990
Best bowling: 4–43 Guyana v Trinidad & Tobago, Point-a-Pierre 1988–89

LAST SEASON: BATTING

	I.	N. O.	R.	H. S.	AV.
TEST					
1ST	5	4	152	69*	152.00
INT					
RAL					
N.W.					
B&H	-	-	-	-	-

LAST SEASON: BOWLING

	O.	M.	R.	W.	AV.
TEST					
1ST	102	16	462	7	66.00
INT					
RAL					
N.W.					
B&H	11	1	38	0	-

CAREER: BATTING

	I.	N. O.	R.	H. S.	AV.
TEST					
1ST	20	6	347	69*	24.78
INT					
RAL					
N.W.					
B&H	-	-	-	-	-

CAREER: BOWLING

	O.	M.	R.	W.	AV.
TEST					
1ST	416.1	55	1565	46	34.02
INT					
RAL					
N.W.					
B&H	11	1	38	0	-

KALLICHARRAN, A. I. Warwickshire

Name: Alvin Isaac Kallicharran
Role: Left-hand bat, right-arm
off-spin bowler
Born: 21 March 1949, Guyana
Height: 5ft 4in
Nickname: Kalli
County debut: 1971
County cap: 1972
Benefit: 1983 (34,094)
Test debut: 1971–72
Tests: 66
One-Day Internationals: 31
1000 runs in a season: 12
1st-Class 50s scored: 160
1st-Class 100s scored: 87
1st-Class 200s scored: 6
1st-Class 5 w. in innings: 1
One-Day 50s: 61
One-Day 100s: 12
Place in batting averages: 201st av.
24.55 (1989 126th av. 26.52)
1st-Class catches: 5 (career 323)
Marital status: Married
Children: One son, Rohan

Family links with cricket: Brother, Derek Isaac, played for Guyana
Overseas tours: With West Indies to England in 1973, 1976, 1980; India, Sri Lanka and Pakistan 1974–75; Australia 1975–76 and 1979–80; India and Sri Lanka 1978–79; New Zealand 1979–80; Pakistan 1980; unofficial West Indies team to South Africa 1982–83, 1983–84
Overseas teams played for: Guyana 1966–81; Queensland in 1977–78; Transvaal 1981–84; Orange Free State 1984–88
Extras: Scored 100* and 101 in first two innings in Test matches v New Zealand in 1971. Signed for World Series Cricket but resigned before playing. He has made his home in England, but only qualified as a non-overseas player in 1989. With Geoff Humpage took part in record English 4th wicket stand of 470 v Lancashire at Southport in July 1982, making 230*. Top of Warwickshire batting averages in 1981, 1982 and 1983. Banned from playing in West Indies for going to South Africa. One of *Wisden's* Five Cricketers of the Year, 1982. Has captained both Transvaal and Orange Free State. Retired from first-class cricket at the end of 1990 season
Opinions on cricket: 'There is so much hypocrisy from politicians over South Africa. Sport should always be free of political pressure. If sportsmen were left alone to maintain their links with all other nations, this world might be a better place for it. Sport brings people of all colours and persuasions together – it doesn't drive people

219

apart as political extremists do. Sport allows ordinary people to see we are all the same underneath.'

Best batting: 243* Warwickshire v Glamorgan, Edgbaston 1983
Best bowling: 5–45 Transvaal v Western Province, Cape Town 1982–83

LAST SEASON: BATTING

	I.	N. O.	R.	H. S.	AV.
TEST					
1ST	10	1	221	72	24.55
INT					
RAL	6	1	210	76	42.00
N.W.	1	0	41	41	41.00
B&H	4	0	77	32	19.25

LAST SEASON: BOWLING

	O.	M.	R.	W.	AV.
TEST					
1ST					
INT					
RAL					
N.W.					
B&H					

CAREER: BATTING

	I.	N. O.	R.	H. S.	AV.
TEST	109	10	4399	187	44.43
1ST	725	76	28251	243*	43.53
INT	28	4	826	78	34.41
RAL	178	19	5039	104	31.69
N.W.	30	3	1372	206	50.81
B&H	64	7	2392	122*	41.96

CAREER: BOWLING

	O.	M.	R.	W.	AV.
TEST	67.5	14	158	4	39.50
1ST	992	166	3872	80	48.40
INT	17.3	3	64	3	21.33
RAL	165.1	5	914	14	65.28
N.W.	92.4	9	319	14	22.78
B&H	22	0	111	0	

KELLEHER, D. J. M. Kent

Name: Daniel John Michael Kelleher
Role: Right-hand bat, right-arm medium bowler, outfielder
Born: 5 May 1966, London
Height: 6ft **Weight:** 12st 13lbs
Nickname: Donk, Shots
County debut: 1987
1st-Class 50s scored: 2
1st-Class 5 w. in innings: 2
Place in batting averages: 262nd
av. 12.62 (1989 203rd av. 17.63)
1st-Class catches: 2 (career 8)
Parents: John and Joan
Marital status: Single
Family links with cricket: Uncle played county cricket for Surrey and Northamptonshire. Father played club cricket
Education: St Mary's Grammar School, Sidcup; Erith College of Technology
Qualifications: O-levels

Cricketers particularly admired: Ian Botham, David Gower, Richard Davis
Other sports followed: Rugby, American football, tennis, golf, skiing
Relaxations: Watching TV, music, 'watching Richard Davis bat.'
Extras: Played rugby and cricket for Kent schools
Opinions on cricket: 'Too much cricket is played.'
Best batting: 53* Kent v Derbyshire, Dartford 1989
Best bowling: 6–109 Kent v Somerset, Bath 1987

LAST SEASON: BATTING

	I.	N. O.	R.	H. S.	AV.
TEST					
1ST	8	0	101	44	12.62
INT					
RAL	1	0	2	2	2.00
N.W.	1	0	21	21	21.00
B&H					

LAST SEASON: BATTING

	O.	M.	R.	W.	AV.
TEST					
1ST	112.5	20	398	7	56.85
INT					
RAL	15.5	2	70	1	70.00
N.W.	9	3	16	3	5.33
B&H					

CAREER: BATTING

	I.	N. O.	R.	H. S.	AV.
TEST					
1ST	41	5	526	53*	14.61
INT					
RAL	11	2	55	19	6.11
N.W.	2	1	21	21	21.00
B&H	3	3	15	11*	–

CAREER: BOWLING

	O.	M.	R.	W.	AV.
TEST					
1ST	791.4	178	2486	74	33.59
INT					
RAL	145.5	10	556	11	50.54
N.W.	26.2	5	95	5	19.00
B&H	76	7	269	6	44.83

43. What did Ashley Metcalfe, David Ward and Alan Butcher have in common last season?

44. Who was the first man to hit four consecutive sixes in one Test over?

45. Who captained New Zealand v England last season?

KELLETT, S. A. Yorkshire

Name: Simon Andrew Kellett
Role: Opening bat, occasional
right-arm medium bowler
Born: 16 October 1967, Mirfield
Height: 6ft 2in **Weight:** 13st
Nickname: Kell
County debut: 1989
1st-class 50s scored: 6
Place in batting averages: 158th av.
27.82
1st-Class catches: 8 (career 9)
Parents: Brian and Valerie
Marital status: Single
Family links with cricket: Father
played local league cricket
Education: Whitcliffe Mount High
School; Huddersfield Technical College
Qualifications: 2 O-levels (Maths and
Economics); Sports Management course
Off-season: 'Working for Trust Motors
in Bradford, keeping fit and watching
Bradford Northern RLFC.'

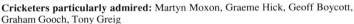

Cricketers particularly admired: Martyn Moxon, Graeme Hick, Geoff Boycott,
Graham Gooch, Tony Greig
Other sports followed: Rugby League, horse racing, football (Bradford City)
Injuries: Viral infection (missed four weeks); broken finger (three weeks)
Relaxations: 'Going out for meals with girlfriend Sarah, watching sport, playing
golf
Extras: Captained NAYC against MCC; captained Yorkshire U–19s to Cambridge
Festival win; was out to first ball in first-class cricket
Opinions on cricket: 'I think the move to one overseas player for each county will
be good for the game.'
Best batting: 75* Yorkshire v Warwickshire, Sheffield 1990

LAST SEASON: BATTING	I.	N. O.	R.	H. S.	AV.
TEST					
1ST	28	3	774	75*	30.96
INT					
RAL	4	0	70	32	17.50
N.W.	1	0	0	0	0.00
B&H	3	0	96	45	32.00

CAREER: BATTING	I.	N. O.	R.	H. S.	AV.
TEST					
1ST	31	3	779	75*	27.82
INT					
RAL	4	0	70	32	17.50
N.W.	1	0	0	0	0.00
B&H	3	0	96	45	32.00

KENDRICK, N. M. Surrey

Name: Neil Michael Kendrick
Role: Right-hand bat, slow left-arm
bowler, gully fielder
Born: 11 November 1967, Bromley
Height: 5ft 11in **Weight:** 11st 7lbs
Nickname: Kendo, Rat, Merson
County debut: 1988
1st-class 50s scored: 1
Place in batting averages: 250th av.
15.50
Place in bowling averages: 122nd av.
47.76
Strike rate: 83.52 (career 82.82)
1st-Class catches: 14 (career 18)
Parents: Michael Hall and Anne
Patricia
Marital status: Single
Family links with cricket: Father
plays club cricket for Old Wilsonians,
and sister has represented Kent Ladies
Education: Hayes Primary; Wilsons
Grammar School

Qualifications: 7 O-levels, 1 A-level; coaching certificate
Career outside cricket: Working for office equipment company
Cricketers particularly admired: Phil Edmonds, Bishen Bedi, 'for the way they
made it look so easy'
Other sports followed: 'Support Arsenal but saw a lot of Charlton last year.'
Injuries: Inflammation of joint in left shoulder

LAST SEASON: BATTING

	I.	N.O.	R.	H.S.	AV.
TEST					
1ST	12	4	124	52*	15.50
INT					
RAL	1	1	2	2*	-
N.W.					
B&H					

LAST SEASON: BOWLING

	O.	M.	R.	W.	AV.
TEST					
1ST	348	66	1194	25	47.76
INT					
RAL	3	0	20	0	-
N.W.					
B&H					

CAREER: BATTING

	I.	N.O.	R.	H.S.	AV.
TEST					
1ST	16	6	149	52*	14.90
INT					
RAL	1	1	2	2*	-
N.W.					
B&H					

CAREER: BOWLING

	O.	M.	R.	W.	AV.
TEST					
1ST	438.5	94	1430	32	44.68
INT					
RAL	3	0	20	0	-
N.W.					
B&H					

Relaxations: 'Listening to music – mainly soul plus Stone Roses and Happy Mondays.'

Opinions on cricket: 'Please can we have four-day cricket. The pitches must remain good, but the balls have too small a seam. As a spinner they are very difficult to grip.'

Best batting: 52* Surrey v Middlesex, Lord's 1990

Best bowling: 4–110 Surrey v Kent, Guildford 1990

KRIKKEN, K. M.   Derbyshire

Name: Karl Matthew Krikken

Role: Right-hand bat, wicket-keeper

Born: 9 April 1969, Bolton

Height: 5ft 10in **Weight:** 12st 6lbs

Nickname: Krikk, Wizard

County debut: 1987 (Sunday League), 1989 (first-class)

1st-class 50s scored: 2

Place in batting averages: 231st av. 18.07

Parents: Brian and Irene

Marital status: Engaged to Liz

Family links with cricket: Father played for Lancashire and Worcestershire in late 1960s as wicket-keeper

Education: Horwich Parish Church School, Rivington; Blackrod High School

Qualifications: 6 O-levels, 3 A-levels; qualified coach

Off-season: Playing in Dunedin, New Zealand

Overseas teams played for: Griqualand West, South Africa 1988–89

Cricketers particularly admired: Alan Knott, Bob Taylor, Rod Marsh

Other sports followed: Football (Wigan Athletic), Rugby League (Wigan)

Injuries: Left cartilage torn in early season

Relaxations: Music, exercise, most sports

Extras: Played first first-class game in South Africa as an overseas professional. Wicket-keeper with most dismissals in 1990 season

Best batting: 77* Derbyshire v Somerset, Taunton 1990

	I.	N. O.	R.	H. S.	AV.
TEST					
1ST	29	2	488	77*	18.07
INT					
RAL	2	0	14	14	7.00
N.W.					
B&H					

LAST SEASON: WICKET-KEEPING

	CT	ST			
TEST					
1ST	60	3			
INT					
RAL	2	0			
N.W.					
B&H					

CAREER: BATTING

	I.	N. O.	R.	H. S.	AV.
TEST					
1ST	39	5	596	77*	17.52
INT					
RAL	3	0	30	16	10.00
N.W.					
B&H					

CAREER: WICKET-KEEPING

	CT	ST			
TEST					
1ST	65	4			
INT					
RAL	3	0			
N.W.					
B&H					

KUIPER, A. P. Derbyshire

Name: Adrian Paul Kuiper
Role: Right-hand bat, right-arm medium bowler
Born: 24 August 1959, Johannesburg
Height: 5ft 11in **Weight:** 13st 8lbs
Nickname: Kuips
County debut: 1990
1st-Class 50s scored: 32
1st-Class 100s scored: 5
1st-Class 5 w. in innings: 4
One-Day 50s: 4
One-Day 100s: 1
Place in batting averages: 203rd av. 23.94
Place in bowling averages: 45th av. 32.75
Strike rate: 62.75 (career 55.62)
1st-Class catches: 10 (career 76)
Parents: Henri and Ghani
Wife and date of marriage: Jean, 8 September 1984
Children: Clare, 11 April 1988; Sarah, 29 January 1990
Education: Diocesan College, Cape Town; University of Stellenbosch
Qualifications: Agricultural Management
Career outside cricket: Fruit farmer
Off-season: Playing cricket in South Africa
Overseas teams played for: Western Province 1978–90 and South Africa 1982–90
Cricketers particularly admired: Clive Rice, Graeme Pollock

Other sports followed: Rugby and football

Relaxations: 'Reading, the sea, sport.'

Extras: Played for South African XI v West Indies, Australia and England. Top-scored in unofficial Test v Mike Gatting's side. Declined Derbyshire's offer to return in 1991

Best batting: 161* Western Province v Natal, Durban 1989–90

Best bowling: 6–55 Western Province v Northern Transvaal, Pretoria 1983–84

LAST SEASON: BATTING

	I.	N. O.	R.	H. S.	AV.
TEST					
1ST	17	0	407	68	23.94
INT					
RAL	18	4	516	74	36.85
N.W.	2	0	74	49	37.00
B&H	4	2	185	106*	92.50

LAST SEASON: BOWLING

	O.	M.	R.	W.	AV.
TEST					
1ST	125.3	29	393	12	32.75
INT					
RAL	93.4	1	598	20	29.90
N.W.	16	1	45	1	45.00
B&H	37.4	0	235	3	78.33

CAREER: BATTING

	I.	N. O.	R.	H. S.	AV.
TEST					
1ST	176	23	5058	161*	33.05
INT					
RAL	18	4	516	74	36.85
N.W.	2	0	74	49	37.00
B&H	4	2	185	106*	92.50

CAREER: BOWLING

	O.	M.	R.	W.	AV.
TEST					
1ST	1483.2	311	4351	160	27.19
INT					
RAL	93.4	1	598	20	29.90
N.W.	16	1	45	1	45.00
B&H	37.4	0	235	3	78.33

46. What have Gower, Greenidge and Gooch got in common?

47. How old was Tendulkar when he first played in a Test?

48. Who scored Test cricket's first triple century?

LAMB, A. J.
Northamptonshire

Name: Allan Joseph Lamb
Role: Right-hand bat, right-arm
medium bowler, county captain
Born: 20 June 1954, Langebaanweg,
Cape Province, South Africa
Height: 5ft 8in **Weight:** 12st 7lbs
Nickname: Lambie, Legger, Joe
County debut: 1978
County cap: 1978
Benefit: 1988 (134,000)
Test debut: 1982
Tests: 67
One-Day Internationals: 99
1000 runs in a season: 10
1st-Class 50s scored: 127
1st-Class 100s scored: 66
1st-Class 200s scored: 2
One-Day 50s: 67
One-Day 100s: 14
Place in batting averages: 18th av.

63.84 (1989 16th av. 52.35)
1st-Class catches: 9 (career 274)
Parents: Michael and Joan
Wife and date of marriage: Lindsay St Leger, 8 December 1979
Children: Katie-Ann and Richard
Family links with cricket: Father and brother played in the B section of the Currie
Cup
Education: Wynberg Boys' High School; Abbotts College
Qualifications: Matriculation
Off-season: Touring Australia with England as vice-captain
Overseas tours: With England to Australia and New Zealand 1982–83; New
Zealand and Pakistan 1983–84; India and Australia 1984–85; West Indies 1985–86;
Australia 1986–87; World Cup in India and Pakistan 1987–88; India and West Indies
1989–90; Australia 1990–91
Overseas teams played for: Western Province 1972–81; Orange Free State
1987–88
Cricketers particularly admired: Mike Procter, Dennis Lillee
Other sports followed: Tennis, golf, rugby and soccer
Injuries: Torn hamstring – out for three weeks
Relaxations: Salmon fishing
Extras: Was primarily a bowler when he first played school cricket in South Africa.
Made first-class debut for Western Province in 1972–73. Top of first-class batting
averages in 1980. One of *Wisden's* Five Cricketers of the Year, 1980. Qualified to

play for England in 1982. Appointed Northamptonshire captain 1989. Captained England in Tests v West Indies in 1989–90 and v Australia in 1990–91 after injuries to Graham Gooch. Made a century in his first Test as captain v West Indies at Bridgetown. Hit three 100s in consecutive Tests v West Indies 1984

Opinions on cricket: 'The quicker we play four-day cricket, the better for English cricket.'

Best batting: 294 Orange Free State v Eastern Province, Bloemfontein 1987–88

Best bowling: 1–1 Northamptonshire v Derbyshire, Derby 1978

LAST SEASON: BATTING

	I.	N.O.	R.	H.S.	AV.
TEST	11	1	493	139	49.30
1ST	18	3	1103	235	73.53
INT	4	0	81	56	20.25
RAL	9	0	248	70	27.55
N.W.	5	1	195	68*	48.75
B&H	1	0	34	34	34.00

LAST SEASON: BOWLING

	O.	M.	R.	W.	AV.
TEST					
1ST					
INT					
RAL					
N.W.					
B&H					

CAREER: BATTING

	I.	N.O.	R.	H.S.	AV.
TEST	118	10	3981	139	36.86
1ST	486	82	20653	294	51.12
INT	95	16	3305	118	41.83
RAL	129	18	4194	132*	37.78
N.W.	35	2	1317	103	39.90
B&H	51	9	2023	126*	48.16

CAREER: BOWLING

	O.	M.	R.	W.	AV.
TEST	5	1	23	1	23.00
1ST	41.1	10	141	5	28.20
INT	1	0	3	0	-
RAL					
N.W.	1.2	0	12	1	12.00
B&H	1	0	11	1	11.00

49. Who captained India v England last season?

50. Who is the President of MCC?

51. Who are the two new stands at Lord's named after?

LAMPITT, S. R. Worcestershire

Name: Stuart Richard Lampitt
Role: Right-hand bat, right-arm
fast-medium bowler
Born: 29 July 1966, Wolverhampton
Height: 5ft 11in **Weight:** 13st
Nickname: Jed
County debut: 1985
County cap: 1989
50 wickets in a season: 1
1st-Class 5 w. in innings: 4
Place in batting averages: 229th av.
18.73
Place in bowling averages: 44th av.
32.56 (1989 4th av. 16.96)
Strike rate: 58.50 (career 56.91)
1st-Class catches: 11 (career 22)
Parents: Joseph Charles and Muriel
Ann
Marital status: Single
Family links with cricket: 'Dad talks a
good game.'
Education: Kingswinford Secondary School; Dudley College of Technology
Qualifications: 7 O-levels; Diploma in Business Studies ('just')
Off-season: 'Having a winter's rest in Worcester.'
Cricketers particularly admired: Ian Botham, Viv Richards, Richard Hadlee
Other sports followed: 'All except show-jumping and bowls.'
Injuries: Strained intercostal muscles – out for three weeks
Relaxations: 'Watching TV, listening to music, going out with mates for a few

LAST SEASON: BATTING

	I.	N. O.	R.	H. S.	AV.
TEST					
1ST	24	5	356	45*	18.73
INT					
RAL	9	4	78	25*	15.60
N.W.	1	1	3	3*	-
B&H	4	1	52	41	17.33

LAST SEASON: BOWLING

	O.	M.	R.	W.	AV.
TEST					
1ST	565.3	98	1889	58	32.56
INT					
RAL	89	3	491	19	25.84
N.W.	35.4	2	128	8	16.00
B&H	55	4	250	6	41.66

CAREER: BATTING

	I.	N. O.	R.	H. S.	AV.
TEST					
1ST	47	11	577	46	16.02
INT					
RAL	15	6	138	25*	15.33
N.W.	3	2	12	9*	12.00
B&H	4	1	52	41	17.33

CAREER: BOWLING

	O.	M.	R.	W.	AV.
TEST					
1ST	872.4	167	2710	92	29.45
INT					
RAL	161	4	884	34	26.00
N.W.	63.4	3	242	12	20.16
B&H	55	4	250	6	41.66

drinks, playing golf.'

Extras: Took five wickets and made 42 for Stourbridge in Final of the Cockspur Cup at Lord's in 1987. 'Once took five wickets in an innings in 1990!'

Opinions on cricket: 'After last season is it worth having an opinion?'

Best batting: 46 Worcestershire v Warwickshire, Worcester 1989

Best bowling: 5–32 Worcestershire v Kent, Worcester 1989

LARKINS, W.   Northamptonshire

Name: Wayne Larkins
Role: Right-hand bat, right-arm medium bowler
Born: 22 November 1953
Height: 5ft 11in **Weight:** 12st
Nickname: Ned
County debut: 1972
County cap: 1976
Benefit: 1986
Test debut: 1979–80
Tests: 10
One-Day Internationals: 18
1000 runs in a season: 11
1st-Class 50s scored: 92
1st-Class 100s scored: 49
1st-Class 200s scored: 3
1st-Class 5 w. in innings: 1
One-Day 50s: 47
One-Day 100s: 16
Place in batting averages: 178th av. 28.04 (1989 31st av. 42.54)
1st-Class catches: 8 (career 234)
Parents: Mavis (father deceased)
Wife and date of marriage: Jane Elaine, 22 March 1975
Children: Philippa Jane, 30 May 1981
Family links with cricket: Father was umpire. Brother, Melvin, played for Bedford Town for many years
Education: Bushmead, Eaton Socon, Huntingdon
Off-season: Touring with England in Australia
Overseas tours: England to Australia and India 1979–80; India and Sri Lanka 1981–82; India and West Indies 1989–90; Australia 1990–91; unofficial English team to South Africa 1981–82
Other sports followed: Golf, football (was on Notts County's books), squash
Relaxations: Gardening
Extras: Banned from Test cricket for three years for joining rebel tour of South

Africa in 1982. Recalled to Test team in 1986 but withdrew due to thumb injury and missed another Test recall in 1987 because of a football injury. Eventually returned to Test cricket in the West Indies in 1989–90, nine years after his last appearance

Best batting : 252 Northamptonshire v Glamorgan, Cardiff 1983
Best bowling : 5–59 Northamptonshire v Worcestershire, Worcester 1984

LAST SEASON: BATTING

	I.	N. O.	R.	H. S.	AV.
TEST					
1ST	25	0	701	207	28.04
INT					
RAL	11	0	334	109	30.36
N.W.	4	0	128	52	32.00
B&H	3	0	177	111	59.00

LAST SEASON: BOWLING

	O.	M.	R.	W.	AV.
TEST					
1ST	10	1	45	0	-
INT					
RAL	13	0	80	2	40.00
N.W.					
B&H					

CAREER: BATTING

	I.	N. O.	R.	H. S.	AV.
TEST	19	1	352	54	19.55
1ST	674	41	21926	252	34.65
INT	17	0	427	124	25.11
RAL	222	13	5725	172*	27.39
N.W.	41	3	1397	121*	36.76
B&H	66	3	2088	132	33.14

CAREER: BOWLING

	O.	M.	R.	W.	AV.
TEST	569.1	120	1852	42	44.09
1ST					
INT	2	0	21	0	-
RAL	338.5	9	1679	57	29.45
N.W.	109.1	9	274	4	68.50
B&H	112.3	4	444	16	27.75

LAWRENCE, D. V.   Gloucestershire

Name: David Valentine Lawrence
Role: Right-hand bat, right-arm fast bowler
Born: 28 January 1964, Gloucester
Height: 6ft 3in **Weight:** 15st 7lbs
Nickname: Syd, Bruno
County debut: 1981
County cap: 1985
Test debut: 1988
Tests: 1
50 wickets in a season: 4
1st-Class 50s scored: 1
1st-Class 5 w. in innings: 16
Place in bowling averages: 51st av. 34.12 (1989 90th av. 34.88)
Strike rate: 51.36 (career 53.82)
1st-Class catches: 7 (career 40)
Parents: Joseph and Joyce
Education: Linden School, Gloucester
Qualifications: 3 CSEs
Overseas tours: England B to Sri Lanka 1986; England A to Zimbabwe 1989–90

Cricketers particularly admired: Viv Richards
Other sports followed: Rugby football. 'Was offered terms to play professional Rugby League winter 1985–86, but turned them down.' Also tried his hand at American football in 1990–91
Relaxations: 'Like listening to jazz and funk, and dancing.'
Extras: Called up to join the England A tour in 1989–90 when Chris Lewis joined the senior squad in the West Indies. Took a hat-trick v Nottinghamshire in 1990
Best batting: 65* Gloucestershire v Glamorgan, Swansea 1987
Best bowling: 7–47 Gloucestershire v Surrey, Cheltenham 1988

LAST SEASON: BATTING

	I.	N. O.	R.	H. S.	AV.
TEST					
1ST	24	3	163	35	7.76
INT					
RAL	2	1	2	1*	2.00
N.W.	1	0	0	0	0.00
B&H	-	-	-	-	-

LAST SEASON: BOWLING

	O.	M.	R.	W.	AV.
TEST					
1ST	497.3	53	1979	58	34.12
INT					
RAL	45	1	223	12	18.58
N.W.	14	0	77	1	77.00
B&H	11	3	36	1	36.00

CAREER: BATTING

	I.	N. O.	R.	H. S.	AV.
TEST	1	0	4	4	4.00
1ST	176	34	1372	65*	9.66
INT					
RAL	16	6	97	21*	9.70
N.W.	8	3	4	2*	0.80
B&H	9	5	43	22*	10.75

CAREER: BOWLING

	O.	M.	R.	W.	AV.
TEST	36	9	111	3	37.00
1ST	3759	532	14061	420	33.47
INT					
RAL	350	5	1830	64	28.59
N.W.	163.4	14	698	21	33.23
B&H	225	17	913	31	29.45

LEATHERDALE, D. A. Worcestershire

Name: David Anthony Leatherdale
Role: Right-hand bat, right-arm medium bowler
Born: 26 November 1967, Bradford
Height: 5ft 10 1/2in **Weight:** 11st
Nickname: Lugs, Spock
County debut: 1988
1st-Class 50s scored: 2
One-Day 50s: 2
Place in batting averages: 194th av. 18.59 (1989 237th av. 13.28)
1st-Class catches: 2 (career 18)
Parents: Paul Anthony and Rosalyn
Wife's name: Vanessa
Children: Callum Edward, 6 July 1990
Family links with cricket: Brother plays in Bradford League. Brother-in-law played for Young England in 1979. Father played representative cricket in Yorkshire
Education: Bolton Royd Primary School; Pudsey Grammar School
Qualifications: 8 O-levels, 2 A-levels; NCA coaching award (stage 1)
Cricketers particularly admired: Mark Scott, George Batty, Peter Kippax
Other sports followed: Golf, football
Relaxations: Listening to music, writing letters
Opinions on cricket: 'A full circuit of 2nd XI cricket will make it easier for 2nd XI players to move up into first-class cricket.'
Best batting: 70 Worcestershire v Lancashire, Kidderminster 1990
Best bowling: 1–12 Worcestershire v Northamptonshire, Worcester 1988

LAST SEASON: BATTING

	I.	N. O.	R.	H. S.	AV.
TEST					
1ST	6	0	154	70	25.66
INT					
RAL	9	1	70	35	8.75
N.W.	-	-	-	-	-
B&H	-	-	-	-	-

CAREER: BATTING

	I.	N. O.	R.	H. S.	AV.
TEST					
1ST	29	2	502	70	18.59
INT					
RAL	19	4	287	62*	19.13
N.W.	6	1	94	43	18.80
B&H	-	-	-	-	-

LEFEBVRE, R. P.   Somerset

Name: Roland Phillippe Lefebvre
Role: Right-hand bat, right-arm medium bowler
Born: 7 February 1963, Rotterdam
Height: 6ft 1in **Weight:** 11st 10lbs
Nickname: Tulip, Lloyds, Clogsy
County debut: 1990
1st-Class 50s scored: 1
1st-Class 5 w. in innings: 1
Place in batting averages: 243rd av. 16.46
Place in bowling averages: 107th av. 41.32
Strike rate: 97.96 (career 97.96)
1st-Class catches: 8 (career 8)
Parents: Pierre Joseph Ernest
Marital status: Single
Family links with cricket: Father still plays veterans cricket; brother Ernest plays for VOC Rotterdam and has represented Holland; brother Boudewijn played for same club

Education: Montessori Lyceum, Rotterdam; Hague Academy of Physiotherapy
Qualifications: Qualified physiotherapist
Career outside cricket: 'Worked as a physiotherapist in several private practices as a relief worker.'
Off-season: 'Playing cricket in New Zealand for Canterbury CA, playing club cricket and working as a physio.'
Overseas tours: Holland tours to England, Canada, Denmark, New Zealand, Barbados, Zimbabwe and Dubai
Overseas teams played for: VOC Rotterdam, Flamingos
Cricketers particularly admired: Anton Bakker, Rob van Weelde, Renee Schoonheim, Dick Abed
Other sports followed: Soccer, golf, cycling, speed skating particularly and most other sports
Injuries: 'Broken finger, but carried on playing with it.'
Relaxations: 'Playing the piano, music of various kinds, golf, travelling, South East Asia.'
Extras: More than 70 caps for Holland. Played in 1986 and 1990 ICC Trophy competitions – voted player of tournament 1990; was a member of the Dutch team that beat England (captained by Peter Roebuck) in 1989
Opinions on cricket: 'The 1990 season hasn't shown a fair contest between bat and ball. There has to be something done either to the ball or the pitches. A real effort

has to be made by the TCCB to allow Holland to play in either the B & H or the NatWest Trophy. It is also necessary for Holland to have a grass wicket so that they can play at home.'

Best batting: 53 Somerset v Northamptonshire, Taunton 1990
Best bowling: 5–30 Somerset v Gloucestershire, Taunton 1990

LAST SEASON / CAREER: BATTING					
	I.	N. O.	R.	H. S.	AV.
TEST					
1ST	16	3	214	53	16.46
INT					
RAL	7	2	86	28	17.20
N.W.	-	-	-	-	-
B&H	3	1	70	37	35.00

LAST SEASON / CAREER: BOWLING					
	O.	M.	R.	W.	AV.
TEST					
1ST	506.1	137	1281	31	41.32
INT					
RAL	82.5	0	468	11	42.54
N.W.	21.3	6	61	9	6.77
B&H	58.2	4	230	5	46.00

LENHAM, N. J. Sussex

Name: Neil John Lenham
Role: Right-hand bat, right-arm medium bowler
Born: 17 December 1965, Worthing
Height: 5ft 11in **Weight:** 11st
Nickname: Archie, Pin
County debut: 1984
County cap: 1990
1st-Class 50s scored: 21
1st-Class 100s scored: 6
One-Day 50s: 7
Place in batting averages: 98th av. 41.57 (1989 127th av. 26.37)
1st-Class catches: 6 (career 33)
Parents: Leslie John and Valerie Anne
Marital status: Single
Family links with cricket: Father ex-Sussex cricketer and NCA National Coach

Education: Broadwater Manor House Prep School; Brighton College
Qualifications: 5 O-levels, 2 A-levels, advanced cricket coach
Overseas tours: England YCs to West Indies (as captain) in 1985
Cricketers particularly admired: Ken McEwan, Barry Richards
Other sports followed: Golf, rugby, squash, hockey
Relaxations: Music, reading, keeping tropical fish, fishing
Extras: Made debut for England YCs in 1983. Broke record for number of runs

scored in season at a public school in 1984 (1534 av. 80.74). Youngest player to appear for County 2nd XI at 14 years old

Opinions on cricket: 'A full season of four-day first-class cricket should now be seriously considered.'

Best batting: 123 Sussex v Somerset, Hove 1990

Best bowling: 4–85 Sussex v Leicestershire, Leicester 1986

LAST SEASON: BATTING

	I.	N. O.	R.	H. S.	AV.
TEST					
1ST	41	1	1663	123	41.57
INT					
RAL	12	1	444	78	40.36
N.W.	2	1	88	47	88.00
B&H	3	0	62	37	20.66

LAST SEASON: BOWLING

	O.	M.	R.	W.	AV.
TEST					
1ST	93	18	309	5	61.80
INT					
RAL	33	0	219	8	27.37
N.W.	9	0	25	3	8.33
B&H	9	0	51	2	25.50

CAREER: BATTING

	I.	N. O.	R.	H. S.	AV.
TEST					
1ST	151	16	4203	123	31.13
INT					
RAL	28	8	660	78	33.00
N.W.	4	1	111	47	37.00
B&H	12	2	287	82	28.70

CAREER: BOWLING

	O.	M.	R.	W.	AV.
TEST					
1ST	290.5	52	946	21	45.04
INT					
RAL	61	0	365	13	28.07
N.W.	18	0	73	4	18.25
B&H	18	0	97	3	32.33

52. How much did the winners of the County Championship get in prize money last season?

53. What is John Morris's nickname?

54. What is Paul Allott's nickname?

LEWIS, C. C.　　　　Leicestershire

Name: Christopher Clairmonte Lewis
Role: Right-hand bat, right-arm
medium bowler
Born: 14 February 1968, Georgetown,
Guyana
Height: 6ft 2 1/2in **Weight:** 13st
Nickname: Carl
County debut: 1987
Test debut: 1990
Tests: 3
One-Day Internationals: 7
50 wickets in a season: 1
1st-Class 50s scored: 4
1st-Class 100s scored: 1
1st-Class 5 w. in innings: 7
1st-Class 10 w. in match: 2
One-Day 50s scored: 4
Place in batting averages: 147th av.
33.19 (1989 220th av. 15.38)
Place in bowling averages: 30th av.
30.30 (1989 23rd av. 21.91)
Strike rate: 57.46 (career 53.06)
1st-Class catches: 15 (career 39)
Parents: Philip and Patricia
Marital status: Single
Education: Willesden High School
Qualifications: 2 O-levels
Off-season: Touring Australia with England

LAST SEASON: BATTING

	I.	N.O.	R.	H.S.	AV.
TEST	3	0	36	32	12.00
1ST	23	5	661	189*	36.72
INT	2	0	13	7	6.50
RAL	11	3	331	93*	41.37
N.W.	1	0	32	32	32.00
B&H	3	1	48	23	24.00

LAST SEASON: BOWLING

	O.	M.	R.	W.	AV.
TEST	106	16	408	9	45.33
1ST	430.2	86	1289	47	27.42
INT	42	1	217	7	31.00
RAL	76.3	2	362	15	24.13
N.W.	12	1	35	1	35.00
B&H	31	4	119	2	59.50

CAREER: BATTING

	I.	N.O.	R.	H.S.	AV.
TEST	3	0	36	32	12.00
1ST	72	10	1424	189*	22.96
INT	2	0	13	7	6.50
RAL	33	11	696	93*	31.63
N.W.	6	0	133	53	22.16
B&H	9	5	119	23*	29.75

CAREER: BOWLING

	O.	M.	R.	W.	AV.
TEST	106	16	408	9	45.33
1ST	1220.3	243	3780	141	26.80
INT	54	2	282	8	35.25
RAL	220.1	10	1001	37	27.05
N.W.	63	5	224	7	32.00
B&H	99.3	8	390	12	32.50

Overseas tours: England YC to Australia for Youth World Cup 1987; England A to Kenya and Zimbabwe 1989–90; England to West Indies 1989–90; Australia and New Zealand 1990–91
Cricketers particularly admired: Richard Hadlee
Other sports followed: Snooker, football, darts, American football
Injuries: Various minor ailments – missed Oval Test with a migraine
Relaxations: Music, sleeping
Extras: Joined England's tour of West Indies in 1989–90 as a replacement for Ricky Ellcock. Suffers from Raynaud's Disease which affects his blood circulation
Best batting: 189* Leicestershire v Essex, Chelmsford 1990
Best bowling: 6–22 Leicestershire v Oxford University, The Parks 1988

LEWIS, J. J. B. Essex

Name: Jonathan James Benjamin Lewis
Role: Right-hand bat
Born: 21 May 1970, Middlesex
Height: 5ft 9in **Weight:** 11st
Nickname: Scrub Head
County debut: 1990
1st-Class 100s scored: 1
1st-Class catches: 1 (career 1)
Parents: Edward and Regina
Marital status: Single
Education: King Edward VI School, Chelmsford; Roehampton Institute of Higher Education
Qualifications: 5 O-levels, 3 A-levels, basic coaching qualification
Off-season: Student
Cricketers particularly admired: Graham Gooch and Greg Matthews
Other sports followed: Soccer, rugby and basketball
Relaxations: Music, food, cinema
Extras: Hit century on first-class debut in Essex's final Championship match of the 1990 season

LAST SEASON / CAREER: BATTING

	I.	N. O.	R.	H. S.	AV.
TEST					
1ST	1	1	116	116*	-
INT					
RAL					
N.W.					
B&H					

LAST SEASON / CAREER: BOWLING

	O.	M.	R.	W.	AV.
TEST					
1ST					
INT					
RAL					
N.W.					
B&H					

Opinions on cricket: 'I do not believe close fielders should be prevented from wearing shin pads or helmet for protection, as has been suggested.'
Best batting: 116* Essex v Surrey, The Oval 1990

LILLEY, A. W.   Essex

Name: Alan William Lilley
Role: Right-hand bat, right-arm
medium bowler, cover fielder
Born: 8 May 1959, Ilford, Essex
Height: 6ft 2in **Weight:** 14st
Nickname: Lil
County debut: 1978
County cap: 1986
1st-Class 50s scored: 24
1st-Class 100s scored: 3
One-Day 50s: 8
One-Day 100s: 2
1st-Class catches: 0 (career 67)
Parents: Min and Ron
Wife and date of marriage: Helen,
6 October 1984 (separated)
Family links with cricket: Father
played for Osborne CC as a bowler for
eighteen years
Education: Caterham High School, Ilford
Off-season: 'Taken over from Ray East as Essex's Youth Development Officer.'
Other sports followed: 'Most ball games.'
Injuries: 'First season for a while with no broken bones.'

LAST SEASON: BATTING

	I.	N. O.	R.	H. S.	AV.
TEST					
1ST	1	0	1	1	1.00
INT					
RAL	5	1	41	10	10.25
N.W.					
B&H	2	0	30	23	15.00

LAST SEASON: BOWLING

	O.	M.	R.	W.	AV.
TEST					
1ST	1	0	7	0	-
INT					
RAL					
N.W.					
B&H	2	0	7	0	-

CAREER: BATTING

	I.	N. O.	R.	H. S.	AV.
TEST					
1ST	190	15	4495	113*	25.68
INT					
RAL	115	11	1657	60	15.93
N.W.	15	2	352	113	27.07
B&H	37	4	741	119	22.45

CAREER: BOWLING

	O.	M.	R.	W.	AV.
TEST					
1ST	86.3	4	565	8	70.62
INT					
RAL	4.3	0	23	3	7.66
N.W.	8	3	33	2	16.50
B&H	3	0	11	1	11.00

Extras: Was on MCC staff at Lord's one season after leaving school. Scored century in second innings of debut v Nottinghamshire. Has broken every finger of both hands twice
Best batting: 113* Essex v Derbyshire, Chesterfield 1989
Best bowling: 3–116 Essex v Glamorgan, Swansea 1985

LLOYD, G. D. Lancashire

Name: Graham David Lloyd
Role: Right-hand bat
Born: 1 July 1969, Accrington
Height: 5ft 9in **Weight:** 11st 7lbs
Nickname: Bumble, Geoff
County debut: 1988
1st-Class 50s scored: 8
1st-Class 100s scored: 3
One-Day 50s: 5
One-day 100s: 1
Place in batting averages: 84th
av. 44.22 (1989 40th av. 40.18)
1st-Class catches: 9 (career 12)
Parents: David and Susan
Marital status: Single
Family links with cricket: Father
played for Lancashire and England
Education: Hollins County High School,
Accrington
Qualifications: 3 O-levels; cricket coach
Off-season: Playing cricket in Queensland
Cricketers particularly admired: Graeme Hick, Allan Lamb, David Makinson, Gary Yates, Gordon Parsons
Other sports followed: Football, horse racing
Injuries: Kept splitting webbing on left hand
Relaxations: Watching Manchester United and playing cards
Extras: His school did not play cricket, so he learnt at Accrington CC, playing in the same team as his father

LAST SEASON: BATTING

	I.	N. O.	R.	H. S.	AV.
TEST					
1ST	20	2	796	96	44.22
INT					
RAL	14	2	577	100*	48.08
N.W.	1	0	36	36	36.00
B&H					

CAREER: BATTING

	I.	N. O.	R.	H. S.	AV.
TEST					
1ST	34	3	1260	117	40.64
INT					
RAL	14	2	577	100*	48.08
N.W.	1	0	36	36	36.00
B&H					

240

Opinions on cricket: 'I would like to see some sort of day/night competition with coloured clothing.'
Best batting: 117 Lancashire v Nottinghamshire, Worksop 1989

LLOYD, T. A. Warwickshire

Name: Timothy Andrew Lloyd
Role: Left-hand bat, off-break bowler, county captain
Born: 5 November 1956, Oswestry
Height: 5ft 11in **Weight:** 12st
Nickname: Towser
County debut: 1977
County cap: 1980
Benefit: 1990
Test debut: 1984
Tests: 1
One-Day Internationals: 3
1000 runs in a season: 8
1st-Class 50s scored: 72
1st-Class 100s scored: 29
1st-Class 200s scored: 1
One-Day 50s: 47
One-Day 100s: 2
Place in batting averages: 198th av. 24.84 (1989 54th av. 36.70)
1st-Class catches: 7 (career 132)
Parents: John Romer and Gwen
Wife: Gilly
Children: Georgia, Sophie
Education: Oswestry Boys' High School; Dorset College of Higher Education
Qualifications: O-levels, 2 A-levels, HND Tourism, NCA advanced coach
Career outside cricket: Business entertainment/corporate hospitality executive
Overseas tours: English Counties XI to Zimbabwe 1984–85
Overseas teams played for: Orange Free State 1978–80
Cricketers particularly admired: Allan Border, Dennis Amiss
Other sports followed: 'Most sports, but particularly racing.'
Injuries: Broken finger, hamstring and calf injuries
Relaxations: 'Enjoying my home, drinking good wine and beer, eating various cuisines. Also greyhounds, playing golf and walking.'
Extras: Played for Shropshire and Warwickshire 2nd XI in 1975. Has been captain of Warwickshire since 1988. Was Gladstone Small's best man
Opinions on cricket: 'After-match arrangements at some grounds must be looked into more closely. Hygiene and refreshment seem low on some counties' list of

priorities.'
Best batting: 208* Warwickshire v Gloucestershire, Edgbaston 1983
Best bowling: 3–62 Warwickshire v Surrey, Edgbaston 1985

LAST SEASON: BATTING

	I.	N. O.	R.	H. S.	AV.
TEST					
1ST	27	1	646	101	24.84
INT					
RAL	10	2	173	63	21.62
N.W.	1	0	15	15	15.00
B&H	3	0	90	72	30.00

LAST SEASON: BOWLING

	O.	M.	R.	W.	AV.
TEST					
1ST	9	1	58	1	58.00
INT					
RAL					
N.W.					
B&H					

CAREER: BATTING

	I.	N. O.	R.	H. S.	AV.
TEST	1	1	10	10*	-
1ST	470	40	15170	208*	35.27
INT	3	0	101	49	33.66
RAL	147	15	3748	90	28.39
N.W.	29	3	1081	121	41.57
B&H	44	3	1304	137*	31.80

CAREER: BOWLING

	O.	M.	R.	W.	AV.
TEST	302	50	1358	17	79.88
INT					
RAL	23.1	0	149	1	149.00
N.W.	9	1	47	2	23.50
B&H	15	1	76	0	-

LLOYDS, J. W. Gloucestershire

Name: Jeremy William Lloyds
Role: Left-hand bat, off-break
bowler, close fielder
Born: 17 November 1954, Penang,
Malaysia
Height: 5ft 11in **Weight:** 12st
Nickname: Jo'burg, JJ or Jerry
County debut: 1979 (Somerset), 1985
(Gloucs)
County cap: 1982 (Somerset), 1985
(Gloucs)
1000 runs in a season: 3
1st-Class 50s scored: 54
1st-Class 100s scored: 10
1st-Class 5 w. in innings: 12
1st-Class 10 w. in match: 1
One-Day 50s: 5
Place in batting averages: 117th av. 38.13 (1989 113th av. 28.66)
Place in bowling averages: 136th av. 57.16 (1989 83rd av. 33.00)
Strike rate: 91.88 (career 69.80)
1st-Class catches: 15 (career 207)
Parents: Edwin William and Grace Cicely
Wife and date of marriage: Corne, March 1989

Family links with cricket: Father played for Blundell's 1st XI 1932–35, was selected for Public Schools and also played in Malaya and Singapore 1950–55. Brother, Christopher Edwin Lloyds played for Blundell's 1st XI 1964–66 and Somerset 2nd XI in 1966

Education: St Dunstan's Prep School; Blundell's School

Qualifications: 10 O-levels, NCA advanced coach

Overseas teams played for: Orange Free State 1983–88

Cricketers particularly admired: John Hampshire, Graeme Pollock, Viv Richards, Ian Botham, Derek Underwood, Brian Davison

Other sports followed: Motor racing, tennis, American football

Relaxations: Music, cinema, driving, reading

Opinions on cricket: 'Coloured clothing and white ball for all one-day cricket; 16 four-day games played Wednesday to Saturday. Play the B & H in May. Season to finish early in September – it drags on too long.'

Best batting: 132* Somerset v Northamptonshire, Northampton 1982

Best bowling: 7–88 Somerset v Essex, Chelmsford 1982

LAST SEASON: BATTING

	I.	N. O.	R.	H. S.	AV.
TEST					
1ST	34	12	839	93	38.13
INT					
RAL	10	3	122	38*	17.42
N.W.	3	2	79	73*	79.00
B&H	2	1	59	53*	59.00

LAST SEASON: BOWLING

	O.	M.	R.	W.	AV.
TEST					
1ST	382.5	60	1429	25	57.16
INT					
RAL	12.3	0	88	2	44.00
N.W.	6	0	50	1	50.00
B&H					

CAREER: BATTING

	I.	N. O.	R.	H. S.	AV.
TEST					
1ST	373	58	9876	132*	31.35
INT					
RAL	92	14	1129	65	14.47
N.W.	18	5	293	73*	22.53
B&H	22	4	329	53*	18.27

CAREER: BOWLING

	O.	M.	R.	W.	AV.
TEST					
1ST	3478.5	723	11293	299	37.76
INT					
RAL	113.5	6	603	13	46.38
N.W.	52.5	5	209	4	52.25
B&H	30.2	2	100	4	25.00

LORD, G. J.   Worcestershire

Name: Gordon John Lord
Role: Left-hand bat, slow left-arm
bowler, specialist third-man
Born: 25 April 1961, Birmingham
Height: 5ft 10in **Weight:** 'Variable
and confidential!'
Nickname: Plum
County debut: 1983 (Warwicks),
1987 (Worcs)
County cap: 1990 (Worcs)
1000 runs in a season: 1
1st-Class 50s scored: 15
1st-Class 100s scored: 5
One-Day 50s: 2
One-Day 100s: 1
Place in batting averages: 73rd
av. 45.59 (1989 195th av. 18.71)
1st-Class catches: 4 (career 19)
Parents: Michael David and Christine
Frances
Marital status: Single
Family links with cricket: Uncle Charles Watts played for Leicestershire
Education: Warwick School; Durham University
Qualifications: 7 O-levels, 4 A-levels, BA General Studies, NCA coaching award
Overseas tours: England YCs to Australia 1978–79 and West Indies 1979–80
Cricketers particularly admired: Dennis Amiss, Graeme Hick
Other sports followed: Watches rugby, squash, snooker
Relaxations: All forms of music, particularly church organ music; astronomy,
reading, people, Indian cooking and eating
Best batting: 199 Warwickshire v Yorkshire, Edgbaston 1985

LAST SEASON: BATTING

	I.	N. O.	R.	H. S.	AV.
TEST					
1ST	24	2	1003	190	45.59
INT					
RAL	3	0	102	78	34.00
N.W.					
B&H	2	0	26	26	13.00

CAREER: BATTING

	I.	N. O.	R.	H. S.	AV.
TEST					
1ST	118	10	2988	199	27.66
INT					
RAL	16	1	351	103	23.40
N.W.	1	0	0	0	0.00
B&H	8	0	67	26	8.37

LYNCH, M. A.   Surrey

Name: Monte Allan Lynch
Role: Right-hand bat, right-arm
medium and off-break bowler
Born: 21 May 1958, Georgetown,
Guyana
Height: 5ft 8in **Weight:** 12st
Nickname: Mont
County debut: 1977
County cap: 1982
Benefit: 1991
One-Day Internationals: 3
1000 runs in a season: 8
1st-Class 50s scored: 65
1st-Class 100s scored: 30
One-Day 50s: 31
One-Day 100s: 4
Place in batting averages: 75th av.
45.44 (1989 10th av. 54.71)
1st-Class catches: 30 (career 252)
Parents: Lawrence and Doreen Austin
Marital status: Single
Family links with cricket: 'Father and most of family played at some time or
another.'
Education: Ryden's School, Walton-on-Thames
Overseas tours: West Indies XI to South Africa 1983–84
Overseas teams played for: Guyana 1982–83
Other sports followed: Football, table tennis
Extras: Hitting 141* for Surrey v Glamorgan at Guildford in August 1982, off 78

LAST SEASON: BATTING

	I.	N. O.	R.	H. S.	AV.
TEST					
1ST	32	5	1227	104	45.44
INT					
RAL	15	2	399	58	30.69
N.W.	1	0	59	59	59.00
B&H	5	0	33	24	6.60

LAST SEASON: BOWLING

	O.	M.	R.	W.	AV.
TEST					
1ST	27	5	130	1	130.00
INT					
RAL	7	0	51	2	25.50
N.W.					
B&H	12	0	66	0	-

CAREER: BATTING

	I.	N. O.	R.	H. S.	AV.
TEST					
1ST	426	51	13570	172*	35.77
INT	3	0	8	6	2.66
RAL	149	22	3738	136	29.43
N.W.	25	4	656	129	31.23
B&H	42	3	1008	112*	25.84

CAREER: BOWLING

	O.	M.	R.	W.	AV.
TEST					
1ST	322.5	61	1246	25	49.84
INT					
RAL	18.5	0	146	7	20.85
N.W.	23	6	80	2	40.00
B&H	18	0	108	0	

balls in 88 minutes, one six hit his captain Roger Knight's car. Joined West Indies Rebels in South Africa 1983–84, although qualified for England. Appeared in all three One-Day Internationals v West Indies 1988

Best batting: 172* Surrey v Kent, The Oval 1989
Best bowling: 3–6 Surrey v Glamorgan, Swansea 1981

MALCOLM, D. E. Derbyshire

Name: Devon Eugene Malcolm
Role: Right-hand bat, right-arm fast bowler
Born: 22 February 1963, Kingston, Jamaica
Height: 6ft 2in **Weight:** 14st 8lbs
Nickname: Dude
County debut: 1984
Test debut: 1989
Tests: 11
One-Day Internationals: 2
50 wickets in a season: 2
1st-Class 50s scored: 1
1st-Class 5 w. in innings: 6
1st-Class 10 w. in innings: 1
Place in bowling averages: 42nd av. 32.46 (1989 35th av. 23.87)
Strike rate: 59.80 (career 51.86)
1st-Class catches: 0 (career 15)
Parents: Albert and Brendalee (deceased)

LAST SEASON: BATTING

	I.	N. O.	R.	H. S.	AV.
TEST	6	3	32	15*	10.66
1ST	7	2	44	20*	8.80
INT	1	0	4	4	4.00
RAL	4	1	9	9	3.00
N.W.	1	0	0	0	0.00
B&H	2	1	5	5	5.00

LAST SEASON: BOWLING

	O.	M.	R.	W.	AV.
TEST	228.4	54	705	22	32.04
1ST	289.4	45	983	30	32.76
INT	22	5	76	3	25.33
RAL	92	2	467	17	27.47
N.W.	24	4	85	3	28.33
B&H	30	2	131	4	32.75

CAREER: BATTING

	I.	N. O.	R.	H. S.	AV.
TEST	14	6	83	15*	7.87
1ST	77	23	467	51	8.64
INT	1	0	4	4	4.00
RAL	6	1	25	16	5.00
N.W.	6	0	11	6	1.83
B&H	4	2	5	5	2.50

CAREER: BOWLING

	O.	M.	R.	W.	AV.
TEST	434.2	75	1448	42	34.47
1ST	1813.2	323	6505	218	29.83
INT	22	5	76	3	25.33
RAL	132	2	644	24	26.83
N.W.	75	8	290	9	32.22
B&H	77	6	280	12	23.33

Wife and date of marriage: Jennifer, October 1989
Education: St Elizabeth Technical High School; Richmond College; Derby College
Qualifications: College certificates, O-levels, coaching certificate
Off-season: Touring Australia with England
Overseas tours: England to West Indies 1989–90, Australia 1990–91
Cricketers particularly admired: Michael Holding, Richard Hadlee
Relaxations: Music and swimming. Collection of 500 records and tapes – reggae, soca, jazz funk 'and especially singers like Anita Baker and Gregory Isaacs.'
Extras: Became eligible to play for England in 1987. Played league cricket for Sheffield Works and Sheffield United. Took 10 for 137 v West Indies in Port of Spain Test, 1989–90
Best batting: 51 Derbyshire v Surrey, Derby 1989
Best bowling: 6–68 Derbyshire v Warwickshire, Derby 1988

MALLENDER, N. A. Somerset

Name: Neil Alan Mallender
Role: Right-hand bat, right-arm fast-medium bowler
Born: 13 August 1961, Kirk Sandall, nr Doncaster
Height: 6ft **Weight:** 13st
Nickname: Ghostie
County debut: 1980 (Northants), 1987 (Somerset)
County cap: 1984 (Northants), 1987 (Somerset)
50 wickets in a season: 5
1st-Class 50s scored: 7
1st-Class 5 w. in innings: 18
1st-Class 10 w. in match: 3
Place in batting averages: 196th av. 25.28 (1989 237th av. 13.28)
Place in bowling averages: 35th av. 31.07 (1989 53rd av. 27.78)
Strike rate: 65.21 (career 69.08)
1st-Class catches: 3 (career 91)
Parents: Ron and Jean
Wife and date of marriage: Caroline, 1 October 1984
Children: Kirstie Jane, 18 May 1988
Family links with cricket: Brother Graham used to play good representative cricket before joining the RAF
Education: Beverley Grammar School, East Yorkshire
Qualifications: 7 O-levels

Off-season: Playing for Otago in New Zealand
Overseas tours: England YC to West Indies 1980
Overseas teams played for: Otago 1983–90
Cricketers particularly admired: Richard Hadlee, Dennis Lillee, Warren Lees and Jimmy Cook
Other sports followed: Golf, Rugby League
Injuries: Groin strain – missed two weeks
Relaxations: Watching sports
Extras: Signed a 3-year contract to play for Somerset in 1987. Equalled Somerset record for 9th wicket v Sussex at Hove in 1990 – batting with Chris Tavare
Best batting: 88 Otago v Central Districts, Oamaru 1984–85
Best bowling: 7–27 Otago v Auckland, Auckland 1984–85

LAST SEASON: BATTING

	I.	N. O.	R.	H. S.	AV.
TEST					
1ST	10	3	177	87*	25.28
INT					
RAL	4	2	44	24	22.00
N.W.	-	-	-	-	-
B&H	3	2	12	6*	12.00

LAST SEASON: BOWLING

	O.	M.	R.	W.	AV.
TEST					
1ST	554.2	116	1585	51	31.07
INT					
RAL	100.5	4	436	13	33.53
N.W.	16	5	33	2	16.50
B&H	35	6	102	3	34.00

CAREER: BATTING

	I.	N. O.	R.	H. S.	AV.
TEST					
1ST	282	89	2985	88	15.46
INT					
RAL	57	30	338	24	12.51
N.W.	9	3	43	11*	7.16
B&H	17	7	54	16*	5.40

CAREER: BOWLING

	O.	M.	R.	W.	AV.
TEST					
1ST	6563.3	1481	18721	666	28.10
INT					
RAL	881.1	50	3934	151	26.05
N.W.	215.4	33	608	32	19.00
B&H	390.3	49	1405	51	27.54

MARSH, S. A. — Kent

Name: Steven Andrew Marsh
Role: Right-hand bat, wicket-keeper,
county vice-captain
Born: 27 January 1961, Westminster
Height: 5ft 11in **Weight:** 12st
County debut: 1982
County cap: 1986
Nickname: Marshy
1st-Class 50s scored: 19
1st-Class 100s scored: 3
One-Day 50s scored: 1
Place in batting averages: 141st
av. 33.74 (1989 141st av. 24.56)
Parents: Melvyn Graham and Valerie
Ann
Wife and date of marriage: Julie,
27 September 1986
Children: Hayley Ann, 15 May 1987
Family links with cricket: Father
played local cricket for Lordswood.
Father-in-law, Bob Wilson, played for
Kent 1954–66
Education: Walderslade Secondary School for Boys; Mid-Kent College of Higher
and Further Education
Qualifications: 6 O-levels, 2 A-levels, OND in Business Studies
Off-season: 'Working for my car sponsor, Swale Motor Co., as a computer operator
and accounts clerk.'
Cricketers particularly admired: Gary Sobers, Alan Knott

LAST SEASON: BATTING

	I.	N. O.	R.	H. S.	AV.
TEST					
1ST	35	8	911	114*	33.74
INT					
RAL	12	3	227	38	25.22
N.W.	1	0	0	0	0.00
B&H	3	0	35	17	11.66

LAST SEASON: WICKET-KEEPING

	CT	ST		
TEST				
1ST	49	5		
INT				
RAL	10	0		
N.W.	1	0		
B&H	3	0		

CAREER: BATTING

	I.	N. O.	R.	H. S.	AV.
TEST					
1ST	178	36	3686	120	25.95
INT					
RAL	52	11	678	53	16.53
N.W.	4	1	31	24*	10.33
B&H	18	4	179	41*	12.78

CAREER: WICKET-KEEPING

	CT	ST		
TEST				
1ST	258	19		
INT				
RAL	76	9		
N.W.	14	1		
B&H	31	2		

Other sports followed: Golf, horse racing
Extras: Once swallowed one of Graham Cowdrey's contact lenses, when Cowdrey left it in a glass of water overnight and Marsh drank the water. Appointed Kent vice-captain for 1991
Best batting: 120 Kent v Essex, Chelmsford 1988

MARSHALL, M. D. Hampshire

Name: Malcolm Denzil Marshall
Role: Right-hand bat, right-arm fast bowler
Born: 18 April 1958, Barbados
Height: 5ft 10 1/2in **Weight:** 12st 8lbs
Nickname: Macko
County debut: 1979
County cap: 1981
Benefit: 1987 (61,006)
Test debut: 1978–79
Tests: 68
One-Day Internationals: 113
50 wickets in a season: 9
1st-Class 50s scored: 44
1st-Class 100s scored: 6
1st-Class 5 w. in innings: 82
1st-Class 10 w. in match: 13
One-Day 50s: 4
Place in batting averages: 70th av. 45.81 (1989 132nd av. 25.75)
Place in bowling averages: 2nd av. 19.18 (1989 3rd av. 16.67)
Strike rate: 46.19 (career 42.83)
1st-Class catches: 7 (career 118)
Parents: Mrs Eleanor Inniss
Children: Shelly, 24 November 1984
Family links with cricket: Cousin Errol Yearwood plays for Texaco in Barbados as a fast bowler
Education: St Giles Boys' School; Parkinson Comprehensive School, Barbados
Qualifications: School passes in Maths and English
Career outside cricket: Working for Banks Brewery
Off-season: Playing for West Indies
Overseas tours: With West Indies to India and Sri Lanka 1978–79; Australia and New Zealand 1979–80; England 1980; Pakistan 1980–81; Australia 1981–82; India 1983–84; England 1984; Australia 1984–85; Pakistan and New Zealand 1986–87; England 1988; Australia 1988–89; Pakistan 1990–91; Young West Indies to

Zimbabwe 1981–82
Overseas teams played for: Barbados 1977–90
Cricketers particularly admired: Wes Hall and Gary Sobers
Other sports followed: Tennis, golf
Injuries: Hand, back and knee problems – missed two Tests of the West Indies v England series
Relaxations: Soul music, reggae
Extras: Took nine wickets in debut match v Glamorgan in May 1979. Scored his first first-class century (109) in Zimbabwe, October 1981. Became the leading West Indies Test wicket-taker when he overtook Lance Gibbs's total of 309. Broke record for number of wickets taken in a 22-match English season (i. e. since 1969) with 133. Published autobiography *Marshall Arts* (1987). Nearly chose to become a wicket-keeper. 'Even now I wish sometimes I was in Jeff Dujon's place behind the stumps.' One of *Wisden's* Five Cricketers of the Year, 1982. After considering retirement, he has signed a new three-year contract with Hampshire
Opinions on cricket: 'Cricket has been my life since I could stand upright and hold a cricket bat or at least our home-made apology, built from anything that looked like one. I played morning, noon and night every day of my life. Not even school could get in the way of my obsession with the game. There was no question of playing football, or anything else, for very long. It was cricket, cricket and more cricket.'
Best batting: 117 Hampshire v Yorkshire, Headingley 1990
Best bowling: 8–71 Hampshire v Worcestershire, Southampton 1982

LAST SEASON: BATTING

	I.	N. O.	R.	H. S.	AV.
TEST					
1ST	24	3	962	117	45.81
INT					
RAL	14	3	259	46	23.54
N.W.	4	0	96	77	24.00
B&H	2	0	55	31	27.50

LAST SEASON: BOWLING

	O.	M.	R.	W.	AV.
TEST					
1ST	554.2	141	1381	72	19.18
INT					
RAL	104	5	458	14	32.71
N.W.	44	6	131	7	18.71
B&H	25	1	125	0	-

CAREER: BATTING

	I.	N. O.	R.	H. S.	AV.
TEST	88	9	1457	92	18.44
1ST	323	44	7300	117	25.97
INT	62	17	781	66	17.35
RAL	78	19	1120	46	18.98
N.W.	19	8	310	77	28.18
B&H	25	1	340	34	14.16

CAREER: BOWLING

	O.	M.	R.	W.	AV.
TEST	2537	537	6831	329	20.76
1ST	7428.5	2052	18612	1067	17.44
INT	998.5	105	3412	137	24.90
RAL	869.3	77	3086	128	24.10
N.W.	280.5	57	762	32	23.81
B&H	290.1	52	862	37	23.29

Name: Peter James Martin
Role: Right-hand bat, right-arm
fast-medium bowler
Born: 15 November 1968,
Accrington
Height: 6ft 4 1/2in **Weight:** 15st 7lbs
Nickname: Digger, Maurice, Astin
County debut: 1989
Place in bowling averages: 94th av.
39.45
Strike rate: 75.13 (career 83.08)
1st-Class catches: 5 (career 6)
Parents: Keith and Catherine Lina
Marital status: Single
Education: Danum Grammar
School, Doncaster
Qualifications: 6 O-levels, 2 A-levels
Off-season: Playing cricket for South
Canberra CC in Australia
Overseas tours: England YC to
Australia for Youth World Cup, 1988
Cricketers particularly admired: Ian Botham, Richard Hadlee, 'Ian Austin and
Nick Speak for their vision and guidance.'
Other sports followed: Soccer (Man United), golf, swimming, 'play most ball
sports if I get the chance.'
Injuries: Rib injury
Relaxations: Bailey's Irish Cream, 'setting the game to rights.'
Extras: Played district football and basketball for Doncaster

LAST SEASON: BATTING

	I.	N. O.	R.	H. S.	AV.
TEST					
1ST	7	3	44	21	11.00
INT					
RAL	-	-	-	-	-
N.W.	-	-	-	-	-
B&H					

LAST SEASON: BOWLING

	O.	M.	R.	W.	AV.
TEST					
1ST	275.3	52	868	22	39.45
INT					
RAL	14	0	79	0	-
N.W.	8	0	53	0	-
B&H					

CAREER: BATTING

	I.	N. O.	R.	H. S.	AV.
TEST					
1ST	9	3	64	21	10.66
INT					
RAL	-	-	-	-	-
N.W.	-	-	-	-	-
B&H					

CAREER: BOWLING

	O.	M.	R.	W.	AV.
TEST					
1ST	318.3	58	1001	23	43.52
INT					
RAL	14	0	79	0	-
N.W.	8	0	53	0	-
B&H					

Opinions on cricket: 'Have uncovered wickets and get rid of water hogs.'
Best batting: 21 Lancashire v Nottinghamshire, Trent Bridge 1990
Best bowling: 4–68 Lancashire v Nottinghamshire, Trent Bridge 1990

MARTINDALE, D. J. R.   Nottinghamshire

Name: Duncan John Richardson Martindale
Role: Right-hand bat, cover fielder
Born: 13 December 1963, Harrogate
Height: 5ft 11 1/2in **Weight:** 11st 11lbs
Nickname: Blowers
County debut: 1985
1st-Class 50s scored: 7
1st-Class 100s scored: 4
One-Day 50s scored: 1
Place in batting averages: 166th av. 30.04 (1989 179th av. 20.09)
1st-Class catches: 5 (career 23)
Parents: Don and Isabel
Marital status: Single
Family links with cricket: Father and grandfather played club cricket; great uncle played for Nottinghamshire 2nd XI
Education: Lymm Grammar School; Trent Polytechnic
Qualifications: 9 O-levels, 2 A-levels, HND Business Studies, NCA senior coaching award
Off-season: 'Touring, teaching and coaching in India.'
Cricketers particularly admired: Geoff Boycott, Viv Richards, Richard Hadlee, Clive Rice
Other sports followed: Most sports
Injuries: Broken big toe
Relaxations: Reading, travelling, meeting people, active in other sports
Extras: Scored a century (104*) in fifth first-class innings. First one-day match was

LAST SEASON: BATTING

	I.	N. O.	R.	H. S.	AV.
TEST					
1ST	28	3	751	138	30.04
INT					
RAL					
N.W.					
B&H	1	0	0	0	0.00

CAREER: BATTING

	I.	N. O.	R.	H. S.	AV.
TEST					
1ST	84	9	1857	138	24.76
INT					
RAL	12	1	276	53	25.09
N.W.	2	1	67	47	67.00
B&H	1	0	0	0	0.00

1985 NatWest Final. Member of Christians in Sport
Opinions on cricket: 'There is too much cricket. There should be 12-month contracts for all players, with the county club helping players to develop careers in and out of the game.'
Best batting: 138 Nottinghamshire v Cambridge University, Fenner's 1990

MARU, R. J.   Hampshire

Name: Rajesh Jamnadass Maru
Role: Right-hand bat, slow
left-arm bowler, close fielder
Born: 28 October 1962, Nairobi
Height: 5ft 6in **Weight:** 10st 7lbs
Nickname: Raj
County debut: 1980 (Middlesex),
1984 (Hampshire)
County cap: 1986 (Hampshire)
50 wickets in a season: 4
1st-Class 50s scored: 5
1st-Class 5 w. in innings: 14
1st-Class 10 w. in match: 1
Place in batting averages: 172nd av.
28.88 (1989 253rd av. 11.29)
Place in bowling averages: 67th av.
36.66 (1989 87th av. 33.89)
Strike rate: 77.37 (career 70.69)
1st-Class catches: 30 (career 170)
Parents: Jamnadass and Prabhavati
Family links with cricket: Brother Pradip has played for Middlesex 2nd XI and now plays for Wembley in Middlesex League
Education: Harrow College (Pinner Sixth Form); Rooks Heath High; Okington Manor
Qualifications: NCA senior cricket coach
Off-season: 'Running my own coaching school; coaching for Hampshire CCC; working on my own game and fitness; playing a little golf.'
Overseas tours: England YCs to West Indies 1980
Cricketers particularly admired: Jack Robertson, Derek Underwood, Malcolm Marshall, Les Lenham
Other sports followed: Badminton, table tennis, squash, swimming, hockey, football, Rugby Union
Relaxations: Music, reading
Extras: Played for Middlesex 1980–83
Best batting: 74 Hampshire v Gloucestershire, Gloucester 1988
Best bowling: 8–41 Hampshire v Kent, Southampton 1989

	I.	N. O.	R.	H. S.	AV.
TEST					
1ST	20	2	520	59	28.88
INT					
RAL	6	2	29	12*	7.25
N.W.	3	1	38	22	19.00
B&H	1	0	9	9	9.00

LAST SEASON: BOWLING

	O.	M.	R.	W.	AV.
TEST					
1ST	851.1	219	2420	66	36.66
INT					
RAL	70.5	0	394	12	32.83
N.W.	45	1	211	6	35.16
B&H	27	2	149	4	37.25

CAREER: BATTING

	I.	N. O.	R.	H. S.	AV.
TEST					
1ST	135	38	1329	74	13.70
INT					
RAL	11	6	47	18*	9.40
N.W.	3	1	38	22	19.00
B&H	1	0	9	9	9.00

CAREER: BOWLING

	O.	M.	R.	W.	AV.
TEST					
1ST	4972.1	1364	13453	422	31.87
INT					
RAL	153	5	795	23	34.56
N.W.	71	2	270	9	30.00
B&H	27	2	149	4	37.25

MAYNARD, M. P.   Glamorgan

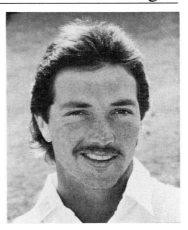

Name: Matthew Peter Maynard
Role: Right-hand bat, right-arm medium bowler, slip fielder
Born: 21 March 1966, Oldham
Height: 5ft 10 1/2in **Weight:** 12st 9lbs
Nickname: The Kid
County debut: 1985
County cap: 1987
Test debut: 1988
Tests: 1
1000 runs in a season: 5
1st-Class 50s scored: 44
1st-Class 100s scored: 11
One-Day 50s: 14
One-Day 100s: 3
Place in batting averages: 86th av. 44.14 (1989 116th av. 27.97)
1st-Class catches: 15 (career 105)
Parents: Pat and Ken (deceased)
Wife and date of marriage: Susan, 27 September 1986
Children: Thomas, 25 March 1989
Family links with cricket: Father pro'd for Duckinfield. Brothers play club cricket
Education: Ysgol David Hughes, Anglesey
Qualifications: Cricket coach
Overseas tours: Unofficial England XI to South Africa 1989–90
Cricketers particularly admired: Richard Hadlee, Ian Botham, Barry Richards

Other sports followed: Rugby, golf, snooker
Relaxations: 'Socialising, playing golf, and spending time with my wife and son.'
Extras: Scored century on debut v Yorkshire at Swansea. Youngest centurion for Glamorgan and scored 1000 runs in first full season. Fastest ever 50 for Glamorgan (14 mins) v Yorkshire and youngest player to be awarded Glamorgan cap. Voted Young Cricketer of the Year 1988 by the Cricket Writers Club. Banned from Test cricket for joining tour of South Africa, 1989–90
Opinions on cricket: 'We should play 16 four-day matches.'
Best batting: 191* Glamorgan v Gloucestershire, Cardiff 1989
Best bowling: 3–21 Glamorgan v Oxford University, The Parks 1987

LAST SEASON: BATTING

	I.	N. O.	R.	H. S.	AV.
TEST					
1ST	41	7	1501	125*	44.14
INT					
RAL	14	1	479	100	36.84
N.W.	3	0	33	24	11.00
B&H	5	0	230	84	46.00

CAREER: BATTING

	I.	N. O.	R.	H. S.	AV.
TEST	2	0	13	10	6.50
1ST	205	25	6842	191*	38.01
INT					
RAL	71	4	1641	100	24.49
N.W.	12	0	254	64	21.16
B&H	20	3	746	115	43.88

McEWAN, S. M. — Worcestershire

Name: Steven Michael McEwan
Role: Right-hand bat, right-arm fast-medium bowler
Born: 5 May 1962, Worcester
Height: 6ft 1in **Weight:** 13st 7lbs
Nickname: IG, Macca
County debut: 1985
County cap: 1989
50 wickets in a season: 1
1st-Class 50s scored: 1
1st-Class 5 w. in innings: 3
Place in batting averages: 207th av. 23.42 (1989 152nd av. 23.16)
Place in bowling averages: 36th av. 31.28 (1989 9th av. 19.21)
Strike rate: 59.26 (career 55.06)
1st-Class catches: 5 (career 17)

Parents: Michael James and Valerie Jeanette
Wife and date of marriage: Debbie, 30 September 1989
Family links with cricket: Father and uncle played club cricket
Education: Worcester Royal Grammar School
Qualifications: 6 O-levels, 3 A-levels. Technician's certificate in building

Off-season: Working for accountants Pearson & Price in Dudley
Cricketers particularly admired: Richard Hadlee, Malcolm Marshall
Other sports followed: American football
Injuries: Pulled hamstring – missed a month of the season
Relaxations: Reading, golf, skittles, watching films
Extras: Took 10 wickets for 13 runs in an innings in 1983 for Worcester Nomads against Moreton-in-Marsh. Also broke school bowling record, 60 wickets, at WRGS, 1982. Took hat-trick for Worcestershire v Leicestershire at Leicester, 1990
Opinions on cricket: 'Second team games should be played on first-class grounds. It seems every year a new rule is introduced which is detrimental towards the bowler. It is probably only a matter of time before limited run-ups and the use of a tennis ball instead of a cricket ball.'
Best batting: 54 Worcestershire v Yorkshire, Worcester 1990
Best bowling: 6–34 Worcestershire v Leicestershire, Kidderminster 1989

LAST SEASON: BATTING

	I.	N. O.	R.	H. S.	AV.
TEST					
1ST	12	5	164	54	23.42
INT					
RAL	4	2	26	18*	13.00
N.W.	-	-	-	-	-
B&H	-	-	-	-	-

LAST SEASON: BOWLING

	O.	M.	R.	W.	AV.
TEST					
1ST	375.2	75	1189	38	31.28
INT					
RAL	75.4	0	437	13	33.61
N.W.	3	0	15	0	-
B&H	11	0	53	2	26.50

CAREER: BATTING

	I.	N. O.	R.	H. S.	AV.
TEST					
1ST	35	16	348	54	18.31
INT					
RAL	12	7	47	18*	9.40
N.W.	1	0	6	6	6.00
B&H	-	-	-	-	-

CAREER: BOWLING

	O.	M.	R.	W.	AV.
TEST					
1ST	1275.4	234	4069	139	29.27
INT					
RAL	236.4	2	1269	39	32.53
N.W.	14	3	66	3	22.00
B&H	11	0	53	2	26.50

MEDLYCOTT, K. T. Surrey

Name: Keith Thomas Medlycott
Role: Right-hand bat, slow
left-arm bowler, slip fielder
Born: 12 May 1965, Whitechapel
Height: 5ft 11in **Weight:** 13st
Nickname: Medders
County debut: 1984
County cap: 1988
50 wickets in a season: 3
1st-Class 50s scored: 17
1st-Class 100s scored: 2
1st-Class 5 w. in innings: 16
1st-Class 10 w. in match: 5
Place in batting averages: 195th av.
25.62 (1989 93rd av. 30.93)
Place in bowling averages: 90th av.
39.04 (1989 96th av. 33.32)
Strike rate: 73.65 (career 63.11)
1st-Class catches: 14 (career 84)
Parents: Thomas Alfred (deceased) and
June Elizabeth
Marital status: Single
Family links with cricket: 'Father played club cricket for Colposa. Twin brother Paul plays very occasionally.'
Education: Parmiters Grammar School; Wandsworth Comprehensive
Qualifications: 2 O-levels
Off-season: Touring Pakistan with England A
Overseas tours: England to West Indies 1989–90; England A to Pakistan 1990–91
Overseas teams played for: Natal B 1988–89
Cricketers particularly admired: Tom Medlycott, David Ward – 'always plays with a smile.'
Other sports followed: Rugby, football
Relaxations: 'Sport in general.'
Extras: Scored 100 on debut (117* v Cambridge University) in 1984. Took first hat-trick of career against Hampshire 2nd XI, 1988. Capped in last game of season, against Kent. First bowler to take 50 wickets in 1990 season. Spent season on Lord's ground staff. Offered a contract by Northamptonshire in 1984. Directed to Surrey by Micky Stewart
Opinions on cricket: 'We should have four-day cricket. The TCCB should pay groundsmen instead of the clubs, and then sack the bad ones!'
Best batting: 153 Surrey v Kent, The Oval 1987
Best bowling: 8–52 Surrey v Sussex, Hove 1988

LAST SEASON: BATTING

	I.	N. O.	R.	H. S.	AV.
TEST					
1ST	25	9	410	44	25.62
INT					
RAL	7	3	96	44*	24.00
N.W.	1	0	38	38	38.00
B&H	1	0	1	1	1.00

LAST SEASON: BOWLING

	O.	M.	R.	W.	AV.
TEST					
1ST	748.5	170	2382	61	39.04
INT					
RAL	93	1	485	17	28.52
N.W.	24	1	91	1	91.00
B&H	44	0	198	5	39.60

CAREER: BATTING

	I.	N. O.	R.	H. S.	AV.
TEST					
1ST	153	36	3060	153	26.15
INT					
RAL	28	7	291	44*	13.85
N.W.	4	2	65	38	32.50
B&H	3	0	14	11	4.66

CAREER: BOWLING

	O.	M.	R.	W.	AV.
TEST					
1ST	3240	812	9814	308	31.86
INT					
RAL	184	4	962	40	24.05
N.W.	50	6	185	2	82.50
B&H	48.3	0	235	7	33.57

MENDIS, G. D.   Lancashire

Name: Gehan Dixon Mendis
Role: Right-hand opening bat
Born: 24 April 1955, Colombo, Ceylon
Height: 5ft 8in **Weight:** 11st
Nickname: Mendo, Dix
County debut: 1974 (Sussex), 1986 (Lancs)
County cap: 1980 (Sussex), 1986 (Lancs)
1000 runs in a season: 11
1st-Class 50s scored: 98
1st-Class 100s scored: 36
1st-Class 200s scored: 3
One-Day 50s: 35
One-Day 100s: 7
Place in batting averages: 41st av. 53.48 (1989 25th av. 44.09)
1st-Class catches: 15 (career 131 & 1 stumping)
Parents: Sam Dixon Charles and Sonia Marcelle (both deceased)
Children: Hayley, 11 December 1982
Education: St Thomas College, Mount Lavinia, Sri Lanka; Brighton, Hove & Sussex Grammar School; Bede College, Durham University
Qualifications: BEd Mathematics, Durham; NCA coaching certificate
Cricketers particularly admired: Barry Richards, Richard Hadlee
Other sports followed: Formula One motor racing

Relaxations: Music, 'getting away from cricket.'

Extras: Turned down invitations to play for Sri Lanka in order to be free to be chosen for England. Left Sussex at end of 1985 to join Lancashire. Played table tennis for Sussex at junior level

Opinions on cricket: 'None, any more, as cricketers have not much say in the running of the game. Sign of old age, I guess!'

Best batting: 209* Sussex v Somerset, Hove 1984

Best bowling: 1–65 Sussex v Yorkshire, Hove 1985

LAST SEASON: BATTING

	I.	N. O.	R.	H. S.	AV.
TEST					
1ST	35	6	1551	180	53.48
INT					
RAL	7	1	202	71	33.66
N.W.	5	2	327	121*	109.00
B&H	7	0	145	40	20.71

CAREER: BATTING

	I.	N. O.	R.	H. S.	AV.
TEST					
1ST	558	55	18798	209*	37.37
INT					
RAL	171	15	4335	125*	27.78
N.W.	38	4	1359	141*	39.97
B&H	61	2	1612	109	27.32

55. What is Chris Smith's nickname?

56. What is Robin Smith's nickname?

57. What is Graeme Fowler's nickname?

MERRICK, T. A. Kent

Name: Tyrone Anthony Merrick
Role: Right-hand bat, right-arm fast-medium bowler
Born: 10 June 1963, Antigua
Height: 6ft
County debut: 1987 (Warwicks), 1990 (Kent)
County cap: 1988 (Warwicks)
50 wickets in a season: 2
1st-Class 50s scored: 2
1st-Class 5 w. in innings: 14
1st-Class 10 w. in match: 2
One-Day 50s: 1
Place in batting averages: 271st av. 11.00
Place in bowling averages: 23rd av. 28.70
Strike rate: 65.11 (career 47.15)
1st-Class catches: 1 (career 26)
Children: Anthea, 6 January 1987
Education: All Saints Primary and Secondary Schools
Jobs outside cricket: Physical Education teacher
Off-season: Playing in West Indies
Overseas tours: West Indies YC to England 1982; West Indies B to Zimbabwe 1986
Overseas teams played for: Leeward Islands 1982–89
Cricketers particularly admired: Andy Roberts, Eldine Baptiste
Other sports followed: Soccer, lawn tennis
Relaxations: Listening to music

LAST SEASON: BATTING

	I.	N. O.	R.	H. S.	AV.
TEST					
1ST	8	2	66	35	11.00
INT					
RAL	4	2	32	12*	16.00
N.W.					
B&H	2	1	15	14	15.00

LAST SEASON: BOWLING

	O.	M.	R.	W.	AV.
TEST					
1ST	184.3	45	488	17	28.70
INT					
RAL	74.3	3	319	15	21.26
N.W.					
B&H	19.4	2	76	2	38.00

CAREER: BATTING

	I.	N. O.	R.	H. S.	AV.
TEST					
1ST	88	17	1061	74*	14.94
INT					
RAL	15	5	158	59	15.80
N.W.	2	0	15	13	7.50
B&H	6	2	42	14	10.50

CAREER: BOWLING

	O.	M.	R.	W.	AV.
TEST					
1ST	1964.5	269	6131	250	24.52
INT					
RAL	214	21	862	40	21.55
N.W.	21	9	39	3	13.00
B&H	68.4	8	203	7	29.00

Extras: Played for Rawtenstall in Lancashire League 1985 and 1986. Released by Warwickshire at end of 1989 season
Best batting: 74* Warwickshire v Gloucestershire, Edgbaston 1987
Best bowling: 7–45 Warwickshire v Lancashire, Edgbaston 1987

METCALFE, A. A. Yorkshire

Name: Ashley Anthony Metcalfe
Role: Right-hand bat, off-break bowler, county vice-captain
Born: 25 December 1963, Horsforth, Leeds
Height: 5ft 9 1/2in **Weight:** 11st 7lbs
County debut: 1983
County cap: 1986
1000 runs in a season: 5
1st-Class 50s scored: 40
1st-Class 100s scored: 21
1st-Class 200s scored: 1
One-Day 50s: 28
One-Day 100s: 2
Place in batting averages: 46th av. 51.17 (1989 74th av. 34.44)
1st-Class catches: 10 (career 50)
Parents: Tony and Ann
Wife and date of marriage: Diane, 20 April 1986
Family links with cricket: Father played in local league; father-in-law Ray Illingworth (Yorkshire and England)
Education: Ladderbanks Middle School; Bradford Grammar School; University College, London
Qualifications: 9 O-levels, 3 A-levels, NCA coaching certificate
Career outside cricket: 'Metcalfe & Sidebottom Associates – Sports Promotion Company.'
Off-season: 'Predominantly obtaining sponsorship for Yorkshire CCC and pro-motional work for the players.'
Overseas teams played for: Orange Free State 1988–89
Cricketers particularly admired: Barry Richards and Martyn Moxon
Other sports followed: Golf and most other sports
Relaxations: 'Relaxing at home with my wife.'
Extras: Made 122 on debut v Nottinghamshire at Park Avenue in 1983, the youngest ever Yorkshire player to do so and it was the highest ever score by a Yorkshireman on debut. Reached 2000 runs for the season in the last match of the 1990 season with 194* and 107 v Nottinghamshire at Trent Bridge

Opinions on cricket: 'Politics should not interfere with sport – South Africa should be eligible for Test cricket.'
Best batting: 216* Yorkshire v Middlesex, Headingley 1988
Best bowling: 2–18 Yorkshire v Warwickshire, Scarborough 1987

LAST SEASON: BATTING

	I.	N. O.	R.	H. S.	AV.
TEST					
1ST	44	4	2047	194*	51.17
INT					
RAL	15	0	403	84	26.86
N.W.	3	2	175	127*	175.00
B&H	4	0	113	38	28.25

CAREER: BATTING

	I.	N. O.	R.	H. S.	AV.
TEST					
1ST	245	15	8473	216*	36.83
INT					
RAL	92	2	2404	115*	26.71
N.W.	15	3	584	127*	48.66
B&H	21	3	848	94*	47.11

METSON, C. P.   Glamorgan

Name: Colin Peter Metson
Role: Right-hand bat, wicket-keeper
Born: 2 July 1963, Cuffley, Herts
Height: 5ft 6in **Weight:** 10st 9lbs
Nickname: Dempster, Reggie, Jazzer
County debut: 1981 (Middlesex), 1987 (Glamorgan)
County cap: 1987 (Glamorgan)
1st-Class 50s scored: 4
Place in batting averages: 246th av. 16.00 (1989 216th av. 15.96)
Parents: Denis Alwyn and Jean Mary
Marital status: Single
Family links with cricket: Father played good club cricket and for MCC; brother plays for Winchmore Hill CC
Education: Stanborough School, Welwyn Garden City; Enfield Grammar School; Durham University
Qualifications: 10 O-levels, 5 A-levels, BA (Hons) Economic History, NCA senior coaching award

Cricketers particularly admired: Bob Taylor, Mike Brearley
Other sports followed: American football, golf, football, all sports except wrestling
Relaxations: Daily Telegraph crossword, reading, drinking good wine, Mexican food, watching most sports programmes
Extras: Young Wicket-keeper of the Year 1981. Played for England YCs v India 1981. Captain Durham University 1984, losing finalists in UAU competition. Left Middlesex at end of 1986 season

Opinions on cricket: 'Cricket must find ways to market itself better, and must give the sponsors value for money. I am in favour of 16 four-day matches.'
Best batting: 96 Middlesex v Gloucestershire, Uxbridge 1984

LAST SEASON: BATTING

	I.	N. O.	R.	H. S.	AV.
TEST					
1ST	27	5	352	50*	16.00
INT					
RAL	10	5	95	30*	19.00
N.W.	1	0	9	9	9.00
B&H	5	1	78	23	19.50

LAST SEASON: WICKET-KEEPING

	CT	ST
TEST		
1ST	59	0
INT		
RAL	10	2
N.W.	2	0
B&H	3	0

CAREER: BATTING

	I.	N. O.	R.	H. S.	AV.
TEST					
1ST	158	37	2021	96	16.70
INT					
RAL	46	24	354	30*	16.09
N.W.	5	1	19	9	4.75
B&H	12	1	124	23	11.27

CAREER: WICKET-KEEPING

	CT	ST
TEST		
1ST	264	22
INT		
RAL	66	18
N.W.	8	0
B&H	10	2

MIDDLETON, T. C.   Hampshire

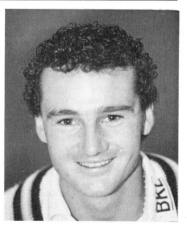

Name: Tony Charles Middleton
Role: Right-hand bat, slow left-arm bowler
Born: 1 February 1964, Winchester
Height: 5ft 11in **Weight:** 11st
Nickname: Roo, Midders, TC
County debut: 1984
1000 runs in a season: 1
1st-Class 50s scored: 8
1st-Class 100s scored: 5
One-Day 50s: 1
Place in batting averages: 62nd av. 47.61 (1989 121st av. 27.40)
1st-Class catches: 9 (career 25)
Parents: Pete and Molly
Wife and date of marriage: Sherralyn, 23 September 1989
Family links with cricket: Brother plays local club cricket in Hampshire
Education: Weeke Infants and Junior Schools; Montgomery of Alamein Comprehensive; Peter Symonds Sixth Form College, Winchester
Qualifications: 1 A-level, 5 O-levels
Off-season: 'Selling safety gear for Southampton Group Safety.'

Cricketers particularly admired: Barry Richards, Gordon Greenidge
Other sports followed: Football, Rugby Union, badminton, squash
Relaxations: Watching and playing other sports, gardening, real ale pubs
Extras: Played for England Schools 1982. Scored six consecutive 100s for Hampshire in May 1990: 104 & 144 v Somerset II; 121 v Yorkshire II; 100 & 124 v Leics II; 104* for 1st XI v Essex
Opinions on cricket: 'Four-day matches in the County Championship would produce better Test players and, played on good wickets, it would provide more interesting cricket for spectators. Unfortunately it would reduce vital income for clubs. Perhaps a better compromise could be reached in the future.'
Best batting: 127 Hampshire v Kent, Canterbury 1990
Best bowling: 1–13 Hampshire v Middlesex, Lord's 1986

LAST SEASON: BATTING

	I.	N. O.	R.	H. S.	AV.
TEST					
1ST	29	3	1238	127	47.61
INT					
RAL	1	0	72	72	72.00
N.W.					
B&H					

CAREER: BATTING

	I.	N. O.	R.	H. S.	AV.
TEST					
1ST	59	7	1878	127	36.11
INT					
RAL	2	1	76	72	76.00
N.W.					
B&H					

58. What is Trevor Jesty's nickname?

59. What is Bruce French's nickname?

60. What is Paul Downton's nickname?

MIKE, G. W.　　　　　　　Nottinghamshire

Name: Gregory Wentworth Mike
Role: Right-hand bat, right-arm
fast-medium bowler
Born: 14 August 1966, Nottingham
Height: 6ft 1in **Weight:** 14st
Nickname: Wenters
County debut: 1988 (RAL), 1989
(first-class)
1st-Class 50s scored: 1
1st-Class catches: 4 (career 4)
Parents: Clinton and Kathleen
Marital status: Single
Family links with cricket: 'My father
played.'
Education: Claremount Comprehensive;
Basford Hall College
Qualifications: 2 O-levels, 5 CSEs
Career outside cricket: Youth worker
Off-season: Playing abroad
Cricketers particularly admired: Ian
Botham, Viv Richards
Other sports followed: Snooker, football
Relaxations: Listening to music, playing snooker
Opinions on cricket: 'Great game to play and watch!'
Best batting: 56* Nottinghamshire v Cambridge University, Fenner's 1989
Best bowling: 2–62 Nottinghamshire v Cambridge University, Fenner's 1989

LAST SEASON: BATTING

	I.	N. O.	R.	H. S.	AV.
TEST					
1ST	5	1	45	18*	11.25
INT					
RAL	4	0	33	13	8.25
N.W.					
B&H					

CAREER: BATTING

	I.	N. O.	R.	H. S.	AV.
TEST					
1ST	7	2	116	56*	23.20
INT					
RAL	8	1	58	25*	8.28
N.W.					
B&H					

MILBURN, E. T.   Gloucestershire

Name: Edward Thomas Milburn
Role: Right-hand bat, right-arm
medium-fast bowler
Born: 15 September 1967, Nuneaton
Height: 6ft 1in **Weight:** 12st
Nickname: Ed
County debut: 1987 (Warwicks), 1990
(Gloucs)
1st-Class catches: 0 (career 2)
Family links with cricket: 'My father
has always loved the game.'
Education: Bablake School, Coventry;
King Edward VI College, Nuneaton
Qualifications: 1 A-level, 8 O-levels
Cricketers particularly admired:
Richard Hadlee
Other sports followed: Golf, squash
Relaxations: Reading science fiction
novels

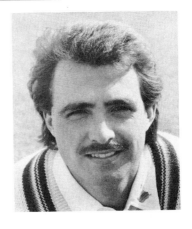

Extras: Released by Warwickshire at
end of 1988 season. Taken on to Gloucestershire staff in 1990 after playing for
Leicestershire and Gloucestershire 2nd XIs in 1989
Best batting: 35 Gloucestershire v Indians, Bristol 1990
Best bowling: 3–43 Gloucestershire v Indians, Bristol 1990

LAST SEASON: BATTING

	I.	N. O.	R.	H. S.	AV.
TEST					
1ST	4	2	49	35	24.50
INT					
RAL	2	2	9	5*	-
N.W.					
B&H	-	-	-	-	-

LAST SEASON: BOWLING

	O.	M.	R.	W.	AV.
TEST					
1ST	32.3	4	150	3	50.00
INT					
RAL	24	0	163	3	54.33
N.W.					
B&H	5	1	23	1	23.00

CAREER: BATTING

	I.	N. O.	R.	H. S.	AV.
TEST					
1ST	8	4	86	35	21.50
INT					
RAL	2	2	9	5*	-
N.W.					
B&H	-	-	-	-	-

CAREER: BOWLING

	O.	M.	R.	H. S.	AV.
TEST					
1ST	68.3	10	278	5	55.60
INT					
RAL	24	0	163	3	54.33
N.W.					
B&H	5	1	23	1	23.00

MILLER, G. Derbyshire

Name: Geoffrey Miller
Role: Right-hand bat, off-break bowler
Born: 8 September 1952, Chesterfield
Height: 6ft 2in **Weight:** 11st 6lbs
Nickname: Dusty
County debut: 1973 (Derbys), 1987 (Essex)
County cap: 1976 (Derbys), 1988 (Essex)
Benefit: 1985
Test debut: 1976
Tests: 34
One-Day Internationals: 25
50 wickets in a season: 4
1st-Class 50s scored: 72
1st-Class 100s scored: 2
1st-Class 5 w. in innings: 39
1st-Class 10 w. in match: 7
One-Day 50s: 17
Place in batting averages: 111th av. 38.83 (1989 91st av. 31.45)
Place in bowling averages: 74th av. 37.37 (1989 115th av. 46.40)
Strike rate: 79.02 (career 67.23)
1st-Class catches: 7 (career 309)
Parents: Keith and Gwen
Wife: Carol
Children: Helen Jane; Anna Louise; James Daniel
Family links with cricket: Father and brother played local cricket in Chesterfield
Education: Chesterfield Grammar School
Qualifications: 5 O-levels
Career outside cricket: Owner of two sports shops
Overseas tours: With England YCs to India 1970–71 and West Indies 1972; England to India, Sri Lanka, Australia 1976–77; Pakistan and New Zealand 1977–78; Australia 1978–79 and 1979–80 (returned early); West Indies 1980–81; Australia and New Zealand 1982–83
Overseas teams played for: Natal 1983–84
Cricketers particularly admired: 'The late Ken Barrington.'
Other sports followed: Golf, table tennis, football
Relaxations: 'Crosswords, reading, television, family life. Watching Chesterfield FC particularly, and all sports in general.'
Extras: Became captain of Derbyshire halfway through 1979 season, but resigned halfway through 1981 season in favour of Barry Wood. After almost leaving in 1982, he left Derbyshire at the end of 1986 and joined Essex. Released by Essex at end of

1989 season, and returned to Derbyshire. Retired at end of 1990
Best batting: 130 Derbyshire v Lancashire, Old Trafford 1984
Best bowling: 8–70 Derbyshire v Leicestershire, Coalville 1982

LAST SEASON: BATTING

	I.	N.O.	R.	H.S.	AV.
TEST					
1ST	14	8	233	47*	38.83
INT					
RAL	2	1	16	14*	16.00
N.W.	1	0	0	0	0.00
B&H	-	-	-	-	-

LAST SEASON: BOWLING

	O.	M.	R.	W.	AV.
TEST					
1ST	461	114	1308	35	37.37
INT					
RAL	72	2	397	6	66.16
N.W.	22	1	87	1	87.00
B&H	22	0	88	1	88.00

CAREER: BATTING

	I.	N.O.	R.	H.S.	AV.
TEST	51	4	1213	98*	25.80
1ST	497	90	10814	130	26.57
INT	18	2	136	46	8.50
RAL	159	35	2580	84	20.80
N.W.	21	4	357	59*	21.00
B&H	54	13	1027	88*	25.04

CAREER: BOWLING

	O.	M.	R.	W.	AV.
TEST	858.1	219	1859	60	30.98
1ST	9092	2476	22995	828	27.77
INT	211.4	20	813	25	32.52
RAL	1082.3	70	4623	153	30.21
N.W.	257.3	54	736	24	30.66
B&H	566	102	1687	62	27.21

MILLNS, D. J.   Leicestershire

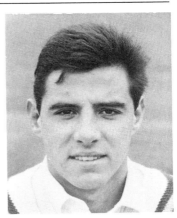

Name: David James Millns
Role: Left-hand bat, right-arm fast medium bowler, slip fielder
Born: 27 February 1965, Mansfield
Height: 6ft 3in **Weight:** 14st
Nickname: Lendus
County debut: 1988 (Notts), 1990 (Leics)
1st-class 5 w. in innings: 2
Place in bowling averages: 3rd av. 21.35
Strike rate: 39.99 (career 52.10)
1st-Class catches: 3 (career 9)
Parents: Bernard and Brenda
Marital status: Single
Family links with cricket: Father and brother both play club cricket
Education: Garibaldi Comprehensive
Qualifications: 9 CSEs; qualified coach
Career outside cricket: Worked for British Coal as a linesman on the surveying staff at Clipstone Colliery
Off-season: Playing club cricket and coaching in Auckland

Cricketers particularly admired: Justin Benson, Russell Evans
Other sports followed: All sports
Relaxations: Watching films, eating, walking, reading
Extras: Left Nottinghamshire and joined Leicestershire for the 1990 season. Finished third in national bowling averages
Opinions on cricket: 'Over-rate fines should be scrapped. With the new balls and better pitches quality bowling is what the TCCB are aiming for not quantity. They can't have it both ways.'
Best batting: 10* Leicestershire v Kent, Dartford 1990
Best bowling: 6–63 Leicestershire v Northamptonshire, Leicester 1990

LAST SEASON: BATTING

	I.	N. O.	R.	H. S.	AV.
TEST					
1ST	10	5	23	10*	4.60
INT					
RAL	1	0	0	0	0.00
N.W.					
B&H					

LAST SEASON: BOWLING

	O.	M.	R.	W.	AV.
TEST					
1ST	206.4	36	662	31	21.35
INT					
RAL	29	2	187	6	31.16
N.W.					
B&H					

CAREER: BATTING

	I.	N. O.	R.	H. S.	AV.
TEST					
1ST	25	11	59	10*	4.21
INT					
RAL	3	2	0	0*	0.00
N.W.					
B&H					

CAREER: BOWLING

	O.	M.	R.	W.	AV.
TEST					
1ST	503.4	80	1744	58	30.06
INT					
RAL	58	2	366	9	40.66
N.W.					
B&H					

MOLES, A. J.

Warwickshire

Name: Andrew James Moles
Role: Right-hand opening bat, right-arm medium bowler
Born: 12 February 1961, Solihull
Height: 5ft 10in **Weight:** 'Above average'
Nickname: Moler
County debut: 1986
County cap: 1987
1000 runs in a season: 3
1st-Class 50s scored: 39
1st-Class 100s scored: 20
1st-Class 200s scored: 3
One-Day 50s: 13
One-Day 100s: 1
Place in batting averages: 56th av. 48.78 (1989 73rd av. 34.48)
1st-Class catches: 12 (career 88)
Parents: Stuart Francis and Gillian Margaret
Wife and date of marriage: Jacquie, 17 December 1988
Children: Daniel
Family links with cricket: Brother plays club cricket
Education: Finham Park Comprehensive, Coventry; Henley College of Further Education; Butts College of Further Education
Qualifications: 3 O-levels, 4 CSEs, Toolmaker/Standard Room Inspector City & Guilds
Career outside cricket: Host and sell corporate hospitality

LAST SEASON: BATTING

	I.	N. O.	R.	H. S.	AV.
TEST					
1ST	46	8	1854	224*	48.78
INT					
RAL	6	0	229	81	38.16
N.W.	2	0	87	60	43.50
B&H	2	0	109	57	54.50

LAST SEASON: BOWLING

	O.	M.	R.	W.	AV.
TEST					
1ST	22	2	133	2	66.50
INT					
RAL					
N.W.					
B&H					

CAREER: BATTING

	I.	N. O.	R.	H. S.	AV.
TEST					
1ST	214	25	8118	230*	42.95
INT					
RAL	37	2	857	85	24.48
N.W.	13	0	397	127	30.53
B&H	14	0	428	72	30.57

CAREER: BOWLING

	O.	M.	R.	W.	AV.
TEST					
1ST	465	97	1517	33	45.97
INT					
RAL	63	0	358	7	51.14
N.W.	15	0	81	0	-
B&H	31	0	151	2	75.50

Off-season: 'Getting fit!!! Working for West Midland Travel.'
Overseas teams played for: Griqualand West, South Africa 1986–88
Cricketers particularly admired: Dennis Amiss, Fred Gardner, Tom Moody
Other sports followed: Football, golf
Relaxations: Playing golf and spending time with family
Opinions on cricket: 'We should play 16 four-day matches.'
Best batting: 230* Griqualand West v Northern Transvaal B, Verwoerdburn 1988–89
Best bowling: 3–21 Warwickshire v Oxford University, The Parks 1987

MOODY, T. M.   Worcestershire

Name: Thomas Masson Moody
Role: Right-hand bat, right-arm medium bowler
Born: 2 October 1965, Adelaide
Height: 6ft 6in
County debut: 1990 (Warwicks)
County cap: 1990 (Warwicks)
Test debut: 1989–90
Tests: 4
One-Day Internationals: 13
1000 runs in a season: 1
1st-Class 50s scored: 20
1st-Class 100s scored: 16
1st-Class 200s scored: 1
One-Day 50s: 8
Place in batting averages: 3rd av. 89.46
1st-Class catches: 4 (career 36)
Off-season: Playing cricket in Australia
Overseas tours: Australia to England 1989
Overseas teams played for: Western Australia 1985–90
Extras: Scored 150s in both innings of 1988–89 Sheffield Shield Final for Western Australia v Queensland; hit a century against Warwickshire during Australia's 1989 tour – signed on a one-year contract for 1990. Hit centuries in first three first-class matches for Warwickshire, and seven in first eight matches – a unique achievement. Scored the fastest ever first-class century v Glamorgan in 26 minutes – taking advantage of deliberate declaration bowling. Reached 1000 first-class runs in first season of county cricket in only 12 innings – another record. Released by Warwickshire at the end of the 1990 season after they had chosen Allan Donald as their one overseas player. Signed by Worcestershire for 1991 as Graeme Hick's replacement

Best batting: 202 Western Australia v Victoria, Perth 1988–89
Best bowling: 4–30 Australians v Kent, Canterbury 1989

LAST SEASON: BATTING

	I.	N. O.	R.	H. S.	AV.
TEST					
1ST	15	2	1163	168	89.46
INT					
RAL	14	1	382	64	29.38
N.W.	2	0	109	58	54.50
B&H	3	0	90	41	30.00

LAST SEASON: BOWLING

	O.	M.	R.	W.	AV.
TEST					
1ST	59	15	212	3	70.66
INT					
RAL	55.3	2	315	6	52.50
N.W.	10.1	0	41	1	41.00
B&H	25	1	152	0	-

CAREER: BATTING

	I.	N. O.	R.	H. S.	AV.
TEST	6	0	234	106	39.00
1ST	117	9	5005	202	46.34
INT	13	2	281	89	25.54
RAL	14	1	382	64	29.38
N.W.	2	0	109	58	54.50
B&H	3	0	90	41	30.00

CAREER: BOWLING

	O.	M.	R.	W.	AV.
TEST	39	15	53	1	53.00
1ST	415.3	129	1093	31	35.25
INT	17	0	81	1	81.00
RAL	55.3	2	315	6	52.50
N.W.	10.1	0	41	1	41.00
B&H	25	1	152	0	-

MOORES, P. Sussex

Name: Peter Moores
Role: Right-hand bat, wicket-keeper
Born: 18 December 1962, Macclesfield, Cheshire
Height: 6ft **Weight:** 13st
Nickname: Stumper, Billy
County debut: 1983 (Worcs), 1985 (Sussex)
1st-Class 50s scored: 8
1st-Class 100s scored: 2
Place in batting averages: 214th av. 21.68 (1989 130th av. 26.20)
Parents: Bernard and Winifred
Wife and date of marriage: Karen, 28 September 1989
Family links with cricket: Three brothers, Anthony, Stephen and Robert, all play club cricket
Education: King Edward VI School, Macclesfield
Qualifications: 7 O-levels, 3 A-levels. Senior NCA coaching award
Off-season: Christians in Sport to India; working with the Britannia Building Society in their research and development department
Overseas teams played for: Orange Free State, South Africa 1988–89

Cricketers particularly admired: Bob Taylor, Alan Knott, Clive Lloyd
Other sports followed: Football, golf
Relaxations: Photography, golf, music and real ale
Extras: On the MCC ground staff in 1982 before joining Worcestershire in latter half of 1982 season. Joined Sussex in 1985
Opinions on cricket: 'The B&H should be spread over more of the season so more Championship cricket can be played early on. I am in favour of four-day cricket as it would give players a rest day each week and allow for more genuine results. This would only raise the quality of cricket played.'
Best batting: 116 Sussex v Somerset, Hove 1989

LAST SEASON: BATTING

	I.	N. O.	R.	H. S.	AV.
TEST					
1ST	36	4	694	106*	21.68
INT					
RAL	11	4	67	17*	9.57
N.W.	1	0	0	0	0.00
B&H	3	0	130	76	43.33

LAST SEASON: WICKET-KEEPING

	CT	ST			
TEST					
1ST	53	10			
INT					
RAL	14	4			
N.W.	2	1			
B&H	1	1			

CAREER: BATTING

	I.	N. O.	R.	H. S.	AV.
TEST					
1ST	130	17	2368	116	20.95
INT					
RAL	37	15	244	34	11.09
N.W.	5	1	48	20	12.00
B&H	6	1	134	76	26.80

CAREER: WICKET-KEEPING

	CT	ST			
TEST					
1ST	182	21			
INT					
RAL	50	15			
N.W.	8	2			
B&H	7	2			

61. Which was Viv Richards's previous county?

62. Which was Raj Maru's previous county?

63. Which was Graham Dilley's previous county?

MORRIS, H.   Glamorgan

Name: Hugh Morris
Role: Left-hand bat, right-arm medium bowler, slip fielder
Born: 5 October 1963, Cardiff
Height: 5ft 8in **Weight:** 12st 4lbs
Nickname: H, Banacek
County debut: 1981
County cap: 1986
1000 runs in a season: 4
1st-Class 50s scored: 45
1st-Class 100s scored: 19
One-Day 50s: 18
One-Day 100s: 6
Place in batting averages: 34th av. 55.51 (1989 79th av. 32.95)
1st-Class catches: 14 (career 85)
Parents: Roger and Anne
Marital status: Single
Family links with cricket: Brother played for Wales U–16. Father played league cricket
Education: Blundell's School; South Glamorgan Institute of HE
Qualifications: 9 O-levels, 3 A-levels, 1 AO-level, BA (Hons), NCA coaching award
Career outside cricket: Marketing Department, Glamorgan CCC; sales representative; journalist with local paper
Off-season: Captaining England A in Pakistan – also flew out to Australia as batting cover after Graham Gooch's hand injury
Overseas tours: English Public Schoolboys to West Indies 1980–81; to Sri Lanka 1982–83; England A to Pakistan 1990–91; (called up to join England tour party in Australia)
Cricketers particularly admired: Ian Botham, Javed Miandad, Viv Richards, Jimmy Cook
Other sports followed: Rugby, golf, football
Injuries: 'Fortunately I had an injury-free season.'
Relaxations: Music, watching movies, travelling and holiday at end of the season
Extras: Highest schoolboy cricket average in 1979 (89.71), 1981 (184.6) and 1982 (149.2). Captain of England U–19 Schoolboys in 1981 and 1982. Played for England YCs v West Indies 1982, and captain v Australia 1983. Played first-class rugby for Aberavon 1984–85 and South Glamorgan Institute, scoring over 150 points. Appointed youngest ever Glamorgan captain 1986, but resigned in 1989 to concentrate on batting. In 1990 scored most runs in a season by a Glamorgan player (2276) and hit most 100s (10). After missing selection for the tour of Australia,

appointed captain for England A's tour of Pakistan; then, after Gooch had required a hand operation and England had lost the First Test to Australia, he flew out to join the senior tour until the England captain recovered

Best batting: 160* Glamorgan v Derbyshire, Cardiff 1990
Best bowling: 1–6 Glamorgan v Oxford University, The Parks 1987

LAST SEASON: BATTING

	I.	N. O.	R.	H. S.	AV.
TEST					
1ST	46	5	2276	160*	55.51
INT					
RAL	15	0	311	68	20.73
N.W.	3	0	200	116	66.66
B&H	5	0	203	106	40.60

CAREER: BATTING

	I.	N. O.	R.	H. S.	AV.
TEST					
1ST	274	28	8664	160*	35.22
INT					
RAL	84	8	2149	100	28.27
N.W.	14	2	684	154*	57.00
B&H	23	2	642	143*	30.57

MORRIS, J. E. Derbyshire

Name: John Edward Morris
Role: Right-hand bat, right-arm medium bowler, county vice-captain
Born: 1 April 1964, Crewe
Height: 5ft 10 1/2in **Weight:** 13st 6lbs
Nickname: Animal
County debut: 1982
County cap: 1986
Test debut: 1990
Tests: 3
1000 runs in a season: 5
1st-Class 50s scored: 46
1st-Class 100s scored: 23
One-Day 50s: 15
One-Day 100s: 5
Place in batting averages: 38th av. 54.03 (1989 28th av. 43.10)
1st-Class catches: 12 (career 76)
Parents: George (Eddie) and Jean
Wife and date of marriage: Sally, 30 September 1990

Family links with cricket: Father played for Crewe CC for many years as an opening bowler
Education: Shavington Comprehensive School; Dane Bank College of Further Education
Qualifications: O-levels
Career outside cricket: BMW car sales and promotion

Off-season: Touring Australia with England
Overseas teams played for: Griqualand West, South Africa 1988–89
Other sports followed: Athletics, motor racing, football, snooker
Relaxations: Movies, music, good food, fly-fishing
Extras: Youngest player to score a Sunday League 100
Best batting: 191 Derbyshire v Kent, Derby 1986
Best bowling: 1–13 Derbyshire v Yorkshire, Harrogate 1987

LAST SEASON: BATTING

	I.	N. O.	R.	H. S.	AV.
TEST	5	2	71	32	23.66
1ST	28	4	1388	157*	57.83
INT					
RAL	15	0	508	134	33.86
N.W.	2	1	168	94*	168.00
B&H	4	0	152	123	38.00

CAREER: BATTING

	I.	N. O.	R.	H. S.	AV.
TEST	5	2	71	32	23.66
1ST	278	22	9727	191	37.99
INT					
RAL	103	8	2688	134	28.29
N.W.	15	3	350	94*	29.16
B&H	27	3	605	123	25.20

MORTENSEN, O. H.   Derbyshire

Name: Ole Henrik Mortensen
Role: Right-hand bat, right-arm
fast-medium bowler
Born: 29 January 1958, Vejle, Denmark
Height: 6ft 4in **Weight:** 14st 2lbs
Nickname: Stan, Blood-Axe
County debut: 1983
County cap: 1986
50 wickets in a season: 2
1st-Class 50s scored: 1
1st-Class 5 w. in innings: 13
1st-Class 10 w. in match: 1
Place in bowling averages: 5th av.
22.42 (1989 14th av. 20.41)
Strike rate: 54.22 (career 49.17)
1st-Class catches: 5 (career 35)
Parents: Will Ernst and Inge Wicka
Wife: Jette Jepmond
Children: Julie Jepmond, 30 August
1982
Family links with cricket: 'My small brother, Michael, used to play cricket. He is
now a professional tennis player, and has played in Davis Cup for Denmark.'
Education: Brondbyoster School; Avedore School
Career outside cricket: Worked as a tax assistant in Denmark
Overseas tours: Danish national side to East Africa, England, Scotland, Wales,
Ireland and Holland

Cricketers particularly admired: Dennis Lillee, Bob Taylor
Other sports played: Tennis, golf, football
Relaxations: Music, books, movies
Extras: *Derbyshire's Dane* by Peter Hargreaves, published 1984. Played for Denmark in the ICC Trophy. Most economical bowler in Refuge League 1990
Opinions on cricket: 'Too much cricket; seam bowlers turn into robots by August.'
Best batting: 74* Derbyshire v Yorkshire, Chesterfield 1987
Best bowling: 6–27 Derbyshire v Yorkshire, Sheffield 1983

LAST SEASON: BATTING

	I.	N. O.	R.	H. S.	AV.
TEST					
1ST	11	9	20	5*	10.00
INT					
RAL	2	2	2	2*	-
N.W.	1	0	0	0	0.00
B&H	1	1	2	2*	-

LAST SEASON: BOWLING

	O.	M.	R.	W.	AV.
TEST					
1ST	316.2	91	785	35	22.42
INT					
RAL	118	9	364	10	36.40
N.W.	23	6	51	4	12.75
B&H	40	9	131	2	65.50

CAREER: BATTING

	I.	N. O.	R.	H. S.	AV.
TEST					
1ST	129	70	560	74*	9.49
INT					
RAL	37	26	67	11	6.09
N.W.	10	6	24	11	6.00
B&H	7	4	8	3*	2.66

CAREER: BOWLING

	O.	M.	R.	W.	AV.
TEST					
1ST	2403.2	688	6730	298	22.58
INT					
RAL	750.3	76	2691	100	26.91
N.W.	147	38	390	26	15.00
B&H	268.2	41	797	37	21.54

64. Which was Phillip DeFreitas's previous county?

65. Which was Neal Radford's previous county?

66. Who succeeded Clive Lloyd as West Indies' manager?

MOXON, M. D.   Yorkshire

Name: Martyn Douglas Moxon
Role: Right-hand bat, right-arm medium
bowler, slip fielder, county captain
Born: 4 May 1960, Barnsley
Height: 6ft 1in **Weight:** 13st 7lbs
Nickname: Frog
County debut: 1981
County cap: 1984
Test debut: 1986
Tests: 10
One-Day Internationals: 8
1000 runs in a season: 6
1st-Class 50s scored: 63
1st-Class 100s scored: 25
1st-class 200s scored: 1
One-Day 50s: 27
One-Day 100s: 3
Place in batting averages: 59th av.
48.02 (1989 64th av. 35.57)

1st-Class catches: 14 (career 159)
Parents: Audrey and Derek (deceased)
Wife and date of marriage: Sue, October 1985
Children: Charlotte Louise, 13 March 1990
Family links with cricket: Father and grandfather played local league cricket
Education: Holgate Grammar School, Barnsley
Qualifications: 8 O-levels, 3 A-levels, HNC in Business Studies, NCA coaching
award
Overseas tours: England to India and Australia 1984–85; Australia and New

LAST SEASON: BATTING

	I.	N. O.	R.	H. S.	AV.
TEST					
1ST	40	6	1633	218*	48.02
INT					
RAL	10	0	455	105	45.50
N.W.	3	2	164	107*	164.00
B&H	3	0	24	11	8.00

LAST SEASON: BOWLING

	O.	M.	R.	W.	AV.
TEST					
1ST	57	9	175	3	58.33
INT					
RAL	24.5	0	128	6	21.33
N.W.	7	2	19	2	9.50
B&H					

CAREER: BATTING

	I.	N. O.	R.	H. S.	AV.
TEST	17	1	455	99	28.43
1ST	319	24	11725	218*	39.74
INT	8	0	174	70	21.75
RAL	73	5	2088	105	30.70
N.W.	18	6	737	107*	61.41
B&H	29	4	1081	106*	43.24

CAREER: BOWLING

	O.	M.	R.	W.	AV.
TEST	8	2	30	0	-
1ST	415.4	69	1410	26	54.23
INT					
RAL	136.2	3	738	16	46.12
N.W.	26	6	85	5	17.00
B&H	42	1	168	4	42.00

Zealand 1987–88; England B to Sri Lanka 1985–86
Overseas teams played for: Griqualand West, South Africa 1982–83 and 1983–84
Cricketers particularly admired: Viv Richards
Other sports followed: Football (supporter of Barnsley FC) and golf
Injuries: Broken left big toe, split webbing on right hand
Relaxations: Listening to most types of music, having a drink with friends
Extras: Captained Yorkshire Schools U–15s, North of England U–15s and Yorkshire Senior Schools. Played for Wombwell Cricket Lovers' Society U–18 side. First Yorkshire player to make centuries in his first two Championship games in Yorkshire, 116 v Essex at Headingley (on debut) and 111 v Derbyshire at Sheffield, and scored 153 in his first innings in a Roses Match. Picked for Lord's Test of 1984 v West Indies, but had to withdraw through injury and had to wait until 1986 to make Test debut. Appointed Yorkshire captain in 1990
Best batting: 218* Yorkshire v Sussex, Eastbourne 1990
Best bowling: 3–24 Yorkshire v Hampshire, Southampton 1989

MULLALLY, A. D. Leicestershire

Name: Alan David Mullally
Role: Right-hand bat, left-arm fast-medium bowler
Born: 12 July 1969, Southend
Height: 6ft 5in **Weight:** 13st 5lb
Nickname: Spider
County debut: 1988 (Hampshire), 1990 (Leics)
Place in bowling averages: 79th av. 38.05
Strike rate: 76.94 (career 82.52)
1st-Class catches: 4 (career 9)
Parents: Michael and Ann
Marital status: Single
Education: Cannington High, Perth, Australia
Qualifications: Radio technician
Off-season: Playing Shield cricket in Australia

Overseas teams played for: Western Australia
Cricketers particularly admired: Dennis Lillee, Wayne Andrews, Neil Mullally
Other sports followed: Hockey, hurling, Australian Rules
Injuries: Hip strain
Relaxations: 'Music (UB40 etc), pubs, beaches – especially North Cottesloe.'
Extras: English-qualified as he was born in Southend, he made his first-class debut for Western Australia in the 1987–88 Sheffield Shield final, and played one match

for Hampshire in 1988. Joined Leicestershire for 1990 season
Opinions on cricket: 'Too much cricket is played. Reduce the number of playing days and the stupid over-rate fines.'
Best batting: 34 Western Australia v Tasmania, Perth 1989–90
Best bowling: 4–59 Leicestershire v Yorkshire, Sheffield 1990

LAST SEASON: BATTING

	I.	N. O.	R.	H. S.	AV.
TEST					
1ST	18	6	113	29	9.41
INT					
RAL	6	3	26	10*	8.66
N.W.	-	-	-	-	-
B&H	-	-	-	-	-

LAST SEASON: BOWLING

	O.	M.	R.	W.	AV.
TEST					
1ST	487.2	117	1446	38	38.05
INT					
RAL	97.1	3	431	12	35.91
N.W.	12	0	55	2	27.50
B&H	21	5	75	2	37.50

CAREER: BATTING

	I.	N. O.	R.	H. S.	AV.
TEST					
1ST	30	10	177	34	8.85
INT					
RAL	6	3	26	10*	8.66
N.W.	-	-	-	-	-
B&H	-	-	-	-	-

CAREER: BOWLING

	O.	M.	R.	W.	AV.
TEST					
1ST	1037.5	236	3053	75	40.72
INT					
RAL	97.1	3	431	12	35.91
N.W.	12	0	55	2	27.50
B&H	21	5	75	2	37.50

MUNTON, T. A. Warwickshire

Name: Timothy Alan Munton
Role: Right-hand bat, right-arm fast-medium bowler
Born: 30 July 1965, Melton Mowbray
Height: 6ft 6in **Weight:** 15st 7lbs
Nickname: Harry, Herman
County debut: 1985
County cap: 1990
50 wickets in a season: 2
1st-Class 5 w. in innings: 7
Place in bowling averages: 25th av. 28.89 (1989 39th av. 26.06)
Strike rate: 63.62 (career 59.38)
1st-Class catches: 9 (career 26)
Parents: Alan and Brenda
Wife and date of marriage: Helen, 20 September 1986
Children: Camilla, 13 August 1988
Education: Sarson High School, King Edward VII Upper School, Melton Mowbray
Qualifications: 8 O-levels, 1 A-level; NCA coaching certificate

Career outside cricket: Brewery salesman
Off-season: Touring Pakistan with England A
Cricketers particularly admired: Richard Hadlee
Other sports followed: Basketball, soccer
Relaxations: 'Playing basketball, spending time with my family.'
Extras: Appeared for Leicestershire 2nd XI 1982–84. Second highest wicket-taker in 1990 with 78
Opinions on cricket: 'The four-day game is a must. Coloured clothing should be introduced for Sunday cricket.'
Best batting: 38 Warwickshire v Yorkshire, Scarborough 1987
Best bowling: 6–21 Warwickshire v Worcestershire, Edgbaston 1988

LAST SEASON: BATTING

	I.	N. O.	R.	H. S.	AV.
TEST					
1ST	24	9	125	29*	8.33
INT					
RAL	5	4	17	6*	17.00
N.W.	1	1	1	1*	-
B&H	2	1	1	1	1.00

CAREER: BATTING

	I.	N. O.	R.	H. S.	AV.
TEST					
1ST	97	38	473	38	8.01
INT					
RAL	18	15	50	7*	16.66
N.W.	3	3	2	1*	-
B&H	7	5	23	13	11.50

LAST SEASON: BOWLING

	O.	M.	R.	W.	AV.
TEST					
1ST	827.1	199	2254	78	28.89
INT					
RAL	111.5	13	424	16	26.50
N.W.	18	1	77	3	25.66
B&H	39	3	143	4	35.75

CAREER: BOWLING

	O.	M.	R.	W.	AV.
TEST					
1ST	2513.5	643	4685	179	26.17
INT					
RAL	439.2	46	1762	59	29.86
N.W.	89.4	11	314	11	28.54
B&H	155	13	537	16	33.56

MURPHY, A. J. Surrey

Name: Anthony John Murphy
Role: Right-hand bat, right-arm medium bowler
Born: 6 August 1962, Manchester
Height: 5ft 11in **Weight:** 'Under review'
Nickname: Audi, Headless, Tramp, Compo
County debut: 1985 (Lancs), 1989 (Surrey)
50 wickets in a season: 1
1st-Class 5 w. in innings: 4
Place in bowling averages: 113th av. 45.56 (1989 75th av. 30.89)
Strike rate: 80.86 (career 65.97)
1st-Class catches: 1 (career 8)
Parents: John Desmond and Elizabeth Catherine
Marital status: Single
Family links with cricket: Brother plays club cricket in London; 'distant cousin plays in Ireland.'
Education: Xaverian College, Manchester; Swansea University
Qualifications: 9 O-levels, 4 A-levels
Off-season: 'Working in the City and practising my Swahili in Mombassa.'
Overseas teams played for: Central Districts, New Zealand 1985–86
Cricketers particularly admired: Clive Lloyd, Michael Holding ('both great ambassadors for cricket as well as great exponents of the game')

LAST SEASON: BATTING

	I.	N. O.	R.	H. S.	AV.
TEST					
1ST	6	3	6	4*	2.00
INT					
RAL	-	-	-	-	-
N.W.	-	-	-	-	-
B&H	1	1	0	0*	-

LAST SEASON: BOWLING

	O.	M.	R.	W.	AV.
TEST					
1ST	404.2	76	1367	30	45.56
INT					
RAL	59	1	303	10	30.30
N.W.	12	1	46	1	46.00
B&H	29	5	138	4	34.50

CAREER: BATTING

	I.	N. O.	R.	H. S.	AV.
TEST					
1ST	46	18	109	38	3.89
INT					
RAL	6	2	6	3	1.50
N.W.	-	-	-	-	-
B&H	4	2	5	5*	2.50

CAREER: BOWLING

	O.	M.	R.	W.	AV.
TEST					
1ST	1003.1	151	3276	98	33.42
INT					
RAL	175	7	803	32	25.09
N.W.	47	5	180	5	36.00
B&H	56	7	234	4	58.50

Other sports followed: American football, wrestling
Injuries: Broken thumb – out all of July
Relaxations: 'Boulder-breaking in Shoreham, building an outdoor pool for my house.'
Extras: 'I have too many theories about bowling.'
Opinions on cricket: 'My opinion about the balance between batting and bowling in the 1990 season is not really printable. I think it is just too much in the batsman's favour.'
Best batting: 38 Surrey v Gloucestershire, The Oval 1989
Best bowling: 6–97 Surrey v Derbyshire, Derby 1989

NEALE, P. A.   Worcestershire

Name: Phillip Anthony Neale
Role: Right-hand bat, county captain
Born: 5 June 1954, Scunthorpe
Height: 5ft 11in **Weight:** 12st 5lbs
Nickname: Phil
County debut: 1975
County cap: 1978
Benefit: 1988 (153,005)
1000 runs in a season: 8
1st-Class 50s scored: 87
1st-Class 100s scored: 28
One-Day 50s: 31
One-Day 100s: 2
Place in batting averages: 82nd av. 44.36 (1989 42nd av. 40.04)
1st-Class catches: 12 (career 127)
Parents: Geoff and Margaret
Wife and date of marriage: Christine, 26 September 1976
Children: Kelly Joanne, 9 November 1979; Craig Andrew, 11 February 1982
Education: Frederick Gough Grammar School, Scunthorpe; John Leggot Sixth Form College, Scunthorpe; Leeds University
Qualifications: 10 O-levels, 2 A-levels, BA (Hons) Russian. Preliminary football and cricket coaching awards
Career outside cricket: 'Phil Neale Tours Ltd – sports tours around the world for cricket, rugby and golf, specialising in Zimbabwe.'
Cricketers particularly admired: Basil D'Oliveira, Norman Gifford, Alan Ormrod
Other sports followed: Most sports – mainly via TV
Injuries 1989: Thigh injury needing an operation August 1990
Relaxations: 'Reading, spending time with my family, trying to play golf.'

284

Extras: Played for Lincolnshire 1973–74. Captain of Worcestershire since 1983. Professional footballer with Lincoln City until 1985. Celebrated his benefit season by captaining Worcestershire to a County Championship and Sunday League double in 1988. Autobiography *A Double Life* published in 1990
Best batting: 167 Worcestershire v Sussex, Kidderminster 1988
Best bowling: 1–15 Worcestershire v Derbyshire, Worcester 1976

LAST SEASON: BATTING	I.	N. O.	R.	H. S.	AV.
TEST					
1ST	32	10	976	122	44.36
INT					
RAL	11	1	197	40	19.70
N.W.	1	0	43	43	43.00
B&H	6	1	129	50	25.80

CAREER: BATTING	I.	N. O.	R.	H. S.	AV.
TEST					
1ST	546	88	16879	167	36.85
INT					
RAL	200	47	4457	102	29.13
N.W.	30	3	944	98	34.96
B&H	58	7	1516	128	29.72

NEWELL, M.   Nottinghamshire

Name: Michael Newell
Role: Right-hand opening bat, leg-break bowler, occasional wicket-keeper, short leg
Born: 25 February 1965, Blackburn
Height: 5ft 8in **Weight:** 11st
Nickname: Sam, Tricky, Mott, Merrick
County debut: 1984
County cap: 1987
1000 runs in a season: 1
1st-Class 50s scored: 23
1st-Class 100s scored: 6
1st-Class 200s scored: 1
One-Day 50s: 4
One-Day 100s: 1
Place in batting averages: 138th av. 34.04 (1989 156th av. 22.70)
1st-Class catches: 4
(career 90 & 1 stumping)

Parents: Barry and Janet
Wife and date of marriage: Jayne, 23 September 1989
Family links with cricket: Father chairman of Notts Unity CC. Brother Paul plays for Loughborough University
Education: West Bridgford Comprehensive
Qualifications: 8 O-levels, 3 A-levels. NCA advanced coach
Off-season: Coaching and playing in Rotorua, New Zealand

Cricketers particularly admired: Franklyn Stephenson, John Birch
Other sports followed: Watches Rugby Union and football, horse racing
Relaxations: Good films, music and drinking at the Trent Bridge Inn
Extras: Carried his bat through the Nottinghamshire innings v Warwickshire, scoring 10 out of Nottinghamshire's 44
Opinions on cricket: 'I feel that individuals should not be prevented from playing in South Africa, though rebel team tours are undoubtedly a danger to the future of Test cricket.'
Best batting: 203* Nottinghamshire v Derbyshire, Derby 1987
Best bowling: 2–38 Nottinghamshire v Sri Lankans, Trent Bridge 1988

LAST SEASON: BATTING

	I.	N. O.	R.	H. S.	AV.
TEST					
1ST	27	2	851	112	34.04
INT					
RAL	8	3	312	109*	62.40
N.W.	2	0	39	35	19.50
B&H	1	0	13	13	13.00

LAST SEASON: BOWLING

	O.	M.	R.	W.	AV.
TEST					
1ST	8.2	3	35	1	35.00
INT					
RAL					
N.W.					
B&H					

CAREER: BATTING

	I.	N. O.	R.	H. S.	AV.
TEST					
1ST	174	24	4470	203*	29.80
INT					
RAL	20	4	562	109*	35.12
N.W.	5	0	136	60	27.20
B&H	9	1	187	39	23.37

CAREER: BOWLING

	O.	M.	R.	W.	AV.
TEST					
1ST	60.5	9	282	7	40.28
INT					
RAL					
N.W.	1	0	10	0	-
B&H					

67. Which current county cricketer played soccer for England v Scotland Schoolboys?

68. Who has the better average as an England opener, Boycott or Amiss?

69. What have Jack Russell and Jimmy Cook got in common?

NEWPORT, P. J. — Worcestershire

Name: Philip John Newport
Role: Right-hand bat, right-arm
fast-medium bowler, outfielder
Born: 11 October 1962, High Wycombe
Height: 6ft 2in **Weight:** 13st 7lbs
Nickname: Schnozz, Barney Rubble
County debut: 1982
County cap: 1986
Test debut: 1988
Tests: 2
50 wickets in a season: 3
1st-Class 50s scored: 9
1st-Class 5 w. in innings: 23
1st-Class 10 w. in match: 3
Place in batting averages: 130th av.
35.33 (1989 231st av. 13.80)
Place in bowling averages: 37th av.
31.76 (1989 24th av. 22.00)
Strike rate: 59.65 (career 49.20)
1st-Class catches: 6 (career 45)
Parents: John and Sheila Diana
Wife and date of marriage: Christine, 26 October 1985
Children: Nathan, 10 May 1989
Family links with cricket: 'Father was a good club cricketer, my younger brother Stewart plays for Octopus CC.'
Education: Royal Grammar School, High Wycombe; Portsmouth Polytechnic
Qualifications: 8 O-levels, 3 A-levels, BA (Hons) Geography, basic coaching qualification
Off-season: Touring Pakistan with England A
Overseas tours: Selected for cancelled England tour to India 1988–89; England A to Pakistan 1990–91
Overseas teams played for: Boland, South Africa 1987–88
Cricketers particularly admired: John Lever, Graeme Pollock
Other sports followed: American football, soccer, athletics
Injuries: Side strain – out for ten days
Relaxations: Cinema, eating out
Extras: Had trial as schoolboy for Southampton FC. Played cricket for NAYC England Schoolboys 1981 and for Buckinghamshire in Minor Counties Championship in 1981 and 1982
Opinions on cricket: 'Over-rate fines for one-day games should be abolished. Much of the first-class cricket in 1990 was a farce. If the new ball, dry grassless pitches and four-day cricket recipe was supposed to have improved the ability of players and the game as a spectacle, it has failed. Any seamer taking over 65 wickets deserves a

medal!'
Best batting: 98 Worcestershire v New Zealand, Worcester 1990
Best bowling: 8–52 Worcestershire v Middlesex, Lord's 1988

LAST SEASON: BATTING

	I.	N. O.	R.	H. S.	AV.
TEST					
1ST	18	6	424	98	35.33
INT					
RAL	8	2	57	16*	9.50
N.W.	1	0	0	0	0.00
B&H	4	1	57	28	19.00

LAST SEASON: BOWLING

	O.	M.	R.	W.	AV.
TEST					
1ST	626.2	116	2001	63	31.76
INT					
RAL	102	8	385	16	24.06
N.W.	22	0	100	5	20.00
B&H	62	8	206	9	22.88

CAREER: BATTING

	I.	N. O.	R.	H. S.	AV.
TEST	3	0	70	36	23.33
1ST	151	49	2665	98	26.12
INT					
RAL	38	14	264	26*	11.00
N.W.	8	2	60	25	10.00
B&H	16	4	127	28	10.58

CAREER: BOWLING

	O.	M.	R.	W.	AV.
TEST	91.3	18	339	9	37.66
1ST	3377.3	560	11100	414	26.81
INT					
RAL	618.3	11	2946	88	33.47
N.W.	160	14	678	18	37.66
B&H	285	20	1019	38	26.81

NICHOLAS, M. C. J.   Hampshire

Name: Mark Charles Jefford Nicholas
Role: Right-hand bat, 'I think I bowl, but no-one else does', county captain
Born: 29 September 1957, London
Height: 6ft **Weight:** 12st 5lbs
Nickname: Skip, Dougie, Cappy
County debut: 1978
County cap: 1982
Benefit: 1991
1000 runs in a season: 7
1st-Class 50s scored: 55
1st-Class 100s scored: 28
1st-Class 200s scored: 1
1st-Class 5 w. in innings: 2
One-Day 50s: 29
One-Day 100s: 1
Place in batting averages: 128th av. 35.80 (1989 59th av. 36.25)
1st-Class catches: 9 (career 176)
Parents: Anne
Marital status: Single
Family links with cricket: Grandfather (F. W. H.) played for Essex as batsman and

wicket-keeper and toured with MCC. Father played for Navy
Education: Fernden Prep School; Bradfield College
Qualifications: 9 O-levels, 3 A-levels
Career outside cricket: 'Not at the moment – haven't time.'
Off-season: 'Organising my benefit year.'
Overseas tours: English Counties XI to Zimbabwe 1984–85; captain of England B to Sri Lanka 1985–86; captain of England A to Zimbabwe and Kenya 1989–90
Cricketers particularly admired: Barry Richards, John Snow, Mike Brearley
Other sports followed: Most – football, golf, fives, squash
Injuries: Malaria – caught in Africa
Relaxations: 'Getting rid of malaria! Theatre, music, golf, going out to dinner.'
Extras: Hampshire captain since 1985
Opinions on cricket: 'We play one one-day competition (Sundays) too many. We should play four-day championship cricket. One-day cricket should be solely commercial – mass advertising, numbers and sponsors on clothes etc.'
Best batting: 206* Hampshire v Oxford University, The Parks 1982
Best bowling: 6–37 Hampshire v Somerset, Southampton 1989

LAST SEASON: BATTING

	I.	N. O.	R.	H. S.	AV.
TEST					
1ST	35	10	895	104	35.80
INT					
RAL	13	4	254	59	28.22
N.W.	4	1	107	50	35.66
B&H	-	-	-	-	-

LAST SEASON: BOWLING

	O.	M.	R.	W.	AV.
TEST					
1ST	69.2	9	276	2	138.00
INT					
RAL	6	0	48	1	48.00
N.W.					
B&H	1	0	2	1	2.00

CAREER: BATTING

	I.	N. O.	R.	H. S.	AV.
TEST					
1ST	457	61	13123	206*	33.13
INT					
RAL	141	23	3163	108	26.80
N.W.	32	4	846	71	30.21
B&H	42	4	891	74	23.44

CAREER: BOWLING

	O.	M.	R.	W.	AV.
TEST					
1ST	870.3	168	2819	66	42.71
INT					
RAL	307.1	5	1709	59	28.96
N.W.	83.2	8	332	9	36.88
B&H	166	10	732	22	33.27

NIXON, P. A. Leicestershire

Name: Paul Andrew Nixon
Role: Left-hand bat, wicket-keeper
Born: 21 October 1970, Carlisle
Height: 6ft **Weight:** 12st 7lbs
Nickname: Nico
County debut: 1989
Place in batting averages: 183rd av.
27.40
Parents: Brian and Sylvia
Marital status: Single
Family links with cricket: 'Grand-
father and father played local league
cricket for Edenhall CC and Penrith in
the North Lancashire League. Mum
made teas.'
Education: Langwathby Primary,
Ullswater High
Qualifications: 2 O-levels, 6 CSEs,
NCA cricket coaching certificate
Jobs outside cricket: Working on
father's farm
Off-season: Playing grade cricket in Perth, Australia
Cricketers particularly admired: Allan Knott, Bob Taylor, David Gower, Viv
Richards
Other sports followed: Football (Carlisle and Spurs FCs), golf, rugby, basketball
Relaxations: Music, eating out
Extras: Played for England U–15s, Minor Counties for Cumberland at 16, MCC
Young Pro in 1988. Took eight catches in debut match v Warwickshire at Hinckley

LAST SEASON: BATTING

	I.	N. O.	R.	H. S.	AV.
TEST					
1ST	23	8	411	46	27.40
INT					
RAL	8	3	39	10	7.80
N.W.	1	0	12	12	12.00
B&H					

LAST SEASON: WICKET-KEEPING

	CT	ST			
TEST					
1ST	49	1			
INT					
RAL	15	1			
N.W.	1	0			
B&H					

CAREER: BATTING

	I.	N. O.	R.	H. S.	AV.
TEST					
1ST	30	11	498	46	26.21
INT					
RAL	9	3	40	10	6.66
N.W.	1	0	12	12	12.00
B&H					

CAREER: WICKET-KEEPING

	CT	ST			
TEST					
1ST	61	3			
INT					
RAL	16	1			
N.W.	1	0			
B&H					

in 1989

Opinions on cricket: 'Politics should be kept out of sport. Second XI cricket should be played on first-class grounds as much as possible and there should be more four-day matches.'

Best batting: 46 Leicestershire v Surrey, The Oval 1990

NOON, W. M.　　Northamptonshire

Name: Wayne Michael Noon
Role: Right-hand bat, wicket-keeper
Born: 5 February 1971, Grimsby
Height: 5ft 9in **Weight:** 11st 7lbs
Nickname: Spoon Head, Noonie, Matt
County debut: 1988 (RAL), 1989
(first-class)
Parents: Trafford and Rosemary
Marital status: Single
Education: Caistor Grammar School
Qualifications: 5 O-levels
Career outside cricket: Duck farmer
Overseas tours: England YC to Australia
1989–90
Cricketers particularly admired: Ian
Botham, Bob Taylor, Jack Russell, Geoff
Cook
Other sports followed: Supports Lincoln
City FC

Relaxations: 'Listening to rock music; having a complete day's break from cricket.'
Extras: Played for England YC v New Zealand 1989; captain v Australia 1989–90

LAST SEASON: BATTING

	I.	N. O.	R.	H. S.	AV.
TEST					
1ST	3	0	6	2	2.00
INT					
RAL	4	0	33	21	8.25
N.W.					
B&H					

LAST SEASON: WICKET-KEEPING

	CT	ST			
TEST					
1ST	5	1			
INT					
RAL	2	0			
N.W.					
B&H					

CAREER: BATTING

	I.	N. O.	R.	H. S.	AV.
TEST					
1ST	5	0	43	37	8.60
INT					
RAL	6	1	48	21	9.60
N.W.					
B&H	-	-	-	-	-

CAREER: WICKET-KEEPING

	CT	ST			
TEST					
1ST	8	2			
INT					
RAL	4	0			
N.W.					
B&H	0	0			

and Pakistan 1990

Opinions on cricket: 'I think there is far too much cricket packed into the six-month season. Clubs should do more to help the lads find jobs in the winter.'

Best batting: 37 Northamptonshire v Australians, Northampton 1989

NORTH, J. A. Sussex

Name: John Andrew North
Role: Right-hand bat, right-arm medium-fast bowler
Born: 19 November 1970, Slindon
Height: 5ft 10in **Weight:** 11st 7lbs
Nickname: Ollie
County debut: 1990
1st-Class catches: 1 (career 1)
Parents: John Allan and Margaret Anne
Marital status: Single
Family links with cricket: Brother Mark played county schoolboy cricket
Education: Bishop Luffa Comprehensive School; Slindon College
Qualifications: 10 O-levels, 2 A-levels
Off-season: 'Playing and coaching for University St Heliers, Auckland, New Zealand
Cricketers particularly admired: Ian Botham, Malcolm Marshall, Viv Richards
Other sports followed: 'Any sport without horses.'
Injuries: Sore shins
Relaxations: 'Music, films, eating out, away trips.'
Extras: Played for ESCA U–15 and U–17, NAYC and England YCs v Pakistan 1990
Opinions on cricket: 'Cricketers should be able to choose where they play their cricket without political pressure and interference.'
Best batting: 19* Sussex v Middlesex, Hove 1990
Best bowling: 2–43 Sussex v Cambridge University, Hove 1990

LAST SEASON / CAREER: BATTING

	I.	N. O.	R.	H. S.	AV.
TEST					
1ST	5	1	41	19*	10.25
INT					
RAL	2	1	16	15*	16.00
N.W.					
B&H	-	-	-	-	-

LAST SEASON / CAREER: BOWLING

	O.	M.	R.	W.	AV.
TEST					
1ST	83.1	17	236	6	39.33
INT					
RAL	8	0	45	2	22.50
N.W.					
B&H	8	0	48	1	48.00

O'GORMAN, T. J. G.   Derbyshire

Name: Timothy Joseph Gerard O'Gorman
Role: Right-hand bat
Born: 15 May 1967, Woking
Height: 6ft 2in **Weight:** 11st 7lbs
County debut: 1987
1st-Class 50s scored: 5
1st-Class 100s scored: 3
Place in batting averages: 103rd av. 40.72 (1989 46th av. 38.50)
1st-Class catches: 4 (career 13)
Parents: Brian and Kathleen
Marital status: Single
Family links with cricket: Grandfather played for Surrey; father played for Nigeria, for Sussex 2nd XI and Middlesex 2nd XI
Education: St George's College, Weybridge, Surrey; Durham University
Qualifications: 12 O-levels, 3 A-levels; Honours Law Degree, Durham
Career outside cricket: Working in solicitors' office during holidays
Cricketers particularly admired: David Gower, Greg Chappell
Other sports followed: Tennis, football, golf, hockey, rugby
Relaxations: Arts, theatre, music, movies
Extras: Surrey Young Cricketer of the Year 1984. Captained Surrey Young Cricketers for three years. Trials for England schoolboys at hockey
Best batting: 124 Derbyshire v Gloucestershire, Cheltenham 1989

LAST SEASON: BATTING

	I.	N. O.	R.	H. S.	AV.
TEST					
1ST	12	1	448	100	40.72
INT					
RAL	7	2	85	32	17.00
N.W.					
B&H	1	0	8	8	8.00

CAREER: BATTING

	I.	N. O.	R.	H. S.	AV.
TEST					
1ST	39	4	1081	124	30.88
INT					
RAL	13	4	185	46*	20.55
N.W.					
B&H	7	0	=125	43	17.85

OSTLER, D. P. Warwickshire

Name: Dominic Piers Ostler
Role: Right-hand bat, right-arm medium bowler
Born: 15 July 1970, Solihull
Height: 6ft 3in
County debut: 1990
1st-Class 50s scored: 5
Place in batting averages: 167th av. 30.00
1st-Class catches: 9 (career 9)
Marital status: Single
Education: Princethorpe College, Solihull Technical College
Extras: Warwickshire 2nd XI debut in 1989; plays club cricket for Moseley in the Birmingham League; member of Warwickshire U19 side that won ESSO National Festival in 1988 and 1989; scored 510 runs in 11 matches in his debut first-class season in 1990
Best batting: 71 Warwickshire v Kent, Edgbaston 1990

LAST SEASON / CAREER: BATTING

	I.	N. O.	R.	H. S.	AV.
TEST					
1ST	19	2	510	71	30.00
INT					
RAL	6	2	97	30	24.25
N.W.	1	0	4	4	4.00
B&H					

LAST SEASON / CAREER: BOWLING

	O.	M.	R.	W.	AV.
TEST					
1ST					
INT					
RAL					
N.W.					
B&H					

OWEN, P. A.   Gloucestershire

Name: Paul Andrew Owen
Role: Left-arm spinner
Born: 9 June 1969, Regina,
Saskatchewan, Canada
Height: 5ft 9in **Weight:** 10st 10lbs
Nickname: Doc, Jessie
County debut: 1990
Parents: Rob and Phil
Marital status: Single
Family links with cricket: Father
plays local cricket
Education: Bedford Modern School;
Thames Polytechnic
Qualifications: 7 O-levels, 3 A-levels
Career outside cricket: 'Worked as an
Industrial Radiographer on oil and gas
pipelines.'
Off-season: Coaching
Cricketers particularly admired: Allan
Border, Ian Botham, Abdul Qadir
Other sports followed: Football, golf and rugby
Relaxations: 'I read a few books, listen to music, play golf, spend time with friends.'
Extras: 'Was asked down to nets on 16 July and played in all three Britannic matches
at Cheltenham without having played any 2nd XI matches. After 10 balls of my debut
I got hit in the face at backward short-leg and was off the field for 10 overs.'
Opinions on cricket: 'With a combination of smaller seams, better pitches and drier
summers, the batsmen have become able to dominate almost any bowling attack.
Bowlers need a lot of luck now to take wickets and facts and figures cannot represent
their ability anymore – you can bowl well and go for lots of runs.'
Best batting: 1 Gloucestershire v Yorkshire, Cheltenham 1990 & Gloucestershire
v Surrey, Cheltenham 1990
Best bowling: 2–37 Gloucestershire v Surrey, Cheltenham 1990

LAST SEASON / CAREER: BATTING

	I.	N. O.	R.	H. S.	AV.
TEST					
1ST	2	0	2	1	1.00
INT					
RAL					
N.W.					
B&H					

LAST SEASON / CAREER: BOWLING

	O.	M.	R.	W.	AV.
TEST					
1ST	57	7	239	4	59.75
INT					
RAL					
N.W.					
B&H					

PARKER, P. W. G.   Sussex

Name: Paul William Giles Parker
Role: Right-hand bat, leg-break
bowler, cover fielder, county captain
Born: 15 January 1956, Bulawayo,
Rhodesia
Height: 5ft 10 1/2in **Weight:** 12st
Nickname: Porky, Polly
County debut: 1976
County cap: 1979
Benefit: 1988 (59,400)
Test debut: 1981
Tests: 1
1000 runs in a season: 8
1st-Class 50s scored: 75
1st-Class 100s scored: 40
1st-Class 200s scored: 1
One-Day 50s: 48
One-Day 100s: 5
Place in batting averages: 65th av.
46.90 (1989 49th av. 37.84)
1st-Class catches: 8 (career 220)
Parents: Anthony John and Margaret Edna
Wife and date of marriage: Teresa, 25 January 1980
Children: James William Ralph, 6 November 1980; Jocelyn Elizabeth, 10
September 1984
Family links with cricket: Father played for Essex 2nd XI. Uncle, David Green,
played for Northamptonshire and Worcestershire. Two brothers, Guy and Rupert,
'very keen and active cricketers'. Father wrote *The Village Cricket Match* and was
sports editor of ITN
Education: Collyer's Grammar School; St Catharine's College, Cambridge
Qualifications: MA (Cantab.)
Career outside cricket: 'Have set up own cricket-based company.'
Overseas teams played for: Natal, South Africa 1980–81
Other sports followed: 'Most ball games.'
Injuries: Pulled hamstring in both legs
Relaxations: Reading, crosswords, bridge, music
Extras: Cambridge Blue at cricket and was selected for Varsity rugby match in 1977
but had to withdraw through injury. Was first reserve for England on Australia tour
1979–80. Appointed captain of Sussex 1988
Best batting: 215 Cambridge University v Essex, Fenner's 1976
Best bowling: 2–21 Sussex v Surrey, Guildford 1984

LAST SEASON: BATTING

	I.	N.O.	R.	H.S.	AV.
TEST					
1ST	25	4	985	107	46.90
INT					
RAL	9	0	233	72	25.88
N.W.	2	1	87	83	87.00
B&H	4	1	101	85*	33.66

LAST SEASON: BOWLING

	O.	M.	R.	W.	AV.
TEST					
1ST	8	0	59	0	-
INT					
RAL					
N.W.					
B&H					

CAREER: BATTING

	I.	N.O.	R.	H.S.	AV.
TEST	2	0	13	13	6.50
1ST	538	75	16544	215	35.73
INT					
RAL	170	24	4469	121*	30.61
N.W.	35	6	1128	109	38.89
B&H	60	6	1438	85*	26.63

CAREER: BOWLING

	O.	M.	R.	W.	AV.
TEST					
1ST	158.5	26	658	11	59.81
INT					
RAL	6.3	0	38	2	19.00
N.W.	2	0	17	1	17.00
B&H	1.2	0	6	2	3.00

PARKS, R. J.　　　　Hampshire

Name: Robert James Parks
Role: Right-hand bat, wicket-keeper
Born: 15 June 1959, Cuckfield, Sussex
Height: 5ft 7 3/4in **Weight:** 10st 7lbs
Nickname: Bobby
County debut: 1980
County cap: 1982
1st-Class 50s scored: 14
Place in batting averages: 224th av. 19.63 (1989 137th av. 25.11)
Parents: James and Irene
Wife and date of marriage: Amanda, 30 January 1982
Family links with cricket: Father, Jim Parks, played for Sussex and England, as did grandfather, J. H. Parks. Uncle, H. W. Parks, also played for Sussex
Education: Eastbourne Grammar School; Southampton Institute of Technology

Qualifications: 9 O-levels, 1 A-level, OND and HND in Business Studies
Off-season: Working for computer software company, Capsco Software Europe Ltd
Overseas tours: English Counties XI to Zimbabwe 1985
Cricketers particularly admired: Bob Taylor, Nick Pocock
Other sports followed: 'Keen follower of Spurs, especially when they beat Arsenal.'
Relaxations: Stamp collecting, crosswords

Injuries: Dislocated finger
Extras: Broke the Hampshire record for the number of dismissals in a match, v Derbyshire, 1982 (10 catches). Took over from Bob Taylor as stand-in wicket-keeper for England v New Zealand at Lord's after injury to Bruce French
Opinions on cricket: 'Cricketers are playing far too much international cricket which is proving detrimental to their fitness and performance at county level.'
Best batting: 89 Hampshire v Cambridge University, Fenner's 1984

LAST SEASON: BATTING

	I.	N. O.	R.	H. S.	AV.
TEST					
1ST	21	10	216	36*	19.63
INT					
RAL	6	1	56	23*	11.20
N.W.	3	2	45	27*	45.00
B&H	2	2	26	20*	-

LAST SEASON: WICKET-KEEPING

	CT	ST			
TEST					
1ST	49	4			
INT					
RAL	10	2			
N.W.	5	1			
B&H	6	1			

CAREER: BATTING

	I.	N. O.	R.	H. S.	AV.
TEST					
1ST	274	79	3775	89	19.35
INT					
RAL	60	29	580	38*	18.71
N.W.	14	6	133	27*	16.62
B&H	27	11	190	23*	11.87

CAREER: WICKET-KEEPING

	CT	ST			
TEST					
1ST	617	70			
INT					
RAL	153	29			
N.W.	38	8			
B&H	57	6			

PARSONS, G. J.   Leicestershire

Name: Gordon James Parsons
Role: Left-hand bat, right-arm medium bowler, outfielder
Born: 17 October 1959, Slough
Height: 6ft 1in **Weight:** 13st 7lbs 'too heavy!'
Nickname: Bullhead ('thousands of others non-complimentary!')
County debut: 1978 (Leics), 1986 (Warwicks)
County cap: 1984 (Leics), 1987 (Warwicks)
50 wickets in a season: 2
1st-Class 50s scored: 20
1st-Class 5 w. in innings: 16
1st-Class 10 w. in match: 1
One-day 50s: 1
Place in batting averages: 268th av. 11.20 (1989 128th av. 26.33)

Place in bowling averages: 16th av. 27.51 (1989 92nd av. 35.48)
Strike rate: 52.25 (career 58.65)
1st-Class catches: 4 (career 72)
Parents: Dave and Evelyn
Marital status: 'Hopeful'
Family links with cricket: 'Father played club cricket for Stoke Green in Slough for more years than he would care to remember.'
Education: Woodside County Secondary School, Slough
Qualifications: 5 O-levels
Off-season: 'Playing for Orange Free State in South Africa and as little coaching as I can get away with!'
Overseas tours: England Schools tour to India 1977–78
Overseas teams played for: Boland, South Africa 1983–84; Griqualand West 1984–86; Orange Free State 1988–91
Cricketers particularly admired: Jonathan Agnew, Mike Garnham, David Allett, Peter Hepworth, David Cotton, Chris Howell
Other sports followed: Golf
Injuries: Disc in lower back (missed a week in early season)
Extras: Played for Leicester 2nd XI since 1976 and for Buckinghamshire in 1977. Left Leicestershire after 1985 season and joined Warwickshire. Capped by Warwickshire while in plaster and on crutches. Released at end of 1988 season and returned to his old county
Opinions on cricket: 'It may be worth considering bonus points for both innings in an attempt to stop declaration bowling and the vast first innings totals that cause some four-day matches being reduced to two and a half innings. Would like over-rates scrapped and a minimum 105 overs bowled in a day.'
Best batting: 76 Boland v Western Province B, Cape Town 1984–85
Best bowling: 9–72 Boland v Transvaal B, Johannesburg 1984–85

LAST SEASON: BATTING

	I.	N. O.	R.	H. S.	AV.
TEST					
1ST	13	3	112	20	11.20
INT					
RAL	4	2	60	19*	30.00
N.W.					
B&H	-	-	-	-	-

LAST SEASON: BOWLING

	O.	M.	R.	W.	AV.
TEST					
1ST	304.5	77	963	35	27.51
INT					
RAL	40	1	247	4	61.75
N.W.					
B&H	4	1	26	0	-

CAREER: BATTING

	I.	N. O.	R.	H. S.	AV.
TEST					
1ST	309	71	4512	76	18.95
INT					
RAL	70	23	568	26*	12.08
N.W.	12	3	121	23	13.44
B&H	20	9	252	63*	22.90

CAREER: BOWLING

	O.	M.	R.	W.	AV.
TEST					
1ST	5386.3	1171	16792	551	30.47
INT					
RAL	818.2	40	3715	112	33.17
N.W.	195.1	25	755	16	47.18
B&H	377.3	47	1340	48	27.91

PATEL, M. M.   Kent

Name: Minal Mahesh Patel
Role: Right-hand bat, left-arm spinner
Born: 7 August 1970, Bombay, India
Height: 5ft 9in **Weight:** 9st
Nickname: Min
County debut: 1989
1st-class 5 w. in innings: 2
1st-class 10 w. in match: 1
Place in batting averages: 253rd av. 14.85
Place in bowling averages: 109th av. 41.80
Strike rate: 89.35 (career 87.95)
1st-Class catches: 2 (career 3)
Parents: Mahesh and Aruna
Marital status: Single
Family links with cricket: 'Dad played good club cricket in India, Africa and England.'
Education: Dartford Grammar School; Erith College of Technology
Qualifications: 6 O-levels, 3 A-levels (Maths, Chemistry, Geography)
Off-season: Studying for a (BA) Economics Degree
Cricketers particularly admired: Bishen Bedi, Derek Underwood, Sunil Gavaskar
Other sports followed: 'All except anything to do with horses!'
Injuries: Split spinning finger – off for one week
Relaxations: 'Listening to soul and hip-hop music. Going to concerts.'

LAST SEASON: BATTING

	I.	N. O.	R.	H. S.	AV.
TEST					
1ST	12	5	104	41*	14.85
INT					
RAL					
N.W.	-	-	-	-	-
B&H					

LAST SEASON: BOWLING

	O.	M.	R.	W.	AV.
TEST					
1ST	297.5	72	836	20	41.80
INT					
RAL					
N.W.	12	6	29	2	14.50
B&H					

CAREER: BATTING

	I.	N. O.	R.	H. S.	AV.
TEST					
1ST	13	5	107	41*	13.37
INT					
RAL					
N.W.	-	-	-	-	-
B&H					

CAREER: BOWLING

	O.	M.	R.	W.	AV.
TEST					
1ST	307.5	74	870	21	41.42
INT					
RAL					
N.W.	12	6	29	2	14.50
B&H					

Extras: Played for ESCA 1988, 1989, and NCA England South 1989. Kent League Young Player of the Year 1987, playing for Blackheath CC
Opinions on cricket: 'There should be more four-day cricket.'
Best batting: 41* Kent v Northamptonshire, Northampton 1990
Best bowling: 6–57 Kent v Leicestershire, Dartford 1990

PATTERSON, B. P.   Lancashire

Name: Balfour Patrick Patterson
Role: Right-hand bat, right-arm fast bowler, outfielder
Born: 15 September 1961, Portland, Jamaica
Height: 6ft 2 1/2in **Weight:** 14st
Nickname: Balf, Pato
County debut: 1984
County cap: 1987
Test debut: 1985–86
Tests: 18
One-Day Internationals: 27
50 wickets in a season: 1
1st-Class 5 w. in innings: 20
1st-Class 10 w. in match: 2
Place in bowling averages: 55th av. 35.00 (1989 11th av. 19.31)
Strike rate: 58.27 (career 49.01)
1st-Class catches: 2 (career 24)
Parents: Maurice and Emelda
Marital status: Single

LAST SEASON: BATTING

	I.	N.O.	R.	H.S.	AV.
TEST					
1ST	4	1	5	4*	1.66
INT					
RAL	-	-	-	-	-
N.W.					
B&H	-	-	-	-	-

CAREER: BATTING

	I.	N.O.	R.	H.S.	AV.
TEST	23	11	90	21*	7.50
1ST	109	38	415	29	5.84
INT	6	5	22	13*	22.00
RAL	2	2	5	3*	-
N.W.	2	1	4	4	4.00
B&H	2	2	18	15*	-

LAST SEASON: BOWLING

	O.	M.	R.	W.	AV.
TEST					
1ST	281.4	45	1015	29	35.00
INT					
RAL	8	0	55	0	-
N.W.					
B&H	31.1	9	73	3	24.33

CAREER: BOWLING

	O.	M.	R.	W.	AV.
TEST	495.2	65	1844	60	30.73
1ST	2797	463	9196	343	26.81
INT	269.5	17	1230	54	22.77
RAL	30.2	0	153	5	30.60
N.W.	24	0	120	1	120.00
B&H	62.1	13	181	7	25.85

Family links with cricket: Father and grandfather played for parish in Jamaica
Education: Happy Grove High School; Wolmers High School for Boys
Qualifications: Jamaica School Certificates, O-levels
Off-season: Playing in West Indies
Overseas tours: West Indies to Pakistan and New Zealand 1986–87; India 1987–88;
England 1988; Australia 1989–90; Young West Indies to Zimbabwe 1990–91
Overseas teams played for: Tasmania 1984–85; Jamaica 1982–90
Cricketers particularly admired: Present West Indian team, Dennis Lillee
Other sports followed: Watches football, basketball
Relaxations: Swimming, listening to music, watching television
Extras: Released by Lancashire at end of 1990
Best batting: 29 Lancashire v Northamptonshire, Northampton 1987
Best bowling: 7–24 Jamaica v Guyana, Kingston 1985–86

PENBERTHY, A. L. Northamptonshire

Name: Anthony Leonard Penberthy
Role: Left-hand bat, right-arm
medium-pace bowler
Born: 1 September 1969, Troon,
Cornwall
Height: 6ft 1in **Weight:** 11st 7lbs
Nickname: Berth, Penbers, After
County debut: 1989
1st-class 50s scored: 3
1st-class 100s scored: 1
Place in batting averages: 156th av.
31.07
Place in bowling averages: 62nd av.
35.95
Strike rate: 56.63 (career 61.36)
1st-Class catches: 8 (career 12)
Parents: Gerald and Wendy
Marital status: Single
Family links with cricket: Father

played in local leagues in Cornwall and
is now a qualified umpire instructor
Education: Troon County Primary; Camborne Comprehensive
Qualifications: 3 O-levels, 3 CSEs, coaching certificate
Off-season: Working back home in Cornwall
Cricketers particularly admired: Ian Botham, David Gower, Geoff Boycott, Viv
Richards, Dennis Lillee
Other sports followed: Football, snooker, rugby, golf

Injuries: Tendonitis in left shin, damaged ankle ligaments, broken toe – missed five weeks in total

Relaxations: Listening to music, watching videos and comedy programmes

Extras: Had trials for Plymouth Argyle at football but came to Northampton for cricket trials instead. Took wicket with first ball in first-class cricket, Mark Taylor caught behind June 1989. Played for England YC v New Zealand 1989. Made first first-class 100 of 1990 season

Opinions on cricket: 'Too much one-day cricket. Lunch and tea intervals should be longer. 16 four-day matches. Over-rate fines too strict.'

Best batting: 101* Northamptonshire v Cambridge University, Fenner's 1990

Best bowling: 4–91 Northamptonshire v Warwickshire, Northampton 1990

LAST SEASON: BATTING

	I.	N. O.	R.	H. S.	AV.
TEST					
1ST	17	3	435	101*	31.07
INT					
RAL	3	1	10	6	5.00
N.W.					
B&H	1	0	10	10	10.00

LAST SEASON: BOWLING

	O.	M.	R.	W.	AV.
TEST					
1ST	207.4	29	791	22	35.95
INT					
RAL	15	0	124	2	62.00
N.W.					
B&H					

CAREER: BATTING

	I.	N. O.	R.	H. S.	AV.
TEST					
1ST	25	3	510	101*	23.18
INT					
RAL	6	1	56	35	11.20
N.W.					
B&H	1	0	10	10	10.00

CAREER: BOWLING

	O.	M.	R.	W.	AV.
TEST					
1ST	255.4	36	953	25	38.12
INT					
RAL	27	1	174	5	34.80
N.W.					
B&H					

Name: Christopher Penn
Role: Left-hand bat, right-arm
medium bowler
Born: 19 June 1963, Dover
Height: 6ft 1in **Weight:** 14st
Nickname: Penny, Gazza
County debut: 1982
County cap: 1987
50 wickets in a season: 1
1st-Class 50s scored: 5
1st-Class 100s scored: 1
1st-Class 5 w. in innings: 9
Place in bowling averages: 138th av.
57.81 (1989 109th av. 43.70)
Strike rate: 85.84 (career 62.81)
1st-Class catches: 2 (career 45)
Parents: Reg and Brenda
Wife and date of marriage: Caroline
Ann, 22 March 1986
Children: Matthew Thomas, 14 October
1987; David Thomas 30 March 1990
Family links with cricket: Father played club cricket for Dover CC for twenty-six
years; father-in-law keen Kent follower
Education: River Primary School; Dover Grammar School
Qualifications: 9 O-levels, 3 A-levels
Off-season: 'Playing and coaching in South Africa.'
Cricketers particularly admired: 'Alan Knott, Dennis Lillee, Malcolm Marshall
and long-serving county pros.'

LAST SEASON: BATTING

	I.	N. O.	R.	H. S.	AV.
TEST					
1ST	6	2	66	23*	16.50
INT					
RAL	2	1	20	20*	20.00
N.W.					
B&H	1	1	8	8*	-

CAREER: BATTING

	I.	N. O.	R.	H. S.	AV.
TEST					
1ST	114	30	1648	115	19.61
INT					
RAL	33	9	231	40	9.62
N.W.	3	0	8	5	2.66
B&H	15	7	97	24*	12.12

LAST SEASON: BOWLING

	O.	M.	R.	W.	AV.
TEST					
1ST	186	35	636	11	57.81
INT					
RAL	39.3	2	208	5	41.60
N.W.					
B&H	10.5	1	40	2	20.00

CAREER: BOWLING

	O.	M.	R.	W.	AV.
TEST					
1ST	2366.1	448	7693	226	34.04
INT					
RAL	391.1	16	1900	61	31.14
N.W.	62	8	180	8	22.50
B&H	362.3	20	780	25	31.20

Other sports followed: All sports – Dover FC
Injuries: Groin injury towards end of season
Relaxations: Music, art and art history, Indian food, local sport, keeping fit
Extras: Played for Young England and England Schools. Took hat-trick in first 2nd XI match v Middlesex when 16 years old. Kent Player of the Year 1988
Opinions on cricket: 'Too many people have opinions on cricket when they really know nothing about the game and some of them are running cricket at all levels – now the seam has gone from the ball, let's take the springs out of the bat!'
Best batting: 115 Kent v Lancashire, Old Trafford 1984
Best bowling: 7–70 Kent v Middlesex, Lord's 1988

PICK, R. A.   Nottinghamshire

Name: Robert Andrew Pick
Role: Left-hand bat, right-arm fast-medium bowler
Born: 19 November 1963, Nottingham
Height: 5ft 10in **Weight:** 13st
Nickname: Dad
County debut: 1983
County cap: 1987
50 wickets in a season: 2
1st-Class 50s scored: 2
1st-Class 5 w. in innings: 6
1st-Class 10 w. in match: 2
Place in batting averages: 219th av. 20.40
Place in bowling averages: 43rd av. 32.49 (1989 89th av. 34.47)
Strike rate: 58.21 (career 58.84)
1st-Class catches: 6 (career 23)
Parents: Bob and Lillian
Wife and date of marriage: Jennie Ruth, 8 April 1989
Family links with cricket: Father, uncles and cousins all play local cricket; David Millns is brother-in-law
Education: Alderman Derbyshire Comprehensive; High Pavement College
Qualifications: 7 O-levels, 1 A-level, coaching qualification
Off-season: Touring with England A to Pakistan
Overseas tours: England A to Pakistan 1990–91
Overseas teams played for: Wellington, New Zealand 1989–90
Cricketers particularly admired: Bob White, Mike Hendrick, Mike Harris, Franklyn Stephenson
Other sports followed: Ice-hockey, soccer and American football
Injuries: 'Torn rib muscle and head injury sustained during collision with Andy

Afford's elbow.'

Relaxations: 'As much fishing as possible and listening to a wide range of music; eating and drinking; going to the pictures.'

Extras: Played for England YCs v Australia 1983. Played soccer for Nottingham Schoolboys

Opinions on cricket: 'Coloured clothing should be introduced for all one-day cricket.'

Best batting: 63 Nottinghamshire v Warwickshire, Nuneaton 1985

Best bowling: 7–128 Nottinghamshire v Leicestershire, Leicester 1990

LAST SEASON: BATTING

	I.	N. O.	R.	H. S.	AV.
TEST					
1ST	16	6	204	35	20.40
INT					
RAL	2	1	12	12	12.00
N.W.	2	2	9	5*	-
B&H	-	-	-	-	-

LAST SEASON: BOWLING

	O.	M.	R.	W.	AV.
TEST					
1ST	494.5	83	1657	51	32.49
INT					
RAL	24	0	113	3	37.66
N.W.	21	3	86	3	28.66
B&H	63.4	2	284	8	35.50

CAREER: BATTING

	I.	N. O.	R.	H. S.	AV.
TEST					
1ST	99	28	1094	63	15.40
INT					
RAL	23	11	130	24	10.83
N.W.	10	8	72	34*	36.00
B&H	9	5	17	4	4.25

CAREER: BOWLING

	O.	M.	R.	W.	AV.
TEST					
1ST	2353.4	429	8075	240	33.64
INT					
RAL	436.2	14	2262	74	30.56
N.W.	177.1	20	658	25	26.32
B&H	241.3	18	1004	33	30.42

70. Which country, other than West Indies, have both Greenidge and Haynes played for?

71. Who does Mark Waugh play for in the Sheffield Shield?

72. Which member of the cabinet was chosen as Best Young Cricketer of the Year at the age of 12 by the *London Evening Standard*?

Name: Christopher Stephen Pickles
Role: Right-hand bat, right-arm medium bowler
Born: 30 January 1966, Cleckheaton
Height: 6ft 1in **Weight:** 13st
Nickname: Pick, Piccolo
County debut: 1985
1st-Class 50s scored: 5
Place in batting averages: 136th av. 34.14 (1989 155th av. 22.82)
Place in bowling averages: 108th av. 41.53 (1989 102nd av. 40.58)
Strike rate: 69.67 (career 77.65)
1st-Class catches: 6 (career 20)
Parents: Ronald Albert and Christine Mary
Wife and date of marriage: Janet Elizabeth, 22 October 1988
Children: Samantha Janet, 10 October 1989
Family links with cricket: Father and brother both play local league cricket
Education: Whitcliffe Mount Comprehensive
Qualifications: Qualified cricket coach
Career outside cricket: Work for carpet manufacturers
Cricketers particularly admired: Richard Hadlee, Malcolm Marshall
Other sports followed: Ruby Union and Cleckheaton RFC
Relaxations: 'Pint, fish and chips, watching TV.'
Opinions on cricket: 'Nobody should qualify as English unless they were born in

LAST SEASON: BATTING

	I.	N. O.	R.	H. S.	AV.
TEST					
1ST	22	8	478	57*	34.14
INT					
RAL	5	1	7	6	1.75
N.W.					
B&H					

LAST SEASON: BOWLING

	O.	M.	R.	W.	AV.
TEST					
1ST	325.1	72	1163	28	41.53
INT					
RAL	57	0	305	7	43.57
N.W.					
B&H					

CAREER: BATTING

	I.	N. O.	R.	H. S.	AV.
TEST					
1ST	51	17	921	66	27.08
INT					
RAL	20	9	101	19	9.18
N.W.	1	0	3	3	3.00
B&H	3	1	22	13*	11.00

CAREER: BOWLING

	O.	M.	R.	W.	AV.
TEST					
1ST	815.2	169	2783	63	44.17
INT					
RAL	237.4	10	1192	34	35.05
N.W.	12	1	41	1	41.00
B&H	49	11	170	1	170.00

this country.'
Best batting: 66 Yorkshire v Somerset, Taunton 1989
Best bowling: 4–92 Yorkshire v Northamptonshire, Northampton 1989

PIERSON, A. R. K.   Warwickshire

Name: Adrian Roger Kirshaw Pierson
Role: Right-hand bat, off-break bowler
Born: 21 July 1963, Enfield, Middlesex
Height: 6ft 4 1/2in **Weight:** 12st
Nickname: Skirlog, Stick
County debut: 1985
1st-Class 5 w. in innings: 3
Place in bowling averages: 83rd
av. 38.60 (1989 96th av. 37.40)
Strike rate: 72.64 (career 79.72)
1st-Class catches: 1 (career 16)
Parents: Patrick Blake Kirshaw and
Patricia Margaret
Wife and date of marriage: Helen
Marjella, 29 September 1990
Education: Lochinver House Primary;
Kent College, Canterbury; Hatfield
Polytechnic
Qualifications: 8 O-levels, 2 A-levels,
NCA senior coach
Off-season: 'Working in London, for design consultants, Tobasgo.'
Cricketers particularly admired: John Emburey, Phil Edmonds, Tony Greig
Other sports followed: All sports ' – except horse racing'

LAST SEASON: BATTING

	I.	N. O.	R.	H. S.	AV.
TEST					
1ST	9	5	57	16*	14.25
INT					
RAL	1	0	1	1	1.00
N.W.	-	-	-	-	-
B&H					

LAST SEASON: BOWLING

	O.	M.	R.	W.	AV.
TEST					
1ST	302.4	55	965	25	38.60
INT					
RAL	23	3	107	4	26.75
N.W.	12	1	49	0	-
B&H					

CAREER: BATTING

	I.	N. O.	R.	H. S.	AV.
TEST					
1ST	58	25	372	42*	11.27
INT					
RAL	16	8	79	21*	9.87
N.W.	1	1	1	1*	-
B&H	6	2	19	11	4.75

CAREER: BOWLING

	O.	M.	R.	W.	AV.
TEST					
1ST	1076.2	215	3474	81	42.88
INT					
RAL	189.2	10	896	20	44.80
N.W.	53	9	160	4	40.00
B&H	78	10	258	6	43.00

Injuries: 'Tendonitis. All over!'
Relaxations: Music, driving, reading, golf, hockey, chess
Extras: On Lord's ground staff 1984–85. Shoulder operation while in Zimbabwe in 1989–90
Opinions on cricket: 'Make the game more commercial with coloured clothing and clear team sponsor logos, etc and be more accommodating towards public opinion. For example, make the bad light law less ambiguous. Keep the present pitches but return to something like the old ball.'
Best batting: 42* Warwickshire v Northamptonshire, Northampton 1986
Best bowling: 6–82 Warwickshire v Derbyshire, Nuneaton 1989

PIGOTT, A. C. S. Sussex

Name: Anthony Charles Shackleton Pigott
Role: Right-hand bat, right-arm fast bowler, slip fielder
Born: 4 June 1958, London
Height: 6ft 1in **Weight:** 13st
Nickname: Lester
County debut: 1978
County cap: 1982
Test debut: 1983–84
Tests: 1
50 wickets in a season: 5
1st-Class 50s scored: 18
1st-Class 100s scored: 1
1st-Class 5 w. in innings: 22
1st-Class 10 w. in match: 1
One-Day 50s: 2
Place in batting averages: 228th av. 18.79 (1989 134th av. 25.27)
Place in bowling averages: 70th av. 36.98 (1989 81st av. 31.57)
Strike rate: 60.11 (career 53.33)
1st-Class catches: 10 (career 105)
Parents: Tom and Juliet
Marital status: Divorced
Children: Elliot Sebastion, 15 March 1983
Family links with cricket: Father captained club side
Education: Harrow School
Qualifications: 5 O-levels, 2 A-levels; junior coaching certificate
Career outside cricket: Sportsmaster at Claremont Prep School, Hastings. Owner of squash club at county ground

Overseas tours: Part of England tour to New Zealand 1983–84
Overseas teams played for: Wellington, New Zealand 1982–83 and 1983–84
Cricketers particularly admired: Ian Botham, John Snow
Other sports followed: Football, golf, squash, tennis – 'all of them'
Relaxations: Squash club. 'Spending time with my son.'
Extras: Public Schools Racquets champion 1975. First three wickets in first-class cricket were a hat-trick. Had operation on back, April 1981, missing most of season, and was told by a specialist he would never play cricket again. Postponed wedding to make Test debut when called into England party on tour of New Zealand. Originally going to Somerset for 1984 season, but remained with Sussex. Was diagnosed as a diabetic after he lost 11lbs in two weeks in 1987, but recovered to take 74 wickets in 1988 season
Opinions on cricket: 'We should start playing total four-day cricket.'
Best batting: 104* Sussex v Warwickshire, Edgbaston 1986
Best bowling: 7–74 Sussex v Northamptonshire, Eastbourne 1982

LAST SEASON: BATTING

	I.	N. O.	R.	H. S.	AV.
TEST					
1ST	29	5	451	64*	18.79
INT					
RAL	10	2	195	37	24.37
N.W.	1	0	1	1	1.00
B&H	2	1	50	38*	50.00

LAST SEASON: BOWLING

	O.	M.	R.	W.	AV.
TEST					
1ST	541	94	1997	54	36.98
INT					
RAL	95	3	509	25	20.36
N.W.	19	2	70	1	70.00
B&H	31	5	109	3	36.33

CAREER: BATTING

	I.	N. O.	R.	H. S.	AV.
TEST	2	1	12	8*	12.00
1ST	239	50	3929	104*	20.78
INT					
RAL	65	25	865	51*	21.62
N.W.	9	0	153	53	17.00
B&H	20	8	175	49*	14.58

CAREER: BOWLING

	O.	M.	R.	W.	AV.
TEST	17	7	75	2	37.50
1ST	4756.2	849	15886	535	29.69
INT					
RAL	791.1	26	3861	178	21.69
N.W.	163.4	22	596	21	28.38
B&H	265	33	1102	38	29.00

PIPER, K. J.   Warwickshire

Name: Keith John Piper
Role: Right-hand bat, wicket-keeper
Born: 18 December 1969
Height: 5ft 6in **Weight:** 10st 7lbs
Nickname: Tubbsy, Tuba
County debut: 1989
1st-class 50s scored: 1
1st-Class 100s scored: 1
Place in batting averages: 208th av.
23.05 (1989 215th av. 16.00)
Parents: John and Charlotte
Marital status: Single
Family links with cricket: 'Dad plays
club cricket in Leicester.'
Education: Seven Sisters Junior;
Somerset Senior
Qualifications: Cricket coaching award,
basketball coaching award
Cricketers particularly admired: Jack
Russell, Andy Brassington, Dermot
Reeve, Paul Smith, Viv Richards, Desmond Haynes
Other sports followed: Snooker, football, squash
Relaxations: 'Music, videos, eating a bit.'
Extras: Attended Haringey Cricket College and went on several tours to the West
Indies
Best batting: 111 Warwickshire v Somerset, Edgbaston 1990

LAST SEASON: BATTING

	I.	N. O.	R.	H. S.	AV.
TEST					
1ST	21	1	461	111	23.05
INT					
RAL	5	1	40	30	10.00
N.W.					
B&H					

LAST SEASON: WICKET-KEEPING

	CT	ST
TEST		
1ST	40	4
INT		
RAL	3	4
N.W.		
B&H		

CAREER: BATTING

	I.	N. O.	R.	H. S.	AV.
TEST					
1ST	36	3	669	111	20.27
INT					
RAL	10	3	86	30	12.28
N.W.	-	-	-	-	-
B&H					

CAREER: WICKET-KEEPING

	CT	ST
TEST		
1ST	65	5
INT		
RAL	6	4
N.W.	1	0
B&H		

POLLARD, P.   Nottinghamshire

Name: Paul Pollard
Role: Left-hand bat, right-arm medium bowler
Born: 24 September 1968, Carlton, Nottinghamshire
Height: 5ft 10in **Weight:** 12st
Nickname: Polly
County debut: 1987
1000 runs in a season: 1
1st-Class 50s scored: 7
1st-Class 100s scored: 3
One-Day 50s scored: 1
One-Day 100s scored: 2
Place in batting averages: 216th av. 21.30 (1989 78th av. 33.25)
1st-Class catches: 5 (career 34)
Parents: Eric and Mary
Education: Gedling Comprehensive
Cricketers particularly admired: Clive Rice, Graeme Pollock, Richard Hadlee, David Gower
Other sports followed: Ice-hockey, golf, football, snooker
Relaxations: Watching videos, playing golf, 'spending time with my girlfriend'
Extras: Made debut for Nottinghamshire 2nd XI in 1985. Worked in Nottinghamshire CCC office on a Youth Training Scheme. Shared stands of 222 and 282 with Tim Robinson v Kent 1988. Youngest player to reach 1000 runs for Nottinghamshire
Best batting: 153 Nottinghamshire v Cambridge University, Fenner's 1989

LAST SEASON: BATTING

	I.	N. O.	R.	H. S.	AV.
TEST					
1ST	13	0	277	72	21.30
INT					
RAL	4	0	27	13	6.75
N.W.					
B&H	3	0	15	5	5.00

CAREER: BATTING

	I.	N. O.	R.	H. S.	AV.
TEST					
1ST	69	1	1901	153	27.95
INT					
RAL	20	1	516	123*	27.15
N.W.	2	0	27	23	13.50
B&H	8	0	110	77	13.75

POTTER, L.   Leicestershire

Name: Laurie Potter
Role: Right-hand bat, slow left-arm
bowler, slip fielder
Born: 7 November 1962, Bexley Heath,
Kent
Height: 6ft 1in **Weight:** 14st
Nickname: Pottsie
County debut: 1981 (Kent), 1986
(Leics)
County cap: 1988 (Leics)
1000 runs in a season: 2
1st-Class 50s scored: 38
1st-Class 100s scored: 7
One-Day 50s: 11
One-Day 100s: 2
Place in batting averages: 151st av.
32.72 (1989 86th av. 32.14)
1st-Class catches: 23 (career 147)
Parents: Ronald Henry Ernest and
Audrey Megan
Wife and date of marriage: Helen Louise, October 1989
Children: Michael Laurie, 14 March 1990
Family links with cricket: Father-in-law Kent 2nd XI scorer
Education: Kelmscott Senior High School, Perth, Western Australia
Qualifications: Australian leaving exams
Off-season: 'Coaching in Leicester schools and at home with wife and son.'
Overseas tours: With Australian U–19 team to Pakistan 1981

LAST SEASON: BATTING

	I.	N. O.	R.	H. S.	AV.
TEST					
1ST	38	5	1080	109*	32.72
INT					
RAL	12	2	128	33	12.80
N.W.	1	0	19	19	19.00
B&H	3	0	16	10	5.33

LAST SEASON: BOWLING

	O.	M.	R.	W.	AV.
TEST					
1ST	181	40	623	7	89.00
INT					
RAL	7	0	51	1	51.00
N.W.					
B&H	11	1	34	1	34.00

CAREER: BATTING

	I.	N. O.	R.	H. S.	AV.
TEST					
1ST	264	32	6762	165*	29.14
INT					
RAL	94	9	2016	105	23.71
N.W.	10	1	206	45	22.88
B&H	20	2	423	112	23.50

CAREER: BOWLING

	O.	M.	R.	W.	AV.
TEST					
1ST	1269.5	303	3708	98	37.83
INT					
RAL	123.1	6	595	25	23.80
N.W.	31	7	99	2	49.50
B&H	62	7	253	5	50.60

Overseas teams played for: Griqualand West, South Africa 1984–85 and 1985–86 as captain; Orange Free State 1987–88
Cricketers particularly admired: Derek Underwood, Alan Knott, Victor Trumper
Other sports followed: Most – football (all types), hockey
Injuries: Bad back
Relaxations: Home and family; following sports
Extras: Captained Australia U–19 team to Pakistan 1981. Played for England YCs v India 1981. Parents emigrated to Australia when he was 4. His mother wrote to Kent in 1978 asking for trial for him. Decided to leave Kent after 1985 season and joined Leicestershire
Best batting: 165* Griqualand West v Border, East London 1984–85
Best bowling: 4–52 Griqualand West v Boland, Stellenbosch 1985–86

PRICHARD, P. J. Essex

Name: Paul John Prichard
Role: Right-hand bat, cover/mid-wicket fielder
Born: 7 January 1965, Brentwood
Height: 5ft 10in **Weight:** 12st 7lbs
Nickname: Pablo, Middies
County debut: 1984
County cap: 1986
1000 runs in a season: 3
1st-Class 50s scored: 45
1st-Class 100s scored: 8
1st-Class 200s scored: 1
One-Day 50s: 12
One-Day 100s: 2
Place in batting averages: 57th av. 48.51 (1989 104th av. 29.65)
1st-Class catches: 9 (career 88)
Parents: John and Margaret
Marital status: Separated
Family links with cricket: Father played club cricket in Essex
Education: Brentwood County High School
Qualifications: NCA senior coaching award
Off-season: Playing and coaching for Waverley CC, Sydney, Australia
Cricketers particularly admired: 'Admire and respect all pros.'
Other sports followed: Rugby Union, football, American football, golf
Injuries: Back injury – missed ten days
Relaxations: 'Sailing my boat, listening to music, having a few quiet beers.'

Extras: Shared county record second wicket partnership of 403 with Graham Gooch v Leicestershire in 1990
Opinions on cricket: 'None that will make any difference!'
Best batting: 245 Essex v Leicestershire, Chelmsford 1990

LAST SEASON: BATTING	I.	N. O.	R.	H. S.	AV.
TEST					
1ST	32	3	1407	245	48.51
INT					
RAL	13	1	331	64	27.58
N.W.	2	1	58	37*	58.00
B&H	4	0	175	107	43.75

CAREER: BATTING	I.	N. O.	R.	H. S.	AV.
TEST					
1ST	230	27	7001	245	34.48
INT					
RAL	64	7	1359	103*	23.84
N.W.	11	1	325	94	32.50
B&H	25	6	721	107	37.94

PRINGLE, D. R.   Essex

Name: Derek Raymond Pringle
Role: Right-hand bat, right-arm fast-medium bowler, county vice-captain
Born: 18 September 1958, Nairobi
Height: 6ft 5in **Weight:** 15st 10lbs
Nickname: Ignell, Suggs
County debut: 1978
County cap: 1982
Test debut: 1982
Tests: 21
One-Day Internationals: 26
50 wickets in a season: 6
1st-Class 50s scored: 36
1st-Class 100s scored: 8
1st-Class 5 w. in innings: 22
1st-Class 10 w. in match: 3
One-Day 50s: 25
Place in batting averages: 137th av. 34.07 (1989 163rd av. 22.15)
Place in bowling averages: 27th av. 29.23 (1989 7th av. 18.64)
Strike rate: 63.26 (career 57.85)
1st-Class catches: 9 (career 127)
Parents: Donald James (deceased) and Doris May
Marital status: Single
Family links with cricket: Father represented Kenya and East Africa (played in World Cup 1975)
Education: St Mary's School, Nairobi; Felsted School, Essex; Cambridge University (Fitzwilliam College)

Qualifications: 8 O-levels, 3 A-levels, MA Cantab.

Overseas tours: With England Schools to India 1978–79; England to Australia and New Zealand 1982–83; England B tour to Sri Lanka 1985–86; England A to Zimbabwe and Kenya 1990–91

Cricketers particularly admired: 'Neil Foster for his flexible philosophy about bowling and life.'

Other sports followed: Watches Rugby Union, plays squash and golf

Relaxations: 'Modern music, especially The Smiths, New Order, Billy Bragg and The The, photography, conchology, pub discussions over a pint of Adnams. Good novels: Kunderg, Naipaul, Garcia Marquez etc.'

Extras: Took all ten wickets for Nairobi Schools U–13 1/2 v Up Country Schools U–13 1/2. Captain of Cambridge University in 1982 (Blue 1979–82). Extra in 'Chariots of Fire'. 'Once went shark hunting with Chris Smith of Hampshire (a recklessly brave fellow) in the Maldive Islands.'

Opinions on cricket: 'If four-day cricket will allow more days off in order to mentally prepare oneself for each match, then I'm all for it. Uncovered wickets don't suit our batsmen so scrap that idea. Inception of up-to-date technologies in order to reduce umpiring errors, as there is too much at stake to merely grin and accept bad decisions, i. e. anything to aid the umpires who are now in a very high-pressure situation.'

Best batting: 128 Essex v Kent, Chelmsford 1988

Best bowling: 7–18 Essex v Glamorgan, Swansea 1989

LAST SEASON: BATTING

	I.	N. O.	R.	H. S.	AV.
TEST					
1ST	15	2	443	84	34.07
INT	1	1	30	30*	-
RAL	11	3	305	63	38.12
N.W.	1	0	33	33	33.00
B&H	3	2	151	77*	151.00

LAST SEASON: BOWLING

	O.	M.	R.	W.	AV.
TEST					
1ST	358.3	90	994	34	29.23
INT	7	0	45	0	-
RAL	78	4	438	19	23.05
N.W.	23.3	3	94	4	23.50
B&H	38.4	4	148	4	37.00

CAREER: BATTING

	I.	N. O.	R.	H. S.	AV.
TEST	36	3	512	63	15.51
1ST	303	58	6942	128	28.33
INT	21	9	369	49*	30.75
RAL	89	21	1840	81*	27.05
N.W.	22	5	462	80*	27.17
B&H	51	11	1309	77*	32.72

CAREER: BOWLING

	O.	M.	R.	W.	AV.
TEST	625	133	1807	48	37.64
1ST	5411	1332	14536	578	25.14
INT	239.5	26	1079	23	46.91
RAL	782.3	36	3730	141	26.45
N.W.	240.5	43	761	30	25.36
B&H	575.4	64	2092	84	24.90

RADFORD, N. V. Worcestershire

Name: Neal Victor Radford
Role: Right-hand bat, right-arm
fast-medium bowler, gully fielder
Born: 7 June 1957, Luanshya,
Zambia
Height: 5ft 11in **Weight:** 12st 4lbs
Nickname: Radiz, Vic
County debut: 1980 (Lancs), 1985
(Worcs)
County cap: 1985 (Worcs)
Test debut: 1986
Tests: 3
One-Day Internationals: 6
50 wickets in a season: 5
1st-Class 50s scored: 5
1st-Class 5 w. in innings: 39
1st-Class 10 w. in match: 6
Place in batting averages: 239th av.

16.85 (1989 209th av. 23.00)
Place in bowling averages: 152nd
av. 66.38 (1989 30th av. 23.00)
Strike rate: 100.66 (career 48.98)
1st-Class catches: 6 (career 113)
Parents: Victor Reginald and Edith Joyce
Wife: Lynne
Children: Luke Anthony, 20 November 1988
Family links with cricket: Brother Wayne pro for Gowerton (SWCA) and
Glamorgan 2nd XI. Also played for Orange Free State in Currie Cup
Education: Athlone Boys High School, Johannesburg
Qualifications: Matriculation and university entrance. NCA advanced coach
Overseas teams played for: Transvaal 1979–89
Overseas tours: With England to New Zealand and Australia 1987–88
Cricketers particularly admired: Vincent van der Bijl
Other sports followed: All sports
Relaxations: Music, TV, films
Extras: Only bowler to take 100 first-class wickets in 1985. First player to 100
wickets in 1987. Took most first-class wickets both years. One of *Wisden's* Five
Cricketers of the Year, 1985
Opinions on cricket: 'We play too much cricket! A cut down will result in better
standards all round. Have a day off for travelling as the majority of injuries and
stiffness are caused by travelling hundreds of miles immediately after matches. I do
feel as a professional working person, one should be entitled to accept work where
one so desires.'

Best batting: 76* Lancashire v Derbyshire, Blackpool 1981
Best bowling: 9–70 Worcestershire v Somerset, Worcestershire 1986

LAST SEASON: BATTING

	I.	N. O.	R.	H. S.	AV.
TEST					
1ST	8	1	118	43*	16.85
INT					
RAL	4	1	32	26*	10.66
N.W.	1	0	0	0	0.00
B&H	4	2	98	40	49.00

LAST SEASON: BOWLING

	O.	M.	R.	W.	AV.
TEST					
1ST	302	49	1195	18	66.38
INT					
RAL	41	0	197	3	65.66
N.W.	4	0	23	0	-
B&H	56.3	9	218	10	21.80

CAREER: BATTING

	I.	N. O.	R.	H. S.	AV.
TEST	4	1	21	12*	7.00
1ST	214	48	2701	76*	16.27
INT	3	2	0	0*	0.00
RAL	62	28	648	48*	19.05
N.W.	12	3	90	37	10.00
B&H	22	11	293	40	26.63

CAREER: BOWLING

	O.	M.	R.	W.	AV.
TEST	113	15	351	4	87.75
1ST	6361.5	1244	20004	789	25.35
INT	58	5	230	2	115.00
RAL	679.2	32	3021	139	21.73
N.W.	226	36	715	29	24.65
B&H	679.2	32	3021	139	21.73

RAMPRAKASH, M. R.   Middlesex

Name: Mark Ravindra Ramprakash
Role: Right-hand bat
Born: 5 September 1969, Bushey, Herts
Height: 5ft 9in **Weight:** 12st
Nickname: Ramps, Axe
County debut: 1987
1000 runs in a season: 2
1st-Class 50s scored: 18
1st-Class 100s scored: 6
One-Day 50s: 6
One-Day 100s scored: 2
Place in batting averages: 58th av. 48.15 (1989 58th av. 36.27)
1st-Class catches: 6 (career 28)
Parents: Jennifer and Deo
Marital status: Single
Family links with cricket: Father played club cricket in Guyana
Education: Gayton High School; Harrow Weald College
Qualifications: 6 O-levels; 2 A-levels (Politics and Economics)
Off-season: England A tour to Pakistan; then to Barbados and Trinidad with BWIA

Overseas tours: England YCs to Sri Lanka 1987 and Australia for Youth World Cup 1988; England A to Pakistan 1990–91

Cricketers particularly admired: 'All the great all-rounders.'

Other sports followed: Snooker, tennis, football, athletics

Injuries: 'Being hit on the shin fielding at cover when David Ward was batting... I wanted to borrow short leg's shin pads.'

Relaxations: 'I enjoy playing snooker with friends even though I am hopeless: it helps me concentrate in the same way I try to do when batting, i. e. not to have a rush of blood.'

Extras: Won Best U–15 Schoolboy of 1985 awarded by Cricket Society. Best Young Cricketer 1986. Did not begin to play cricket until he was nine years old. Made debut for Middlesex aged 17. Played for Bessborough CC at age 13. Played for ESCA Under–15s v Public Schools, 1984. Played in NCA Guernsey Festival Tournament and scored 204*. Played for England YCs v Sri Lanka 1987 and New Zealand 1989. Played for Middlesex 2nd XI aged 16. In 1987 played for Stanmore CC and made 186* on his debut. Man of the Match in Middlesex's NatWest Trophy Final win 1988, on his debut in the competition. Cricket Society's Most Promising Player of the Year 1988. Scored three 100s in successive innings during 1990 season

Opinions on cricket: 'I enjoy playing a mix of three and four-day cricket. The benefit system should be revised: every year each club should have a benefit, guarantee the player a sum with the excess to go into a pool for others who do not qualify; committees should take into account the extra workload of fast bowlers; players should concentrate on their cricket, not worry about organising benefits.'

Best batting: 146* Middlesex v Somerset, Uxbridge 1990

Best bowling: 1–17 Middlesex v Surrey, The Oval 1990

LAST SEASON: BATTING

	I.	N. O.	R.	H. S.	AV.
TEST					
1ST	42	10	1541	146*	48.15
INT					
RAL	17	5	638	147*	53.16
N.W.	3	0	152	104	50.66
B&H	5	0	78	44	15.60

CAREER: BATTING

	I.	N. O.	R.	H. S.	AV.
TEST					
1ST	103	22	3335	146*	41.17
INT					
RAL	38	9	1103	147*	38.03
N.W.	9	0	289	104	32.11
B&H	9	1	126	44	15.75

RANDALL, D. W.   Nottinghamshire

Name: Derek William Randall
Role: Right-hand bat, cover fielder
Born: 24 February 1951, Retford,
Nottinghamshire
Height: 5ft 8 1/2in **Weight:** 11st
Nickname: Arkle, Rags
County debut: 1972
County cap: 1973
Benefit: 1983 (42,000)
Test debut: 1976–77
Tests: 47
One-Day Internationals: 49
1000 runs in a season: 12
1st-Class 50s scored: 149
1st-Class 100s scored: 46
1st-Class 200s scored: 3
One-Day 50s: 61
One-Day 100s: 6
Place in batting averages: 126th av.
36.55 (1989 41st av. 40.13)
1st-Class catches: 14 (career 329)
Parents: Frederick and Mavis
Wife and date of marriage: Elizabeth, September 1973
Children: Simon, June 1977
Family links with cricket: Father played local cricket – 'tried to bowl fast off a long run and off the wrong foot too!'
Education: Sir Frederick Milner Secondary Modern School, Retford
Qualifications: ONC mechanical engineering, mechanical draughtsman
Overseas tours: England to India, Sri Lanka and Australia 1976–77; Pakistan and New Zealand 1977–78; Australia 1978–79; Australia and India 1979–80; Australia and New Zealand 1982–83; New Zealand and Pakistan 1983–84; England B to Sri Lanka 1985–86
Cricketers particularly admired: Sir Gary Sobers, Tom Graveney ('boyhood idol'), Reg Simpson
Other sports followed: Football, squash, golf
Relaxations: Listening to varied selection of tapes. Family man
Extras: Before joining Nottinghamshire staff, played for Retford CC in the Basset-law League, and helped in Championship wins of 1968 and 1969. Scored 174 in Centenary Test v Australia 1976–77. One of *Wisden's* Five Cricketers of the Year, 1978
Best batting: 237 Nottinghamshire v Derbyshire, Trent Bridge 1988
Best bowling: 3–15 Nottinghamshire v MCC, Lord's 1982

LAST SEASON: BATTING

	I.	N.O.	R.	H.S.	AV.
TEST					
1ST	28	1	987	178	36.55
INT					
RAL	8	3	198	54*	39.60
N.W.	1	0	56	56	56.00
B&H	6	0	95	39	15.83

LAST SEASON: BOWLING

	O.	M.	R.	W.	AV.
TEST					
1ST					
INT					
RAL					
N.W.					
B&H					

CAREER: BATTING

	I.	N.O.	R.	H.S.	AV.
TEST	79	5	2470	174	33.37
1ST	675	64	23257	237	38.06
INT	45	5	1067	88	26.67
RAL	215	32	5929	123	32.39
N.W.	37	5	943	149*	29.46
B&H	86	12	2458	103*	33.21

CAREER: BOWLING

	O.	M.	R.	W.	AV.
TEST	2.4	0	3	0	-
1ST	73.3	5	383	12	31.91
INT	0.2	0	2	1	2.00
RAL	0.5	0	9	0	-
N.W.	2	0	23	0	-
B&H	2.5	0	5	0	-

RATCLIFFE, J. D.   Warwickshire

Name: Jason David Ratcliffe
Role: Opening bat, right-arm
medium-pace bowler, slip fielder
Born: 19 June 1969, Solihull
Height: 6ft 3in **Weight:** 13st 4lbs
Nickname: Ratters, Roland
County debut: 1988
1st-Class 50s scored: 5
1st-Class 100s scored: 1
One-Day 50s: 1
Place in batting averages: 179th av.
27.85 (1989 61st av. 35.68)
1st-Class catches: 7 (career 14)
Parents: David and Sheila
Marital status: Single
Family links with cricket: Father
(D. P. Ratcliffe) played for Warwickshire
1956–62
Education: Meadow Green Primary
School; Sharmons Cross Secondary
School; Solihull Sixth Form College

Qualifications: 6 O-levels; advanced cricket coach
Off-season: Playing cricket for Belmont District CC in Australia
Overseas teams played for: Westend CC, Kimberley 1987–88
Cricketers particularly admired: Geoff Boycott, Dennis Amiss
Other sports followed: Football and most other sports
Injuries: Hit on shoulder while batting at The Oval – missed one game

Relaxations: 'Listening to music, reading, eating out.'
Opinions on cricket: 'In favour of 16 four-day matches.'
Best batting: 127* Warwickshire v Cambridge University, Fenner's 1989
Best bowling: 1–15 Warwickshire v Yorkshire, Headingley 1989

LAST SEASON: BATTING

	I.	N. O.	R.	H. S.	AV.
TEST					
1ST	31	3	780	81*	27.85
INT					
RAL					
N.W.					
B&H					

CAREER: BATTING

	I.	N. O.	R.	H. S.	AV.
TEST					
1ST	55	7	1382	127*	28.79
INT					
RAL	4	1	47	37	15.66
N.W.	1	0	59	59	59.00
B&H					

REEVE, D. A. Warwickshire

Name: Dermot Alexander Reeve
Role: Right-hand bat, right-arm
fast-medium bowler, county vice-captain
Born: 2 April 1963, Hong Kong
Height: 6ft **Weight:** 12st
Nickname: Legend, Motte
County debut: 1983 (Sussex), 1988
(Warwicks)
County cap: 1986 (Sussex), 1989
(Warwicks)
1000 runs in a season: 1
50 wickets in a season: 2
1st-Class 50s scored: 20
1st-Class 100s scored: 5
1st-Class 200s scored: 1
1st-Class 5 w. in innings: 5
One-Day 50s: 4
Place in batting averages: 36th av.
54.30 (1989 23rd av. 44.69)
Place in bowling averages: 22nd av.
28.48
Strike rate: 68.66 (career 63.78)
1st-Class catches: 26 (career 101)
Parents: Alexander James and Monica
Wife and date of marriage: Julie, 20 December 1986
Children: Emily Kaye, 14 September 1988
Family links with cricket: Father captain of school XI, brother Mark an improving
club cricketer

Education: King George V School, Kowloon, Hong Kong
Qualifications: 7 O-levels
Career outside cricket: Operations manager for Employment Agency
Off-season: 'Working in Birmingham and going on cricket tours. I've played the last eight winters in Perth. Time for a rest!'
Cricketers particularly admired: Wasim Akram, Waqar Younis, Jimmy Cook, Tim Munton, John Barclay
Other sports followed: Football (Man Utd), Aussie Rules
Injuries: 'Had my big toe Wasim'd!'
Relaxations: Music, videos, swimming, Perth beaches, Italian food
Extras: Formerly on Lord's ground staff. Represented Hong Kong in the ICC Trophy competition June 1982. Hong Kong Cricketer of the Year 1980–81. Hong Kong's Cricket Sports Personality of the Year 1981. Man of the Match in 1986 NatWest Final for Sussex and 1989 Final for Warwickshire. Twice Western Australian CA Cricketer of the Year
Opinions on cricket: 'Four-day cricket on covered wickets and 100 overs a day. More One-Day Internationals in England. Over-rate fines too strict. I would also like to see coloured clothing for Sunday cricket.'
Best batting: 202* Warwickshire v Northamptonshire, Northampton 1990
Best bowling: 7–37 Sussex v Lancashire, Lytham 1987

LAST SEASON: BATTING

	I.	N. O.	R.	H. S.	AV.
TEST					
1ST	38	12	1412	202*	54.30
INT					
RAL	13	2	252	41	22.90
N.W.	2	1	36	36*	36.00
B&H	4	1	61	29*	20.33

LAST SEASON: BOWLING

	O.	M.	R.	W.	AV.
TEST					
1ST	377.4	110	940	33	28.48
INT					
RAL	83.1	5	412	12	34.33
N.W.	20	2	62	0	-
B&H	41	4	175	4	43.75

CAREER: BATTING

	I.	N. O.	R.	H. S.	AV.
TEST					
1ST	179	50	4185	202*	32.44
INT					
RAL	65	20	1031	70*	22.91
N.W.	15	7	223	45	27.87
B&H	19	8	213	30*	19.36

CAREER: BOWLING

	O.	M.	R.	W.	AV.
TEST					
1ST	3263.5	864	8581	307	27.95
INT					
RAL	1082.2	20	2737	100	27.37
N.W.	193.5	41	550	20	27.50
B&H	194.4	20	842	22	38.27

REMY, C. C.   Sussex

Name: Carlos Charles Remy
Role: Right-hand bat, right-arm
medium bowler
Born: 24 July 1968, St Lucia,
Windward Islands
Height: 5ft 9in
County debut: 1989
1st-Class catches: 0 (career 1)
Education: St Aloyious School,
Archway, London; Haringey Cricket
College
Extras: Played for Middlesex 2nd XI
1987–88. Plays club cricket for
Littlehampton in the Sussex League
Best batting: 4* Sussex v Gloucester-
shire, Hove 1990
Best bowling: 4–63 Sussex v Cambridge
University, Hove 1990

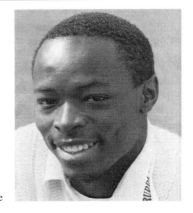

LAST SEASON: BATTING

	I.	N. O.	R.	H. S.	AV.
TEST					
1ST	1	1	4	4*	-
INT					
RAL	5	1	33	12*	8.25
N.W.	1	0	1	1	1.00
B&H					

LAST SEASON: BOWLING

	O.	M.	R.	W.	AV.
TEST					
1ST	54	6	224	5	44.80
INT					
RAL	16.4	0	102	2	51.00
N.W.	10	1	30	0	-
B&H					

CAREER: BATTING

	I.	N. O.	R.	H. S.	AV.
TEST					
1ST	2	1	4	4*	4.00
INT					
RAL	5	1	33	12*	8.25
N.W.	1	0	1	1	1.00
B&H					

CAREER: BOWLING

	O.	M.	R.	W.	AV.
TEST					
1ST	69	9	257	6	42.83
INT					
RAL	16.4	0	102	2	51.00
N.W.	10	1	30	0	-
B&H					

RHODES, S. J.   Worcestershire

Name: Steven John Rhodes
Role: Right-hand bat, wicket-keeper
Born: 17 June 1964, Bradford
Height: 5ft 8in **Weight:** 11st 10lbs
Nickname: Wilf, Bumpy
County debut: 1981 (Yorks), 1985
(Worcs)
County cap: 1988 (Worcs)
One-Day Internationals: 3
1st-Class 50s scored: 18
1st-Class 100s scored: 1
One-Day 50s: 2
Place in batting averages: 81st av.
44.80 (1989 71st av. 34.61)
Parents: Bill and Norma
Marital status: Single
Family links with cricket: Father
played for Nottinghamshire 1961–64
Education: Bradford Moor Junior
School; Lapage St Middle; Carlton-
Bolling Comprehensive, Bradford
Qualifications: 4 O-levels, coaching certificate
Off-season: Touring Pakistan with England A
Overseas tours: England B to Sri Lanka 1986–86; picked for cancelled England
tour of India 1988–89; England A to Zimbabwe and Kenya 1989–90; Pakistan
1990–91
Cricketers particularly admired: Alan Knott ('seemed to have lots of time with
his keeping'), Bob Taylor, Graeme Hick

LAST SEASON: BATTING

	I.	N. O.	R.	H. S.	AV.
TEST					
1ST	25	10	672	96	44.80
INT					
RAL	9	3	117	35*	19.50
N.W.	1	0	2	2	2.00
B&H	3	0	14	8	4.66

LAST SEASON: WICKET-KEEPING

	CT	ST		
TEST				
1ST	61	8		
INT				
RAL	14	3		
N.W.	3	0		
B&H	6	0		

CAREER: BATTING

	I.	N. O.	R.	H. S.	AV.
TEST					
1ST	197	69	3969	108	31.00
INT	2	1	9	8	9.00
RAL	64	15	1044	48*	21.30
N.W.	15	6	154	61	17.11
B&H	23	5	343	51*	19.05

CAREER: WICKET-KEEPING

	CT	ST		
TEST				
1ST	374	42		
INT	3	0		
RAL	102	24		
N.W.	25	4		
B&H	35	5		

Other sports followed: Rugby League (Bradford Northern), golf
Relaxations: 'Playing (and paying) golf with Tim (Bandit) Curtis.' Tropical fish
Extras: England YC v Australia in 1983. Youngest wicket-keeper to play for Yorkshire. Record for most victims in an innings for Young England. Released by Yorkshire to join Worcestershire at end of 1984 season
Opinions on cricket: 'Play four-day matches on good pitches. The TCCB should pay the groundsman. Scrap the 25-point deduction rule as wickets should be good if TCCB employ groundsmen! Do away with one one-day competition to reduce cricket, and keep players fresh. All one-dayers should be a maximum of 50 overs.'
Best batting: 108 Worcestershire v Derbyshire, Derby 1988

RICHARDS, I. V. A.   Glamorgan

Name: Isaac Vivian Alexander Richards
Role: Right-hand bat, off-break bowler
Born: 7 March 1952, St John's, Antigua
Height: 5ft 11in **Weight:** 13st 7lbs
Nickname: Smokey, Vivey
County debut: 1974 (Somerset), 1990 (Glamorgan)
County cap: 1974 (Somerset), 1990 (Glamorgan)
Benefit: 1982 (56,440)
Test debut: 1974
Tests: 111
One-Day Internationals: 179
1000 runs in a season: 13
1st-class 50s scored: 142
1st-class 100s scored: 109
1st-class 200s scored: 7
1st-class 5 w. in innings: 1
One-day 50s: 96
One-day 100s: 23
Place in batting averages: 20th av. 61.95
1st-class catches: 8 (career 413 & 1 stumping)
Parents: Malcolm and Gratel
Wife and date of marriage: Miriam, 24 March 1981
Children: Matara
Family links with cricket: Father played for Antigua as an all-rounder. Half-brother Donald played for Antigua and Leeward Islands and brother Mervyn played for Antigua
Education: St John's Boys School and Antigua Grammar School
Off-season: Playing cricket in West Indies

Overseas tours: West Indies to India, Sri Lanka and Pakistan 1974–75; Australia 1975–76; England 1976; Australia 1979–80; England 1980; Pakistan 1980–81; Australia 1981–82; India 1983–84; England 1984; Australia 1984–85; Pakistan and New Zealand 1986–87; India 1987–88; England 1988; Australia 1988–89
Overseas teams played for: Leeward Islands and Combined Islands since 1971–72; Queensland 1976–77
Other sports followed: Football, basketball, squash. Played football for Antigua and once had a trial with Bath City FC
Injuries: Still troubled by haemorrhoid problem that forced him to miss the whole of the 1989 season
Relaxations: Listening to music
Extras: 'I remain a religious person to the delight of my parents. I pray every night before going to sleep; occasionally I pray for success on the field.' Helps to sponsor young sportsmen in Antigua. 'Sounds mad but I am not a travelling man – I hate it in the air. Planes terrify me.' Captain of West Indies since 1986. Released by Somerset at end of 1986 and played for Rishton in Lancashire League in 1987. Became first West Indian to hit 100 first-class 100s in 1988–89. Signed two-year contract with Glamorgan in 1989 but unable to play at all in his first season due to injury. Made his debut for Glamorgan in 1990 and has signed a further two-year contract for 1992 and 1993
Best batting: 322 Somerset v Warwickshire, Taunton 1985
Best bowling: 5–88 West Indies v Queensland, Brisbane 1981–82

LAST SEASON: BATTING

	I.	N. O.	R.	H. S.	AV.
TEST					
1ST	28	5	1425	164*	61.95
INT					
RAL	14	1	490	77	37.69
N.W.	3	1	201	118	100.50
B&H	5	0	104	28	20.80

LAST SEASON: BOWLING

	O.	M.	R.	W.	AV.
TEST					
1ST	137	26	426	5	85.20
INT					
RAL	69.5	1	431	14	30.78
N.W.	26	0	114	4	28.50
B&H	51	1	200	5	40.00

CAREER: BATTING

	I.	N. O.	R.	H. S.	AV.
TEST	166	10	7990	291	51.21
1ST	542	40	25043	322	48.91
INT	160	24	6501	189*	47.80
RAL	153	17	5235	126*	38.49
N.W.	34	4	1410	139*	47.00
B&H	44	6	1499	132*	39.44

CAREER: BOWLING

	O.	M.	R.	W.	AV.
TEST	833.4	201	1857	32	58.03
1ST	2797	853	7493	178	42.09
INT	923.4	26	4144	118	35.11
RAL	456.5	15	2189	84	26.06
N.W.	161.1	15	592	20	29.60
B&H	118.4	15	425	12	35.41

RIPLEY, D. Northamptonshire

Name: David Ripley
Role: Right-hand bat, wicket-keeper
Born: 13 September 1966, Leeds
Height: 5ft 11in **Weight:** 12st
Nickname: Rips, Spud, Sheridan
County debut: 1984
County cap: 1987
1st-Class 50s scored: 4
1st-Class 100s scored: 4
Place in batting averages: 169th av. 29.81 (1989 147th av. 23.55)
Parents: Arthur and Brenda
Wife and date of marriage: Jackie, 24 September 1988
Family links with cricket: 'My Mum once made the teas at Farsley CC.'
Education: Woodlesford Primary; Royds High, Leeds
Qualifications: 5 O-levels, NCA coaching certificate
Career outside cricket: Director of Gard Sports, Northampton
Overseas tours: England YCs to West Indies 1984–85
Cricketers particularly admired: Alan Knott, Bob Taylor, Ian Botham, Dennis Lillee
Other sports followed: Soccer (Leeds United) and Rugby League (Castleford), golf
Relaxations: Music, eating out
Extras: Finished top of wicket-keepers' dismissals list for 1988 with 87 victims

LAST SEASON: BATTING

	I.	N. O.	R.	H. S.	AV.
TEST					
1ST	28	6	656	109*	29.81
INT					
RAL	9	3	67	26	11.16
N.W.	4	1	23	13	7.66
B&H	4	1	44	27	14.66

LAST SEASON: WICKET-KEEPING

	CT	ST			
TEST					
1ST	28	6			
INT					
RAL	5	1			
N.W.	2	0			
B&H	2	0			

CAREER: BATTING

	I.	N. O.	R.	H. S.	AV.
TEST					
1ST	171	38	2882	134*	21.66
INT					
RAL	45	21	404	36*	16.83
N.W.	13	5	95	27*	11.87
B&H	17	6	227	33	20.63

CAREER: WICKET-KEEPING

	CT	ST			
TEST					
1ST	264	48			
INT					
RAL	41	10			
N.W.	20	2			
B&H	22	3			

Best batting: 134* Northamptonshire v Yorkshire, Scarborough 1986
Best bowling: 2–89 Northamptonshire v Essex, Ilford 1987

ROBERTS, A. R.   Northamptonshire

Name: Andrew Richard Roberts
Role: Right-hand bat, leg-spin bowler
Born: 16 April 1971, Kettering
Height: 5ft 6in **Weight:** 10st 4lbs
Nickname: Reggie
County debut: 1989
1st-Class catches: 1 (career 2)
Parents: David and Shirley
Marital status: Single
Family links with cricket: 'Dad (Dave)
had a couple of games on trial at
Northampton.'
Education: Our Lady's and Bishop
Stopford, Kettering
Qualifications: 3 O-levels, 5 CSEs
Off-season: 'Playing cricket in
Christchurch, New Zealand.'
Cricketers particularly admired:
Richard Williams, Wayne Larkins,
Malcolm Marshall, Derek Randall
Other sports followed: Golf
Relaxations: 'Music, swimming, a curry and a pint!'
Extras: Played for England YCs v Pakistan 1990

LAST SEASON: BATTING

	I.	N. O.	R.	H. S.	AV.
TEST					
1ST	3	0	5	5	1.66
INT					
RAL					
N.W.					
B&H					

LAST SEASON: BOWLING

	O.	M.	R.	W.	AV.
TEST					
1ST	63	14	207	3	69.00
INT					
RAL					
N.W.					
B&H					

CAREER: BATTING

	I.	N. O.	R.	H. S.	AV.
TEST					
1ST	6	1	27	8*	5.40
INT					
RAL					
N.W.					
B&H					

CAREER: BOWLING

	O.	M.	R.	W.	AV.
TEST					
1ST	97	16	364	5	72.80
INT					
RAL					
N.W.					
B&H					

Opinions on cricket: 'Good idea to have first-class umpires standing in 2nd XI Championship matches. Use a seam on the ball mid-way between the 1989 and 1990 versions to level the balance between bat and ball.'
Best batting: 8* Northamptonshire v Glamorgan, Swansea 1989
Best bowling: 2–123 Northamptonshire v Gloucestershire, Cheltenham 1990

ROBERTS, B. Derbyshire

Name: Bruce Roberts
Role: Right-hand bat, right-arm medium bowler, slip fielder
Born: 30 May 1962, Lusaka, Zambia
Height: 6ft 1in **Weight:** 14st
County debut: 1984
County cap: 1986
1000 runs in a season: 3
1st-Class 50s scored: 40
1st-Class 100s scored: 13
1st-Class 5 w. in innings: 1
One-Day 50s: 17
One-Day 100s: 2
Place in batting averages: 129th av. 35.74 (1989 172nd av. 20.80)
1st-Class catches: 23 (career 165 & 1 stumping)
Parents: Arthur William and Sara Ann
Wife: Ingrid
Family links with cricket: Father played for Country Districts

LAST SEASON: BATTING

	I.	N. O.	R.	H. S.	AV.
TEST					
1ST	38	7	1108	124*	35.74
INT					
RAL	14	4	345	77*	34.50
N.W.	2	1	45	31	45.00
B&H	3	1	55	46	27.50

LAST SEASON: BOWLING

	O.	M.	R.	W.	AV.
TEST					
1ST	19	5	52	3	17.33
INT					
RAL					
N.W.					
B&H					

CAREER: BATTING

	I.	N. O.	R.	H. S.	AV.
TEST					
1ST	331	32	9102	184	30.44
INT					
RAL	89	17	2203	101*	30.59
N.W.	14	3	342	64*	31.09
B&H	28	7	716	100	34.09

CAREER: BOWLING

	O.	M.	R.	W.	AV.
TEST					
1ST	898.1	163	2948	89	33.12
INT					
RAL	139.4	2	918	41	22.39
N.W.	23	2	104	2	52.00
B&H	43.1	5	201	5	40.20

Education: Ruzawi, Peterhouse, and Prince Edward, Zimbabwe
Qualifications: O-levels, coaching qualifications
Career outside cricket: Working in family sports shop
Overseas teams played for: Transvaal 1982–89
Cricketers particularly admired: Allan Border, Clive Rice
Other sports followed: Rugby and most other sports
Relaxations: 'Family, watching a good programme on TV, stamps and computers.'
Best batting: 184 Derbyshire v Sussex, Chesterfield 1987
Best bowling: 5–68 Transvaal B v Northern Transvaal B, Johannesburg 1986–87

ROBERTS, M. L. Glamorgan

Name: Martin Leonard Roberts
Role: Right-hand bat, wicket-keeper
Born: 12 April 1966, Mullion, Cornwall
Height: 5ft 11in **Weight:** 11st 7lbs
Nickname: Hen
County debut: 1985
Parents: Leonard and Marianne
Wife and date of marriage: Susan, 20
September 1986
Children: Christopher, 18 May 1989
Family links with cricket: Brother
Kevin plays for Helston; father also used
to play
Education: Helston Comprehensive
School
Qualifications: 5 O-levels; qualified
cricket coach
Off-season: 'Looking for work in and
around Cardiff.'
Cricketers particularly admired: Bob
Taylor, Jack Russell, John Steele (2nd XI
captain/coach)
Other sports followed: Football, golf and American football
Injuries: 'Missed two games – one with a twisted ankle, the other with a dislocated
finger.'
Relaxations: 'Enjoy attempting crosswords, eating out and swimming.'
Extras: Awarded 2nd XI Player of the Year 1989
Opinions on cricket: 'All Championship matches should be four days to give our
batsmen more time at the wicket and condition them for Test cricket.'
Best batting: 25 Glamorgan v Sri Lanka, Ebbw Vale 1990

LAST SEASON: BATTING

	I.	N. O.	R.	H. S.	AV.
TEST					
1ST	5	1	79	25	19.75
INT					
RAL	1	1	12	12*	-
N.W.					
B&H					

LAST SEASON: WICKET-KEEPING

	CT	ST			
TEST					
1ST	10	0			
INT					
RAL	0	0			
N.W.					
B&H					

CAREER: BATTING

	I.	N. O.	R.	H. S.	AV.
TEST					
1ST	8	1	93	25	13.28
INT					
RAL	3	3	19	12*	-
N.W.					
B&H					

CAREER: WICKET-KEEPING

	CT	ST			
TEST					
1ST	14	1			
INT					
RAL	1	0			
N.W.					
B&H					

ROBINSON, J. D.   Surrey

Name: Jonathan David Robinson
Role: Left-hand bat, right-arm medium bowler
Born: 3 August 1966, Epsom, Surrey
Height: 5ft 10 1/2in **Weight:** 12st 4lbs
Nickname: Robbo, Johnny Yamamoto
County debut: 1988
1st-Class 50s: 1
Place in batting averages: 235th av. 17.50 (1989 188th av. 19.44)
1st-Class catches: 1 (career 4)
Parents: Peter and Wendy
Marital status: Single
Family links with cricket: Father played for Cambridge University and Esher CC; 'Mother bowled at me in the garden!'
Education: Danes Hill Preparatory School; Lancing College; West Sussex Institute of Higher Education
Qualifications: 6 O-levels, 3 A-levels, BA degree in Sports Studies, cricket coaching award
Cricketers particularly admired: Ian Botham, David Gower, Robin Smith
Other sports followed: Rugby, squash, soccer, horse racing (brother Michael is a trainer)
Relaxations: Theatre, restaurants, TV, music, pubs, all sports, cinema, clubs, friends, travel

Extras: Did a major study at college about the commercialisation of cricket
Opinions on cricket: 'Four-day Championship matches can only be beneficial to English cricket, as a build-up to Test cricket. One-day matches, however, are a lot of fun to play in and for spectators.'
Best batting: 72 Surrey v Middlesex, The Oval 1990
Best bowling: 2–37 Surrey v Leicestershire, Leicester 1989

LAST SEASON: BATTING

	I.	N. O.	R.	H. S.	AV.
TEST					
1ST	10	0	175	72	17.50
INT					
RAL	4	0	40	16	10.00
N.W.					
B&H	1	1	2	2*	-

LAST SEASON: BOWLING

	O.	M.	R.	W.	AV.
TEST					
1ST	146.3	28	476	7	68.00
INT					
RAL	11	0	63	0	-
N.W.					
B&H	11	0	41	2	20.50

CAREER: BATTING

	I.	N. O.	R.	H. S.	AV.
TEST					
1ST	26	4	405	72	18.40
INT					
RAL	13	3	111	18*	11.10
N.W.					
B&H	2	1	2	2*	2.00

CAREER: BOWLING

	O.	M.	R.	W.	AV.
TEST					
1ST	198.5	37	701	13	53.92
INT					
RAL	49.2	0	272	2	136.00
N.W.					
B&H	11	0	41	2	20.50

ROBINSON, M. A.   Yorkshire

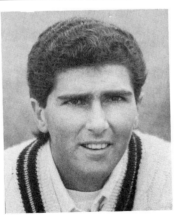

Name: Mark Andrew Robinson
Role: Right-hand bat, right-arm fast-medium bowler
Born: 23 November 1966, Hull
Height: 6ft 3in **Weight:** 12st 12lbs
Nickname: Smokey, Coddy
County debut: 1987 (Northants)
Place in bowling averages: 119th av. 47.22 (1989 73rd av. 30.78)
Strike rate: 83.87 (career 68.36)
1st-Class catches: 5 (career 14)
Parents: Joan Margaret and Malcolm
Marital status: Single
Family links with cricket: Maternal grandfather an established local cricketer. Father was hostile cricketer in back garden
Education: Fifth Avenue Primary; Endike Junior High; Hull Grammar School
Qualifications: 6 O-levels, 2 A-levels, 1st NCA cricket coaching award

Off-season: Coaching in Hull
Overseas teams played for: Canterbury, New Zealand 1988–89
Cricketers particularly admired: Dennis Lillee, Richard Hadlee, Winston Davis, Neil Foster, Mike Gatting, John Emburey
Other sports followed: Hull City FC ('The Tigers'), and all sports
Injuries: 'Sore shins and tendonitis in shoulder and knee.'
Relaxations: Cinema, soap operas, reading, music, hot baths
Extras: Took part in Leeds to London relay run around all county headquarters, in aid of Leukaemia Research. Took hat-trick with first three balls of innings in Yorkshire League, playing for Hull v Doncaster. First player to win Yorkshire U–19s Bowler of the Season Award in two successive years. Northamptonshire Uncapped Player of the Year 1989. Endured a world record 11 innings without scoring a run during 1990 season and has joined Yorkshire for 1991
Opinions on cricket: 'The balance of bat and ball was too one-sided in 1990 and the powers that be must address the problem for the good of the game. The NatWest dates should be swapped with the B & H – avoiding the toss of a coin deciding the outcome of one of English cricket's showpiece events.'
Best batting: 19* Northamptonshire v Essex, Chelmsford 1988
Best bowling: 4–19 Northamptonshire v Glamorgan, Wellingborough 1988

LAST SEASON: BATTING

	I.	N. O.	R.	H. S.	AV.
TEST					
1ST	16	10	3	1*	0.50
INT					
RAL	3	2	0	0*	-
N.W.	3	2	3	3*	3.00
B&H	3	2	1	1	1.00

LAST SEASON: BOWLING

	O.	M.	R.	W.	AV.
TEST					
1ST	559.1	105	1889	40	47.22
INT					
RAL	88.3	7	528	11	48.00
N.W.	56	5	206	9	22.88
B&H	38.4	1	176	4	44.00

CAREER: BATTING

	I.	N. O.	R.	H. S.	AV.
TEST					
1ST	68	32	72	19*	2.00
INT					
RAL	11	3	3	3	0.37
N.W.	3	2	3	3*	3.00
B&H	3	2	1	1	1.00

CAREER: BOWLING

	O.	M.	R.	W.	AV.
TEST					
1ST	1720.3	336	5193	151	34.39
INT					
RAL	224.4	12	1117	22	50.77
N.W.	79.4	9	268	14	19.14
B&H	82.4	6	286	9	31.77

ROBINSON, P. E.   Yorkshire

Name: Phillip Edward Robinson
Role: Right-hand middle-order bat,
left-arm 'declaraton bowler'
Born: 3 August 1963, Keighley
Height: 5ft 9in **Weight:** 13st 6lbs
Nickname: Billy, Red
County debut: 1984
County cap: 1988
1000 runs in a season: 2
1st-Class 50s scored: 36
1st-Class 100s scored: 5
One-Day 50s: 12
Place in batting averages: 88th av.
43.81 (1989 106th av. 28.92)
1st-Class catches: 20 (career 76)
Parents: Keith and Lesley
Wife and date of marriage: Jane,
19 September 1986
Family links with cricket: Father and
brothers play in Bradford League.
Younger brother at Park Avenue Cricket
Academy
Education: Long Lee Primary; Hartington Middle; Greenhead Grammar
Qualifications: 2 O-levels
Off-season: Playing and coaching in New Zealand for Riverside CC, Lower Hutt
Cricketers particularly admired: Gary Sobers, Geoff Boycott
Other sports followed: 'I follow most sports.'
Relaxations: Watching TV, computers, health food
Extras: Scored the highest score by a Yorkshire 2nd XI player when he made 233
in 1983 v Kent at Canterbury. Scored most runs by an overseas player in the Auckland
Cricket League for Eden Roskill 1989–90
Opinions on cricket: 'The fixture list should be sorted out. There seems to be far
too much travelling between matches. It will only be a matter of time before someone
gets killed because of the long journeys between games – in 1990 Yorkshire played
at Headingley, then Eastbourne and back to Middlesbrough.'

LAST SEASON: BATTING

	I.	N. O.	R.	H. S.	AV.
TEST					
1ST	39	7	1402	150*	43.81
INT					
RAL	14	1	257	58*	19.76
N.W.	1	0	7	7	7.00
B&H	4	2	173	73*	86.50

CAREER: BATTING

	I.	N. O.	R.	H. S.	AV.
TEST					
1ST	176	24	5375	150*	35.36
INT					
RAL	85	9	1893	78*	24.90
N.W.	4	0	73	66	18.25
B&H	13	2	339	73*	30.81

Best batting: 150* Yorkshire v Derbyshire, Scarborough 1990
Best bowling: 1–10 Yorkshire v Somerset, Scarborough 1990

ROBINSON, R. T.   Nottinghamshire

Name: Robert Timothy Robinson
Role: Right-hand opening bat, right-arm bowler, county captain
Born: 21 November 1958, Sutton-in-Ashfield, Nottinghamshire
Height: 5ft 11 1/2in **Weight:** 12st 4lbs
Nickname: Robbo, Chop
County debut: 1978
County cap: 1983
Test debut: 1984–85
Tests: 29
One-Day Internationals: 26
1000 runs in a season: 8
1st-Class 50s scored: 82
1st-Class 100s scored: 39
1st-Class 200s scored: 2
One-Day 50s: 44
One-Day 100s: 6
Place in batting averages: 89th av. 43.67 (1989 35th av. 42.11)

1st-Class catches: 12 (career 168)
Parents: Eddy and Christine
Wife and date of marriage: Patricia, 2 November 1985
Children: Philip, 14 December 1986
Family links with cricket: Father, uncle, cousin and brother all played local cricket.
Education: Dunstable Grammar School; High Pavement College, Nottingham; Sheffield University
Qualifications: Degree in Accounting and Financial Management
Overseas tours: England to India and Australia 1984–85; West Indies 1985–86; World Cup, India, New Zealand 1987–88; unofficial English team to South Africa 1989–90
Cricketers particularly admired: Geoffrey Boycott
Other sports followed: Soccer, rugby
Relaxations: Television, reading, spending time with family
Extras: Played for Northamptonshire 2nd XI in 1974–75 and for Nottinghamshire 2nd XI in 1977. Had soccer trials with Portsmouth, Chelsea and QPR. One of *Wisden's* Five Cricketers of the Year, 1985. Banned from Test cricket for joining 1990 tour of South Africa
Opinions on cricket: 'There should be a four-day County Championship.'

Best batting: 220* Nottinghamshire v Yorkshire, Trent Bridge 1990
Best bowling: 1–22 Nottinghamshire v Northamptonshire, Northampton 1982

LAST SEASON: BATTING

	I.	N. O.	R.	H. S.	AV.
TEST					
1ST	45	5	1747	220*	43.67
INT					
RAL	17	4	610	116	46.92
N.W.	2	0	91	61	45.50
B&H	6	4	355	106*	177.50

CAREER: BATTING

	I.	N. O.	R.	H. S.	AV.
TEST	49	5	1601	175	36.38
1ST	425	53	15388	220*	41.36
INT	26	0	597	83	22.96
RAL	136	16	3931	116	32.75
N.W.	26	2	1006	139	41.91
B&H	52	7	1785	120	39.66

ROEBUCK, P. M. Somerset

Name: Peter Michael Roebuck
Role: Right-hand bat, right-arm
'fast off-break bowler', slip fielder
Born: 6 March 1956, Oxford
Height: 'am slowly shrinking' **Weight:**
'a few pounds more since the benefit'
Nickname: Professor
County debut: 1974
County cap: 1978
Benefit: 1990
1000 runs in a season: 9
1st-Class 50s scored: 88
1st-Class 100s scored: 32
1st-Class 200s scored: 2
1st-Class 5 w. in innings: 1
One-Day 50s: 34
One-Day 100s: 5
Place in batting averages: 53rd av.
49.30 (1989 38th av. 41.14)
1st-Class catches: 6 (career 157)
Parents: James and Elizabeth
Marital status: Single
Family links with cricket: Mother and sister both played for Oxford University
Ladies. Younger brother Paul played for Glamorgan
Education: Park School, Bath; Millfield School; Emmanuel College, Cambridge
University
Qualifications: 1st Class Hons degree in law
Career outside cricket: 'Interested in writing, education, politics, travel and
pontificating; might run a Catholic shool.'
Off-season: 'In Australia – watching Alderman bowl to Gooch, hopefully for ages.'

337

Overseas tours: 'None apart from England to Holland, 1989.'

Cricketers particularly admired: Keith Fletcher

Other sports followed: 'Not synchronised swimming – I follow Bath Rugby (since 12 years of age) and Somerset cricket.'

Injuries: 'Not even any mental aberrations. Tried to discover an injury allowing me to bat but not bowl. No joy.'

Relaxations: 'Reading Massie, Kuderan, Marquez and lots of other people I won't mention as it might be bad for the image.'

Extras: Cambridge Blue 1975–77. Youngest Minor County cricketer, playing for Somerset 2nd XI at age of 13. Books published include: *Slice of Cricket, It Never Rains, It Sort of Clicks* and *Great Innings*. Writes for *Sunday Times* and 'anyone else who asks'. Somerset captain 1986 to 1988. One of *Wisden's* Five Cricketers of the Year, 1988.

Opinions on cricket: 'Don't like insipid pitches or soft balls. Supposed to be a contest between bat and ball not an orgy.'

Best batting: 221* Somerset v Nottinghamshire, Trent Bridge 1986

Best bowling: 6–50 Cambridge University v Kent, Canterbury 1977

LAST SEASON: BATTING

	I.	N. O.	R.	H. S.	AV.
TEST					
1ST	28	5	1134	201*	49.30
INT					
RAL	8	0	195	85	24.37
N.W.	2	0	63	43	31.50
B&H	4	0	129	91	32.25

LAST SEASON: BOWLING

	O.	M.	R.	W.	AV.
TEST					
1ST	182.3	42	529	8	66.12
INT					
RAL	19	1	131	3	43.66
N.W.	5.2	0	22	0	-
B&H	14	0	70	2	35.00

CAREER: BATTING

	I.	N. O.	R.	H. S.	AV.
TEST					
1ST	523	78	16719	221*	37.57
INT					
RAL	159	23	4039	105	29.69
N.W.	35	2	988	102	29.93
B&H	60	6	1597	120	29.57

CAREER: BOWLING

	O.	M.	R.	W.	AV.
TEST					
1ST	1137.4	280	3225	63	51.19
INT					
RAL	68.1	1	382	17	22.47
N.W.	15.2	0	77	2	38.50
B&H	37.2	3	154	8	19.25

Name: Paul William Romaines
Role: Right-hand opening bat,
off-break bowler
Born: 25 December 1955, Bishop
Auckland, Co Durham
Height: 6ft **Weight:** 12st 8lbs
Nickname: Canny, Human
County debut: 1975 (Northants), 1982
(Gloucs)
County cap: 1983 (Gloucs)
Benefit: 1991
1000 runs in a season: 3
1st-Class 50s scored: 41
1st-Class 100s scored: 13
One-Day 50s: 20
One-Day 100s: 2
Place in batting averages: 149th av.
32.77 (1989 180th av. 20.00)
1st-Class catches: 2 (career 67)
Parents: George and Freda
Wife and date of marriage: Julie Anne, 1979
Children: Claire Louise
Family links with cricket: Father played local cricket and is still an avid watcher.
Grandfather, W. R. Romaines, represented Durham in Minor Counties cricket, and
played v Australia in 1926
Education: Leeholme School, Bishop Auckland
Qualifications: 8 O-levels, NCA qualified coach
Off-season: 'MCC tour to Pennsylvania and organising my Benefit year for 1991.'
Overseas teams played for: Griqualand West, South Africa 1984–85
Cricketers particularly admired: Zaheer Abbas, Graham Gooch, Clive Radley,
Gordon Greenidge
Other sports followed: Athletics, squash, golf, soccer
Relaxations: 'Listening to music, having a good pint, antiques, people, writing
letters, good conversation.'
Extras: Debut for Northamptonshire 1975. Played Minor County cricket with

LAST SEASON: BATTING

	I.	N. O.	R.	H. S.	AV.
TEST					
1ST	11	2	295	95	32.77
INT					
RAL	12	3	227	47	25.22
N.W.	1	0	20	20	20.00
B&H					

CAREER: BATTING

	I.	N. O.	R.	H. S.	AV.
TEST					
1ST	304	23	8085	186	28.77
INT					
RAL	102	11	2499	105	27.46
N.W.	16	2	400	82	28.57
B&H	20	1	663	125	34.89

Durham 1977–81. Joined Gloucestershire in 1982

Opinions on cricket: 'Cricket balls should be totally standardised. I hope that Durham's proposals for first-class status are accepted.'

Best batting: 186 Gloucestershire v Warwickshire, Nuneaton 1982

Best bowling: 3–42 Gloucestershire v Surrey, The Oval 1985

ROSE, G. D.   Somerset

Name: Graham David Rose

Role: Right-hand bat, right-arm fast-medium bowler

Born: 12 April 1964, Tottenham

Height: 6ft 4in **Weight:** 14st 7lbs

Nickname: Rosie

County debut: 1985 (Middlesex), 1987 (Somerset)

County cap: 1988 (Somerset)

1000 runs in a season: 1

50 wickets in a season: 2

1st-Class 50s scored: 12

1st-Class 5 w. in innings: 4

One-Day 50s: 4

One-day 100s: 2

Place in batting averages: 33rd av. 55.55 (1989 183rd av. 19.84)

Place in bowling averages: 69th av. 36.81 (1989 38th av. 24.31)

Strike rate: 64.71 (career 54.55)

1st-Class catches: 14 (career 39)

Parents: William and Edna

Wife and date of marriage: Teresa Julie, 19 September 1987

Family links with cricket: Father and brother played club cricket in North London

Education: Northumberland Park School, Tottenham

Qualifications: 6 O-levels, 4 A-levels. NCA coaching certificate

Cricketers particularly admired: Steve Waugh, Wayne Daniel, Richard Hadlee

Other sports followed: 'Follow Spurs for my sins', golf and squash

Relaxations: Music – Dire Straits, Beatles, Pink Floyd, U2

Extras: Played for England YCs v Australia 1983. Took 6 wickets for 41 on Middlesex debut. Joined Somerset for 1987 season and scored 95 on debut. Completed double of 1000 runs and 50 wickets in first-class cricket in 1990 and scored fastest recorded 100s in NatWest Trophy (v Devon) and Sunday League (v Glamorgan)

Opinions on cricket: 'Four-day cricket is definitely a success. Over-rate fines should not be levied if quotas are reached by 6.30 pm. Counties should do more to

find winter employment for their players, especially the younger ones.'
Best batting: 97* Somerset v Glamorgan, Bath 1990
Best bowling: 6–41 Middlesex v Worcestershire, Worcester 1985

LAST SEASON: BATTING

	I.	N.O.	R.	H.S.	AV.
TEST					
1ST	29	11	1000	97*	55.55
INT					
RAL	15	2	430	148	33.07
N.W.	2	0	126	110	63.00
B&H	6	1	163	64	32.60

LAST SEASON: BOWLING

	O.	M.	R.	W.	AV.
TEST					
1ST	571.4	99	1951	53	36.81
INT					
RAL	113.3	1	610	18	33.88
N.W.	14	1	51	1	51.00
B&H	55	6	240	10	24.00

CAREER: BATTING

	I.	N.O.	R.	H.S.	AV.
TEST					
1ST	105	29	2206	97*	29.02
INT					
RAL	53	9	1132	148	25.72
N.W.	5	0	163	110	32.60
B&H	16	3	280	64	21.53

CAREER: BOWLING

	O.	M.	R.	W.	AV.
TEST					
1ST	1918.4	203	6015	211	28.50
INT					
RAL	450.1	12	2019	69	29.26
N.W.	46.5	1	154	5	30.80
B&H	208.2	12	833	28	29.75

ROSEBERRY, M. A.　　Middlesex

Name: Michael Anthony Roseberry
Role: Right-hand bat, right-arm occasional off-break and swing bowler, close-to-wicket fielder
Born: 28 November 1966, Houghton-le-Spring, Sunderland
Height: 6ft **Weight:** 14st
Nickname: Zorro
County debut: 1985
County cap: 1990
1000 runs in a season: 1
1st-Class 50s scored: 20
1st-Class 100s scored: 4
One-Day 50s scored: 9
Place in batting averages: 107th av. 39.82 (1989 77th av. 33.41)
1st-Class catches: 23 (career 50)
Parents: Matthew and Jean
Wife and date of marriage: Helen Louise, 22 February 1991
Family links with cricket: Uncle, Peter Wyness, played for Royal Navy; brother Andrew has joined Leicester

341

Education: Tonstall Preparatory School; Durham School

Qualifications: 5 O-levels, 1 A-level, advanced cricket coach

Off-season: 'Coaching cricket and rugby and organising my wedding with Helen.'

Overseas tours: England YCs to West Indies 1985

Cricketers particularly admired: Desmond Haynes, Geoff Boycott

Other sports followed: Football, rugby, 'I tend to follow and take part in most.'

Relaxations: 'I love eating out with Helen, listening to music, going out to a pub.'

Extras: Won Lord's Taverners/MCC Cricketer of the Year 1983. Won Cricket Society's Award for Best Young Cricketer of the Year 1984 and also twice won Cricket Society award for best all-rounder in schools cricket. Played in Durham League as a professional while still at school. At age 16, playing for Durham School v St Bees, he hit 216 in 160 minutes

Opinions on cricket: 'Championship cricket should be all four days with teams still encouraged to be positive. Coloured clothing and more razzamattazz in Refuge games.'

Best batting: 135 Middlesex v Essex, Ilford 1990

Best bowling: 1–1 Middlesex v Sussex, Hove 1988

LAST SEASON: BATTING

	I.	N. O.	R.	H. S.	AV.
TEST					
1ST	44	4	1593	135	39.82
INT					
RAL	18	1	678	86	39.88
N.W.	4	0	115	48	28.75
B&H	4	0	73	38	18.25

CAREER: BATTING

	I.	N. O.	R.	H. S.	AV.
TEST					
1ST	116	16	3225	135	32.25
INT					
RAL	36	3	1054	86	31.93
N.W.	7	0	179	48	25.57
B&H	6	0	81	38	13.50

73. How do you pronounce the name of South African cricketer, Adrian Kuiper?

74. Who is Chairman of the TCCB?

75. Who is captain of Somerset?

RUSSELL, R. C.   Gloucestershire

Name: Robert Charles Russell
Role: Left-hand bat, wicket-keeper
Born: 15 August 1963, Stroud
Height: 5ft 8 1/2in **Weight:** 9st 8lbs
Nickname: Jack, Bob (after Bob
Taylor), Whispering Gloves
County debut: 1981
County cap: 1985
Test debut: 1988
Tests: 17
One-Day Internationals: 17
1st-Class 50s scored: 22
1st-Class 100s scored: 3
One-Day 50s: 5
One-Day 100s: 1
Place in batting averages: 119th av.
37.81 (1989 124th av. 26.63)

Parents: John and Jennifer
Wife and date of marriage: Aileen
Ann, 6 March 1985
Children: Stepson, Marcus Anthony;
Elizabeth Ann, March 1988; Victoria, 1989
Education: Uplands County Primary School; Archway Comprehensive School
Qualifications: 7 O-levels, 2 A-levels
Off-season: Touring with England to Australia
Overseas tours: England to Pakistan 1987–88; to India and West Indies 1989–90;
Australia 1990–91
Cricketers particularly admired: Alan Knott, Bob Taylor
Other sports followed: Football ('a Tottenham Hotspur supporter, but only on
television'), snooker
Relaxations: Drawing, sketching, painting (oil and watercolour). Watching comedy,
Rory Bremner and Phil Cool especially
Extras: Spotted at age 9 by Gloucestershire coach, Graham Wiltshire. Record for
most dismissals in a match on first-class debut: 8 (7 caught, 1 stumped) for
Gloucestershire v Sri Lankans at Bristol, 1981. Youngest Gloucestershire
wicket-keeper (17 years 307 days). Represented England YC v West Indies in 1982.
Hat-trick of catches v Surrey at The Oval 1986. Had a three-week exhibition of his
drawings in Bristol 1988 and published a book of his work entitled *A Cricketer's
Art*. Was chosen as England's Man of the Test Series, England v Australia 1989.
Commissioned by Dean of Gloucester to do a drawing of Gloucester Cathedral to
raise funds for 900th Anniversary. Still turns out for his original club, Stroud CC,
whenever he can. Runs six miles a day to keep fit and drinks up to 20 cups of tea a
day. One of *Wisden's* Five Cricketers of the Year, 1990

Best batting: 128* England v Australia, Old Trafford 1989

LAST SEASON: BATTING

	I.	N. O.	R.	H. S.	AV.
TEST	7	1	143	43	23.83
1ST	16	1	651	120	43.40
INT	4	1	124	50	41.33
RAL	9	0	191	62	21.22
N.W.	1	0	12	12	12.00
B&H	3	1	76	46*	38.00

LAST SEASON: WICKET-KEEPING

	CT	ST			
TEST	18	1			
1ST	27	0			
INT	2	2			
RAL	6	2			
N.W.	3	1			
B&H	4	0			

CAREER: BATTING

	I.	N. O.	R.	H. S.	AV.
TEST	26	5	690	128*	32.85
1ST	238	57	4622	120	25.53
INT	12	6	210	50	35.00
RAL	68	19	1098	108	22.40
N.W.	13	4	200	42*	22.22
B&H	21	7	258	46*	18.42

CAREER: WICKET-KEEPING

	CT	ST			
TEST	49	5			
1ST	381	67			
INT	12	4			
RAL	79	20			
N.W.	21	6			
B&H	33	7			

SADIQ, Z. A.   Derbyshire

Name: Zahid Asa Sadiq
Role: Right-hand bat
Born: 6 May 1965, Nairobi
Height: 5ft 11in **Weight:** 11st 2lbs
Nickname: Zeidi, Munch, Shag
County debut: 1987 (Surrey), 1990 (Derbys)
1st-Class 50s scored: 1
One-Day 50s: 1
1st-Class catches: 0 (career 5)
Parents: Mohammed Sadiq
Marital status: Single
Education: Rutlish School
Qualifications: 2 O-levels
Cricketers particularly admired: Viv Richards, Monte Lynch, Imran Khan
Other sports followed: Rugby, squash
Relaxations: Listening to music, parties
Extras: Released by Surrey at end of 1989 season. Made debut for Derbyshire in last match of 1990 season
Best batting: 64 Surrey v Cambridge University, Fenner's 1988

	I.	N. O.	R.	H. S.	AV.
TEST					
1ST	1	0	0	0	0.00
INT					
RAL					
N.W.					
B&H					

	I.	N. O.	R.	H. S.	AV.
TEST					
1ST	11	0	213	64	19.36
INT					
RAL	18	0	241	53	13.38
N.W.					
B&H	2	0	10	9	5.00

SALISBURY, I. D. K.   Sussex

Name: Ian David Kenneth Salisbury
Role: Right-hand bat, right-arm
leg-spinner
Born: 2 January 1970, Northampton
Height: 5ft 11in **Weight:** 12st
Nickname: Budgie
County debut: 1989
1st-Class 50s scored: 1
1st-Class 5 w. in innings: 2
Place in batting averages: 202nd av.
24.07 (1989 260th av. 10.33)
Place in bowling averages: 129th av.
49.40 (1989 123rd av. 62.13)
Strike rate: 85.88 (career 92.50)
1st-Class catches: 13 (career 17)
Parents: Dave and Margaret
Marital status: Single
Family links with cricket: 'Dad
is vice-president of my first club,
Brixworth.'
Education: Moulton Comprehensive,
Northampton
Qualifications: 7 O-levels; NCA coaching certificate
Off-season: 'Club cricket in New Zealand, then England A tour after Christmas.'
Overseas tours: England A to Pakistan 1990–91
Cricketers particularly admired: Desmond Haynes, Viv Richards, Richard
Blakey, Richie Benaud and all of Sussex CCC
Other sports followed: 'All sports.'
Injuries: 'Broke little finger on right hand – out for three weeks.'
Relaxations: Music and socialising
Opinions on cricket: 'Four-day cricket must be introduced. We should have at least
a day off a week, so travelling can be much safer, rather than having to drive straight
after a game.'
Best batting: 68 Sussex v Derbyshire, Hove 1990
Best bowling: 5–32 Sussex v Worcestershire, Worcester 1990

LAST SEASON: BATTING

	I.	N. O.	R.	H. S.	AV.
TEST					
1ST	23	10	313	68	24.07
INT					
RAL	4	1	10	7	3.33
N.W.	1	1	2	2*	-
B&H	1	0	2	2	2.00

LAST SEASON: BOWLING

	O.	M.	R.	W.	AV.
TEST					
1ST	601.1	113	2075	42	49.40
INT					
RAL	52	2	296	9	32.88
N.W.	17	3	66	0	-
B&H	17	0	92	1	92.00

CAREER: BATTING

	I.	N. O.	R.	H. S.	AV.
TEST					
1ST	33	14	375	68	19.73
INT					
RAL	6	3	29	12*	9.66
N.W.	1	1	2	2*	-
B&H	1	0	2	2	2.00

CAREER: BOWLING

	O.	M.	R.	W.	AV.
TEST					
1ST	878.5	174	3007	57	52.75
INT					
RAL	74	2	386	12	32.16
N.W.	17	3	66	0	-
B&H	17	0	92	1	92.00

SARGEANT, N. F.　　　　　Surrey

Name: Neil Fredrick Sargeant
Role: Right-hand bat, wicket-keeper
Born: 8 November 1965, Hammersmith
Height: 5ft 7in **Weight:** 10st 7lbs
Nickname: Sarge, Bilko, Dusty
County debut: 1989
Parents: Barry and Christine
Marital status: Single
Education: Grange Primary School;
Whitmore High School
Qualifications: 2 O-levels
Cricketers particularly admired: Alan
Knott, Bob Taylor, Ray Jennings
Other sports followed: Football, golf,
horse racing
Relaxations: Horse racing, music
Extras: Played football for Tottenham
Hotspur Youth Team
Best batting: 18 Surrey v Indians,
The Oval 1990

	I.	N.O.	R.	H.S.	AV.
TEST					
1ST	2	0	19	18	9.50
INT					
RAL	1	0	22	22	22.00
N.W.					
B&H					

LAST SEASON: WICKET-KEEPING

	CT	ST			
TEST					
1ST	6	1			
INT					
RAL	3	0			
N.W.					
B&H					

CAREER: BATTING

	I.	N.O.	R.	H.S.	AV.
TEST					
1ST	5	1	45	18	11.25
INT					
RAL	1	0	22	22	22.00
N.W.					
B&H					

CAREER: WICKET-KEEPING

	CT	ST			
TEST					
1ST	10	2			
INT					
RAL	3	0			
N.W.					
B&H					

SAXELBY, K.   Nottinghamshire

Name: Kevin Saxelby
Role: Right-hand bat, right-arm fast medium bowler
Born: 23 February 1959, Worksop
Height: 6ft 2in **Weight:** 14st
Nickname: Sax
County debut: 1978
County cap: 1984
1st-Class 50s scored: 1
1st-Class 5 w. in innings: 6
1st-Class 10 w. in match: 1
1st-Class catches: 3 (career 31)
Parents: George Kenneth and Hilda Margaret
Wife and date of marriage: Peta Jean Wendy, 24 September 1983
Children: Craig Robert, 6 June 1985
Family links with cricket: Father played in local league cricket. Brother plays for Nottinghamshire
Education: Magnus Grammar School, Newark
Qualifications: 10 O-levels, 4 A-levels
Career outside cricket: Farmer
Off-season: Working on family farm
Cricketers particularly admired: Dennis Lillee, John Snow
Other sports followed: 'Most sports – not anything to do with horses.'
Relaxations: Gardening, DIY, playing rugby

Opinions on cricket: 'I believe there should be no limit on over-rates in four-day cricket, in order to encourage genuine fast bowlers.'
Best batting: 59* Nottinghamshire v Derbyshire, Chesterfield 1982
Best bowling: 6–49 Nottinghamshire v Sussex, Trent Bridge 1987

LAST SEASON: BATTING

	I.	N. O.	R.	H. S.	AV.
TEST					
1ST	6	0	42	20	7.00
INT					
RAL	2	2	12	6*	-
N.W.					
B&H	-	-	-	-	-

LAST SEASON: BOWLING

	O.	M.	R.	W.	AV.
TEST					
1ST	91	19	319	7	45.57
INT					
RAL	53.5	0	378	9	42.00
N.W.					
B&H	11	3	39	2	19.50

CAREER: BATTING

	I.	N. O.	R.	H. S.	AV.
TEST					
1ST	137	42	1112	59*	11.70
INT					
RAL	40	27	170	23*	13.07
N.W.	5	3	26	12	13.00
B&H	12	7	53	13*	10.60

CAREER: BOWLING

	O.	M.	R.	W.	AV.
TEST					
1ST	3105	734	9705	300	32.35
INT					
RAL	748.4	25	3829	147	26.04
N.W.	195.1	22	753	30	25.10
B&H	302.4	36	1196	47	25.44

SAXELBY, M. Nottinghamshire

Name: Mark Saxelby
Role: Left-hand bat, right-arm medium bowler
Born: 4 January 1969, Newark
Height: 6ft 3in **Weight:** 14st 7lbs
Nickname: Sax
County debut: 1989
1st-class 50s scored: 2
Place in batting averages: 163rd av. 30.45
1st-Class catches: 3 (career 3)
Parents: George Kenneth and Hilda Margaret
Marital status: Single
Family links with cricket: Brother plays for Nottinghamshire; father played local cricket
Education: Nottingham High School
Qualifications: 7 O-levels, 2 A-levels
Career outside cricket: Lab technician
Off-season: Coaching and playing for Geelong in Victoria
Cricketers particularly admired: Richard Hadlee, Derek Randall

Other sports followed: Rugby Union and League, football, American football
Injuries: 'Operation to cure kidney complaint at start of season and operation on shoulder in September.'
Relaxations: 'Good pubs, cinema, watching most sports.'
Opinions on cricket: 'Put the seam back on the ball fast. You're killing bowlers off. These flat pitches do nothing for the game. I would like to see more four-day cricket. Captains have become so adept at contrived finishes that spectators are bored.'
Best batting: 73 Nottinghamshire v Cambridge University, Fenner's 1990
Best bowling: 2–25 Nottinghamshire v Cambridge University, Fenner's 1989

LAST SEASON: BATTING

	I.	N. O.	R.	H. S.	AV.
TEST					
1ST	15	4	335	73	30.45
INT					
RAL	9	2	188	34	26.85
N.W.	1	0	41	41	41.00
B&H	1	0	0	0	0.00

LAST SEASON: BOWLING

	O.	M.	R.	W.	AV.
TEST					
1ST	61.4	9	270	3	90.00
INT					
RAL	40	0	259	6	43.16
N.W.					
B&H					

CAREER: BATTING

	I.	N. O.	R.	H. S.	AV.
TEST					
1ST	17	5	371	73	30.91
INT					
RAL	9	2	188	34	26.85
N.W.	1	0	41	41	41.00
B&H	1	0	0	0	0.00

CAREER: BOWLING

	O.	M.	R.	W.	AV.
TEST					
1ST	77.4	12	320	5	64.00
INT					
RAL	40	0	259	6	43.16
N.W.					
B&H					

76. Who is captain of Lancashire?

77. Who is captain of Yorkshire?

78. Who is captain of Glamorgan?

SCOTT, R. J.   Hampshire

Name: Richard James Scott
Role: Left-hand bat, right-arm
medium pace bowler
Born: 2 November 1963, Bournemouth
Height: 5ft 11in **Weight:** 14st
Nickname: Gazza, Scotty-Boy
County debut: 1986
1st-Class 50s scored: 5
1st-Class 100s scored: 1
One-Day 50s: 7
One-Day 100s: 1
Place in batting averages: 232nd av.
18.00 (1989 170th av. 21.00)
1st-Class catches: 4 (career 20)
Parents: Andrew and Ann
Marital status: Engaged
Family links with cricket: 'Dad
played for Colehill. Two brothers also
play for same side in Dorset League.'
Education: Queen Elizabeth School,
Wimborne
Qualifications: 2 O-levels, CSEs, coaching award
Cricketers particularly admired: Ian Botham, Malcolm Marshall
Other sports followed: Golf, football, snooker
Relaxations: 'Like to relax down any nice pub testing out local brews. Also like
taking dog for walks deep in Dorset countryside.'
Extras: Played Minor Counties cricket for Dorset since 1981. Represented Minor
Counties Cricket Association in 1985

LAST SEASON: BATTING

	I.	N. O.	R.	H. S.	AV.
TEST					
1ST	10	2	144	71	18.00
INT					
RAL	12	0	386	76	32.16
N.W.					
B&H	2	0	54	47	27.00

LAST SEASON: BOWLING

	O.	M.	R.	W.	AV.
TEST					
1ST	36.4	5	165	5	33.00
INT					
RAL	30.4	0	171	6	28.50
N.W.					
B&H	11	0	56	0	-

CAREER: BATTING

	I.	N. O.	R.	H. S.	AV.
TEST					
1ST	46	4	917	107*	21.83
INT					
RAL	27	2	724	116*	28.96
N.W.	2	0	22	22	11.00
B&H	6	0	218	69	36.33

CAREER: BOWLING

	O.	M.	R.	W.	AV.
TEST					
1ST	63.1	5	257	5	51.40
INT					
RAL	30.4	0	171	6	28.50
N.W.					
B&H	11	0	56	0	-

Opinions on cricket: 'Four-day game a revelation. Best side will always win Championship.'
Best batting: 107* Hampshire v Sri Lankans, Southampton 1988
Best bowling: 2–5 Hampshire v Middlesex, Bournemouth 1990

SEYMOUR, A. C. Essex

Name: Adam Charles Seymour
Role: Left-hand bat, right-arm medium bowler
Born: 7 December 1967, Royston, Cambridgeshire
Height: 6ft 2in
County debut: 1988
1st-Class 50s scored: 1
1st-Class catches: 1 (career 1)
Education: Millfield School
Injuries: Suffered broken arm when batting for Essex v Gloucestershire in June
Extras: First played for Essex 2nd XI in 1984, aged 16. In 1989 was the county's leading batsman in second team cricket
Best batting: 89 Essex v Cambridge University, Fenner's 1990

LAST SEASON: BATTING

	I.	N. O.	R.	H. S.	AV.
TEST					
1ST	5	2	131	89	43.66
INT					
RAL					
N.W.					
B&H					

CAREER: BATTING

	I.	N. O.	R.	H. S.	AV.
TEST					
1ST	6	3	164	89	54.66
INT					
RAL					
N.W.					
B&H					

SHAHID, N

Essex

Name: Nadeem Shahid
Role: Right-hand bat, right-arm
leg-spinner
Born: 23 April 1969, Karachi
Height: 6ft **Weight:** 11st 7lbs
Nickname: Prince, Binyani II, Nads
County debut: 1989
1000 runs in a season: 1
1st-Class 50s scored: 7
1st-class 100s scored: 1
Place in batting averages: 74th av.
45.59 (1989 55th av. 36.42)
1st-Class catches: 22 (career 28)
Parents: Ahmed and Salma
Marital status: Single
Family links with cricket: Brother
plays in the local league
Education: Stoke High; Northgate
High; Ipswich School; Plymouth
Polytechnic
Qualifications: 6 O-levels, 1 A-level; coaching certificate
Off-season: Playing for Gosnells CC in Perth, Western Australia
Cricketers particularly admired: Abdul Qadir, Ian Botham and John Garnham
(Copdock CC)
Other sports played: Golf, badminton, tennis, golf, football and rugby
Relaxations: 'Listening to music, dining out, going to the cinema.'
Extras: Youngest Suffolk player aged 17. Played for HMC, MCC Schools, ESCA
U–19, NCA Young Cricketers (Lord's and International Youth tournament in

LAST SEASON: BATTING

	I.	N. O.	R.	H. S.	AV.
TEST					
1ST	29	7	1003	125	45.59
INT					
RAL	4	1	79	31	26.33
N.W.					
B&H					

LAST SEASON: BOWLING

	O.	M.	R.	W.	AV.
TEST					
1ST	111.2	18	454	7	64.85
INT					
RAL					
N.W.					
B&H					

CAREER: BATTING

	I.	N. O.	R.	H. S.	AV.
TEST					
1ST	38	9	1258	125	43.37
INT					
RAL	5	1	90	31	22.50
N.W.					
B&H					

CAREER: BOWLING

	O.	M.	R.	W.	AV.
TEST					
1ST	192.3	31	780	15	52.00
INT					
RAL					
N.W.					
B&H					

Belfast), and at every level for Suffolk. TSB Young Player of the Year 1986, winner of *The Daily Telegraph* bowling award 1987 and 1988, and Cricket Society's All-rounder of the Year, 1988

Opinions on cricket: 'Old Reader balls should be re-introduced for the 1991 season in order to improve the imbalance between bat and ball. Captains should play more attacking cricket and perhaps be prepared to lose in order to win – setting reasonable targets rather than killing the game.'

Best batting: 125 Essex v Lancashire, Colchester 1990
Best bowling: 3–91 Essex v Surrey, The Oval 1990

SHARP, K. Yorkshire

Name: Kevin Sharp
Role: Left-hand bat, off-break bowler
Born: 6 April 1959, Leeds
Height: 5ft 9in **Weight:** 12st 7lbs
Nickname: Lambsy, Poodle
County debut: 1976
County cap: 1982
Benefit: 1991
1000 runs in a season: 1
1st-Class 50s scored: 47
1st-Class 100s scored: 14
One-Day 50s: 27
One-Day 100s: 3
Place in batting averages: 108th av. 39.75 (1989 75th av. 34.13)
1st-Class catches: 1 (career 107)
Parents: Gordon and Joyce
Wife and date of marriage: Karen, 1 October 1983
Children: Amy Lauren, 28 December 1985; Nicholas Richard, 21 October 1989
Family links with cricket: Father played with Woodhouse in Leeds League for many years. Younger brother David now playing local cricket
Education: Abbey Grange C of E High School, Leeds
Qualifications: CSE Grade I Religious Education. Coaching award
Career outside cricket: Working for Credit Collections UK Ltd
Off-season: 'Organising benefit year in 1991.'
Overseas teams played for: Griqualand West, South Africa 1981–84
Cricketers particularly admired: Richard Hadlee, Malcolm Marshall
Other sports followed: Snooker, soccer, golf, squash
Injuries: Groin strain, broken nose, broken thumb
Relaxations: Decorating and maintaining the house

Extras: Scored 260* for England YCs v West Indies 1977 – a record score for England in Youth Tests

Opinions on cricket: 'Too much continuous cricket. Because of travelling and playing every day I believe cricket is not up to the standard it could be. There should be more time between matches to allow players to prepare properly.'

Best batting: 181 Yorkshire v Gloucestershire, Harrogate 1986
Best bowling: 2–13 Yorkshire v Glamorgan, Bradford 1984

LAST SEASON: BATTING

	I.	N. O.	R.	H. S.	AV.
TEST					
1ST	13	5	318	53*	39.75
INT					
RAL	7	2	207	71	41.40
N.W.	-	-	-	-	-
B&H					

LAST SEASON: BOWLING

	O.	M.	R.	W.	AV.
TEST					
1ST					
INT					
RAL					
N.W.					
B&H					

CAREER: BATTING

	I.	N. O.	R.	H. S.	AV.
TEST					
1ST	361	38	9962	181	30.84
INT					
RAL	133	13	3315	114	27.62
N.W.	13	2	228	50	20.72
B&H	39	3	1073	105*	29.80

CAREER: BOWLING

	O.	M.	R.	W.	AV.
TEST					
1ST	210.2	43	887	12	73.91
INT					
RAL	0.1	0	1	0	-
N.W.	10	0	47	4	11.75
B&H					

79. Who is captain of Northants?

80. Who is captain of Hampshire?

81. Who is Leicestershire's team manager?

SHINE, K. J.   Hampshire

Name: Kevin James Shine
Role: Right-hand bat, right-arm medium bowler
Born: 22 February 1969, Bracknell, Berkshire
Height: 6ft 3in **Weight:** 15st
Nickname: Shirely, Shoe, Don
County debut: 1989
Place in bowling averages: 93rd av. 39.42
Strike rate: 67.14 (career 66.70)
1st-Class catches: 1 (career 1)
Parents: Joe and Clair
Marital status: Single
Education: Winnerish County Primary; Maiden Erleigh Comprehensive
Qualifications: 5 O-levels, gave up A-levels to pursue a cricket career
Off-season: 'Going to Newcastle in Australia with Cardigan Connor to play for Merryweather CC.'
Cricketers particularly admired: Malcolm Marshall, Cardigan Connor ('the fittest cricketer in the country'), Peter Sainsbury
Other sports followed: Football, basketball
Injuries: Stress fracture of left foot
Relaxations: Swimming, driving and visiting night clubs
Extras: Plays club cricket for Reading. Hampshire 2nd XI debut in 1986

LAST SEASON: BATTING

	I.	N. O.	R.	H. S.	AV.
TEST					
1ST	1	1	24	24*	-
INT					
RAL					
N.W.					
B&H	1	0	0	0	0.00

LAST SEASON: BOWLING

	O.	M.	R.	W.	AV.
TEST					
1ST	156.4	30	552	14	39.42
INT					
RAL					
N.W.					
B&H	32.2	1	167	4	41.75

CAREER: BATTING

	I.	N. O.	R.	H. S.	AV.
TEST					
1ST	3	2	53	26*	53.00
INT					
RAL					
N.W.					
B&H	1	0	0	0	0.00

CAREER: BOWLING

	O.	M.	R.	W.	AV.
TEST					
1ST	189	38	640	17	37.64
INT					
RAL					
N.W.					
B&H	32.2	1	167	4	41.75

Best batting: 26* Hampshire v Middlesex, Lord's 1989
Best bowling: 4–52 Hampshire v Yorkshire, Headingley 1990

SIDEBOTTOM, A.   Yorkshire

Name: Arnold Sidebottom
Role: Right-hand bat, right-arm
fast-medium bowler, outfielder
Born: 1 April 1954, Barnsley
Height: 6ft 2in **Weight:** 13st 10lbs
Nickname: Woofer, Red Setter, Arnie
County debut: 1973
County cap: 1980
Benefit: 1988 (103,240)
Test debut: 1985
Tests: 1
50 wickets in a season: 4
1st-Class 50s scored: 13
1st-Class 100s scored: 1
1st-Class 5 w. in innings: 23
1st-Class 10 w. in match: 3
One-Day 50s: 1
1st-Class catches: 1 (career 62)
Parents: Jack and Florence
Wife and date of marriage: Gillian,
17 June 1977
Children: Ryan Jay, 1978; Dale, 1980
Family links with cricket: Father good cricketer
Education: Barnsley Broadway Grammar School
Career outside cricket: Professional footballer with Manchester United for five years, Huddersfield Town for two years and Halifax Town
Overseas teams played for: Orange Free State 1981–84
Overseas tours: Rebel England team to South Africa 1981–82
Cricketers particularly admired: Steve Oldham, David Bairstow, Graham Stevenson
Other sports followed: Most sports
Relaxations: Watching television, horse racing, playing with sons
Extras: Banned from Test cricket for three years for joining rebel team to South Africa in 1982. Injured toe during Test debut in 1985 and not picked for England again. Yorkshire Player of the Year 1989
Best batting: 124 Yorkshire v Glamorgan, Cardiff 1977
Best bowling: 8–72 Yorkshire v Leicestershire, Middlesbrough 1986

	I.	N.O.	R.	H.S.	AV.
TEST					
1ST	4	0	104	38	26.00
INT					
RAL	4	2	14	8*	7.00
N.W.	1	0	1	1	1.00
B&H	2	1	11	9*	11.00

LAST SEASON: BOWLING

	O.	M.	R.	W.	AV.
TEST					
1ST	60.5	11	190	4	47.50
INT					
RAL	69	7	230	7	32.85
N.W.	34	8	76	2	38.00
B&H	40.1	7	156	3	52.00

CAREER: BATTING

	I.	N.O.	R.	H.S.	AV.
TEST	1	0	2	2	2.00
1ST	261	61	4488	124	22.44
INT					
RAL	82	31	811	52*	15.90
N.W.	16	5	192	45	17.45
B&H	27	9	246	32	13.66

CAREER: BOWLING

	O.	M.	R.	W.	AV.
TEST	18.4	3	65	1	65.00
1ST	5080.1	1121	14467	594	24.35
INT					
RAL	1051.4	55	4446	147	30.24
N.W.	256.2	41	700	37	18.91
B&H	465.5	75	1528	68	22.47

SMALL, G. C.   Warwickshire

Name: Gladstone Cleophas Small
Role: Right-hand bat, right-arm
fast-medium bowler
Born: 18 October 1961, St George,
Barbados
Height: 5ft 11st **Weight:** 12st
Nickname: Gladys
County debut: 1980
County cap: 1982
Test debut: 1986
Tests: 13
One-Day Internationals: 40
50 wickets in a season: 6
1st-Class 50s scored: 6
1st-Class 5 w. in innings: 27
1st-Class 10 w. in match: 2
Place in batting averages: 244th av.
16.44 (1989 224th av. 14.55)
Place in bowling averages: 72nd av.
37.18 (1989 34th av. 25.45)
Strike rate: 79.81 (career 55.70)
1st-Class catches: 4 (career 65)
Parents: Chelston and Gladys
Wife: Lois
Children: Zak
Family links with cricket: Cousin, Milton Small, toured England with West Indies
in 1984

Education: Moseley School; Hall Green Technical College, Birmingham
Qualifications: 2 O-levels
Off-season: Touring with England to Australia
Overseas tours: England YC to New Zealand 1979–80; England to Australia 1986–87; World Cup 1987; India and West Indies 1989–90; Australia 1990–91
Overseas teams played for: South Australia 1985–86
Cricketers particularly admired: Dennis Lillee, Malcolm Marshall, Richard Hadlee, Bob Willis
Other sports followed: Athletics, golf, tennis, soccer
Relaxations: 'Playing a round of golf; listening to music and relaxing with my wife.'
Extras: Was called up for England Test squad v Pakistan at Edgbaston, July 1982, but did not play. Bowled 18-ball over v Middlesex in August 1982, with 11 no balls. Grandfather watched him take eight wickets in the Barbados Test v West Indies in 1989–90 on his return to the land of his birth. Was Andy Lloyd's best man
Opinions on cricket: 'The introduction of four-day Championship cricket will improve the first-class game: teams will have to bowl out the opposition twice instead of relying on contrived results. We should play on hard, fast and true wickets that would be beneficial to both batsmen and bowlers.'
Best batting: 70 Warwickshire v Lancashire, Old Trafford 1988
Best bowling: 7–15 Warwickshire v Nottinghamshire, Edgbaston 1988

LAST SEASON: BATTING

	I.	N. O.	R.	H. S.	AV.
TEST	4	2	84	44*	42.00
1ST	18	2	212	55	13.25
INT	1	0	4	4	4.00
RAL	3	1	9	4*	4.50
N.W.	2	0	8	8	4.00
B&H	3	0	28	22	9.33

LAST SEASON: BOWLING

	O.	M.	R.	W.	AV.
TEST	104	27	290	5	58.00
1ST	321.4	78	900	27	33.33
INT	32	1	175	3	58.33
RAL	62.3	3	290	5	58.00
N.W.	15	1	58	0	-
B&H	44	4	123	11	11.18

CAREER: BATTING

	I.	N. O.	R.	H. S.	AV.
TEST	18	6	221	59	18.41
1ST	273	60	3114	70	14.61
INT	17	8	59	18*	6.55
RAL	59	19	304	40*	7.60
N.W.	16	6	143	33	14.30
B&H	25	6	126	22	6.63

CAREER: BOWLING

	O.	M.	R.	W.	AV.
TEST	505.5	88	1447	46	31.45
1ST	5584.5	1220	16926	610	27.74
INT	365.5	22	1528	45	33.95
RAL	846.5	55	3825	158	24.20
N.W.	255.1	44	829	28	29.60
B&H	371.2	61	1332	52	25.61

SMITH, B. F.   Leicestershire

Name: Benjamin Francis Smith
Role: Right-hand bat
Born: 3 April 1972, Corby
Height: 5ft 8in **Weight:** 9st 7lbs
Nickname: Chucker
County debut: 1990
1st-Class catches: 1 (career 1)
Parents: Janet and Keith
Marital status: Single
Family links with cricket: Both
uncles played for ESCA, dad played for
Northamptonshire Schools
Education: Tugby, Kibworth, Market
Harborough
Qualifications: 8 GCSEs
Off-season: Touring New Zealand with
England YCs
Overseas tours: England YCs to New
Zealand 1990–91
Cricketers particularly admired: Paul
Parker, Graeme Hick
Other sports followed: Tennis, football, golf
Relaxations: 'Listening to music, going to the cinema, driving.'
Extras: Played tennis for Leicestershire aged 12
Best batting: 15* Leicestershire v Glamorgan, Hinckley 1990

LAST SEASON / CAREER: BATTING

	I.	N. O.	R.	H. S.	AV.
TEST					
1ST	2	1	19	15*	19.00
INT					
RAL	4	0	55	29	13.75
N.W.					
B&H					

LAST SEASON / CAREER: BOWLING

	O.	M.	R.	W.	AV.
TEST					
1ST					
INT					
RAL					
N.W.					
B&H					

SMITH, C. L. Hampshire

Name: Christopher Lyall Smith
Role: Right-hand bat, off-spin bowler
Born: 15 October 1958, Durban, South Africa
Height: 5ft 11in **Weight:** 13st 10lbs
Nickname: Kippy
County debut: 1979 (Glamorgan), 1980 (Hampshire)
County cap: 1981 (Hampshire)
Benefit: 1990
Test debut: 1983
Tests: 8
One-Day Internationals: 4
1000 runs in a season: 9
1st-Class 50s scored: 81
1st-Class 100s scored: 41
1st-Class 200s scored: 1
1st-Class 5 w. in innings: 1
One-Day 50s: 34
One-Day 100s: 7
Place in batting averages: 22nd av. 60.83 (1989 32nd av. 42.41)

1st-Class catches: 14 (career 172)
Parents: John Arnold and Joy Lyall
Wife and date of marriage: Julie Owen, August 1989
Family links with cricket: Grandfather, Vernon Lyall Shearer, played for Natal; brother Robin also plays for Hampshire and England
Education: Northlands High School, Durban, South Africa
Qualifications: Matriculation (2 A-level equivalents)
Career outside cricket: 'Running Chris Smith Sports Entertainment which specialises in corporate entertaining. Also run a travel business and am involved with Car-phone Group's activities around Hampshire.'
Overseas tours: England to New Zealand and Pakistan 1983–84; England B to Sri Lanka 1985–86
Overseas teams played for: Natal (debut 1978)
Cricketers particularly admired: Barry Richards, Grayson Heath (coach in South Africa)
Other sports followed: Watches football (Southampton FC), squash, golf
Relaxations: 'Walking in the countryside with my dog or lying on the beach, swimming, listening to music.'
Extras: Made debut for Glamorgan in 1979. Played for Gorseinon in South Wales League in 1979. Made Hampshire debut 1980. Captained Hampshire 2nd XI in 1981. Became eligible to play for England in 1983. One of *Wisden's* Five Cricketers of the

Year, 1983
Opinions on cricket: 'Still feel the game is undersold and that too few clubs employ successful, proven, get-up-and-go marketing managers. Welcome four-day cricket as it should help to produce more potential Test players.'
Best batting: 217 Hampshire v Warwickshire, Edgbaston 1987
Best bowling: 5–69 Hampshire v Sussex, Southampton 1988

LAST SEASON: BATTING

	I.	N.O.	R.	H.S.	AV.
TEST					
1ST	38	7	1886	148	60.83
INT					
RAL	9	2	237	89	33.85
N.W.	4	0	188	106	47.00
B&H	3	1	201	154*	100.50

LAST SEASON: BOWLING

	O.	M.	R.	W.	AV.
TEST					
1ST	28	9	97	5	19.40
INT					
RAL					
N.W.					
B&H	1	0	2	0	-

CAREER: BATTING

	I.	N.O.	R.	H.S.	AV.
TEST	14	1	392	91	30.15
1ST	425	56	16083	217	43.58
INT	4	0	109	70	27.25
RAL	108	22	3171	95	36.87
N.W.	28	4	1237	159	51.54
B&H	29	5	852	154*	35.50

CAREER: BOWLING

	O.	M.	R.	W.	AV.
TEST	17	4	39	3	13.00
1ST	706.5	139	2583	47	54.95
INT	6	0	28	2	14.00
RAL	3.3	1	10	2	5.00
N.W.	15	3	59	5	11.80
B&H	1	0	2	0	-

SMITH, D. M. — Sussex

Name: David Mark Smith
Role: Left-hand bat, right-arm medium bowler
Born: 9 January 1956, Balham
Height: 6ft 4in **Weight:** 15st
Nickname: Smudger, Tom
County debut: 1973 (Surrey), 1984 (Worcs), 1989 (Sussex)
County cap: 1980 (Surrey), 1984 (Worcs)
Test debut: 1985–86
Tests: 2
One-Day Internationals: 2
1000 runs in a season: 5
1st-Class 50s scored: 56
1st-Class 100s scored: 23
One-Day 50s: 29
One-Day 100s: 4
Place in batting averages: 197th av. 25.21 (1989 22nd av. 45.00)
1st-Class catches: 2 (career 157)

Parents: Dennis Henry and Tina
Wife and date of marriage: Jacqui, 7 January 1977
Children: Sarah Jane Louise, 4 April 1982
Family links with cricket: Father played cricket for the BBC
Education: Battersea Grammar School
Qualifications: 3 O-levels
Career outside cricket: Contracts manager, painting and decorating firm
Overseas tours: England to West Indies 1985–86; joined tour to West Indies 1989–90 as a replacement
Cricketers particularly admired: Graham Gooch, Malcolm Marshall, Ian Botham
Other sports followed: Football, motor racing
Injuries: Suffered broken thumb in West Indies and rebroke it as soon as he returned to county cricket
Relaxations: 'I own my own racing car.'
Extras: Played for Surrey 2nd XI in 1972. Was not retained after 1977 but was re-instated in 1978. Sacked by Surrey during 1983 season and joined Worcestershire in 1984. Rejoined Surrey in 1987, but released by Surrey at end of 1988 season. Joined Sussex for 1989. Called up as a replacement for England's tour of West Indies in 1989–90 – played in one match before breaking his thumb
Best batting: 189* Worcestershire v Kent, Worcester 1984
Best bowling: 3–40 Surrey v Sussex, The Oval 1976

LAST SEASON: BATTING

	I.	N. O.	R.	H. S.	AV.
TEST					
1ST	16	2	353	71	25.21
INT					
RAL	2	0	18	18	9.00
N.W.					
B&H	1	0	3	3	3.00

LAST SEASON: BOWLING

	O.	M.	R.	W.	AV.
TEST					
1ST					
INT					
RAL					
N.W.					
B&H					

CAREER: BATTING

	I.	N. O.	R.	H. S.	AV.
TEST	4	0	80	47	20.00
1ST	404	79	11743	189*	36.13
INT	2	1	15	10*	15.00
RAL	137	27	3022	87*	27.47
N.W.	30	6	1202	109	50.08
B&H	55	9	1608	126	34.95

CAREER: BOWLING

	O.	M.	R.	W.	AV.
TEST					
1ST	460.1	96	1541	30	51.36
INT					
RAL	124.5	6	606	12	50.50
N.W.	31	6	118	4	29.50
B&H	56	4	266	8	33.25

SMITH, G. Warwickshire

Name: Gareth Smith
Role: Right-hand bat, left-arm
fast-medium bowler
Born: 20 July 1966, Jarrow,
County Durham
Height: 6ft 1in **Weight:** 12st 7lbs
Nickname: Smudger, Headless, Ethel
County debut: 1986 (Northants), 1990
(Warwicks)
1st-Class 5 w. in innings: 1
1st-Class catches: 1 (career 3)
Parents: John and Patricia
Wife and date of marriage:
Katharine Jane, 6 October 1990
Family links with cricket: Father on
selection committee at Boldon CC
Education: Boldon Comprehensive
School; South Tyneside College
Qualifications: 6 O-levels, BTec
ONC/OND in Computer Studies

Off-season: Working for Mailforce Ltd as a computer operator
Cricketers particularly admired: Geoff Cook, Tim Munton ('for his ability to stay
fit'), Ian Botham, Wayne Larkins
Other sports followed: Golf, football (Sunderland FC)
Injuries: 'You name it. Bill, the physio, is sick to death of me!'
Relaxations: 'Lager and Bon Jovi. Going out for a good meal. Golf (to a low
standard).'
Extras: 'Took wicket of Sunil Gavaskar with second ball in first-class cricket, after

LAST SEASON: BATTING

	I.	N. O.	R.	H. S.	AV.
TEST					
1ST	1	0	30	30	30.00
INT					
RAL	1	0	5	5	5.00
N.W.					
B&H					

LAST SEASON: BOWLING

	O.	M.	R.	W.	AV.
TEST					
1ST	26.5	3	81	4	20.25
INT					
RAL	11	0	65	4	16.25
N.W.					
B&H					

CAREER: BATTING

	I.	N. O.	R.	H. S.	AV.
TEST					
1ST	11	2	90	30	10.00
INT					
RAL	1	0	5	5	5.00
N.W.					
B&H					

CAREER: BOWLING

	O.	M.	R.	W.	AV.
TEST					
1ST	178.5	26	633	21	30.14
INT					
RAL	22	0	145	4	36.25
N.W.					
B&H					

the first had disappeared over long-on for four.'

Opinions on cricket: 'When top order batsmen reach 50 they should be made to retire, so I can bowl at batsmen such as myself whilst still reasonably fresh. Four-day cricket should be introduced and those ridiculous seamless balls should be outlawed.'

Best batting: 30 Warwickshire v Sussex, Eastbourne 1990

Best bowling: 6–72 Northamptonshire v Sussex, Hove 1987

SMITH, I.   Glamorgan

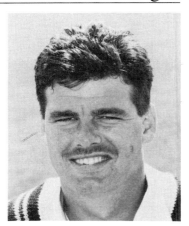

Name: Ian Smith
Role: Right-hand bat, right-arm medium bowler
Born: 11 March 1967, Consett, County Durham
Height: 6ft 3in **Weight:** 14st 5lbs
Nickname: Smudga, Cyril, Gilbert
County debut: 1985
1st-Class 50s scored: 5
1st-Class 100s scored: 3
One-Day 50s: 1
Place in batting averages: 102nd av. 41.00 (1989 81st av. 32.75)
1st-Class catches: 1 (career 17)
Parents: Jim and Mary
Marital status: Single
Family links with cricket: Father NCA Coach, brother played in League cricket. 'No relation to Chris, Robin, David, Neil, Paul, Gareth, etc, etc.'
Education: Ryton Comprehensive
Qualifications: 4 O-levels, CSE; studying for Open University degree in Social Psychology
Off-season: 'Playing football for Blyth Spartans; watching Newcastle Utd drop to Division 3; getting to know my local again; studying.'
Overseas tours: England YC to West Indies 1985
Cricketers particularly admired: Ian Botham, Mike Fatkin, Viv Richards
Other sports followed: Football, table tennis
Injuries: 'Tonsilitis (three times).'
Relaxations: Music, wine, theatre, golf
Extras: Glamorgan Young Player of the Year 1989. Offered terms by several football clubs
Opinions on cricket: 'Can't believe that four-day cricket wasn't introduced for 1991. It's by far the best form of cricket, particularly with wickets and balls as they were in 1990.'

Best batting: 116 Glamorgan v Kent, Canterbury 1989
Best bowling: 3–48 Glamorgan v Hampshire, Cardiff 1989

LAST SEASON: BATTING

	I.	N. O.	R.	H. S.	AV.
TEST					
1ST	10	2	328	112*	41.00
INT					
RAL	9	2	185	46	26.42
N.W.	1	0	22	22	22.00
B&H	4	0	32	21	8.00

CAREER: BATTING

	I.	N. O.	R.	H. S.	AV.
TEST					
1ST	68	11	1429	116	25.07
INT					
RAL	33	8	485	56*	19.40
N.W.	3	0	60	33	20.00
B&H	7	0	47	21	6.71

LAST SEASON: BOWLING

	O.	M.	R.	W.	AV.
TEST					
1ST	39	3	181	1	181.00
INT					
RAL	2	0	17	0	-
N.W.	4	0	20	1	20.00
B&H					

CAREER: BOWLING

	O.	M.	R.	W.	AV.
TEST					
1ST	532.2	31	2140	47	45.53
INT					
RAL	96	1	515	14	36.78
N.W.	16	0	63	2	31.50
B&H	14	0	69	1	69.00

SMITH, N. M. K.   Warwickshire

Name: Neil Michael Knight Smith
Role: Right-hand bat, off-spin bowler
Born: 27 July 1967, Solihull
Height: 6ft 1in **Weight:** 13st 7lbs
Nickname: Gurt
County debut: 1987
1st-Class 50s scored: 1
1st-Class 100s scored: 1
Place in batting averages: 160th av.
30.83
1st-Class catches: 4 (career 7)
Parents: Mike (M. J. K.) and Diana
Marital status: Single
Family links with cricket: Father
captained Warwickshire and England
Education: Warwick School
Qualifications: 3 O-levels (Maths,
English, French); cricket coach Grade 1
Off-season: Coaching
Cricketers particularly admired: Paul Smith, Tim Munton, Joe Benjamin
Other sports followed: Rugby, squash, golf, football
Injuries: Broken finger – missed six weeks cricket
Relaxations: Sport and music

Best batting: 161 Warwickshire v Yorkshire, Headingley 1989
Best bowling: 3–62 Warwickshire v Yorkshire, Headingley 1989

LAST SEASON: BATTING

	I.	N. O.	R.	H. S.	AV.
TEST					
1ST	14	2	370	83*	30.83
INT					
RAL	8	1	122	38*	17.42
N.W.	1	0	52	52	52.00
B&H	2	1	41	30*	41.00

LAST SEASON: BOWLING

	O.	M.	R.	W.	AV.
TEST					
1ST	177.5	37	535	7	76.42
INT					
RAL	67.3	3	399	11	36.27
N.W.	8	0	41	0	-
B&H	15	0	63	1	63.00

CAREER: BATTING

	I.	N. O.	R.	H. S.	AV.
TEST					
1ST	30	5	677	161	27.08
INT					
RAL	19	3	197	38*	12.31
N.W.	4	2	83	52	41.50
B&H	2	1	41	30*	41.00

CAREER: BOWLING

	O.	M.	R.	W.	AV.
TEST					
1ST	355.3	72	1134	22	51.54
INT					
RAL	144.3	3	797	18	44.27
N.W.	19	0	80	2	40.00
B&H	15	0	63	1	63.00

SMITH, P. A.   Warwickshire

Name: Paul Andrew Smith
Role: Right-hand bat, right-arm fast-medium bowler
Born: 15 April 1964, Newcastle-on-Tyne
Height: 6ft 2in **Weight:** 12st
Nickname: Smithy, Jim
County debut: 1982
County cap: 1986
1000 runs in a season: 2
1st-Class 50s scored: 42
1st-Class 100s scored: 4
1st-Class 5 w. in innings: 2
One-Day 50s: 8
Place in batting averages: 153rd av. 32.50 (1989 70th av. 34.63)
Place in bowling averages: 10th av. 24.85 (1989 48th av. 27.21)
Strike rate: 44.65 (career 56.02)
1st-Class catches: 1 (career 45)
Parents: Kenneth and Joy
Wife and date of marriage: Caroline, 31 July 1987
Children: Oliver James, 5 February 1988
Family links with cricket: Father played for Leicestershire and Northumberland.

Both brothers played for Warwickshire

Education: Heaton Grammar School, Newcastle

Qualifications: 5 O-levels

Career outside cricket: Worked for *Birmingham Post and Mail* for three winters; restoring classic cars

Cricketers particularly admired: Ian Botham, Wayne Larkins, Dennis Amiss, Bob Willis, Tim Munton. 'I admire most players who play professionally, as it's not easy.'

Other sports followed: 'None.'

Injuries: Two operations on knee repairing cartilage and taking out pieces of floating bone – missed 16 Championship matches

Relaxations: 'Working on my car, listening to music, reading – no sport.'

Extras: Along with Andy Moles set a new world record for most consecutive opening partnerships of over 50. In 1989, scored 140 v Worcestershire, during which scored 100 out of partnership of 123 with Dermot Reeve and took a hat-trick against Northamptonshire. In 1990 took a hat-trick against Sussex, bowling in Tim Munton's boots – two sizes too big ('it's your's Tim!')

Opinions on cricket: 'I disagree with people who think the 1990 season with the flat wickets and balls with smaller seams was bad for the game. Seam bowlers had to work hard for their wickets in comparison to the 1987, 1988 and 1989 seasons, but didn't they have it a bit easy then? Slow bowlers did more bowling last year and it must have been more interesting to watch and better for cricket.'

Best batting: 140 Warwickshire v Worcestershire, Worcester 1989

Best bowling: 5–48 Warwickshire v Somerset, Edgbaston 1990

LAST SEASON: BATTING

	I.	N. O.	R.	H. S.	AV.
TEST					
1ST	20	4	520	117	32.50
INT					
RAL	7	0	102	33	14.57
N.W.					
B&H	1	0	13	13	13.00

LAST SEASON: BOWLING

	O.	M.	R.	W.	AV.
TEST					
1ST	148.5	34	497	20	24.85
INT					
RAL	29	1	162	5	32.40
N.W.					
B&H	5	0	15	0	-

CAREER: BATTING

	I.	N. O.	R.	H. S.	AV.
TEST					
1ST	259	32	6534	140	28.78
INT					
RAL	87	19	1660	93*	24.41
N.W.	17	2	301	79	20.06
B&H	26	4	455	74	20.68

CAREER: BOWLING

	O.	M.	R.	W.	AV.
TEST					
1ST	1708.5	220	6823	183	37.28
INT					
RAL	396.3	11	2135	60	35.58
N.W.	107.4	6	432	17	25.41
B&H	115.2	10	496	15	33.06

SMITH, R. A.   Hampshire

Name: Robin Arnold Smith
Role: Right-hand bat, slip fielder
Born: 13 September 1963, Durban, South Africa
Height: 5ft 11 3/4in **Weight:** 15st 3lbs
Nickname: The Judge
County debut: 1982
County cap: 1985
Test debut: 1988
Tests: 18
One-Day Internationals: 20
1000 runs in a season: 5
1st-Class 50s scored: 51
1st-Class 100s scored: 27
1st-Class 200s scored: 1
One-Day 50s: 26
One-Day 100s: 10
Place in batting averages: 15th av. 66.09 (1989 4th av. 58.40)
1st-Class catches: 11 (career 114)

Parents: John Arnold and Joy Lyall
Wife and date of marriage: Katherine, 21 September 1988
Family links with cricket: Grandfather played for Natal in Currie Cup. Brother Chris plays for Hampshire and England
Education: Northlands Boys High, Durban
Qualifications: 'Highly qualified.'
Off-season: Touring with England in Australia
Overseas tours: England to India and West Indies 1989–90; Australia 1990–91
Overseas teams played for: Natal 1980–84
Cricketers particularly admired: Malcolm Marshall, Graeme Hick, Graham Gooch. 'I learnt most from brother Chris, Barry Richards and Grayson Heath, my coach in south Africa.'
Other sports followed: Soccer, athletics, most sports
Relaxations: 'Reading Sidney Sheldon novels, trout fishing, siestas, keeping fit and spending as much time as possible with my lovely wife.'
Extras: Played rugby for Natal Schools and for Romsey RFC as a full-back. Held nineteen school athletics records and two South African schools records in shot put and 100-metre hurdles. One of *Wisden*'s Five Cricketers of the Year, 1990. First child was born while he was on tour in Australia last winter
Opinions on cricket: 'I think four-day cricket so far has been a great success. I think the standard of umpiring in England is of a very high quality in comparison to umpiring in other parts of the world.'
Best batting: 209* Hampshire v Essex, Southampton 1987

Best bowling: 2–11 Hampshire v Surrey, Southampton 1985

LAST SEASON: BATTING

	I.	N. O.	R.	H. S.	AV.
TEST	11	4	513	121*	73.28
1ST	19	4	941	181	62.73
INT	4	0	242	128	60.50
RAL	10	0	517	122	51.70
N.W.	4	0	141	59	35.25
B&H	3	2	185	132	185.00

CAREER: BATTING

	I.	N. O.	R.	H. S.	AV.
TEST	34	8	1397	143	53.73
1ST	269	47	9444	209*	42.54
INT	19	3	691	128	43.18
RAL	73	10	2475	131	39.28
N.W.	18	3	797	125*	53.13
B&H	24	7	964	155*	56.70

LAST SEASON: BOWLING

	O.	M.	R.	W.	AV.
TEST					
1ST	0.3	0	3	0	-
INT					
RAL					
N.W.					
B&H					

CAREER: BOWLING

	O.	M.	R.	W.	AV.
TEST					
1ST	115.5	18	520	9	57.77
INT					
RAL					
N.W.	2.5	0	13	2	6.50
B&H	1	0	2	0	

SPEAK, N. J. — Lancashire

Name: Nicholas Jason Speak
Role: Right-hand opening bat, off-spin bowler
Born: 21 October 1966, Manchester
Height: 6ft **Weight:** 11st 7lbs
Nickname: Twenty, Vision, Pod
County debut: 1986–87 in Jamaica
1st-Class 50s scored: 4
1st-Class 100s scored: 1
Place in batting averages: 76th av. 45.44 (1989 173rd av. 20.66)
1st-Class catches: 3 (career 9)
Parents: John and Irene
Marital status: Single
Family links with cricket: Father was league professional in Lancashire and Yorkshire
Education: Parrs Wood High School and Sixth Form College
Qualifications: 6 O-levels; NCA coaching certificate
Off-season: Working in the City
Cricketers particularly admired: Martin Crowe, Dexter Fitton, Neil Fairbrother
Other sports followed: Most sports – Manchester City FC

Relaxations: 'Sharing a lager with Graham Lloyd and discussing the finer points of the game. Indian food and red wine.'
Opinions on cricket: 'To see Holland reach Test level, along with Zimbabwe. More under–25 county cricket. Tea should be 10 minutes longer.'
Best batting: 138 Lancashire v Zimbabwe, Old Trafford 1990

LAST SEASON: BATTING

	I.	N. O.	R.	H. S.	AV.
TEST					
1ST	9	0	409	138	45.44
INT					
RAL					
N.W.					
B&H					

CAREER: BATTING

	I.	N. O.	R.	H. S.	AV.
TEST					
1ST	23	1	644	138	29.27
INT					
RAL	1	0	13	13	13.00
N.W.					
B&H					

SPEIGHT, M. P. Sussex

Name: Martin Peter Speight
Role: Right-hand bat, wicket-keeper/close fielder
Born: 24 October 1967, Walsall
Height: 5ft 10 1/2in **Weight:** 11st 7lbs
Nickname: Sprog, Hoover, Ginger, Ronald
County debut: 1986
1st-Class 50s scored: 18
1st-Class 100s scored: 2
One-Day 50s: 6
Place in batting averages: 106th av. 40.44 (1989 125th av. 26.56)
1st-Class catches: 14 (career 36)
Parents: Peter John and Valerie
Marital status: Single
Education: Hassocks' Infants School; The Windmill's School, Hassocks; Hurstpierpoint College Junior and Senior Schools; Durham University
Qualifications: 13 O-levels, 3 A-levels; BA (Hons) Dunelm (Archaeology/Ancient History)
Off-season: 'Going to Bangladesh with Alan Fordham to coach and play for national youth team; relaxing and doing a bit of painting.'
Overseas tours: England YCs tour to Sri Lanka 1987
Overseas teams played for: Wellington CC, New Zealand 1989–90
Cricketers particularly admired: Nasser Hussain, James Boiling
Other sports followed: Golf, tennis, football, hockey, squash, horse racing

Relaxations: 'Going to the races, especially at Newmarket. Painting.'
Extras: Member of Durham University UAU winning side 1987; played for Combined Universities in B&H Cup 1987 and 1988; Member of Durham University's men's hockey team to Barbados 1988. Sussex CCC's Most Promising Player, 1989. 'Painted an oil painting of the maiden first-class game at Arundel Castle between Sussex and Hampshire which was later auctioned to raise money for the Sussex Young Cricketers' tour to India 1990–91.'
Opinions on cricket: 'Too much cricket and too many different games (Sunday slog / 55 / 60 overs / first-class).'
Best batting: 131 Sussex v Glamorgan, Hove 1990
Best bowling: 1–2 Sussex v Middlesex, Hove 1988

LAST SEASON: BATTING

	I.	N.O.	R.	H.S.	AV.
TEST					
1ST	41	7	1375	131	40.44
INT					
RAL	13	1	353	77	29.41
N.W.	1	0	4	4	4.00
B&H	4	0	160	71	40.00

CAREER: BATTING

	I.	N.O.	R.	H.S.	AV.
TEST					
1ST	77	9	2230	131	32.79
INT					
RAL	24	2	676	77	30.72
N.W.	3	0	59	48	19.66
B&H	15	0	421	83	28.06

STEMP, R. D. Worcestershire

Name: Richard David Stemp
Role: Slow left-arm bowler
Born: 11 December 1967, Edgbaston
Height: 6ft **Weight:** 12st 4lbs
Nickname: Stempy, Stempez, Stencho
County debut: 1990
1st-Class catches: 1 (career 1)
Parents: Rita and Arnold Homer
Marital status: Single
Family links with cricket: Father played Birmingham League cricket for Old Hill
Education: Britannia High School, Rowley Regis
Qualifications: NCA coaching award
Off-season: 'Selling fax machines for Photostatic Copiers.'
Cricketers particularly admired:

Graeme Hick ('for natural talent'); Steve Rhodes ('for energy'); Mark Scott ('for patience')
Other sports followed: Indoor cricket, Australian Rules and American football
Relaxations: 'Ornithology, reading, driving, music.'

Extras: Played for England Indoor cricket team v Australia in Manulife Test series, 1990
Opinions on cricket: 'I am not interested or intelligent enough to be a politician, so why am I subject to politics when I want to go abroad in winter. Cricket for cricketers, politics for politicians.'
Best batting: 3* Worcestershire v Yorkshire, Worcester 1990
Best bowling: 1–32 Worcestershire v Yorkshire, Worcester 1990

LAST SEASON / CAREER: BATTING

	I.	N.O.	R.	H.S.	AV.
TEST					
1ST	2	2	3	3*	-
INT					
RAL	2	1	4	3*	4.00
N.W.					
B&H	-	-	-	-	-

LAST SEASON / CAREER: BOWLING

	O.	M.	R.	W.	AV.
TEST					
1ST	45	14	123	1	123.00
INT					
RAL	12	0	65	0	-
N.W.					
B&H	8	1	38	0	-

STEPHENSON, F. D.   Nottinghamshire

Name: Franklyn Dacosta Stephenson
Role: Right-hand bat, right-arm fast bowler
Born: 8 April 1959, Barbados
Height: 6ft 4in **Weight:** 13st 7lbs
Nickname: Cookie
County debut: 1982 (Gloucs), 1988 (Notts)
County cap: 1988 (Notts)
1000 runs in a season: 1
50 wickets in a season: 3
1st-Class 50s scored: 21
1st-Class 100s scored: 4
1st-Class 5 w. in innings: 25
1st-Class 10 w. in match: 6
One-Day 50s: 3
Place in batting averages: 174th av. 28.82 (1989 164th av. 22.11)
Place in bowling averages: 86th av. 38.85 (1989 8th av. 18.77)
Strike rate: 67.85 (career 45.35)
1st-Class catches: 5 (career 43)
Parents: Leonard Young and Violet
Wife and date of marriage: Julia, 2 April 1981
Children: Amanda, Orissa

Education: St John Baptist Mixed School; Samuel Jackson Prescod Polytechnic
Career outside cricket: Professional golfer
Off-season: 'Cricketing, golfing and training.'
Overseas tours: With West Indies U–19s to England 1978; rebel West Indies team to South Africa 1982–83 and 1983–84
Overseas teams played for: Tasmania 1981–82; Barbados 1981–82 and 1989–90
Cricketers particularly admired: Sir Garfield Sobers, Sylvester Clarke, Collis King, Richard Hadlee
Other sports followed: Golf and tennis
Injuries: Hamstring trouble
Relaxations: 'Playing golf, listening to music, spending time with my wife and kids.'
Extras: Played League cricket for Littleborough in the Central Lancashire League in 1979, Royton in 1980 (100 wickets and 621 runs), Rawtenstall in 1981 and 1982 (100+ wickets and 500+ runs both years). Hit 165 for Barbados in 1982 having been sent in as night-watchman. Took 10 wickets in match on debut for Tasmania. In 1988 did the double when he scored 1018 runs and took 125 wickets in first-class cricket. Britannic Assurance Player of the Year, 1988. One of *Wisden's* Five Cricketers of the Year, 1988. Now again eligible to play for West Indies, having been banned for playing in South Africa
Opinions on cricket: 'I fail to see how the further limitation of overseas players can be the answer to the lack of outstanding English players; or, for that matter, the low gate receipts being experienced by the county clubs.'
Best batting: 165 Barbados v Leeward Islands, Basseterre 1981–82
Best bowling: 8–47 Nottinghamshire v Essex, Trent Bridge 1989

LAST SEASON: BATTING

	I.	N. O.	R.	H. S.	AV.
TEST					
1ST	35	7	807	121	28.82
INT					
RAL	13	2	207	42	18.81
N.W.	2	0	33	29	16.50
B&H	6	3	162	98*	54.00

LAST SEASON: BOWLING

	O.	M.	R.	W.	AV.
TEST					
1ST	610.4	94	2098	54	38.85
INT					
RAL	123	11	577	24	24.04
N.W.	17	3	52	2	26.00
B&H	66	4	249	9	27.66

CAREER: BATTING

	I.	N. O.	R.	H. S.	AV.
TEST					
1ST	154	17	3575	165	26.09
INT					
RAL	45	10	728	69	20.80
N.W.	5	1	73	29	18.25
B&H	15	5	298	98*	29.80

CAREER: BOWLING

	O.	M.	R.	W.	AV.
TEST					
1ST	2970.4	622	9011	393	22.92
INT					
RAL	404.5	36	1765	83	21.26
N.W.	85	18	236	9	26.22
B&H	165.2	20	545	25	21.80

STEPHENSON, J. P.   Essex

Name: John Patrick Stephenson
Role: Right-hand opening bat,
right-arm medium bowler
Born: 14 March 1965, Stebbing
Height: 6ft 1in **Weight:** 13st
Nickname: Stan
County debut: 1985
Test debut: 1989
Tests: 1
1000 runs in a season: 2
1st-Class 50s scored: 32
1st-Class 100s scored: 9
1st-Class 200s scored: 1
One-Day 50s: 5
One-Day 100s: 5
Place in batting averages: 30th av.
57.18 (1989 50th av. 37.61)
1st-Class catches: 16 (career 60)

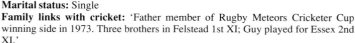

Parents: Patrick and Eve
Marital status: Single
Family links with cricket: 'Father member of Rugby Meteors Cricketer Cup winning side in 1973. Three brothers in Felstead 1st XI; Guy played for Essex 2nd XI.'
Education: Felstead Prep School; Felstead Senior School; Durham University
Qualifications: 7 O-levels, 3 A-levels; NCA coaching award; General Arts BA
Overseas tours: England A to Zimbabwe and Kenya 1989–90
Overseas teams played for: Boland, South Africa 1988–89
Cricketers particularly admired: Graham Gooch, Brian Hardie and many others

LAST SEASON: BATTING

	I.	N. O.	R.	H. S.	AV.
TEST					
1ST	41	8	1887	202*	57.18
INT					
RAL	12	1	341	109	31.00
N.W.	1	0	44	44	44.00
B&H	3	1	8	4*	4.00

LAST SEASON: BOWLING

	O.	M.	R.	W.	AV.
TEST					
1ST	123	28	485	5	97.00
INT					
RAL	11	0	73	3	24.33
N.W.	4	0	24	1	24.00
B&H	20	0	80	7	11.42

CAREER: BATTING

	I.	N. O.	R.	H. S.	AV.
TEST	2	0	36	25	18.00
1ST	176	21	5704	202*	36.80
INT					
RAL	40	8	711	109	22.21
N.W.	6	1	142	55	28.40
B&H	11	2	296	75	32.88

CAREER: BOWLING

	O.	M.	R.	W.	AV.
TEST					
1ST	419.1	89	1390	30	46.33
INT					
RAL	104.2	2	497	15	33.13
N.W.	8	1	46	1	46.00
B&H	67	3	262	15	17.46

Other sports followed: 'There are far too many other interesting things to watch or follow than sport when you do it for a living.'

Relaxations: 'Reading, writing and listening to the Meatpuppets, REM, Pixies, T'Pau, DBs, Mock Turtles, etc.'

Extras: Awarded 2nd XI cap in 1984 when leading run-scorer with Essex 2nd XI. Essex Young Player of the Year, 1985. Captained Durham University to victory in UAU Competition 1986 and captain of Combined Universities team 1987 in the first year that it was drawn from all universities

Opinions on cricket: 'Four-day cricket to stay and hopefully take over for all Championship matches. Less 40-over cricket. No restraint of trade.'

Best batting: 202* Essex v Somerset, Bath 1990

Best bowling: 3–22 England A v Zimbabwe, Bulawayo 1989–90

STEWART, A. J. Surrey

Name: Alec James Stewart
Role: Right-hand bat, wicket-keeper, county vice-captain
Born: 8 April 1963, Merton
Nickname: Stewie
Height: 5ft 10in **Weight:** 12st
County debut: 1981
County cap: 1985
Test debut: 1989–90
Tests: 7
One-Day Internationals: 13
1000 runs in a season: 5
1st-Class 50s scored: 54
1st-Class 100s scored: 16
1st-Class 200s scored: 1
One-Day 50s: 23
One-Day 100s: 4
Place in batting averages: 93rd av. 42.78 (1989 24th av. 44.51)
1st-Class catches: 24 (career 208 & 6 stumpings)

Parents: Michael James and Sheila Marie Macdonald
Marital status: Engaged to Lynn
Family links with cricket: Father played for England (1962–64) and Surrey (1954 – 72). Brother Neil captains Malden Wanderers CC
Education: Tiffin Boys School
Qualifications: 4 O-levels
Off-season: Touring Australia with England
Overseas tours: England and West Indies 1989–90; Australia 1990–91

Cricketers particularly admired: Geoff Arnold, Kevin Gartrell, Tony Mann, Graham Monkhouse
Other sports followed: All sports, watches Chelsea FC
Injuries: Various minor injuries – lost place in England side after series v New Zealand
Relaxations: 'Visiting Durham, theatre, listening to Neil 'Oracle' Kendrick, watching Rehan Alikhan bat.'
Opinions on cricket: 'In favour of four-day cricket. No over-rate fines.'
Best batting: 206* Surrey v Essex, The Oval 1989
Best bowling: 1–7 Surrey v Lancashire, Old Trafford 1989

LAST SEASON: BATTING

	I.	N. O.	R.	H. S.	AV.
TEST	5	0	147	54	29.40
1ST	24	6	837	100*	46.50
INT	2	0	61	33	30.50
RAL	7	0	258	125	36.85
N.W.	1	0	48	48	48.00
B&H	5	1	334	84*	83.50

CAREER: BATTING

	I.	N. O.	R.	H. S.	AV.
TEST	13	1	317	54	26.41
1ST	259	39	8849	206*	38.64
INT	11	1	194	61	19.40
RAL	87	8	2213	125	28.01
N.W.	15	2	548	107*	42.15
B&H	25	3	727	84*	33.04

STOVOLD, A. W. Gloucestershire

Name: Andrew Willis-Stovold
Role: Right-hand bat, former wicket-keeper
Born: 19 March 1953, Bristol
Height: 5ft 7in **Weight:** 12st 4lbs
Nickname: Stumper, Squeak, Stov, Stovers, Stubble
County debut: 1973
County cap: 1976
Benefit: 1987 (75,000)
1000 runs in a season: 8
1st-Class 50s scored: 97
1st-Class 100s scored: 20
1st-Class 200s scored: 1
One-Day 50s: 35
One-Day 100s: 4
1st-Class catches: 0 (career 289 & 45 stumpings)
Parents: Lancelot Walter and Dorothy Patricia
Wife and date of marriage: Kay Elizabeth, 30 September 1978
Children: Nicholas, 18 June 1981; Neil, 24 February 1983

Family links with cricket: Father played local club cricket for Old Down CC. Brother Martin also played county cricket for Gloucestershire
Education: Filton High School; Loughborough College of Education
Qualifications: Certificate of Education
Career outside cricket: Teacher at Tockington Manor Prep School
Overseas tours: England Schools to India 1970–71; England YCs to West Indies 1972
Overseas teams played for: Orange Free State 1974–76
Cricketers particularly admired: Mike Procter, Barry Richards, Richard Hadlee
Other sports followed: Rugby, hunting, horse racing, football, golf
Relaxations: Gardening, walking
Extras: His 1987 benefit produced 75,000 – a record for a Gloucestershire player
Opinions on cricket: 'Worried about the sudden increase in player transfers. We must not let it get too much like football.'
Best batting: 212* Gloucestershire v Northamptonshire, Northampton 1982
Best bowling: 1-0 Gloucestershire v Derbyshire, Bristol 1976

LAST SEASON: BATTING

	I.	N. O.	R.	H. S.	AV.
TEST					
1ST	4	0	104	74	26.00
INT					
RAL					
N.W.					
B&H	3	0	14	8	4.66

CAREER: BATTING

	I.	N. O.	R.	H. S.	AV.
TEST					
1ST	630	35	17705	212*	29.75
INT					
RAL	181	21	3835	98*	23.96
N.W.	33	3	1138	104*	37.93
B&H	68	8	2148	123	35.80

82. Of whom did Brian Close say, 'He was the greatest player I ever laid eyes on.... a gentleman and a genius.'?

83. Which American citizen played English county cricket last season?

84. When Wasim Akram was asked last season which player he would choose to play for his life, what name did he give?

SUCH, P. M. Essex

Name: Peter Mark Such
Role: Right-hand bat, off-spin bowler
Born: 12 June 1964, Helensburgh, Scotland
Height: 6ft 1in **Weight:** 11st 7lbs
Nickname: Suchy
County debut: 1982 (Notts), 1987 (Leics), 1990 (Essex)
1st-Class 5 w. in innings: 6
Place in bowling averages: 60th av. 35.75 (1989 105th av. 41.06)
Strike rate: 81.80 (career 68.74)
1st-Class catches: 2 (career 41)
Parents: John and Margaret
Marital status: Single
Family links with cricket: Father and brother village cricketers
Education: Lantern Lane Primary School; Harry Carlton Comprehensive, East Leake
Qualifications: 9 O-levels, 3 A-levels, qualified cricket coach (senior)
Off-season: 'Coaching at the Essex CCC Indoor School and visiting schools.'
Cricketers particularly admired: Bob White, Eddie Hemmings, John Childs, Ray East, Keith Fletcher
Other sports followed: Golf, American football and most other sports
Relaxations: 'Reading, gardening, watching movies, playing golf, listening to music and keeping Steve Andrew company in a local wine bar.'

LAST SEASON: BATTING

	I.	N. O.	R.	H. S.	AV.
TEST					
1ST	5	3	44	27	22.00
INT					
RAL	1	0	5	5	5.00
N.W.					
B&H					

LAST SEASON: BOWLING

	O.	M.	R.	W.	AV.
TEST					
1ST	272.4	67	715	20	35.75
INT					
RAL	20	0	106	2	53.00
N.W.					
B&H					

CAREER: BATTING

	I.	N. O.	R.	H. S.	AV.
TEST					
1ST	86	33	171	27	3.22
INT					
RAL	4	2	13	8*	6.50
N.W.					
B&H	-	-	-	-	-

CAREER: BOWLING

	O.	M.	R.	W.	AV.
TEST					
1ST	2600.4	686	7086	227	31.21
INT					
RAL	87	2	514	10	51.40
N.W.					
B&H	44	3	186	5	37.20

Extras: Played for England YC v Australia 1983. Left Nottinghamshire at end of 1986 season. Joined Leicestershire in 1987 and released at the end of 1989. Signed by Essex for 1990

Opinions on cricket: 'The balance has tipped too far in favour of batsmen. Wickets need pace and bounce to encourage batsmen but the bowlers have to have a chance with a small amount of sideways movement. Both green and flat wickets produce boring cricket.'

Best batting: 27 Essex v Middlesex, Ilford 1990
Best bowling: 6–123 Nottinghamshire v Kent, Trent Bridge 1983

SWALLOW, I. G. Somerset

Name: Ian Geoffrey Swallow
Role: Right-hand bat, off-break bowler, cover or slip fielder
Born: 18 December 1962, Barnsley
Height: 5ft 7in **Weight:** 10st
Nickname: Chicken, Swal
County debut: 1983 (Yorks), 1990 (Somerset)
1st-Class 50s scored: 2
1st-Class 100s scored: 1
1st-Class 5 w. in innings: 1
Place in batting averages: 230th av. 18.70 (1989 217th av. 15.94)
Place in bowling averages: 148th av. 63.94 (1989 113th av. 45.50)
Strike rate: 121.61 (career 108.36)
1st-Class catches: 12 (career 40)
Parents: Geoffrey and Joyce
Marital status: Single
Family links with cricket: Father and brother both played for Elsecar Village CC
Education: Hayland Kirk, Balk, Comprehensive School; Barnsley Technical College
Qualifications: 3 O-levels
Cricketers particularly admired: Viv Richards, John Emburey
Other sports followed: Barnsley FC, all sports, 'play for fun.'
Relaxations: Sports in general
Extras: Took hat-trick v Warwickshire 2nd XI 1984. Figures: 4–3–2–4. Released by Yorkshire at end of 1989 season
Best batting: 114 Yorkshire v MCC, Scarborough 1987

Best bowling: 7–95 Yorkshire v Nottinghamshire, Trent Bridge 1987

LAST SEASON: BATTING

	I.	N. O.	R.	H. S.	AV.
TEST					
1ST	17	7	187	32	18.70
INT					
RAL	8	5	77	31	25.66
N.W.	-	-	-	-	-
B&H	3	0	26	18	8.66

LAST SEASON: BOWLING

	O.	M.	R.	W.	AV.
TEST					
1ST	689.1	161	2174	34	63.94
INT					
RAL	69	2	365	6	60.83
N.W.	13	0	69	0	-
B&H	45.5	3	207	4	51.75

CAREER: BATTING

	I.	N. O.	R.	H. S.	AV.
TEST					
1ST	99	25	1483	114	20.04
INT					
RAL	9	5	79	31	19.75
N.W.	1	1	17	17*	-
B&H	6	2	44	18	11.00

CAREER: BOWLING

	O.	M.	R.	W.	AV.
TEST					
1ST	1770	410	5444	98	55.55
INT					
RAL	73	2	396	6	66.00
N.W.	17	0	85	0	-
B&H	81.5	7	358	6	59.66

TAVARE, C. J. Somerset

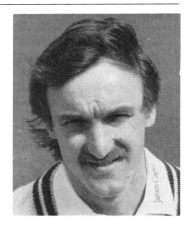

Name: Christopher James Tavaré
Role: Right-hand bat, off-break bowler, slip fielder, county captain
Born: 27 October 1954, Orpington
Height: 6ft 1 1/2in **Weight:** 12st 12lbs
Nickname: Tav, Rowdy
County debut: 1974 (Kent), 1989 (Somerset)
County cap: 1978 (Kent), 1989 (Somerset)
Benefit: 1988 (92,318) (Kent)
Test debut: 1980
Tests: 31
One-Day Internationals: 29
1000 runs in a season: 14
1st-Class 50s scored: 123
1st-Class 100s scored: 39
1st-Class 200s scored: 1
One-Day 50s: 56
One-Day 100s: 13
Place in batting averages: 25th av. 58.50 (1989 57th av. 36.29)
1st-Class catches: 16 (career 362)
Parents: Andrew and June
Wife and date of marriage: Vanessa, 22 March 1980
Family links with cricket: Father, Uncle Jack Tavaré, and Uncle Derrick Attwood,

all played school and club cricket. Elder brother Stephen and younger brother Jeremy also both play

Education: Sevenoaks School; Oxford University

Qualifications: Zoology degree

Off-season: Working for Ministry of Agriculture, Fisheries & Food, in Exeter

Overseas tours: England to India and Sri Lanka 1981–82; Australia and New Zealand 1982–83; New Zealand and Pakistan 1983–84

Other sports followed: 'Take an interest in most sports, especially American football in winter.'

Relaxations: Music, zoology, films, gardening, woodwork, golf

Extras: Played for England Schools v India at Birmingham in 1973, scoring 124*. Oxford University cricket Blue 1975–77. Whitbread Scholarship to Perth, Australia, 1978–79. Suffers from asthma and hay-fever. Captain of Kent 1983–84. Rejected Kent's offer of a new contract for 1989 and joined Somerset as vice-captain. Appointed Somerset captain for 1990 after retirement of Vic Marks

Best batting: 219 Somerset v Sussex, Hove 1990

Best bowling: 1–3 Kent v Hampshire, Canterbury 1986

LAST SEASON: BATTING

	I.	N. O.	R.	H. S.	AV.
TEST					
1ST	32	4	1638	219	58.50
INT					
RAL	16	1	421	86	28.06
N.W.	2	2	261	162*	-
B&H	6	1	233	93	46.60

CAREER: BATTING

	I.	N. O.	R.	H. S.	AV.
TEST	56	2	1755	149	32.50
1ST	567	63	19765	219	39.21
INT	28	2	720	83*	27.69
RAL	187	25	5179	136*	31.96
N.W.	32	7	1367	162*	54.68
B&H	82	8	2457	143	33.20

LAST SEASON: BOWLING

	O.	M.	R.	W.	AV.
TEST					
1ST	17.2	0	162	0	-
INT					
RAL					
N.W.					
B&H					

CAREER: BOWLING

	O.	M.	R.	W.	AV.
TEST	5	3	11	0	-
1ST	123.1	15	676	5	135.20
INT	2	0	3	0	-
RAL					
N&W					
B&H					

Name: Charles William Taylor
Role: Left-hand bat, left-arm seam
bowler
Born: 12 August 1966, Banbury,
Oxfordshire
Height: 6ft 5in **Weight:** 13st 7lbs
Nickname: Chas
County debut: 1990
1st-Class 5 w. in innings: 1
Parents: Richard and Ann
Marital status: Single
Education: Spendlove Comprehensive
School, Charlbury; Banbury Technical
College
Qualifications: City and Guilds
Certificate in farming; 1 O-level
Career outside cricket: Farming
Off-season: 'Working on family farm.'
Cricketers particularly admired: David
Gower
Other sports followed: National Hunt Racing
Injuries: 'Dog bite on left wrist.'
Extras: Returned figures of 5 for 33 in second first-class match as Middlesex gained
an important win on the way to the 1990 Championship title
Best batting: 13 Middlesex v Nottinghamshire, Trent Bridge 1990
Best bowling: 5–33 Middlesex v Yorkshire, Headingley 1990

LAST SEASON / CAREER: BATTING

	I.	N. O.	R.	H. S.	AV.
TEST					
1ST	2	1	13	13	13.00
INT					
RAL					
N.W.					
B&H					

LAST SEASON / CAREER: BOWLING

	O.	M.	R.	W.	AV.
TEST					
1ST	47.5	7	139	6	23.16
INT					
RAL					
N.W.					
B&H					

TAYLOR, L. B. Leicestershire

Name: Leslie Brian Taylor
Role: Right-hand bat, right-arm fast-medium bowler
Born: 25 October 1953, Earl Shilton, Leicestershire
Height: 6ft 3 1/2in **Weight:** 14st 7lbs
Nickname: Les
County debut: 1977
County cap: 1981
Benefit: 1989
Test debut: 1985
Tests: 2
One-Day Internationals: 2
1st-Class 50s scored: 1
1st-Class 5 w. in innings: 18
1st-Class 10 w. in match: 1
1st-Class catches: 0 (career 53)
Parents: Peggy and Cyril
Wife and date of marriage: Susan, 12 July 1973
Children: Jamie, 24 June 1976; Donna, 10 November 1978; Suzy, 3 June 1981
Family links with cricket: Relation of the late Sam Coe, holder of highest individual score for Leicestershire, 252* v Northamptonshire at Leicester in 1914
Education: Heathfield High School, Earl Shilton
Qualifications: Qualified carpenter and joiner
Overseas tours: Rebel English team to South Africa 1981–82; England to West Indies 1985–86
Overseas teams played for: Natal 1981–84

LAST SEASON: BATTING

	I.	N. O.	R.	H. S.	AV.
TEST					
1ST	-	-	-	-	-
INT					
RAL	2	1	0	0*	0.00
N.W.					
B&H					

LAST SEASON: BOWLING

	O.	M.	R.	W.	AV.
TEST					
1ST	9	1	34	0	-
INT					
RAL	46	2	244	6	40.66
N.W.					
B&H					

CAREER: BATTING

	I.	N. O.	R.	H. S.	AV.
TEST	1	1	1	1*	-
1ST	198	86	1060	60	9.38
INT	1	1	1	1*	-
RAL	41	28	117	15*	9.00
N.W.	6	5	18	6*	18.00
B&H	10	5	18	5	3.60

CAREER: BOWLING

	O.	M.	R.	W.	AV.
TEST	63.3	11	178	4	44.50
1ST	5183.2	1128	14470	577	25.07
INT	14	3	47	0	-
RAL	906.5	61	4019	184	21.84
N.W.	169.1	23	603	32	18.84
B&H	331.4	58	1115	56	19.91

Other sports followed: Swimming and football
Relaxations: Game-shooting, fox-hunting with the Atherstone Hunt
Extras: Was banned from Test cricket for three years for joining rebel England tour of South Africa in 1982. Retired at end of 1990 season
Opinions on cricket: 'We should not be subjected to over-rate fines in one-day cricket.'
Best batting: 60 Leicestershire v Essex, Chelmsford 1988
Best bowling: 7–28 Leicestershire v Derbyshire, Leicester 1981

TAYLOR, N. R.   Middlesex

Name: Neil Raymond Taylor
Role: Right-arm medium bowler
Born: 9 February 1964, Boscombe, Bournemouth
Height: 6ft **Weight:** 13st 7lbs
County debut: 1990
1st-Class catches: 1 (career 1)
Parents: Ray and Molly
Wife and date of marriage: Nicola, 21 May 1988
Education: Arnewood Comprehensive
Qualifications: 6 O-levels, HNC in Communications Engineering
Career outside cricket: British Telecom Engineer
Off-season: Working for British Telecom
Cricketers particularly admired: Ian Botham, Dennis Lillee and Malcolm Marshall
Other sports followed: Football, golf
Relaxations: 'TV, playing football and cricket.'
Extras: Plays Minor County cricket for Dorset and for Minor Counties in the B & H Cup; first-class debut for Minor Counties v Indians 1990; contracted to play Refuge matches for Middlesex
Opinions on cricket: 'I am in favour of playing on uncovered pitches or extending all Championship games to four days.'
Best bowling: 3–44 Middlesex v Hampshire, Bournemouth 1990

	I.	N. O.	R.	H. S.	AV.
TEST					
1ST	2	0	0	0	0.00
INT					
RAL	2	2	9	5*	-
N.W.	1	0	7	7	7.00
B&H	1	0	3	3	3.00

LAST SEASON: BOWLING

	O.	M.	R.	W.	AV.
TEST					
1ST	37	7	131	4	32.75
INT					
RAL	34.5	0	181	3	60.33
N.W.	10	0	55	0	-
B&H	41	5	165	7	23.57

CAREER: BATTING

	I.	N. O.	R.	H. S.	AV.
TEST					
1ST	2	0	0	0	0.00
INT					
RAL	2	2	9	5*	-
N.W.	2	0	7	7	3.50
B&H	3	1	18	14	9.00

CAREER: BOWLING

	O.	M.	R.	W.	AV.
TEST					
1ST	37	7	131	4	32.75
INT					
RAL	34.5	0	181	3	60.33
N.W.	22	3	120	1	120.00
B&H	84.4	11	295	14	21.07

TAYLOR, N. R.   Kent

Name: Neil Royston Taylor
Role: Right-hand bat, off-break bowler
Born: 21 July 1959, Farnborough, Kent
Height: 6ft 1in **Weight:** 14st 7lbs
Nickname: Map
County debut: 1979
County cap: 1982
1000 runs in a season: 7
1st-Class 50s scored: 56
1st-Class 100s scored: 30
1st-class 200s scored: 1
One-Day 50s: 23
One-Day 100s: 4
Place in batting averages: 21st av. 61.84 (1989 30th av. 42.71)
1st-Class catches: 9 (career 119)
Parents: Leonard and Audrey
Wife and date of marriage: Jane Claire, 25 September 1982
Children: Amy Louise, 7 November 1985; Lauren, 21 July 1988
Family links with cricket: Brother Colin played for Kent U–19s. Father played club cricket
Education: Cray Valley Technical High School
Qualifications: 8 O-levels, 2 A-levels, NCA coaching certificate
Off-season: Coaching for Kent CCC
Overseas tours: With England Schools Team to India 1977–78

Cricketers particularly admired: Chris Tavare, Mark Benson and Robin Smith
Other sports followed: Rugby Union, golf
Relaxations: 'Reading Wilbur Smith, Frederick Forsyth and cricket autobiographies, listening to music.'
Extras: Made 110 on debut for Kent CCC v Sri Lanka, 1979. Won four Man of the Match awards in first five matches. Scored three successive centuries in the B & H. Played for England B v Pakistan, 1982. Fielded twice as 12th man for England v India in 1982 and West Indies in 1988, both matches at The Oval
Opinions on cricket: 'Perhaps the groundsmen could be employed by the TCCB, so that they do not feel pressured by their county club. They can then produce their best pitches, instead of inferior ones!'
Best batting: 204 Kent v Surrey, Canterbury 1990
Best bowling: 2–20 Kent v Somerset, Canterbury 1985

LAST SEASON: BATTING

	I.	N. O.	R.	H. S.	AV.
TEST					
1ST	37	5	1979	204	61.84
INT					
RAL	13	0	614	95	47.23
N.W.	2	1	13	13*	13.00
B&H	3	0	117	90	39.00

LAST SEASON: BOWLING

	O.	M.	R.	W.	AV.
TEST					
1ST	21	5	57	1	57.00
INT					
RAL					
N.W.					
B&H					

CAREER: BATTING

	I.	N. O.	R.	H. S.	AV.
TEST					
1ST	379	50	12308	204	37.41
INT					
RAL	93	8	2539	95	29.87
N.W.	18	1	406	85	23.88
B&H	34	1	1370	137	41.51

CAREER: BOWLING

	O.	M.	R.	W.	AV.
TEST					
1ST	259.3	46	865	16	54.06
INT					
RAL					
N.W.	15.5	3	48	3	16.00
B&H	2	1	5	0	-

Name: Geoffrey Alan Tedstone
Role: Right-hand bat, wicket-keeper
Born: 19 January 1961, Southport
Height: 5ft 6 1/2in **Weight:** 10st 7lbs
Nickname: Ted, Super
County debut: 1982 (Warwicks), 1989 (Gloucs)
1st-Class 50s scored: 4
One-Day 50s: 1
Place in batting averages: 233rd av. 13.73 (1988 200th av. 18.87)
Parents: Ken and Win
Wife and date of marriage: Jane, 17 September 1988
Family links with cricket: Sister, Janet Aspinall, plays for England Ladies. Father played club cricket for Leamington. Brother Roger plays for Leamington
Education: Warwick School; St Pauls College, Cheltenham
Qualifications: 6 O-levels, 4 A-levels, BEd degree, qualified teacher, FA coach
Career outside cricket: PE teacher
Overseas tours: England YCs to West Indies 1980
Cricketers particularly admired: Dennis Amiss, Bob Taylor
Other sports followed: Soccer (Wolverhampton Wanderers FC), hockey (played for Coventry and Warwickshire)
Relaxations: Playing or watching most sports, listening to music, watching films,

LAST SEASON: BATTING

	I.	N. O.	R.	H. S.	AV.
TEST					
1ST	5	0	88	23	17.60
INT					
RAL	2	1	26	25	26.00
N.W.					
B&H					

CAREER: BATTING

	I.	N. O.	R.	H. S.	AV.
TEST					
1ST	67	9	935	67*	16.12
INT					
RAL	12	5	128	31*	18.28
N.W.	1	1	55	55*	-
B&H	-	-	-	-	-

LAST SEASON: WICKET-KEEPING

	CT	ST			
TEST					
1ST	9	1			
INT					
RAL					
N.W.					
B&H					

CAREER: WICKET-KEEPING

	CT	ST			
TEST					
1ST	82	14			
INT					
RAL	12	2			
N.W.					
B&H					

being sociable
Best batting: 67* Warwickshire v Cambridge University, Fenner's 1983

TERRY, V. P. Hampshire

Name: Vivian Paul Terry
Role: Right-hand bat, right-arm medium bowler, slip or cover fielder
Born: 14 January 1959, Osnabruck, West Germany
Height: 6ft **Weight:** 13st 6lbs
County debut: 1978
County cap: 1983
Test debut: 1984
Tests: 2
1000 runs in a season: 7
1st-Class 50s scored: 57
1st-Class 100s scored: 22
One-Day 50s: 3
One-Day 100s: 8
Place in batting averages: 97th av. 41.62 (1989 88th av. 31.92)
1st-Class catches: 23 (career 218)
Parents: Michael and Patricia
Wife and date of marriage: Bernadette, 4 June 1986
Children: Siobhan Catherine, 13 September 1987
Education: Durlston Court, Hampshire; Millfield School, Somerset
Qualifications: 8 O-levels, 1 A-level, advanced cricket coach
Off-season: 'In the main, coaching in Hampshire.'
Overseas tours: ESCA tour to India 1977–78; English Counties tour to Zimbabwe 1985
Cricketers particularly admired: Gordon Greenidge, Chris Smith, Viv and Barry Richards, Malcolm Marshall, Gary Sobers
Other sports followed: Most sports – golf, squash, football
Injuries: Chickenpox – missed three games; knock on the jaw – missed one game
Relaxations: Music, sport
Opinions on cricket: 'Not enough done to ease pressures on cricketers during the winter. We are expected to reach April at a level of fitness and skill but always in our own time.'
Best batting: 190 Hampshire v Sri Lankans, Southampton 1988

	I.	N.O.	R.	H.S.	AV.
TEST					
1ST	35	3	1332	165	41.62
INT					
RAL	14	1	482	113*	37.07
N.W.	4	0	137	76	34.25
B&H	4	0	180	134	45.00

CAREER: BATTING

	I.	N.O.	R.	H.S.	AV.
TEST	3	0	16	8	5.33
1ST	324	33	10255	190	35.24
INT					
RAL	128	16	3457	142	30.86
N.W.	25	1	926	165*	38.58
B&H	39	3	1365	134	37.91

THOMAS, J. G. Northamptonshire

Name: John Gregory Thomas
Role: Right-hand bat, right-arm fast bowler
Born: 12 August 1960, Trebanos, Swansea
Height: 6ft 3in **Weight:** 14st
Nickname: Blodwen
County debut: 1979 (Glamorgan), 1989 (Northants)
County cap: 1986 (Glamorgan)
Test debut: 1985–86
Tests: 5
One-Day Internationals: 3
50 wickets in a season: 1
1st-Class 50s scored: 6
1st-Class 100s scored: 2
1st-Class 5 w. in innings: 16
1st-Class 10 w. in match: 1
Place in batting averages: 252nd av. 15.20 (1989 248th av. 11.93)
Place in bowling averages: 101st av. 40.37 (1989 62nd av. 29.04)
Strike rate: 63.17 (career 52.84)
1st-Class catches: 9 (career 71)
Parents: Illtyd and Margaret
Marital status: Single
Family links with cricket: Father played village cricket
Education: Cwmtawe Comprehensive School; South Glamorgan Institute of Higher Education
Qualifications: Qualified teacher, advanced cricket coach
Overseas tours: England to West Indies 1985–86; unofficial English team to South Africa 1989–90
Overseas teams played for: Border 1983–87; Eastern Province 1987–89
Relaxations: Any sport, music
Extras: Having never hit a first-class century before, hit two in August 1988. Signed

389

for Northamptonshire in 1989. Banned from Test cricket for joining tour to South Africa in 1989–90. Career best bowling figures against his old county in 1990

Best batting: 110 Glamorgan v Warwickshire, Edgbaston 1988
Best bowling: 7–75 Northamptonshire v Glamorgan, Northampton 1990

LAST SEASON: BATTING

	I.	N. O.	R.	H. S.	AV.
TEST					
1ST	13	3	152	48	15.20
INT					
RAL	7	2	35	19*	7.00
N.W.	-	-	-	-	-
B&H	3	0	35	32	11.66

LAST SEASON: BOWLING

	O.	M.	R.	W.	AV.
TEST					
1ST	305.2	51	1171	29	40.37
INT					
RAL	59	3	313	10	31.30
N.W.	10	2	21	1	21.00
B&H	39	0	204	6	34.00

CAREER: BATTING

	I.	N. O.	R.	H. S.	AV.
TEST	10	4	83	31*	13.83
1ST	231	38	3130	110	16.21
INT	3	2	1	1*	1.00
RAL	76	17	692	37	11.72
N.W.	11	3	151	34	18.87
B&H	23	2	197	32	9.38

CAREER: BOWLING

	O.	M.	R.	W.	AV.
TEST	129	18	504	10	50.40
1ST	4248	751	14862	487	30.51
INT	26	2	144	3	48.00
RAL	617.1	38	2973	114	26.07
N.W.	117.5	9	427	18	23.72
B&H	277.2	32	1100	39	28.20

THORPE, G. P. Surrey

Name: Graham Paul Thorpe
Role: Left-hand bat, right-arm medium bowler
Born: 1 August 1969, Farnham
Height: 5ft 10in **Weight:** 12st
Nickname: Chalky
County debut: 1988
1000 runs in a season: 1
1st-Class 50s scored: 12
1st-Class 100s scored: 3
One-Day 50s: 9
Place in batting averages: 182nd av. 27.63 (1989 20th av. 45.28)
1st-Class catches: 9 (career 26)
Parents: Geoff and Toni
Marital status: Single
Family links with cricket: 'Both brothers play cricket at Farnham.'
Education: Weydon Comprehensive; Farnham Sixth-Form College
Qualifications: 6 O-levels, PE Diploma

Off-season: Touring Pakistan with England A
Overseas tours: England A to Zimbabwe and Kenya 1989–90; Pakistan 1990–91
Cricketers particularly admired: Mark Ramprakash, Grahame Clinton, David Smith
Other sports followed: Football, ice hockey, athletics
Relaxations: Swimming and reading
Extras: Played England Schools cricket U–15 and U–19 and England Schools football U–18
Opinions on cricket: 'There should be 16 four-day matches, with two limited-overs competitions.'
Best batting: 154 Surrey v Kent, The Oval 1989
Best bowling: 2–31 Surrey v Essex, The Oval 1989

LAST SEASON: BATTING

	I.	N. O.	R.	H. S.	AV.
TEST					
1ST	28	6	608	86	27.63
INT					
RAL	15	3	514	85	42.83
N.W.	2	1	31	16	31.00
B&H	5	1	89	50*	22.25

LAST SEASON: BOWLING

	O.	M.	R.	W.	AV.
TEST					
1ST	23	7	99	1	99.00
INT					
RAL					
N.W.					
B&H	7	0	45	1	45.00

CAREER: BATTING

	I.	N. O.	R.	H. S.	AV.
TEST					
1ST	66	13	2040	154	38.49
INT					
RAL	28	4	878	85	36.58
N.W.	5	1	114	74	28.50
B&H	6	1	111	50*	22.20

CAREER: BOWLING

	O.	M.	R.	W.	AV.
TEST					
1ST	108	15	381	9	42.33
INT					
RAL	21	1	125	2	62.50
N.W.	2	0	12	0	-
B&H	18	2	80	4	20.00

Name: Martin John Thursfield
Role: Right-hand bat, right-arm medium bowler
Born: 14 December 1971, South Shields, Tyne and Wear
Height: 6ft 3 1/2ins **Weight:** 13st
Nickname: Thursy, Kettle
County debut: 1990 (Middlesex)
Parents: Anthony John and Maureen
Marital status: Single
Education: Boldon Comprehensive School
Qualifications: GCSEs
Off-season: 'Keeping fit and praticising.'
Cricketers particularly admired: Don Wilson, Martin Robinson, John Hampshire, Gary Brown
Other sports followed: Most sports, especially football and golf (8 handicap)

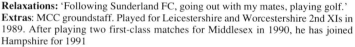

Injuries: Groin strain, sore shins
Relaxations: 'Following Sunderland FC, going out with my mates, playing golf.'
Extras: MCC groundstaff. Played for Leicestershire and Worcestershire 2nd XIs in 1989. After playing two first-class matches for Middlesex in 1990, he has joined Hampshire for 1991
Opinions on cricket: 'With the improved pitches and the new ball I think the game has leant towards the side of the batsmen. The wider-seamed ball should be re-instated.'
Best bowling: 1–24 Middlesex v Essex, Ilford 1990

LAST SEASON / CAREER: BATTING

	I.	N. O.	R.	H. S.	AV.
TEST					
1ST	-	-	-	-	-
INT					
RAL					
N.W.					
B&H					

LAST SEASON / CAREER: BOWLING

	O.	M.	R.	W.	AV.
TEST					
1ST	42	11	130	2	65.00
INT					
RAL					
N.W.					
B&H					

Name: Christopher Mark Tolley
Role: Right-hand bat, left-arm medium bowler
Born: 30 December 1967, Kidderminster
Height: 5ft 9in **Weight:** 10st 8lbs
Nickname: Treefrog
County debut: 1989
One-Day 50s scored: 2
1st-class catches: 2 (career 2)
Parents: Ray and Elisabeth
Marital status: Single
Family links with cricket: Father played local league; brother Richard plays for Stourbridge in the Birmingham League
Education: Oldswinford Primary School; Redhill Comprehensive School; King Edward VI College, Stourbridge; Loughborough University
Qualifications: 9 O-levels, 3 A-levels, BSc PE Sports Science and Recreation Management
Off-season: 'Working as a PE teacher.'
Overseas tours: British Universities Sports Federation tour to Barbados October 1989
Cricketers particularly admired: Ian Botham, Richard Hadlee, Graeme Hick
Other sports followed: 'I watch most sports but particularly enjoy hockey, tennis

LAST SEASON: BATTING

	I.	N. O.	R.	H. S.	AV.
TEST					
1ST	6	1	79	29	15.80
INT					
RAL	2	1	2	1*	2.00
N.W.	-	-	-	-	-
B&H	4	0	171	77	42.75

LAST SEASON: BOWLING

	O.	M.	R.	W.	AV.
TEST					
1ST	88	14	326	5	65.20
INT					
RAL	14	0	46	2	23.00
N.W.	6	0	32	0	-
B&H	38	6	169	0	-

CAREER: BATTING

	I.	N. O.	R.	H. S.	AV.
TEST					
1ST	12	3	199	37	22.11
INT					
RAL	2	1	2	1*	2.00
N.W.	-	-	-	-	-
B&H	8	1	201	77	28.71

CAREER: BOWLING

	O.	M.	R.	W.	AV.
TEST					
1ST	149	30	464	6	77.33
INT					
RAL	27	1	83	3	27.66
N.W.	6	0	32	0	-
B&H	87	12	336	4	84.00

and athletics.'

Injuries: 'Injured left shoulder during the winter; strained side prevented me bowling for two weeks.'

Relaxations: Listening to music, watching TV, eating out

Extras: Played for ESCA U–19 in 1986; played for the Combined Universities in the B & H Cup

Opinions on cricket: 'There is too much cricket played resulting in too little time for players to prepare mentally and physically for each game.'

Best batting: 37 Worcestershire v Kent, Worcester 1989

Best bowling: 2–66 Worcestershire v Somerset, Worcester 1990

TOPLEY, T. D. Essex

Name: Thomas Donald Topley
Role: Right-hand bat, right-arm fast-medium bowler
Born: 25 February 1964, Canterbury
Height: 6ft 3in **Weight:** 14st 5lbs
Nickname: Toppers, Wimble
County debut: 1985 (Surrey), 1985 (Essex)
County cap: 1988 (Essex)
50 wickets in a season: 2
1st-Class 50s scored: 2
1st-Class 5 w. in innings: 11
1st-Class 10 w. in match: 2
Place in bowling averages: 41st av. 32.40 (1989 37th av. 24.03)
Strike rate: 60.81 (career 50.84)
1st-Class catches: 6 (career 44)
Parents: Tom (deceased) and Rhoda
Marital status: Single
Family links with cricket: Brother Peter played for Kent (1972–76). Father played for Royal Navy
Education: Royal Hospital School, Ipswich
Qualifications: 6 O-levels, NCA advanced coach
Jobs outside cricket: Coaching cricket or PE
Off-season: Playing and coaching abroad
Overseas teams played for: Griqualand West, South Africa 1987–88
Cricketers particularly admired: Don Wilson, Geoff Arnold, John Lever, Graham Gooch, Keith Fletcher, Richard Hadlee
Other sports followed: Rugby, soccer, badminton and all other ball sports
Injuries: 'Prolonged shin soreness and a back spasm.'

Relaxations: Photography, food, travelling. Supporting Colchester United FC

Extras: Spent three years prior to joining Essex on the MCC Young Professionals at Lord's. As 12th man held famous one-handed 'catch' for England v West Indies at Lord's in 1984, stepping over the boundary in taking it. Also played for Norfolk and Surrey

Opinions on cricket: 'Bring back higher seam ball as current ball v bat contest is boring and one-sided. Produce a ball that encourages swing bowling. Abolish fines on over-rates and reduce the amount of cricket we play.'

Best batting: 66 Essex v Yorkshire, Headingley 1987

Best bowling: 7–75 Essex v Derbyshire, Chesterfield 1988

LAST SEASON: BATTING

	I.	N. O.	R.	H. S.	AV.
TEST					
1ST	6	2	78	23*	19.50
INT					
RAL	8	2	22	10	3.66
N.W.	-	-	-	-	-
B&H	1	1	10	10*	-

CAREER: BATTING

	I.	N. O.	R.	H. S.	AV.
TEST					
1ST	94	22	1116	66	15.50
INT					
RAL	28	9	132	23	6.94
N.W.	3	1	25	15*	12.50
B&H	3	3	19	10*	-

LAST SEASON: BOWLING

	O.	M.	R.	W.	AV.
TEST					
1ST	223	33	713	22	32.40
INT					
RAL	93.5	2	488	13	37.53
N.W.	18	0	98	0	-
B&H	31	2	101	1	101.00

CAREER: BOWLING

	O.	M.	R.	W.	AV.
TEST					
1ST	2305.1	467	6927	272	25.46
INT					
RAL	407.5	18	1818	70	25.97
N.W.	79.2	9	286	12	23.83
B&H	169	26	546	23	23.73

Name: Gareth Terence John Townsend
Role: Opening batsman and cover fielder ('short leg when in 1st team')
Born: 28 June 1968, Tiverton, Devon
Height: 6ft **Weight:** 11st 7lbs
Nickname: Gobbler
County debut: 1990
1st-Class catches: 3 (career 3)
Parents: Terry and Sheila
Marital status: Single
Family links with cricket: 'Father played before giving up time to help me with my career; older brother played Devon Schools cricket and club cricket.'
Education: Tiverton Comprehensive School and Birmingham University
Qualifications: 7 O-levels, 4 A-levels, BA (Hons) General Studies, majoring in Sport and Exercise Science
Career outside cricket: 'Unsure at present, though after previous winter in Australia definitely not cauliflower picking!'
Off-season: Teaching PE at Park Grove School, Birmingham, and coaching cricket at Birmingham University
Cricketers particularly admired: Gordon Greenidge, Jimmy Cook, Peter Roebuck
Other sports followed: Most sports – 'an avid follower of Five Nations Rugby championship and West Ham United.'
Relaxations: 'Keeping in touch with the outside world by following newspapers, etc. and enjoying a bottle of red wine or a lager and blackcurrant.'
Extras: Scored 85 and 115* on 2nd XI debut v Hampshire in 1987
Opinions on cricket: 'Cricketers who enjoy a successful career in county cricket can expect to earn a reasonable living. However, the wellbeing and financial interests of the younger members of county staffs should not be neglected. Young players are

LAST SEASON / CAREER: BATTING

	I.	N. O.	R.	H. S.	AV.
TEST					
1ST	4	1	21	15	7.00
INT					
RAL					
N.W.					
B&H					

LAST SEASON / CAREER: BOWLING

	O.	M.	R.	W.	AV.
TEST					
1ST					
INT					
RAL					
N.W.					
B&H					

expected to develop the attributes of professional sportsmen soon after entering the game: thus they should be rewarded accordingly.'

Best batting: 15 Somerset v Warwickshire, Edgbaston 1990

TREMLETT, T. M. Hampshire

Name: Timothy Maurice Tremlett
Role: Right-hand bat, right-arm medium bowler
Born: 26 July 1956, Wellington, Somerset
Height: 6ft 2in **Weight:** 13st 7lbs
Nickname: Hurricane, Trooper, R2
County debut: 1976
County cap: 1983
50 wickets in a season: 4
1st-Class 50s scored: 18
1st-Class 100s scored: 1
1st-Class 5 w. in innings: 11
Place in bowling averages: 91st av. 39.30 (1989 25th av. 22.25)
Strike rate: 72.50 (career 58.97)
1st-Class catches: 1 (career 73)
Parents: Maurice Fletcher and Melina May
Wife and date of marriage: Carolyn Patricia, 28 September 1979
Children: Christopher Timothy, 2 September 1981; Alastair Jonathan, 1 February 1983; Benjamin Paul, 2 May 1984
Family links with cricket: Father played for Somerset and for England against West Indies in the West Indies 1947–48. Captained Somerset 1958–60. Younger brother plays local club cricket for Deanery CC
Education: Bellemoor Secondary Modern; Richard Taunton Sixth-Form College
Qualifications: 5 O-levels, 1 A-level. Advanced coaching certificate
Career outside cricket: 'Now employed full-time by Hampshire CCC as player / coach with the main responsibility of running the 2nd XI.'
Overseas tours: English Counties tour to Zimbabwe 1985; England B to Sri Lanka 1985–86
Cricketers particularly admired: Vincent van der Bijl, Mike Hendrick, Malcolm Marshall, Richard Hadlee
Other sports followed: Golf, table tennis, squash, swimming, badminton
Relaxations: Collecting cricket books and records, gardening, cinema
Opinions on cricket: 'With ever increasing numbers of top-class cricketers withdrawing from international fixtures, the cricketing authorities must begin to

reduce the amount of cricket played in this country, especially one-day cricket. With the emphasis still geared towards one-day matches, specialists are still outnumbered heavily by bits-and-pieces performers, with young spin-bowlers particularly at a disadvantage. To ensure that the highest standards are maintained, the structure of English first-class cricket is in further need of streamlining.'

Best batting: 102* Hampshire v Somerset, Taunton 1985
Best bowling: 6–53 Hampshire v Somerset, Weston-super-Mare 1987

LAST SEASON: BATTING

	I.	N. O.	R.	H. S.	AV.
TEST					
1ST	5	3	143	78	71.50
INT					
RAL	3	1	41	21	20.50
N.W.					
B&H					

LAST SEASON: BOWLING

	O.	M.	R.	W.	AV.
TEST					
1ST	120.5	30	393	10	39.30
INT					
RAL	45	2	167	12	13.91
N.W.					
B&H					

CAREER: BATTING

	I.	N. O.	R.	H. S.	AV.
TEST					
1ST	249	66	3862	102*	21.10
INT					
RAL	58	26	362	35	11.31
N.W.	13	4	142	43*	15.77
B&H	25	10	213	36*	14.20

CAREER: BOWLING

	O.	M.	R.	W.	AV.
TEST					
1ST	4413.2	1269	10759	449	23.96
INT					
RAL	937.4	39	4322	176	24.55
N.W.	213.2	37	697	28	24.89
B&H	325.5	50	1063	46	23.10

85. Which Australian team does Graeme Hick play for?

86. Who was the only Lancastrian before Mike Atherton to hit a Test century for England at Old Trafford?

87. What is Chris Broad's first name?

TRUMP, H. R. J.   Somerset

Name: Harvey Russell John Trump
Role: Right-hand bat, off-spin bowler
Born: 11 October 1968, Taunton
Height: 6ft 2in **Weight:** 13st 7lbs
Nickname: Trumptonian, Trumpy, Gupta, Snagger
County debut: 1988
1st-Class catches: 3 (career 16)
Marital status: Single
Family links with cricket: Father played for Somerset 2nd XI and captained Devon
Education: Edgarley Hall (Millfield Jnr School); Millfield School; Chester College of Higher Education
Qualifications: 7 O-levels, 2 A-levels, BA (Hons) in Combined Studies (History and PE)
Career outside cricket: Teacher
Off-season: Teaching at Stamford School in Lincs
Overseas tours: England YCs to Sri Lanka 1987; to Australia for Junior World Cup 1988
Cricketers particularly admired: John Emburey, Vic Marks, Viv Richards, Jimmy Cook
Other sports followed: Hockey and most ball games
Relaxations: Reading, walking, cinema, 'working with disabled children.'
Extras: Played county hockey for Somerset U–19s. Qualified lifeguard, attaining

LAST SEASON: BATTING

	I.	N. O.	R.	H. S.	AV.
TEST					
1ST	5	1	11	4*	2.75
INT					
RAL	1	0	0	0	0.00
N.W.					
B&H					

LAST SEASON: BOWLING

	O.	M.	R.	W.	AV.
TEST					
1ST	164	41	520	9	57.77
INT					
RAL	14	0	73	2	36.50
N.W.					
B&H					

CAREER: BATTING

	I.	N. O.	R.	H. S.	AV.
TEST					
1ST	26	3	156	48	6.78
INT					
RAL	4	0	6	4	1.50
N.W.	1	0	0	0	0.00
B&H					

CAREER: BOWLING

	O.	M.	R.	W.	AV.
TEST					
1ST	850	208	2349	58	40.50
INT					
RAL	84	2	374	10	37.40
N.W.	21	0	73	2	36.50
B&H					

bronze medallion lifesaving award. Preliminary teacher of disabled swimming certificate

Opinions on cricket: 'Something has got to be done about the seam on the ball. Over-rates need to be looked at and adjusted appropriately. It is vitally important for youngsters to have a good grounding at junior levels in two-and three-day cricket not just one-day cricket.'

Best batting: 48 Somerset v Hampshire, Taunton 1988
Best bowling: 4–17 Somerset v Kent, Canterbury 1988

TUFNELL, P. C. R.   Middlesex

Name: Philip Clive Roderick Tufnell
Role: Right-hand bat, slow left-arm spinner
Born: 29 April 1966, Hadley Wood, Hertfordshire
Height: 6ft **Weight:** 11st 7lbs
Nickname: Tuffers, Brucie
County debut: 1986
50 wickets in a season: 2
1st-Class 5 w. in innings: 6
Place in batting averages: 213th av. 21.76
Place in bowling averages: 58th av. 35.60 (1989 60th av. 28.43)
Strike rate: 84.87 (career 79.86)
1st-Class catches: 8 (career 28)
Parents: Sylvia and Alan
Marital status: Single

Education: Highgate School; Southgate School
Qualifications: O-level in Art; City & Guilds Silversmithing
Off-season: Touring Australia with England
Overseas tours: England YC tour to the West Indies 1985; England to Australia 1990–91
Cricketers particularly admired: Clive Radley, Derek Underwood
Other sports followed: American football, snooker, golf
Relaxations: 'Finding excuses to get out of buying a round.'
Extras: MCC Young Cricketer of the Year 1984. Middlesex Uncapped Bowler of the Year 1987. Was originally a seam bowler and gave up cricket for three years in his mid-teens
Opinions on cricket: 'Tea should be longer. Go back to uncovered wickets.'

Best batting: 37 Middlesex v Yorkshire, Headingley 1990
Best bowling: 6–60 Middlesex v Kent, Canterbury 1987

LAST SEASON: BATTING

	I.	N. O.	R.	H. S.	AV.
TEST					
1ST	22	9	283	37	21.76
INT					
RAL	1	1	0	0*	-
N.W.	-	-	-	-	-
B&H	1	1	7	7*	-

LAST SEASON: BOWLING

	O.	M.	R.	W.	AV.
TEST					
1ST	1036.5	281	2635	74	35.60
INT					
RAL	23	0	142	1	142.00
N.W.	12	2	22	2	11.00
B&H	18	0	78	1	78.00

CAREER: BATTING

	I.	N. O.	R.	H. S.	AV.
TEST					
1ST	60	21	434	37	11.12
INT					
RAL	2	2	13	13*	-
N.W.	-	-	-	-	-
B&H	1	1	7	7*	-

CAREER: BOWLING

	O.	M.	R.	W.	AV.
TEST					
1ST	2565.4	667	6720	192	35.00
INT					
RAL	47	1	248	3	82.66
N.W.	36	6	101	6	16.83
B&H	18	0	78	1	78.0

TURNER, I. J.   Hampshire

Name: Ian John Turner
Role: Right-hand bat, slow left-arm bowler
Born: 18 July 1968, Denmead
Height: 6ft 1in **Weight:** 13st 7lbs
Nickname: Turns, Bunsen
County debut: 1989
1st-Class catches: 2 (career 2)
Parents: Robert and Sheila
Marital status: Single
Family links with cricket: 'Dad plays for Hambledon CC.'
Education: Cowplain Comprehensive School; South Downs College
Qualifications: 7 CSEs, pass in BTec General Diploma in Business Studies
Career outside cricket: Bank clerk
Off-season: 'Staying in England.'
Cricketers particularly admired: Sir Garfield Sobers, Malcolm Marshall, Robin Smith
Other sports followed: 'Football – especially Liverpool – and look at local teams' results.'
Relaxations: Listening to music

Opinions on cricket: 'State of pitches in 2nd XI cricket is inadequate. Why not put the games on county grounds?'
Best batting: 14 Hampshire v Oxford University, The Parks 1990
Best bowling: 3–20 Hampshire v Glamorgan, Southampton 1989

LAST SEASON: BATTING

	I.	N. O.	R.	H. S.	AV.
TEST					
1ST	3	1	15	14	7.50
INT					
RAL					
N.W.					
B&H					

LAST SEASON: BOWLING

	O.	M.	R.	W.	AV.
TEST					
1ST	148.2	39	424	9	47.11
INT					
RAL					
N.W.					
B&H					

CAREER: BATTING

	I.	N. O.	R.	H. S.	AV.
TEST					
1ST	5	2	24	14	8.00
INT					
RAL					
N.W.					
B&H					

CAREER: BOWLING

	O.	M.	R.	W.	AV.
TEST					
1ST	183.2	60	472	13	36.00
INT					
RAL					
N.W.					
B&H					

TWOSE, R. G.   Warwickshire

Name: Roger Graham Twose
Role: Left-hand bat, right-arm fast-medium bowler
Born: 17 April 1968, Torquay ('in a car!')
Height: 6ft **Weight:** 14st
Nickname: Twosey, Buffalo
County debut: 1989
1st-Class 50s scored: 6
One-day 50s: 1
Place in batting averages: 188th av. 26.77 (1989 152nd av. 23.16)
1st-Class catches: 3 (career 10)
Parents: Paul and Patricia
Marital status: Single
Family links with cricket: Father played for Devon, brother Richard plays for Devon. Uncles – Roger

Tolchard (Leicestershire and England) and Jeff Tolchard (Leicestershire)
Education: Wolborough Hill, Newton Abbot, Devon; King's College, Taunton
Qualifications: 7 O-levels, 2 A-levels, NCA coaching certificate

Off-season: In Birmingham – playing rugby for Camp Hill
Overseas teams played for: Northern Districts, New Zealand 1989–90
Cricketers particularly admired: Giles Barber, Rick Pickard, Ken Rogers
Other sports followed: Chess, bridge and billiards
Relaxations: Playing golf
Extras: 'Once took all ten wickets in an innings whilst playing in New Zealand: a feat I plan to reproduce in first-class cricket!'
Opinions on cricket: 'Sixteen four-day matches; coloured clothing for Sunday League; cricket under floodlights.'
Best batting: 64* Warwickshire v Sri Lanka, Edgbaston 1990
Best bowling: 1–10 Warwickshire v Worcestershire, Worcester 1990

LAST SEASON: BATTING

	I.	N. O.	R.	H. S.	AV.
TEST					
1ST	10	1	241	64*	26.77
INT					
RAL	9	2	113	40	16.14
N.W.	1	0	1	1	1.00
B&H	2	0	19	17	9.50

LAST SEASON: BOWLING

	O.	M.	R.	W.	AV.
TEST					
1ST	53	12	185	4	46.25
INT					
RAL	45.4	3	245	8	30.62
N.W.					
B&H	3	0	16	0	-

CAREER: BATTING

	I.	N. O.	R.	H. S.	AV.
TEST					
1ST	34	6	777	64*	27.75
INT					
RAL	15	3	192	40	16.00
N.W.	3	0	66	56	22.00
B&H	2	0	19	17	9.50

CAREER: BOWLING

	O.	M.	R.	W.	AV.
TEST					
1ST	135.5	21	472	6	78.66
INT					
RAL	69.4	3	373	11	33.90
N.W.	20	0	79	2	39.50
B&H	3	0	16	0	-

Name: Shaun David Udal
Role: Right-hand bat, off-spin bowler, field in the deep
Born: 18 March 1969, Farnborough
Height: 6ft 2in **Weight:** 12st 9lbs
Nickname: Prawn
County debut: 1989
Place in bowling averages: 104th av. 40.90
Strike rate: 63.68 (career 66.68)
1st-Class catches: 2 (career 2)
Parents: Robin and Mary
Marital status: Single
Family links with cricket: Grandfather played for Middlesex and Leicestershire; father played for Surrey Colts, and for Camberley; brother plays for Camberley
Education: Tower Hill Infant and Junior Schools; Cove County Secondary School
Qualifications: 8 CSEs, qualified print finisher
Off-season: Working at Omega Print Finishers in Camberley
Cricketers particularly admired: Ian Botham, Malcolm Marshall, Peter Boot ('from my club side who has helped me a lot.')
Other sports played: Football, golf, snooker
Other sports followed: Football, golf and snooker; 'follow Aldershot FC through thick and thin.'

LAST SEASON: BATTING

	I.	N. O.	R.	H. S.	AV.
TEST					
1ST	6	2	79	28*	19.75
INT					
RAL	1	1	2	2*	-
N.W.					
B&H					

LAST SEASON: BOWLING

	O.	M.	R.	W.	AV.
TEST					
1ST	238.3	46	900	22	40.90
INT					
RAL	15	0	56	3	18.66
N.W.					
B&H					

CAREER: BATTING

	I.	N. O.	R.	H. S.	AV.
TEST					
1ST	6	2	79	28*	19.75
INT					
RAL	1	1	2	2*	-
N.W.					
B&H					

CAREER: BOWLING

	O.	M.	R.	W.	AV.
TEST					
1ST	244.3	52	921	22	41.86
INT					
RAL	20	0	92	4	23.00
N.W.					
B&H					

Injuries: 'Pulled intercostal muscle in my side and missed a week of season.'
Relaxations: Watching videos, having a few drinks, going to nightclubs
Extras: Has taken two hat-tricks in club cricket, and scored a double hundred in a 40-over club game
Opinions on cricket: 'More four-day matches to help county players adjust to Test cricket. Too many bad 2nd XI games are played on bad pitches. A better programme must be worked out to cut down the travelling between games.'
Best batting: 28* Hampshire v Surrey, Southampton 1990
Best bowling: 4–139 Hampshire v Sri Lanka, Southampton 1990

WALSH, C. A. — Gloucestershire

Name: Courtney Andrew Walsh
Role: Right-hand bat, right-arm fast bowler
Born: 30 October 1962, Kingston, Jamaica
Height: 6ft 5 1/2in **Weight:** 14st 7lbs
Nickname: Mark, Walshy, Cuddy
County debut: 1984
County cap: 1985
Test debut: 1984–85
Tests: 37
One-Day Internationals: 88
50 wickets in a season: 5
1st-Class 50s scored: 5
1st-Class 5 w. in innings: 44
1st-Class 10 w. in match: 9
Place in batting averages: 184th av. 27.29 (1989 200th av. 18.00)
Place in bowling averages: 19th av. 28.08 (1989 15th av. 20.67)
Strike rate: 50.93 (career 46.56)
1st-Class catches: 6 (career 54)
Parents: Eric and Joan Wollaston
Marital status: Single
Education: Excelsior High School
Qualifications: GCE and CXL
Off-season: Playing for the West Indies
Overseas tours: West Indies YCs to Zimbabwe 1983; West Indies to England 1984; Australia 1984–85; Pakistan, Australia and New Zealand 1986–87; World Cup and India 1987–88; England 1988; Australia 1988–89; Pakistan 1990–91
Overseas teams played for: Jamaica 1981–91
Cricketers particularly admired: Michael Holding, Viv Richards, Lawrence

Rowe, Richard Hadlee, Clive Lloyd, Imran Khan
Other sports followed: Basketball, track and field events
Relaxations: Swimming, reading and listening to music
Extras: Took record 10–43 in Jamaican school cricket in 1979. On tour, he has the reputation as an insatiable collector of souvenirs. David Graveney, when captaining Gloucestershire, reckoned Walsh was the 'best old-ball bowler in the world'. One of *Wisden's* Five Cricketers of the Year, 1986. Took hat-trick for West Indies v Australia in 1988–89
Best batting: 63* Gloucestershire v Yorkshire, Cheltenham 1990
Best bowling: 9–72 Gloucestershire v Somerset, Bristol 1986

LAST SEASON: BATTING

	I.	N. O.	R.	H. S.	AV.
TEST					
1ST	20	3	464	63*	27.29
INT					
RAL	7	1	76	23	12.66
N.W.	1	0	7	7	7.00
B&H	1	0	1	1	1.00

LAST SEASON: BOWLING

	O.	M.	R.	W.	AV.
TEST					
1ST	611.1	107	2022	72	28.08
INT					
RAL	103.5	6	410	18	22.77
N.W.	31	4	106	10	10.60
B&H	23	2	74	2	37.00

CAREER: BATTING

	I.	N. O.	R.	H. S.	AV.
TEST	48	17	302	30*	9.74
1ST	188	44	2041	63*	14.17
INT	27	11	129	18	8.06
RAL	34	7	261	35	9.66
N.W.	8	3	63	25*	12.60
B&H	10	3	74	28	10.57

CAREER: BOWLING

	O.	M.	R.	W.	AV.
TEST	1196.1	253	3201	134	23.88
1ST	4826	859	14828	642	23.09
INT	776.3	61	2977	101	29.47
RAL	432.3	30	1764	84	21.00
N.W.	136	17	451	25	18.04
B&H	166.3	21	574	19	30.21

88. What is Andy Lloyd's first name?

89. What is Viv Richards's first name?

90. What is Tim Robinson's first name?

WAQAR YOUNIS Surrey

Name: Waqar Younis
Role: Right-hand bat, right-arm fast bowler
Born: 16 November 1971, Burewala, Punjab
Height: 5ft 11in **Weight:** 12st
Nickname: Wicky
County debut: 1990
Test debut: 1989–90
Tests: 5
One-Day Internationals: 23
50 wickets in a season: 1
1st-Class 50s scored: 1
1st-Class 5 w. in innings: 7
1st-class 10 w. in match: 2
Place in bowling averages: 7th av. 23.80
Strike rate: 44.52 (career 49.05)
1st-Class catches: 4 (career 7)
Marital status: Single
Education: Pakistani College, Sharjah; Sadiq Public School, Burewala
Qualifications: Studying law
Off-season: Playing for Pakistan
Overseas tours: Pakistan to India, Australia and Sharjah 1989–90
Overseas teams played for: United Bank
Cricketers particularly admired: Imran Khan, Wasim Akram, Geoff Arnold, Alec Stewart
Other sports followed: Football, badminton, squash

LAST SEASON: BATTING

	I.	N. O.	R.	H. S.	AV.
TEST					
1ST	9	7	56	14	28.00
INT					
RAL	2	2	1	1*	-
N.W.	-	-	-	-	-
B&H	1	0	4	4	4.00

LAST SEASON: BOWLING

	O.	M.	R.	W.	AV.
TEST					
1ST	422	70	1357	57	23.80
INT					
RAL	82.2	1	396	31	12.77
N.W.	24	5	62	5	12.40
B&H	11	0	55	2	27.50

CAREER: BATTING

	I.	N. O.	R.	H. S.	AV.
TEST	6	1	43	18	8.60
1ST	32	16	280	51	17.50
INT	8	4	38	20*	9.50
RAL	2	2	1	1*	-
N.W.	-	-	-	-	-
B&H	1	0	4	4	4.00

CAREER: BOWLING

	O.	M.	R.	W.	AV.
TEST	141	23	461	10	46.10
1ST	831.5	121	2834	109	26.00
INT	175	16	688	37	18.59
RAL	82.2	1	396	31	12.77
N.W.	24	5	62	5	12.40
B&H	11	0	55	2	27.50

Relaxations: 'Sleeping and family get-togethers.'

Extras: Made Test debut for Pakistan v India aged 17, taking 4 for 80 at Karachi. Signed by Surrey during 1990 season on recommendation of Imran Khan, who had first seen him bowling on TV. Made county debut in B & H quarter-final v Lancashire. Martin Crowe described his bowling during Pakistan's series with New Zealand as the best display of fast bowling he had ever seen

Opinions on cricket: 'In favour of 16 four-day matches in county championship. There should be no over-rate fines.'

Best batting: 51 United Bank v PIA, Lahore 1989–90

Best bowling: 7–73 Surrey v Warwickshire, The Oval 1990

WARD, D. M.   Surrey

Name: David Mark Ward
Role: Right-hand bat, wicket-keeper
Born: 10 February 1961, Croydon
Height: 6ft **Weight:** 13st 2lbs
Nickname: Cocker, Wardy, Jaws, Gnasher
County debut: 1985
1000 runs in a season: 1
1st-Class 50s scored: 11
1st-Class 100s scored: 10
1st-class 200s scored: 2
One-Day 50s: 10
One-Day 100s: 1
Place in batting averages: 5th av. 76.74 (1989 133rd av. 25.33)
1st-Class catches: 32 & 3 stumpings (career 87 & 3)
Parents: Thomas and Dora Kathleen
Marital status: Single
Education: Haling Manor High School; Croydon Technical College
Qualifications: 2 O-levels, Advanced City and Guilds in Carpentry and Joinery
Cricketers particularly admired: Graham Gooch, Ian Botham, Viv Richards, John Goodey (Banstead CC), Neil Silberry
Other sports followed: Charlton FC – 'seem to spend most of the time with my hands over my eyes!'
Relaxations: Eating out, watching TV, movies, jazz, golf, greyhound racing
Extras: First Surrey batsman since John Edrich to score 2000 runs in a season in 1990 and shared county record stand of 413 for third wicket with Darren Bicknell v Kent at Canterbury
Opinions on cricket: 'Why can't we work where we want? '

Best batting performance: 263 Surrey v Kent, Canterbury 1990

LAST SEASON: BATTING

	I.	N.O.	R.	H.S.	AV.
TEST					
1ST	34	7	2072	263	76.74
INT					
RAL	15	3	394	102*	32.83
N.W.	1	0	11	11	11.00
B&H	5	2	145	46*	48.33

CAREER: BATTING

	I.	N.O.	R.	H.S.	AV.
TEST					
1ST	122	19	4179	263	40.57
INT					
RAL	68	13	1468	102*	26.69
N.W.	8	0	242	97	30.25
B&H	12	2	191	46*	19.10

WARD, T. R.   Kent

Name: Trevor Robert Ward
Role: Right-hand bat, off-spin bowler
Born: 18 January 1968, Farningham, Kent
Height: 5ft 11in **Weight:** 12st 10lbs
Nickname: Chikka
County debut: 1986
1000 runs in a season: 1
1st-Class 50s scored: 17
1st-Class 100s scored: 3
One-Day 50s: 6
Place in batting averages: 155th av. 31.96 (1989 60th av. 35.91)
1st-Class catches: 14 (career 36)
Parents: Robert Henry and Hazel Ann
Wife and date of marriage: Sarah Ann, 29 September 1990
Family links with cricket: Father played club cricket at Farningham
Education: Anthony Roper County Primary; Hextable Comprehensive
Qualifications: 7 O-levels
Off-season: Coaching
Overseas tours: England YCs to Sri Lanka 1987; Australia for Youth World Cup 1988
Cricketers particularly admired: Ian Botham, Richard Hadlee, Gordon Greenidge
Other sports followed: Football, most sports
Injuries: Damaged ankle ligaments (missed six weeks)
Relaxations: Watching films, fishing
Opinions on cricket: 'Four-day cricket is a must on better wickets and less travelling.'
Best batting: 175 Kent v Hampshire, Bournemouth 1990

Best bowling: 2–48 Kent v Worcestershire, Canterbury 1990

LAST SEASON: BATTING

	I.	N. O.	R.	H. S.	AV.
TEST					
1ST	28	1	863	175	31.96
INT					
RAL	11	0	311	80	28.27
N.W.	1	0	47	47	47.00
B&H	4	1	191	94	63.66

LAST SEASON: BOWLING

	O.	M.	R.	W.	AV.
TEST					
1ST	53	6	225	4	56.25
INT					
RAL	14	0	78	2	39.00
N.W.					
B&H					

CAREER: BATTING

	I.	N. O.	R.	H. S.	AV.
TEST					
1ST	89	7	2542	175	31.00
INT					
RAL	31	0	668	80	21.54
N.W.	5	0	183	83	36.60
B&H	10	2	309	94	38.62

CAREER: BOWLING

	O.	M.	R.	W.	AV.
TEST					
1ST	98.5	15	386	5	77.20
INT					
RAL	37	0	176	5	35.20
N.W.	12	0	58	1	58.00
B&H	2	0	10	0	-

WARNER, A. E.   Derbyshire

Name: Allan Esmond Warner
Role: Right-hand bat, right-arm
fast bowler, outfielder
Born: 12 May 1959, Birmingham
Height: 5ft 8in **Weight:** 10st
Nickname: Esis
County debut: 1982 (Worcs), 1985
(Derbys)
County cap: 1987 (Derbys)
1st-Class 50s scored: 11
1st-Class 5 w. in innings: 2
One-Day 50s: 1
Place in bowling averages: 100th av.
40.30 (1989 33rd av. 23.45)
Strike rate: 71.54 (career 62.62)
1st-Class catches: 2 (career 32)
Parents: Edgar and Sarah
Children: Alvin, 6 September 1980
Education: Tabernacle School,
St Kitts, West Indies
Qualifications: CSE Maths
Cricketers particularly admired: Malcolm Marshall, Michael Holding
Other sports followed: Football, boxing and athletics
Relaxations: Watching movies, music (soul, reggae and calypso)

Extras: Released by Worcestershire at end of 1984 and joined Derbyshire
Best batting: 91 Derbyshire v Leicestershire, Chesterfield 1986
Best bowling: 5–27 Worcestershire v Glamorgan, Worcester 1984

LAST SEASON: BATTING

	I.	N.O.	R.	H.S.	AV.
TEST					
1ST	19	2	160	59	9.41
INT					
RAL	7	3	72	28*	18.00
N.W.	1	1	1	1*	-
B&H	2	0	23	16	11.50

LAST SEASON: BOWLING

	O.	M.	R.	W.	AV.
TEST					
1ST	393.3	67	1330	33	40.30
INT					
RAL	101	0	538	16	33.62
N.W.	24	2	84	5	16.80
B&H	33	2	126	8	15.75

CAREER: BATTING

	I.	N.O.	R.	H.S.	AV.
TEST					
1ST	182	35	2544	91	17.30
INT					
RAL	65	16	667	68	13.61
N.W.	7	1	67	32	11.16
B&H	19	6	130	24*	10.00

CAREER: BOWLING

	O.	M.	R.	W.	AV.
TEST					
1ST	2713.5	531	8488	260	32.64
INT					
RAL	613.3	11	3167	103	30.74
N.W.	109.5	13	438	13	33.69
B&H	283.2	24	1172	46	25.47

WASIM AKRAM   Lancashire

Name: Wasim Akram
Role: Left-hand bat, left-arm
fast-medium bowler
Born: 3 June 1966, Lahore, Pakistan
Height: 6ft 3in **Weight:** 12st 7lbs
County debut: 1988
Test debut: 1984–85
Tests: 32
One-Day Internationals: 97
50 wickets in a season: 1
1st-Class 50s scored: 8
1st-Class 100s scored: 2
1st-Class 5 w. in innings: 20
1st-Class 10 w. in match: 4
One-Day 50s: 3
Place in batting averages: 263rd av.
12.27 (1989 175th av. 20.58)
Place in bowling averages: 96th av. 40.00
(1989 5th av. 17.73)
Strike rate: 76.50 (career 58.21)
1st-Class catches: 0 (career 28)
Education: Islamia College

Off-season: Playing for Pakistan

Overseas tours: Pakistan U–23 to Sri Lanka 1984–85; Pakistan to New Zealand 1984–85; Sri Lanka 1985–86; India 1986–87; England 1987; West Indies 1987–88; Australia 1989–90

Overseas teams played for: PACO 1984–86; Lahore Whites 1985–86

Extras: His second first-class match was playing for Pakistan on tour in New Zealand. Imran Khan wrote of him: 'I have great faith in Wasim Akram. I think he will become a great all-rounder, as long as he realises how much hard work is required. As a bowler he is extremely gifted, and has it in him to be the best left-armer since Alan Davidson.' Hit maiden Test 100 v Australia 1989–90 during stand of 191 with Imran

Best batting: 123 Pakistan v Australia, Adelaide 1989–90

Best bowling: 7–42 World XI v MCC, Scarborough 1989

LAST SEASON: BATTING

	I.	N. O.	R.	H. S.	AV.
TEST					
1ST	11	0	135	32	12.27
INT					
RAL	8	1	175	50	25.00
N.W.	3	1	28	14	14.00
B&H	3	1	38	28	19.00

LAST SEASON: BOWLING

	O.	M.	R.	W.	AV.
TEST					
1ST	204	44	640	16	40.00
INT					
RAL	88.1	0	447	19	23.52
N.W.	50.1	3	182	10	18.20
B&H	31	0	98	6	16.33

CAREER: BATTING

	I.	N. O.	R.	H. S.	AV.
TEST	39	6	665	123	20.15
1ST	69	11	1298	116*	22.37
INT	68	14	763	86	14.12
RAL	29	7	567	56	25.77
N.W.	8	1	89	19	12.71
B&H	10	2	206	52	25.75

CAREER: BOWLING

	O.	M.	R.	W.	AV.
TEST	1169.3	293	2967	111	26.72
1ST	1480.4	324	3875	162	23.91
INT	805.3	67	3072	130	23.63
RAL	266.1	9	1138	61	18.65
N.W.	99.1	11	361	16	22.56
B&H	116.4	9	424	22	19.27

Name: Stuart Nicholas Varney Waterton
Role: Right-hand bat, wicket-keeper
Born: 6 December 1960, Dartford, Kent
Height: 6ft **Weight:** 'Variable'
Nickname: Domino
County debut: 1980 (Kent), 1986
(Northants), 1990 (Lancs)
1st-Class 50s scored: 3
Parents: Barry and Olive (deceased)
Marital status: Single
Family links with cricket: 'Father
is an avid armchair critic and has been
known to bowl mean beach leg-breaks.'
Education: Gravesend School for
boys; London School of Economics
Qualifications: 10 O-levels, 3
A-levels, BSc (Hons) Economics, NCA
coaching award
Career outside cricket: Economics
teacher; Non-customer Services
Manager for Gray-Nicholls
Off-season: 'Club Cricket Conference tour of Australasia and working for Grays.'
Cricketers particularly admired: Alan Knott, Bob Taylor, Glenn Turner, Barry
Richards, Graeme Pollock, 'anyone with the enthusiasm to maintain performance
over a county career with little prospect of further representative honours.'
Other sports followed: Hockey, golf, athletics, rugby – most sports but not darts,
horse racing or swimming – 'I'd rather watch paint dry.'
Injuries: Broken thumb in August – missed three Minor County matches

LAST SEASON: BATTING

	I.	N. O.	R.	H. S.	AV.		
TEST							
1ST	1	0	3	3	3.00		
INT							
RAL							
N.W.	1	0	0	0	0.00		
B&H	1	0	6	6	6.00		

LAST SEASON: WICKET-KEEPING

	CT	ST					
TEST							
1ST	4	0					
INT							
RAL							
N.W.	0	1					
B&H	1	0					

CAREER: BATTING

	I.	N. O.	R.	H. S.	AV.		
TEST							
1ST	48	10	757	58*	19.92		
INT							
RAL	6	3	74	28	24.66		
N.W.	4	1	97	92	32.33		
B&H	1	0	6	6	6.00		

CAREER: WICKET-KEEPING

	CT	ST					
TEST							
1ST	79	15					
INT							
RAL	12	5					
N.W.	2	1					
B&H	1	0					

Relaxations: 'Playing sport, sports psychology, nattering, films.'
Extras: Previously played for Kent and Northamptonshire; brought out of semi-retirement by SOS call; now plays Minor County cricket for Oxfordshire ('jealously guarding my amateur status'); scored over 1000 runs in both 1989 and 1990 – only done twice in previous twenty-five years; member of Saints CC
Opinions on cricket: 'Players should regard themselves more as entertainers. They are paid to do a job that many thousands of weekend cricketers would love to do, yet they seldom indicate that they are enjoying it. It is difficult being in the public eye but that is a choice the players have made. They owe more to the fans than most would admit.'
Best batting: 58* Northamptonshire v Worcestershire, Northampton 1986

WATKIN, S. L. Glamorgan

Name: Steven Llewellyn Watkin
Role: Right-hand bat, right-arm fast-medium bowler
Born: 13 September 1964, Duffryn, Rhondda, nr Port Talbot
Height: 6ft 3in **Weight:** 18st 8lbs
Nickname: Watty, Banger
County debut: 1986
County cap: 1989
50 wickets in a season: 2
1st-Class 5 w. in innings: 11
1st-Class 10 w. in match: 3
Place in batting averages: 272nd av. 11.00
Place in bowling averages: 92nd av. 39.30 (1989 40th av. 25.10)
Strike rate: 69.23 (career 61.69)
1st-Class catches: 6 (career 16)

Parents: John and Sandra
Marital status: Single
Family links with cricket: 'Brother plays local cricket.'
Education: Cymer Afan Comprehensive; Swansea College of Further Education; South Glamorgan Institute of Higher Education
Qualifications: 8 O-levels, 2 A-levels, BA degree in Human Movement Studies
Off-season: 'Looking for a job.'
Overseas tours: British Colleges to West Indies 1987; England A to Zimbabwe 1989–90
Cricketers particularly admired: Richard Hadlee, Dennis Lillee, 'all cricketers'
Other sports followed: Football, rugby and all except horse racing
Relaxations: Listening to music, a few beers, car mechanics, DIY

Extras: Joint-highest wicket-taker in 1989 with 94 wickets. Sister Lynda represents Great Britain at hockey

Opinions on cricket: 'The Reader ball should have 12 strands. More four-day cricket should be played. Genuine results can be gained more readily than in three-day cricket where too many results are achieved as a result of captains' agreements.'

Best batting: 31 Glamorgan v Leicestershire, Leicester 1989

Best bowling: 8–59 Glamorgan v Warwickshire, Edgbaston 1988

LAST SEASON: BATTING

	I.	N. O.	R.	H. S.	AV.
TEST					
1ST	25	8	187	25*	11.00
INT					
RAL	5	2	32	28	10.66
N.W.	1	1	6	6*	-
B&H	4	2	14	6	7.00

LAST SEASON: BOWLING

	O.	M.	R.	W.	AV.
TEST					
1ST	796.1	137	2712	69	39.30
INT					
RAL	88.3	5	470	17	27.64
N.W.	35	5	102	5	20.40
B&H	44	7	163	2	81.50

CAREER: BATTING

	I.	N. O.	R.	H. S.	AV.
TEST					
1ST	74	20	436	31	8.07
INT					
RAL	14	6	90	28*	11.25
N.W.	2	2	8	6*	-
B&H	8	5	23	6	7.66

CAREER: BOWLING

	O.	M.	R.	W.	AV.
TEST					
1ST	2231.1	464	6809	217	31.37
INT					
RAL	220.1	13	1103	38	29.02
N.W.	53	10	142	7	20.28
B&H	82.3	17	309	5	61.80

91. What is Paul Terry's first name?

92. Who came top of England's batting averages v India last season?

93. Who are Graeme and Rob Turner?

WATKINSON, M. Lancashire

Name: Michael Watkinson
Role: Right-hand bat, right-arm medium or off-break bowler
Born: 1 August 1961, Westhoughton
Height: 6ft 1 1/2in **Weight:** 13st
Nickname: Winker
County debut: 1982
County cap: 1987
50 wickets in a season: 2
1st-Class 50s scored: 29
1st-Class 100s scored: 2
1st-Class 5 w. in innings: 17
One-Day 50s: 8
Place in batting averages: 127th av. 35.90 (1989 162nd av. 22.31)
Place in bowling averages: 48th av. 33.57 (1989 54th av. 28.06)
Strike rate: 64.89 (career 63.67)
1st-Class catches: 8 (career 81)
Parents: Albert and Marian
Wife and date of marriage: Susan, 12 April 1986
Education: Rivington and Blackrod High School, Horwich
Qualifications: 8 O-levels, HTC Civil Engineering
Career outside cricket: Draughtsman
Cricketers particularly admired: Clive Lloyd, Imran Khan
Other sports followed: Football
Extras: Played for Cheshire CCC in Minor Counties, and NatWest Trophy (v Middlesex) 1982. Man of the Match in the first ever Refuge Assurance Cup

LAST SEASON: BATTING

	I.	N. O.	R.	H. S.	AV.
TEST					
1ST	23	2	754	138	35.90
INT					
RAL	13	6	203	33*	29.00
N.W.	4	1	162	90	54.00
B&H	7	1	174	50	29.00

LAST SEASON: BOWLING

	O.	M.	R.	W.	AV.
TEST					
1ST	508.2	122	1578	47	33.57
INT					
RAL	99	0	562	22	25.54
N.W.	46	3	181	6	30.16
B&H	62.4	3	261	12	21.75

CAREER: BATTING

	I.	N. O.	R.	H. S.	AV.
TEST					
1ST	232	31	4952	138	24.63
INT					
RAL	90	32	1352	58	23.31
N.W.	19	5	407	90	29.07
B&H	25	4	374	70*	17.81

CAREER: BOWLING

	O.	M.	R.	W.	AV.
TEST					
1ST	3618.5	660	11135	341	32.65
INT					
RAL	749.3	32	3589	119	30.16
N.W.	241.5	21	955	22	43.40
B&H	325.5	29	1363	41	33.24

Final 1988 and in 1990 Benson & Hedges Cup Final 1990
Best batting: 138 Lancashire v Yorkshire, Old Trafford 1990
Best bowling: 7–25 Lancashire v Sussex, Lytham 1987

WAUGH, M. E. Essex

Name: Mark Edward Waugh
Role: Right-hand bat, right-arm
medium pace bowler
Born: 2 June 1965, Canterbury,
New South Wales
Height: 6ft **Weight:** 13st 7lbs
Nickname: Bev, Rodger
County debut: 1988
One-Day Internationals: 8
1000 runs in a season: 2
1st-Class 50s scored: 30
1st-Class 100s scored: 23
1st-Class 200s scored: 2
1st-Class 5 w. in innings: 1
One-Day 50s: 9
One-Day 100s: 3
Place in batting averages: 6th av.
76.74 (1989 26th av. 43.91)
Place in bowling averages: 149th av.
64.25 (1989 63rd av. 29.64)
Strike rate: 95.50 (career 69.72)
1st-Class catches: 18 (career 107)
Parents: Rodger and Beverley
Marital status: Single
Family links with cricket: Uncle a 1st Grade cricketer in Sydney for
Bankstown/Canterbury. Twin brother Steve plays for Australia and played for
Somerset in 1988. Younger brother Dean played in Bolton League with Astley
Bridge in 1989 and made debut for NSW in 1990–91
Education: East Hills Boys High School
Qualifications: Higher School Certificate, cricket coach
Off-season: Playing cricket for New South Wales
Overseas teams played for: New South Wales 1985–90
Cricketers particularly admired: 'Allan Border for his guts and determination,
Doug Walters for his ability and sportsmanship, Greg Chappell – pure class.'
Other sports followed: 'Any – but mainly golf, football and horse racing.'
Relaxations: 'Sleeping, eating and gambling.'
Extras: Steve and Mark are only twins to score hundreds in the same innings of a
first-class match and to both play international cricket. Chosen as New South Wales

Cricketer of the Year, 1988 and Sheffield Shield Cricketer of the Year, jointly with D. Tazelaar of Queensland. First batsman to score a century on his Sunday League debut

Opinions on cricket: 'Too much cricket is played.'
Best batting: 207* Essex v Yorkshire, Middlesbrough 1990
Best bowling: 5–37 Essex v Northamptonshire, Northampton 1990

LAST SEASON: BATTING

	I.	N. O.	R.	H. S.	AV.
TEST					
1ST	33	6	2072	207*	76.74
INT					
RAL	15	0	552	111	36.80
N.W.	1	0	47	47	47.00
B&H	4	1	90	62	30.00

LAST SEASON: BOWLING

	O.	M.	R.	W.	AV.
TEST					
1ST	191	33	771	12	64.25
INT					
RAL	52	1	317	9	35.22
N.W.	5	1	17	0	-
B&H	6	0	25	1	25.00

CAREER: BATTING

	I.	N. O.	R.	H. S.	AV.
TEST					
1ST	150	23	6848	207*	53.92
INT	7	0	145	42	20.71
RAL	35	6	1201	112*	41.41
N.W.	2	0	47	47	23.50
B&H	10	1	302	93	33.55

CAREER: BOWLING

	O.	M.	R.	W.	AV.
TEST					
1ST	720.3	131	2544	62	41.03
INT					
RAL	85.1	1	493	16	30.81
N.W.	5	1	17	0	-
B&H	8	0	45	1	45.00

WEEKES, P. N. Middlesex

Name: Paul Nicholas Weekes
Role: Left-hand bat, off-break bowler
Born: 8 July 1969, Hackney
Height: 5ft 10in **Weight:** 10st 7lbs
Nickname: Weekesy, Twiddles
County debut: 1990
1st-Class 50s scored: 1
1st-Class catches: 3 (career 3)
Parents: Robert and Carol
Marital status: Single
Family links with cricket: Father played club cricket
Education: Homerton House Secondary School, Hackney
Qualifications: NCA cricket coach
Career outside cricket: 'Coaching cricket in the innner city schools.'
Off-season: 'Playing in Zimbabwe for five months.'

418

Cricketers particularly admired: David Gower, Richie Richardson
Other sports followed: Boxing
Relaxations: 'Dancing and listening to music.'
Opinions on cricket: 'There should be more entertainment for the spectators during lunch intervals, i. e. competitions for throwing distances and bowling speeds.'
Best batting: 51 Middlesex v Sussex, Lord's 1990
Best bowling: 2–115 Middlesex v Somerset, Uxbridge 1990

LAST SEASON / CAREER: BATTING

	I.	N. O.	R.	H. S.	AV.
TEST					
1ST	3	0	75	51	25.00
INT					
RAL	1	1	29	29*	-
N.W.					
B&H	-	-	-	-	-

LAST SEASON / CAREER: BOWLING

	O.	M.	R.	W.	AV.
TEST					
1ST	80	17	264	4	66.00
INT					
RAL	16	1	92	2	46.00
N.W.					
B&H	7	1	27	0	-

WELLS, A. P. Sussex

Name: Alan Peter Wells
Role: Right-hand bat, right-arm medium bowler
Born: 2 October 1961, Newhaven
Height: 6ft **Weight:** 12st 4lbs
Nickname: Morph, Bomber
County debut: 1981
County cap: 1986
1000 runs in a season: 5
1st-Class 50s scored: 50
1st-Class 100s scored: 14
One-Day 50s: 24
Place in batting averages: 91st av. 43.54 (1989 15th av. 52.54)
1st-Class catches: 12 (career 100)
Parents: Ernest William Charles and Eunice Mae
Wife and date of marriage: Melanie Elizabeth, 26 September 1988
Family links with cricket: Father played for many years for local club. Eldest brother Ray plays club cricket. Colin plays for Sussex
Education: Tideway Comprehensive, Newhaven
Qualifications: 5 O-levels, NCA coaching certificate
Overseas tours: Unofficial England team to South Africa 1989–90
Overseas teams played for: Border, South Africa 1981–82

Injuries: Broken thumb – missed one game
Relaxations: Listening to music, eating out, drinking in country pubs
Extras: Played for England YCs v India 1981. Banned from Test cricket for joining tour of South Africa. 'Scored 100 in first game of acting captain v Leicestershire in 1990 – we won the match.'
Best batting: 161* Sussex v Kent, Hove 1987
Best bowling: 3–67 Sussex v Worcestershire, Worcester 1987

LAST SEASON: BATTING

	I.	N. O.	R.	H. S.	AV.
TEST					
1ST	44	7	1611	144*	43.54
INT					
RAL	13	2	413	98	37.54
N.W.	1	0	85	85	85.00
B&H	4	0	150	74	37.50

CAREER: BATTING

	I.	N. O.	R.	H. S.	AV.
TEST					
1ST	315	53	9232	161*	35.23
INT					
RAL	113	14	2578	98	26.04
N.W.	17	4	406	86*	31.23
B&H	30	2	788	74	28.14

LAST SEASON: BOWLING

	O.	M.	R.	W.	AV.
TEST					
1ST	39	8	169	3	56.33
INT					
RAL					
N.W.					
B&H					

CAREER: BOWLING

	O.	M.	R.	W.	AV.
TEST					
1ST	126.1	15	575	8	71.87
INT					
RAL	10.2	0	69	4	17.25
N.W.	1	0	1	0	-
B&H	10	1	72	3	24.00

94. India had four Test captains in the same team against England last summer. Who were they?

95. How many Derbyshire-born players were on the Derbyshire staff last season?

96. Who is Chairman of the Cricketers' Association?

WELLS, C. M.   Sussex

Name: Colin Mark Wells
Role: Right-hand bat, right-arm medium
bowler, county vice-captain
Born: 3 March 1960, Newhaven
Height: 6ft **Weight:** 13st
Nickname: Bomber, Dougie
County debut: 1979
County cap: 1982
One-Day Internationals: 2
1000 runs in a season: 6
50 wickets in a season: 2
1st-Class 50s scored: 55
1st-Class 100s scored: 20
1st-Class 200s scored: 1
1st-Class 5 w. in innings: 6
One-Day 50s: 23
One-Day 100s: 4

Place in batting averages: 145th av.
33.32 (1989 80th av. 32.93)
Place in bowling averages: 154th av.
72.76 (1989 51st av. 27.57)
Strike rate: 132.00 (career 72.51)
1st-Class catches: 5 (career 82)
Parents: Ernest William Charles and Eunice Mae
Wife and date of marriage: Celia, 25 September 1982
Children: Jessica Louise, 2 October 1987
Family links with cricket: Father, Billy, had trials for Sussex and played for Sussex
Cricket Association. Eldest brother Ray plays club cricket and youngest brother Alan
plays for Sussex
Education: Tideway Comprehensive School, Newhaven
Qualifications: 9 O-levels, 2 CSEs, 1 A-level, intermediate coaching certificate
Overseas tours: With England to Sharjah 1985
Overseas teams played for: Border 1980–81; Western Province 1984–85
Other sports followed: Football, rugby, hockey, basketball, tennis, table tennis
Relaxations: Sea-angling, philately, listening to music
Extras: Played in three John Player League matches in 1978. Was recommended to
Sussex by former Sussex player, Ian Thomson. Vice-captain since 1988
Opinions on cricket: 'Should play four-day cricket as soon as possible. Strongly
believe that we cram in too much cricket, which must have a detrimental effect on
all, especially the fast bowlers, particularly long term.'
Best batting: 203 Sussex v Hampshire, Hove 1984
Best bowling: 7–65 Sussex v Kent, Hove 1990

	I.	N.O.	R.	H.S.	AV.
TEST					
1ST	33	5	933	113*	33.32
INT					
RAL	14	0	220	64	15.71
N.W.	-	-	-	-	-
B&H	4	1	229	101	76.33

LAST SEASON: BOWLING

	O.	M.	R.	W.	AV.
TEST					
1ST	374	68	1237	17	72.76
INT					
RAL	106.5	6	384	7	54.85
N.W.	9	6	6	1	6.00
B&H	42	4	190	1	190.00

CAREER: BATTING

	I.	N.O.	R.	H.S.	AV.
TEST					
1ST	408	62	11567	203	33.43
INT	2	0	22	17	11.00
RAL	149	21	3421	104*	26.72
N.W.	22	3	415	76	21.84
B&H	45	5	1253	117	31.32

CAREER: BOWLING

	O.	M.	R.	W.	AV.
TEST					
1ST	4399.2	1025	12443	364	34.18
INT					
RAL	892.1	67	3302	112	29.48
N.W.	198.4	30	570	13	43.84
B&H	272	36	1049	33	31.78

WELLS, V. J.   Kent

Name: Vincent John Wells
Role: Right-hand bat, right-arm medium pace bowler, wicket-keeper
Born: 6 August 1965, Dartford
Height: 6ft **Weight:** 13st
Nickname: Wellsy, Vinny, Whiplash
County debut: 1987
1st-Class 50s scored: 2
1st-class 5 w. in innings: 1
Place in batting averages: 206th av. 23.46
Place in bowling averages: 4th av. 21.41
Strike rate: 42.50 (career 48.42)
1st-Class catches: 8 (career 10)
Parents: Pat and Jack
Wife and date of marriage: Debbie, 14 October 1989
Family links with cricket: Brother plays club cricket in Kent League
Education: Downs School, Dartford; Sir William Nottidge School, Whitstable
Qualifications: 1 O-level, 8 CSEs
Off-season: 'Winter at Avendale CC, Cape Town.'
Cricketers particularly admired: David Gower, Ian Botham
Other sports followed: Football. 'Enjoy most sports.'
Relaxations: 'Eating out; keeping fit; reading.'
Extras: Was a schoolboy footballer with Leyton Orient. Scored 100* on NatWest debut v Oxfordshire

Opinions on cricket: 'Four-day cricket is a good idea. Sunday League must be livened up, e. g. coloured clothing, names on shirts. Too much 2nd XI is played on poor wickets in contrast to the improving standard in first-class cricket.'
Best batting: 58 Kent v Hampshire, Bournemouth 1990
Best bowling: 5–43 Kent v Leicestershire, Leicester 1990

LAST SEASON: BATTING

	I.	N. O.	R.	H. S.	AV.
TEST					
1ST	15	0	352	58	23.46
INT					
RAL	3	1	36	16	18.00
N.W.	1	1	100	100*	-
B&H					

LAST SEASON: BOWLING

	O.	M.	R.	W.	AV.
TEST					
1ST	85	19	257	12	21.41
INT					
RAL	1	0	5	0	-
N.W.					
B&H					

CAREER: BATTING

	I.	N. O.	R.	H. S.	AV.
TEST					
1ST	21	1	395	58	19.75
INT					
RAL	5	2	48	16	16.00
N.W.	1	1	100	100*	-
B&H	1	1	15	15*	-

CAREER: BOWLING

	O.	M.	R.	W.	AV.
TEST					
1ST	113	25	369	14	26.35
INT					
RAL	23	1	73	7	10.42
N.W.					
B&H	7	1	33	0	-

WESTON, M. J. Worcestershire

Name: Martin John Weston
Role: Right-hand bat, right-arm medium bowler
Born: 8 April 1959, Worcester
Height: 6ft 1in **Weight:** 15st
Nickname: Wesso
County debut: 1979
County cap: 1986
1000 runs in a season: 1
1st-Class 50s scored: 26
1st-Class 100s scored: 3
One-Day 50s: 14
One-Day 100s: 1
Place in batting averages: 274th av. 10.00 (1989 138th av. 24.89)
1st-Class catches: 1 (career 71)
Parents: John Franklyn and Sheila Margaret
Marital status: Single
Family links with cricket: 'Father was a pretty useful all-rounder for the British

Waterways team.'

Education: St George's C of E Junior; Samuel Southall Secondary Modern, – 'and Worcester's Pavilion Bar!'

Qualifications: City & Guilds and Advanced Crafts in Bricklaying

Cricketers particularly admired: Basil D'Oliveira

Other sports followed: Horse racing, football

Relaxations: Reading *Sporting Life*

Opinions on cricket: 'Four-day cricket is a must. Certain one-day games should be played in coloured clothing, with a white ball.'

Best batting: 145* Worcestershire v Northamptonshire, Worcester 1984

Best bowling: 4–24 Worcestershire v Warwickshire, Edgbaston 1988

LAST SEASON: BATTING

	I.	N. O.	R.	H. S.	AV.
TEST					
1ST	10	1	90	38*	10.00
INT					
RAL	10	1	171	90	19.00
N.W.	3	0	152	98	50.66
B&H	4	1	179	99*	59.66

LAST SEASON: BOWLING

	O.	M.	R.	W.	AV.
TEST					
1ST	21	3	74	1	74.00
INT					
RAL	62	0	279	6	46.50
N.W.	4	0	20	0	-
B&H	6	1	21	1	21.00

CAREER: BATTING

	I.	N. O.	R.	H. S.	AV.
TEST					
1ST	239	20	5279	145*	24.10
INT					
RAL	103	15	1780	109	20.22
N.W.	20	4	571	98	35.68
B&H	33	2	714	99*	23.03

CAREER: BOWLING

	O.	M.	R.	W.	AV.
TEST					
1ST	1042.1	254	2998	78	38.43
INT					
RAL	483.3	17	2057	67	30.70
N.W.	108.2	13	410	10	41.00
B&H	96.1	9	346	12	28.83

WHITAKER, J. J. — Leicestershire

Name: John James Whitaker
Role: Right-hand bat, off-break
bowler, county vice-captain
Born: 5 May 1962, Skipton, Yorkshire
Height: 6ft **Weight:** 13st
County debut: 1983
County cap: 1986
Test debut: 1986–87
Tests: 1
One-Day Internationals: 2
1000 runs in a season: 7
1st-Class 50s scored: 49
1st-Class 100s scored: 23
1st-Class 200s scored: 1
One-Day 50s: 16
One-Day 100s: 3
Place in batting averages: 77th av.
45.30 (1989 48th av. 37.88)
1st-Class catches: 14 (career 116)
Parents: John and Anne
Family links with cricket: Father plays club cricket for Skipton
Education: Uppingham School
Qualifications: 7 O-levels
Overseas tours: England to Australia 1986–87; England A to Zimbabwe and Kenya
1989–90
Cricketers particularly admired: Geoff Boycott, Dennis Amiss
Other sports followed: Football, hockey, tennis, Leicester Tigers rugby
Relaxations: Discos, music, reading, eating out
Extras: One of *Wisden's* Five Cricketers of the Year, 1986
Opinions on cricket: 'There is too much first-class cricket.'
Best batting: 200* Leicestershire v Nottinghamshire, Leicester 1986
Best bowling: 1–41 Leicestershire v Essex, Leicester 1986

LAST SEASON: BATTING

	I.	N. O.	R.	H. S.	AV.
TEST					
1ST	45	6	1767	124*	45.30
INT					
RAL	14	1	422	83	32.46
N.W.	1	0	24	24	24.00
B&H	3	0	99	46	33.00

CAREER: BATTING

	I.	N. O.	R.	H. S.	AV.
TEST	1	0	11	11	11.00
1ST	285	37	9873	200*	39.81
INT	2	1	48	44*	48.00
RAL	86	11	2453	132	32.70
N.W.	14	0	503	155	35.92
B&H	25	2	570	73*	24.78

WHITE, C.   Yorkshire

Name: Craig White
Role: Right-hand bat, off-spin bowler,
cover fieldsman
Born: 16 December 1969, Morley,
Yorkshire
Height: 6ft **Weight:** 12st
Nickname: Chalkey
County debut: 1990
1st-Class 5 w. in innings: 1
Place in batting averages: 256th av.
14.11
Place in bowling averages: 115th av.
46.76
Strike rate: 73.38 (career 73.38)
1st-Class catches: 4 (career 4)
Parents: Fred Emsley and Cynthia
Anne
Marital status: Single
Family links with cricket: Father
played with Pudsey St Lawrence
Education: Flora Hill High School and
Bendigo Senior High School (Victoria, Australia)
Career outside cricket: 'Member of Victorian Institute of Sport.'
Off-season: 'I'll always travel back to Australia to play in Victoria.'
Overseas tours: Australian YCs to West Indies 1990
Overseas teams played for: Victoria (debut 1990–91)
Cricketers particularly admired: Greg Chappell, Allan Border, Dean Jones
Other sports followed: Australian Rules football, tennis, golf
Injuries: 'Missed a couple of weeks after being hit in the mouth by Tony Merrick.'
Relaxations: 'Enjoy driving in the countryside or the bush; enjoy reading on the
beach at Surfers Paradise, Queensland, Australia.'
Extras: Recommended to Yorkshire CCC by Victorian Cricket Academy. Eligible
to play for Yorkshire as he was born in the county. 'Fred Trueman and I are the only
Yorkshire players to debut in the firsts before the seconds.'
Opinions on cricket: 'I would love to see South Africa return to Test cricket.'

LAST SEASON / CAREER: BATTING

	I.	N. O.	R.	H. S.	AV.
TEST					
1ST	11	2	127	38	14.11
INT					
RAL	3	3	76	30*	-
N.W.					
B&H	2	1	18	17*	18.00

LAST SEASON / CAREER: BOWLING

	O.	M.	R.	W.	AV.
TEST					
1ST	159	23	608	13	46.76
INT					
RAL	24.1	0	165	5	33.00
N.W.					
B&H	9	0	31	1	31.00

Best batting: 38 Yorkshire v Northamptonshire, Northampton 1990
Best bowling: 5–73 Yorkshire v Surrey, Harrogate 1990

WHITTICASE, P.   Leicestershire

Name: Philip Whitticase
Role: Right-hand bat, wicket-keeper
Born: 15 March 1965, Birmingham
Height: 5ft 8in **Weight:** 10st 7lbs
Nickname: Jasper, Tracy, Roland Rat
County debut: 1984
County cap: 1987
1st-Class 50s scored: 11
Parents: Larry Gordon and Ann
Marital status: Single
Family links with cricket: Grandfather
and father club cricketers (both
wicket-keepers)
Education: Buckpool Secondary;
Crestwood Comprehensive
Qualifications: 5 O-levels, 4 CSEs,
coaching certificate
Cricketers particularly admired: Bob
Taylor, Alan Knott, Philip DeFreitas,
Dennis Amiss
Other sports followed: Football, table tennis, golf. Schoolboy with Birmingham
City FC
Relaxations: Football, golf, listening to music. 'I'm interested in most sports. A
good night out. Playing cards is amusing especially when Les Taylor and Jon Agnew

LAST SEASON: BATTING

	I.	N. O.	R.	H. S.	AV.
TEST					
1ST	7	2	39	11*	7.80
INT					
RAL	2	0	40	38	20.00
N.W.					
B&H	2	1	52	45	52.00

LAST SEASON: WICKET-KEEPING

	CT	ST			
TEST					
1ST	13	0			
INT					
RAL	3	0			
N.W.					
B&H	4	0			

CAREER: BATTING

	I.	N. O.	R.	H. S.	AV.
TEST					
1ST	134	31	2281	71	22.14
INT					
RAL	29	5	270	38	11.25
N.W.	6	1	67	32	13.40
B&H	11	5	189	45	31.50

CAREER: WICKET-KEEPING

	CT	ST			
TEST					
1ST	240	9			
INT					
RAL	49	4			
N.W.	12	0			
B&H	23	1			

are involved.'

Extras: Was Derek Underwood's last first-class victim

Opinions on cricket: 'I would like to see 16 four-day games, so that you play every county just once, during the week. Have the weekends purely for one-day cricket, Refuge League on a Sunday, and have a new competition on a Saturday, possibly involving coloured clothing.'

Best batting: 71 Leicestershire v Somerset, Leicester 1988

WILD, D. J.   Northamptonshire

Name: Duncan James Wild
Role: Left-hand bat, right-arm medium bowler
Born: 28 November 1962, Northampton
Height: 6ft **Weight:** 12st 7lbs
Nickname: Oscar, Wildy, Spunko
County debut: 1980
County cap: 1986
1st-Class 50s scored: 13
1st-Class 100s scored: 5
One-Day 50s: 9
1st-Class catches: 0 (career 40)
Parents: John and Glenys
Marital status: Single
Family links with cricket: Father played for Northamptonshire
Education: Cherry Orchard Middle; Northampton School for Boys
Qualifications: 7 O-levels. Diploma in international trade
Jobs outside cricket: Proprietor of promotional clothing business
Off-season: Running own business in Northampton
Overseas tours: England YCs to West Indies 1980
Cricketers particularly admired: David Gower, Richard Hadlee, Geoff Cook, Martin Crowe
Other sports followed: Rugby, soccer, squash, golf
Relaxations: 'Shopping at Tesco's; drinking Guinness.'
Extras: Played for England YCs v India in 1981 and West Indies in 1982. Retired at end of 1990 season to concentrate on his clothing business
Opinions on cricket: 'Play all four-day games; play each county once; start games on a Saturday.'
Best batting: 144 Northamptonshire v Lancashire, Southport 1984
Best bowling: 4–4 Northamptonshire v Cambridge University, Fenner's 1986

LAST SEASON: BATTING

	I.	N. O.	R.	H. S.	AV.
TEST					
1ST	4	0	80	43	20.00
INT					
RAL	12	2	142	48*	14.20
N.W.					
B&H	3	0	15	15	5.00

LAST SEASON: BOWLING

	O.	M.	R.	W.	AV.
TEST					
1ST	21.5	6	74	1	74.00
INT					
RAL	44.4	0	243	10	24.30
N.W.					
B&H	8	2	33	0	-

CAREER: BATTING

	I.	N. O.	R.	H. S.	AV.
TEST					
1ST	167	21	3688	144	25.26
INT					
RAL	79	24	1150	91	20.90
N.W.	27	5	530	91	24.09
B&H	23	7	247	48	15.43

CAREER: BOWLING

	O.	M.	R.	W.	AV.
TEST					
1ST	899.5	85	2910	66	44.09
INT					
RAL	476.5	13	2337	83	28.15
N.W.	122.3	16	424	14	30.28
B&H	209	7	712	23	30.95

WILLEY, P.　　　　　Leicestershire

Name: Peter Willey
Role: Right-hand bat, off-break bowler
Born: 6 December 1949, Sedgefield, Co Durham
Height: 6ft 1in **Weight:** 13st
Nickname: Chin, Will
County debut: 1966 (Northants), 1984 (Leics)
County cap: 1971 (Northants), 1984 (Leics)
Benefit: 1981 (31,400)
Test debut: 1976
Tests: 26
One-Day Internationals: 26
1000 runs in a season: 10
50 wickets in a season: 2
1st-Class 50s scored: 101
1st-Class 100s scored: 44
1st-Class 200s scored: 1
1st-Class 5 w. in innings: 26
1st-Class 10 w. in match: 3
One-Day 50s: 63
One-Day 100s: 9
Place in batting averages: 140th av. 33.82 (1989 108th av. 28.94)
Place in bowling averages: 120th av. 47.43 (1989 44th av. 26.62)
Strike rate: 110.00 (career 76.81)

1st-Class catches: 10 (career 229)
Parents: Oswald and Maisie
Wife and date of marriage: Charmaine, 23 September 1971
Children: Heather Jane, 11 September 1985
Family links with cricket: Father played local club cricket in County Durham
Education: Secondary School, Seaham, County Durham
Overseas tours: England to Australia and India 1979–80; West Indies 1980–81 and 1985–86; with unofficial England XI to South Africa 1981–82
Overseas teams played for: Eastern Province, South Africa 1982–85
Cricketers particularly admired: Bishen Bedi, Geoffrey Boycott
Other sports followed: Football, golf, rugby
Relaxations: Reading, taking Irish Setter for long walks and shooting, gardening
Extras: With Wayne Larkins, received 2016 pints of beer (seven barrels) from a brewery in Northampton as a reward for their efforts in Australia with England in 1979–80. Youngest player ever to play for Northamptonshire CCC at 16 years 180 days v Cambridge U in 1966. Banned from Test cricket for three years for joining England rebel tour of South Africa in 1982. Left Northamptonshire at end of 1983 and moved to Leicestershire as vice-captain. Appointed Leicestershire captain for 1987, but resigned after only one season
Opinions on cricket: 'Good pitches is the only way to get good cricketers. Four-day cricket won't make people better cricketers. Young players have things made too easy for them.'
Best batting: 227 Northamptonshire v Somerset, Northampton 1976
Best bowling: 7–37 Northamptonshire v Oxford University, The Parks 1975

LAST SEASON: BATTING

	I.	N. O.	R.	H. S.	AV.
TEST					
1ST	40	6	1150	177	33.82
INT					
RAL	10	1	259	68*	28.77
N.W.	1	1	72	72*	-
B&H	1	0	49	49	49.00

LAST SEASON: BOWLING

	O.	M.	R.	W.	AV.
TEST					
1ST	421.4	119	1091	23	47.43
INT					
RAL	58	0	303	9	33.66
N.W.	12	2	54	1	54.00
B&H	11	0	36	0	-

CAREER: BATTING

	I.	N. O.	R.	H. S.	AV.
TEST	50	6	1184	102*	26.90
1ST	850	110	22960	227	31.02
INT	24	1	538	64	23.39
RAL	256	19	6353	107	26.80
N.W.	47	7	1479	154	36.97
B&H	63	11	1689	88*	32.48

CAREER: BOWLING

	O.	M.	R.	W.	AV.
TEST	181.5	49	456	7	65.14
1ST	9432.4	2630	22503	744	30.24
INT	171.5	9	659	13	50.69
RAL	1508.2	124	6167	226	27.28
N.W.	467.3	62	1457	35	41.62
B&H	595.3	92	1661	44	37.75

WILLIAMS, N. F.   Middlesex

Name: Neil Fitzgerald Williams
Role: Right-hand bat, right-arm
fast-medium bowler
Born: 2 July 1962, Hopewell, St
Vincent, West Indies
Height: 5ft 11in **Weight:** 11st 7lbs
Nickname: Joe
County debut: 1982
County cap: 1984
Test debut: 1990
Tests: 1
50 wickets in a season: 3
1st-Class 50s scored: 10
1st-Class 5 w. in innings: 10
1st-Class 10 w. in match: 1
Place in batting averages: 215th av.
21.33 (1989 158th av. 22.64)
Place in bowling averages: 29th av.
29.96 (1989 78th av. 31.29)
Strike rate: 58.77 (career 53.24)
1st-Class catches: 4 (career 35)
Parents: Alexander and Aldreta
Marital status: Single
Family links with cricket: 'Uncle Joe was 12th man for St Vincent and played 1st
Division cricket.'
Education: Cane End Primary School, St Vincent; Acland Burghley School, Tufnell
Park
Qualifications: School Leaver's Certificate, 6 O-levels, 1 A-level

LAST SEASON: BATTING

	I.	N. O.	R.	H. S.	AV.
TEST	1	0	38	38	38.00
1ST	23	3	410	55*	20.50
INT					
RAL	6	3	46	12	15.33
N.W.	-	-	-	-	-
B&H	4	2	55	28	27.50

LAST SEASON: BOWLING

	O.	M.	R.	W.	AV.
TEST	41	5	148	2	74.00
1ST	488.1	93	1470	52	33.46
INT					
RAL	112	4	574	19	30.21
N.W.	41	3	219	0	
B&H	54	7	201	11	18.27

CAREER: BATTING

	I.	N. O.	R.	H. S.	AV.
TEST	1	0	38	38	38.00
1ST	170	40	2739	69*	21.06
INT					
RAL	39	14	377	43	15.08
N.W.	7	3	36	10	9.00
B&H	21	5	209	29*	13.06

CAREER: BOWLING

	O.	M.	R.	W.	AV.
TEST	41	5	148	2	74.00
1ST	3455.4	646	11331	392	28.90
INT					
RAL	562.3	16	2562	97	26.41
N.W.	130.1	17	520	13	40.00
B&H	333.5	30	1282	39	32.87

Overseas tours: English Counties to Zimbabwe 1985
Overseas teams played for: Windward Islands 1982–83 and 1989–90; Tasmania 1983–84
Cricketers particularly admired: Viv Richards, Andy Roberts, Michael Holding, Dennis Lillee, Malcolm Marshall, Lawrence Rowe
Other sports followed: Most
Relaxations: Reggae, soca, soul, cinema
Extras: Was on stand-by for England in New Zealand and Pakistan 1983–84. Test debut v India at The Oval in 1990
Best batting: 69* Middlesex v Hampshire, Lord's 1989
Best bowling: 7–55 English Counties XI v Zimbabwe, Harare 1984–85

WILLIAMS, R. C. J.   Gloucestershire

Name: Richard Charles James Williams
Role: Left-hand bat, wicket-keeper
Born: 8 August 1969, Bristol
Height: 5ft 9in **Weight:** 10st 5lbs
Nickname: Reggie
County debut: 1990
1st-Class 50s scored: 1
Parents: Michael and Angela
Marital status: Single
Family links with cricket: Dad played local cricket
Education: Clifton College Preparatory School, Millfield School
Off-season: 'Playing and coaching in Zimbabwe.'
Cricketers particularly admired: Andy Brassington, Jack Russell, Alan Knott
Other sports followed: 'Most sports.'
Best batting: 50* Gloucestershire v Indians, Bristol 1990

LAST SEASON / CAREER: BATTING

	I.	N. O.	R.	H. S.	AV.
TEST					
1ST	8	4	132	50*	33.00
INT					
RAL	-	-	-	-	-
N.W.					
B&H					

LAST SEASON / CAREER: WICKET-KEEPING

	CT	ST			
TEST					
1ST	27	4			
INT					
RAL	5	0			
N.W.					
B&H					

WILLIAMS, R. G.　　　Northamptonshire

Name: Richard Grenville Williams
Role: Right-hand bat, off-break
bowler
Born: 10 August 1957, Bangor, Wales
Height: 5ft 6in **Weight:** 12st
Nickname: Chippy
County debut: 1974
County cap: 1979
Benefit: 1989 (100,053)
1000 runs in a season: 6
1st-Class 50s scored: 55
1st-Class 100s scored: 17
1st-Class 5 w. in innings: 9
One-Day 50s: 21
Place in batting averages: 185th av.
26.95 (1989 145th av. 23.71)
Place in bowling averages: 85th av.
38.83
Strike rate: 83.70 (career 71.41)
1st-Class catches: 6 (career 98)
Parents: Gordon and Rhianwen
Wife and date of marriage: Helen Laura, 24 April 1982
Family links with cricket: Father played for Caernarvonshire and North Wales
Education: Ellesmere Port Grammar School
Career outside cricket: Qualified carpenter (self-employed)
Overseas tours: England YCs to West Indies 1976; English Counties to Zimbabwe
1985
Other sports followed: Golf

LAST SEASON: BATTING

	I.	N. O.	R.	H. S.	AV.
TEST					
1ST	26	5	566	96	26.95
INT					
RAL	8	3	99	35	19.80
N.W.	4	1	68	44	22.66
B&H	1	0	17	17	17.00

LAST SEASON: BOWLING

	O.	M.	R.	W.	AV.
TEST					
1ST	432.3	119	1204	31	38.83
INT					
RAL	47	0	273	4	68.25
N.W.	51	5	244	7	34.85
B&H					

CAREER: BATTING

	I.	N. O.	R.	H. S.	AV.
TEST					
1ST	433	62	11564	175*	31.17
INT					
RAL	132	24	2470	82	22.87
N.W.	30	6	560	94	23.33
B&H	38	9	916	83	31.58

CAREER: BOWLING

	O.	M.	R.	W.	AV.
TEST					
1ST	4380.1	1124	12380	368	33.64
INT					
RAL	474.2	25	2316	79	29.31
N.W.	216	34	745	33	22.57
B&H	227	32	826	27	30.59

Relaxations: Fly fishing, shooting, fly tying
Extras: Debut for 2nd XI in 1972 aged 14 years 11 months. Made maiden century in 1979 and then scored four centuries in five innings. Hat-trick v Gloucestershire, at Northampton 1980. Was first player to score a century against the 1980 West Indies touring team. Was stand-by for England tour to India 1981–82
Best batting: 175* Northamptonshire v Leicestershire, Leicester 1980
Best bowling: 7–73 Northamptonshire v Cambridge University, Fenner's 1980

WOOD, J. R. Hampshire

Name: Julian Ross Wood
Role: Left-hand bat, right-arm medium bowler
Born: 21 November 1968, Winchester, Hampshire
Height: 5ft 8in **Weight:** 13st 7lbs
Nickname: Woody, Fred
County debut: 1989
1st-Class 50s scored: 4
One-Day 50s: 1
1st-Class catches: 6 (career 7)
Parents: Ross and Susan Keysell
Marital status: Single
Family links with cricket: Father NCA coach, Minor Counties umpire, and also played in local league
Education: St Barts Prep School; Priors Court School; Leighton Park School
Qualifications: CSE, NCA coaching certificate
Off-season: 'Playing grade cricket in Australia for Newcastle City, Sydney. Plus getting very fit for the coming season.'
Cricketers particularly admired: Ian Botham, Robin Smith, Malcolm Marshall, Viv Richards
Other sports followed: 'Follow Man Utd and always look at the Southampton results – but only to have a laugh!'
Injuries: 'Badly torn tendons and ligaments in left ankle prevented me playing for last three months of season.'
Relaxations: 'Watching most sports, having a few beers with my mates, watching videos, music.'
Extras: Hit first ball in first-class cricket for four as he scored 65 on debut v Sussex. England Schools U–15, U–19. MCC Young Professionals groundstaff. Hampshire Young Player of the Year, 1989

Opinions on cricket: 'It is time the authorities realised that cricket today is changing for the better (money and one-day cricket).'
Best batting: 96 Hampshire v Northamptonshire, Northampton 1989
Best bowling: 1–5 Hampshire v Sussex, Southampton 1989

LAST SEASON: BATTING

	I.	N. O.	R.	H. S.	AV.
TEST					
1ST	2	0	28	17	14.00
INT					
RAL	1	0	18	18	18.00
N.W.					
B&H	1	1	43	43*	-

CAREER: BATTING

	I.	N. O.	R.	H. S.	AV.
TEST					
1ST	20	2	616	96	34.22
INT					
RAL	5	0	108	66	21.60
N.W.	1	1	3	3*	-
B&H	1	1	43	43*	-

WREN, T. N. Kent

Name: Timothy Neil Wren
Role: Right-hand bat, left-arm medium bowler
Born: 26 March 1970, Folkestone
Height: 6ft 3in **Weight:** 14st 7lbs
Nickname: Rott, Blockhead
County debut: 1989 (RAL), 1990 (first-class)
1st-Class catches: 2 (career 2)
Parents: James and Gillian
Marital status: Single
Family links with cricket: Father and brother played local cricket
Education: Lyminge Primary; Harvey Grammar School, Folkestone
Qualifications: 6 O-levels
Off-season: 'Working for my father as a plumber and getting fit.'
Cricketers particularly admired: John Lever, Ian Botham, Richard Hadlee

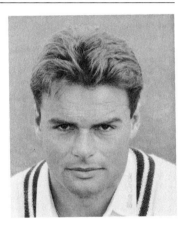

Other sports followed: Any sport, particularly rugby and golf
Injuries: Pulled side – out for three weeks
Relaxations: Listening to music, good food, films, socialising
Extras: First played for Kent 2nd XI in 1987, aged 17
Opinions on cricket: 'Four-day cricket is great, providing they change the ball; 2nd XI cricket should be played under first-class conditions with regard to pitches.'
Best batting: 16 Kent v Essex, Canterbury 1990
Best bowling: 2–78 Kent v Worcestershire, Canterbury 1990

LAST SEASON: BATTING

	I.	N.O.	R.	H.S.	AV.
TEST					
1ST	5	2	23	16	7.66
INT					
RAL	-	-	-	-	-
N.W.					
B&H					

LAST SEASON: BOWLING

	O.	M.	R.	W.	AV.
TEST					
1ST	122	14	489	6	81.50
INT					
RAL	6	0	31	1	31.00
N.W.					
B&H					

CAREER: BATTING

	I.	N.O.	R.	H.S.	AV.
TEST					
1ST	5	2	23	16	7.66
INT					
RAL	-	-	-	-	-
N.W.					
B&H					

CAREER: BOWLING

	O.	M.	R.	W.	AV.
TEST					
1ST	122	14	489	6	81.50
INT					
RAL	13.3	0	72	2	36.00
N.W.					
B&H					

WRIGHT, A. J. — Gloucestershire

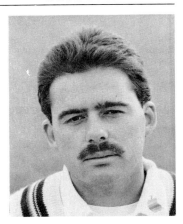

Name: Anthony John Wright
Role: Right-hand bat, off-break bowler, county captain
Born: 27 July 1962, Stevenage
Height: 6ft **Weight:** 14st
Nickname: Billy, Horace
County debut: 1982
County cap: 1987
1000 runs in a season: 3
1st-Class 50s scored: 36
1st-Class 100s scored: 8
One-Day 50s: 16
Place in batting averages: 192nd av. 26.02 (1989 107th av. 28.97)
1st-Class catches: 23 (career 110)
Parents: Michael and Patricia
Wife and date of marriage: Rachel, 21 December 1986
Children: Hannah, 3 April 1988
Education: Alleyn's School, Stevenage
Qualifications: 6 O-levels
Off-season: Working for Gloucestershire CCC
Cricketers particularly admired: Viv Richards, Ian Botham, Malcolm Marshall, Jack Russell
Other sports followed: All sports except motor racing
Relaxations: Eating out, reading, playing golf
Extras: Appointed captain of Gloucestershire for 1990

Opinions on cricket: 'Although 1990 may have had conditions in favour of batsmen, I believe the improvement in surfaces will improve our cricket at Test and county level over the next few years. With a slight adjustment to the ball and a more typical English summer in 1991, we will see a good balance between bat and ball. I would also like to see four-day games on covered pitches which would remove contrived finishes from the first-class game.'
Best batting: 161 Gloucestershire v Glamorgan, Bristol 1987
Best bowling: 1–16 Gloucestershire v Yorkshire, Harrogate 1989

LAST SEASON: BATTING

	I.	N.O.	R.	H.S.	AV.
TEST					
1ST	38	3	911	112	26.02
INT					
RAL	15	1	429	68	30.64
N.W.	3	0	141	92	47.00
B&H	3	0	122	97	40.66

CAREER: BATTING

	I.	N.O.	R.	H.S.	AV.
TEST					
1ST	278	17	6969	161	26.70
INT					
RAL	79	10	1570	81	22.75
N.W.	14	0	539	92	38.50
B&H	19	0	468	97	24.63

YATES, G.   Lancashire

Name: Gary Yates
Role: Right-hand bat, off-spin bowler
Born: 20 September 1967, Ashton-under-Lyne
Height: 6ft 1in **Weight:** 12st 11lbs
Nickname: Yugo, Pearly, Backyard
County debut: 1990
1st-Class 100s scored: 1
1st-Class catches: 1 (career 1)
Parents: Patricia and Alan
Marital status: Single
Family links with cricket: Father played in Lancashire Leagues
Education: Manchester Grammar School
Qualifications: 6 O-levels, Australian Coaching Council coach
Off-season: 'Playing and coaching in New Zealand.'
Cricketers particularly admired: Michael Atherton, Ian Botham, Viv Richards
Other sports followed: All sports, especially football, golf, rallying
Relaxations: Playing golf, watching football
Extras: Played for Worcestershire 2nd XI in 1987; made debut for Lancashire 2nd XI in 1988 and taken on to county staff in 1990; scored century on Championship debut v Nottinghamshire at Trent Bridge

Opinions on cricket: 'Would like to see more four-day cricket.'
Best batting: 106 Lancashire v Nottinghamshire, Trent Bridge 1990
Best bowling: 4–94 Lancashire v Sri Lanka, Old Trafford 1990

LAST SEASON / CAREER: BATTING

	I.	N. O.	R.	H. S.	AV.
TEST					
1ST	4	2	165	106	82.50
INT					
RAL					
N.W.					
B&H					

LAST SEASON / CAREER: BOWLING

	O.	M.	R.	W.	AV.
TEST					
1ST	167	38	420	8	52.50
INT					
RAL					
N.W.					
B&H					

97. Who was Sir Richard Hadlee's last victim in Test cricket?

98. How many runs did Gooch hit in the First Test v India last season?

99. Who has captained a Test team most times?

100. What is the longest recorded hit of a cricket ball, and by whom?

ROLL OF HONOUR

BRITANNIC ASSURANCE CHAMPIONSHIP

Final Table

		P	W	L	D	Bt	Bl	Pts
1	Middlesex (3)	22	10	1	11	73	55	288
2	Essex (2)	22	8	2	12	73	56	257
3	Hampshire (6)	22	8	4	10	67	48	243
4	Worcestershire (1)	22	7	1	14	70	58	240
5	Warwickshire (8)	22	7	7	8	55	64	231
6	Lancashire (4)	22	6	3	13	65	56	217
7	Leicestershire (13)	22	6	7	9	61	53	210
8	Glamorgan (17)	22	5	6	11	64	48	192
9	Surrey (12)	22	4	3	15	54	64	190
10	Yorkshire (16)	22	5	9	8	52	55	187
11	Northamptonshire (5)	22	4	9	9	61	60	185
12	Derbyshire (7)	22	6	7	9	58	52	181
13	Nottinghamshire (11)	22	4	8	10	51	58	173
14	Gloucestershire (9)	22	4	7	11	51	58	173
15	Somerset (14)	22	3	4	15	73	45	166
16	Kent (15)	22	3	6	13	69	35	152
17	Sussex (10)	22	3	9	10	51	44	143

Surrey's total includes 8 points for a drawn match where scores finished level
Derbyshire were penalised 25 points by the TCCB for preparing an unsatisfactory pitch
1989 positions shown in brackets

REFUGE ASSURANCE LEAGUE

Final Table

		P	W	L	NR	Away wins	Pts	Run rate
1	Derbyshire (5)	16	12	3	1	6	50	87.35
2	Lancashire (1)	16	11	3	2	7	48	100.18
3	Middlesex (9)	16	10	5	1	5	42	95.40
4	Nottinghamshire (6)	16	10	5	1	4	42	89.31
5	Hampshire (6)	16	9	5	2	4	40	88.82
6	Yorkshire (11)	16	9	6	1	4	38	83.60
7	Surrey (7)	16	9	6	1	3	38	90.39
8	Somerset (10)	16	8	8	0	4	32	91.25
9	Gloucestershire (16)	16	7	7	2	2	32	87.80
10	Worcestershire (2)	16	7	8	1	4	30	84.96
11	Kent (12)	16	7	8	1	3	30	85.94
12	Essex (3)	16	6	9	1	3	26	90.56
13	Sussex (13)	16	5	9	2	2	24	85.90
14	Warwickshire (15)	16	5	10	1	2	22	80.69
15	Glamorgan (17)	16	4	11	1	2	18	84.20
16	Leicestershire (14)	16	4	11	1	1	18	76.59
17	Northamptonshire (8)	16	3	12	1	1	14	86.40

1989 positions shown in brackets

BENSON & HEDGES CUP

Winners: Lancashire
Runners-up: Worcestershire
Losing semi-finalists: Somerset and Nottinghamshire

NATWEST TROPHY

Winners: Lancashire
Runners-up: Northamptonshire
Losing semi-finalists: Hampshire and Middlesex

REFUGE ASSURANCE CUP

Winners: Middlesex
Runners-up: Derbyshire
Losing semi-finalists: Lancashire and Nottinghamshire

ANSWERS

1. Middlesex
2. Derbyshire
3. Sussex
4. Northamptonshire
5. Lancashire
6. Lancashire
7. Middlesex
8. Warwickshire
9. A. V. Bedser of Surrey and England: 33
10. I. R. Bishop: 40.22
11. *Basingstoke Boy*
12. Philip Mead
13. Sir Richard Hadlee: 431
14. G. A. Gooch
15. They both scored the same number of first-class runs: 2072
16. 92
17. John Morris
18. L. A. Joseph
19. Bill Athey
20. Both were N. R. Taylor
21. R. A. Pick
22. N. J. Lenham
23. A. A. Metcalfe
24. Phil Neale of Worcestershire
25. Leicestershire II
26. 'George'
27. Viv Richards: 40
28. Neil Foster: 94
29. G. A. Gooch
30. 4005
31. Hampshire and Somerset
32. They all won their county caps in 1990
33. They all won their county caps in 1990
34. 24,000
35. He scored 116 not out
36. 9
37. Going for 12 consecutive innings without scoring a run
38. Hertfordshire and Berkshire
39. John Abrahams, ex-Lancashire, for Shropshire
40. Nobody
41. Ex-Essex Stuart Turner, at 47 years old: 40 wickets
42. Courtney Walsh for Gloucestershire v Northants
43. They all hit six County Championship 100s
44. Kapil Dev, for India v England, Lord's 1990
45. John Wright
46. They have all scored successive One-Day International 100s
47. 16
48. A. Sandham of Surrey and England
49. M. Azharuddin
50. Lord Griffiths, of Cambridge and Glamorgan
51. W. J. Edrich and D. C. S. Compton, both of Middlesex and England
52. 40,000
53. Animal
54. Walt or Walter
55. Kippy
56. Judge
57. Fox
58. Jets
59. Frog
60. Nobby
61. Somerset
62. Middlesex
63. Kent
64. Leicestershire
65. Lancashire
66. Lance Gibbs
67. G. P. Thorpe
68. Amiss
69. They were both among *Wisden's* Cricketers of the Year, 1990

70. Scotland
71. New South Wales
72. John Major MP
73. 'Caper'
74. Frank Chamberlain, ex-Northants
75. Chris Tavare
76. David Hughes
77. Martyn Moxon
78. Alan Butcher
79. Allan Lamb
80. Mark Nicholas
81. Bob Simpson
82. Sir Leonard Hutton of Yorkshire and England
83. George Ferris of Antigua and Leicestershire
84. Sir Richard Hadlee
85. Queensland
86. Geoff Pullar
87. Brian
88. Timothy
89. Isaac
90. Robert
91. Vivian
92. Robin Smith
93. This season's captains of Oxford and Cambridge respectively
94. Azharuddin, Vengsarkar, Kapil Dev, Shastri
95. Only three
96. Tim Curtis of Worcestershire and England
97. Devon Malcolm
98. 456
99. Clive Lloyd, West Indies
100. 175 yards from hit to pitch by Rev W. Fellowes, in practice at Oxford in 1856

INDEX OF PLAYERS
BY COUNTY

Jarvis, K. B. S.
Lawrence, D. V.
Lloyds, J. W.
Milburn, E. T.
Owen, P. A.
Romaines, P. W.
Russell, R. C.
Stovold, A. W.
Tedstone, G. A.
Walsh, C. A.
Williams, R. C. J.
Wright, A. J.

HAMPSHIRE

Ayling, J. R.
Aymes, A. N.
Bakker, P. J.
Connor, C. A.
Cox, R. M. F.
Gower, D. I.
James, K. D.
Joseph, L. A.
Marshall, M. D.
Maru, R. J.
Middleton, T. C.
Parks, R. J.
Scott, R. J.
Shine, K. J.
Smith, C. L.
Smith, R. A.
Terry, V. P.
Tremlett, T. M.
Turner, I. J.
Udal, S. D.
Wood, J. R.

KENT

Benson, M. R.
Cowdrey, C. S.
Cowdrey, G. R.
Davis, R. P.
De Villiers, P. S
Dobson, M. C.

Ealham, M. A.
Ellison, R. M.
Fleming, M. V.
Hinks, S. G.
Igglesden, I. P.
Kelleher, D. J. M.
Marsh, S. A.
Merrick, T. A.
Patel, M. M.
Penn, C.
Taylor, N. R.
Ward, T. R.
Wells, V. J.
Wren, T. N.

LANCASHIRE

Allott, P. J. W.
Atherton, M. A.
Austin, I. D.
Bramhall, S.
Crawley, J. P.
DeFreitas, P. A. J.
Fairbrother, N. H.
Fitton, J. D.
Fowler, G.
Hegg, W. K.
Hughes, D. P.
Jesty, T. E.
Lloyd, G. D.
Martin, P. J.
Mendis, G. D.
Patterson, B. P.
Speak, N. J.
Wasim Akram
Waterton, S. N. V.
Watkinson, M.
Yates, G.

LEICESTERSHIRE

Agnew, J. P.
Benjamin, W. K. M.
Benson, J. D. R.
Boon, T. J.

Briers, N. E.
Ferris, G. J. F.
Gidley, M. I.
Hawkes, C. J.
Hepworth, P. N.
Lewis, C. C.
Millns, D. J.
Mullally, A. D.
Nixon, P. A.
Parsons, G. J.
Potter, L.
Smith, B. F.
Taylor, L. B.
Whitaker, J. J.
Whitticase, P.
Willey, P.

Curran, K. M.
Davis, W. W.
Felton, N. A.
Fordham, A.
Govan, J. W.
Hughes, J. G.
Lamb, A. J.
Larkins, W.
Noon, W. M.
Penberthy, A. L.
Ripley, D.
Roberts, A. R.
Robinson, M. A.
Thomas, J. G.
Wild, D. J.
Williams, R. G.

MIDDLESEX

Brown, K. R.
Cowans, N. G.
Downton, P. R.
Emburey, J. E.
Farbrace, P.
Fraser, A. R. C.
Gatting, M. W.
Haynes, D. L.
Hughes, S. P.
Ramprakash, M. R.
Roseberry, M. A.
Taylor, C. W.
Taylor, N. R.
Thursfield, M. J.
Tufnell, P. C. R.
Weekes, P. N.
Williams, N. F.

NORTHAMPTONSHIRE

Ambrose, C. E. L.
Bailey, R. J.
Brown, S. J.
Capel, D. J.
Cook, G.
Cook, N. G. B.

NOTTINGHAMSHIRE

Afford, J. A.
Broad, B. C.
Cooper, K. E.
Evans, K. P.
Evans, R. J.
Field-Buss, M. G.
French, B. N.
Hemmings, E. E.
Johnson, P.
Martindale, D. J. R.
Mike, G. W.
Newell, M.
Pick, R. A.
Pollard, P.
Randall, D. W.
Robinson, R. T.
Saxelby, K.
Saxelby, M.
Stephenson, F. D.

SOMERSET

Bartlett, R. J.
Burns, N. D.
Cook, S. J.
Hallett, J. C.

Harden, R. J.
Hardy, J. J. E.
Hayhurst, A. N.
Lefebvre, R. P.
Mallender, N. A.
Roebuck, P. M.
Rose, G. D.
Swallow, I. G.
Tavare, C. J.
Townsend, G. T. J.
Trump, H. R. J.

Lenham, N. J.
Moores, P.
North, J. A.
Parker, P. W. G.
Pigott, A. C. S.
Remy, C. C.
Salisbury, I. D. K.
Smith, D. M.
Speight, M. P.
Wells, A. P.
Wells, C. M.

SURREY

Alikhan, R. I.
Atkins, P. D.
Bicknell, D. J.
Bicknell, M. P.
Clinton, G. S.
Feltham, M. A.
Gray, A. H.
Greig, I. A.
Kendrick, N. M.
Lynch, M. A.
Medlycott, K. T.
Murphy, A. J.
Robinson, J. D.
Sargeant, N. F.
Stewart, A. J.
Thorpe, G. P.
Waqar Younis
Ward, D. M.

WARWICKSHIRE

Asif Din
Benjamin, J. E.
Booth, P. A.
Donald, A. A.
Humpage, G. W.
Kallicharran, A. I.
Lloyd, T. A.
Moles, A. J.
Munton, T. A.
Ostler, D. P.
Pierson, A. R. K.
Piper, K. J.
Ratcliffe, J. D.
Reeve, D. A.
Small, G. C.
Smith, G.
Smith, N. M. K.
Smith, P. A.
Twose, R. G.

SUSSEX

Babington, A. M.
Bunting, R. A.
Dodemaide, A. I. C.
Donelan, B. T. P.
Gould, I. J.
Greenfield, K.
Hall, J. W.
Hanley, R.
Hansford, A. R.
Jones, A. N.

WORCESTERSHIRE

Bent, P.
Bevins, S. R.
Botham, I. T.
Curtis, T. S.
D'Oliveira, D. B.
Dilley, G. R.
Hick, G. A.
Illingworth, R. K.
Lampitt, S. R.

Leatherdale, D. A.
Lord, G. J.
McEwan, S. M.
Moody, T. M.
Neale, P. A.
Newport, P. J.
Radford, N. V.
Rhodes, S. J.
Stemp, R. D.
Tolley, C. M.
Weston, M. J.

YORKSHIRE

Bairstow, D. L.
Batty, J. D.
Berry, P.
Blakey, R. J.

Byas, D.
Carrick, P.
Chapman, C. M.
Fletcher, S. D.
Gough, D.
Grayson, A. P.
Hartley, P. J.
Houseman, I. J.
Jarvis, P. W.
Kellett, S. A.
Metcalfe, A. A.
Moxon, M. D.
Pickles, C. S.
Robinson, P. E.
Sharp, K.
Sidebottom, A.
White, C.